FRONTIERS AND BOUNDARIES

Previously published in this series:

23. Multiculturalism and the Canon of American Culture, 1993
24. Victorianism in the United States, 1992 *
25. Cultural Transmissions and Receptions, 1993
26. Modern American Landscapes, 1994
27. Fair Representations, 1994
28. Hollywood in Europe, 1994
29. American Photographs in Europe, 1994
30. American Culture in the Netherlands, 1996
31. Connecting Cultures, 1994
32. The Small Town in America, 1995
33. 'Writing' Nation and 'Writing' Region in America, 1996
34. The American Columbiad, 1996 *
35. The Insular Dream, 1995 *
36. Brave New Words, 1995
37. Social and Secure? 1996
38. Living with America, 1946-1996, 1997 *
39. Writing Lives, 1998
40. Through the Cultural Looking Glass, 1999
41. Dynamics of Modernization, 1999
42. Beat Culture, 1999
43. Predecessors, 1999
44. Ceremonies and Spectacles, 2000 *
45. The American Metropolis, 2001
46. Transatlantic Encounters, I en II, 2000
47. Federalism, Citizenship, and Collective Identities in U.S. History, 2001
48. Not English Only, 2001
49. "Nature's Nation" Revisited, 2003 *
50. Straddling Borders, 2004
51. Dreams of Paradise, Visions of Apocalypse, 2004
52. Religion in America, 2004
53. Public Space, Private Lives, 2004
54. First Nations of North America, 2004
55. Post-Cold War Europe, Post-Cold War America, 2004
56. Working Sites, 2004
57. The Cultural Shuttle, 2004 *
58. Frontiers and Boundaries in U.S. History, 2004
    Nation on the Move, 2002 **

* These volumes have been produced for the European Association for American Studies (E.A.A.S.).
** This title is not a volume in the series, but closely connected with it.

FRONTIERS AND BOUNDARIES IN U.S. HISTORY

edited by

Cornelis A. van Minnen and Sylvia L. Hilton

VU UNIVERSITY PRESS
AMSTERDAM 2004

EUROPEAN CONTRIBUTIONS TO AMERICAN STUDIES

This series is published for the Netherlands American Studies Association (N.A.S.A.) and the European Association for American Studies (E.A.A.S.)

General editor:
Rob Kroes
Amerika Instituut
Spuistraat 134
1012 VB Amsterdam

VU University Press is an imprint of
VU Boekhandel/Uitgeverij bv
De Boelelaan 1105
1081 HV Amsterdam
The Netherlands
E-mail: info@vu-uitgeverij.nl

ISBN 90 5383 942 9 (ECAS no 58)
NUR 686

Design cover: De Ontwerperij (Marcel Bakker), Amsterdam
Cover illustration: Frederic S. Remington, *The Fall of the Cowboy*, oil on canvas, 1895, Amon Carter Museum, Fort Worth, Texas, no 1961.230.
Printer: Wilco, Amersfoort

© 2004, Roosevelt Study Center, Middelburg,
       Cornelis A. van Minnen and Sylvia L. Hilton,
       and VU University Press, Amsterdam

All rights reserved. No part of this book may be reproduced, stored in an retrieval system, or transmitted, in any form or by any means, electronic, mechanical, photocopying, recording, or otherwise, without the prior written consent of the publisher.

CONTENTS

Frontiers and Boundaries in U.S. History: An Introduction
   Sylvia L. Hilton and Cornelis A. van Minnen   1

Reassessing American Frontier Theory: Culture, Cultural Relativism, and the Middle Ground in Early America
   Paul Otto   27

Foregrounding the Boundaries of American Literary History
   Michael Boyden   39

Republicanism, Federalism and Territorial Expansion in the United States
   Carmen de la Guardia Herrero   53

Breaking into the Trans-Mississippian Frontiers: Thomas Jefferson's Expeditions to the West
   Marco Sioli   69

Myths and Legends of the Irish Pioneers in Texas
   Graham Davis   89

Yeomen and Yankees across the Mason-Dixon Line: A Different Perspective on the Antebellum North/South Divide?
   Louis Billington and David Brown   101

The Special Message of Rutherford B. Hayes, 8 March 1880, and the "American" Canal Policy
   Joseph Smith   117

On the Frontier of Civilization: Deliberations of Exceptionalism and Environmental Determinism in the Creation of America's Tropical Empire, 1890-1910
   Frank Schumacher   127

Cajun Louisiana: A "French" Borderland in the Twentieth Century
   Robert M. Lewis   143

New Deal, New Frontiers and Borderlands
   David K. Adams   155

Frontiers and Boundaries in Hollywood Film: The Case of *The Grapes of Wrath*
   Melvyn Stokes   173

Along the Ideological Frontier: The Limits of American Democracy,
the Communist Party, and the Need for Historiographical Synthesis
    James G. Ryan   185

Between Avant-Garde and Kitsch: Pragmatic Liberalism, Public Arts Funding,
and the Cold War in the United States
    David Brian Howard   197

Hawaii, Statehood, and the East-West Center: Opening Up the Pacific Frontier
    Giles Scott-Smith   207

The "New" American Frontier in Real and Fictional Las Vegas
    Ingrid Eumann   219

Frontier and Identity: The Case of Alaska
    Tity de Vries   229

Notes on Contributors   247

Acknowledgments   251

FRONTIERS AND BOUNDARIES IN U.S. HISTORY: AN INTRODUCTION[1]

Sylvia L. Hilton and Cornelis A. van Minnen

The essays in this book illustrate the ways in which scholars of U.S. history have studied different kinds of discernible and significant boundaries or zones of separation, differentiation, contact and conflict, from colonial times to the present. One recurring theme is the interfacing of ideology, politics, and academic scholarship in defining thematic boundaries and interpretive divisions in the development of professional historiography. Several essays focus upon geographical factors in the development of the United States; on interpretations of territorial exploration and expansion; and on the ways in which the land and its political or historiographical demarcation have influenced aspects of American history. Others examine the development of "frontier" mythology and its influence on American identity, values, politics, institutions and diplomacy. Internal boundaries based on economic factors, administrative jurisdictions, or ethnic consciousness pose intriguing questions about definitions and changes over time. The expansion of U.S. influences in Panama, Hawaii, and the Philippines raises issues of sovereignty, cultural policies, and the significance of environmental factors on tropical frontiers. The frontier concept also proves useful as a metaphor in analyses of the limits of freedom of expression, and artistic peripheries, as well as cultural and technological vanguards. In short, this volume discusses theoretical and practical aspects of the definition and demarcation of frontiers and boundaries, their transgression, and their relationship with identities and the exercise of power.

The physical and geographical senses of terms such as "frontier" and "boundary" lend themselves readily to figurative, metaphorical and symbolic uses.[2] Historians and even geographers have often deemed it difficult to reach a consensus on the definition of the concept of a territorial boundary, so it is not surprising that the definition of demarcations which are commonly applied for the purpose of social identification and inclusion/exclusion poses even greater problems. A sense of belonging to one group and of differing from others might be based on gender, race, ethnicity, kinship, social class, professional group, religious persuasion, language, ideology, and many other elements that contribute to the definition of individual and collective identities, and of course, on combinations thereof, all of which, in addition, might fluctuate over time or according to circumstances. Historians and other social scientists have used many different terms and phrases to evoke images of separation and delimitation of social identities. Hence, such phrases as the "color

---

[1] Professor Sylvia L. Hilton gratefully acknowledges financial support from the Spanish Ministry of Science and Technology, for research project BHA2000-0709.
[2] Some other terms with similar applications are border, borderland, borderline, bounds, confine(s), curtain, demarcation, divide, edge, fringe, limit, line, march(es), marchland, margin, mark, periphery, perimeter, rim.

line,"[3] or the "glass ceiling" referring to women's difficulties in breaking through an invisible barrier in order to reach the highest levels of authority, income, or responsibility.[4]

The word "frontier," in particular, carries a heavy load of multiple meanings in historiographical, political, and popular usages in the United States. Consequently, the concept itself has become the subject of much scholarly debate. The French philosopher Lucien Febvre provided a useful introduction to the European origins of the term "frontier," through his overview of definitions and examples of *frontière* and related terms in French dictionaries and usage, from the thirteenth century to the nineteenth.[5] The brief study is made more illuminating by Febvre's comments on the evolution of the meanings of this term in France and neighboring countries. From the point of view of North American historiography, it is worthy of note that one early (thirteenth through sixteenth centuries) meaning of the term *frontières* was military, but did not refer to walls, fortifications, trenches or other defensive works, but to the front line of troops facing the enemy. In other words, together with the idea of frontier defence, was clearly the idea that a frontier composed of men was movable. Indeed, if armed men defined the *frontières*, they could just as easily move aggressively forward as stay defensively in one place.[6] During that same period, among other words that were in common usage, two were especially important: *fins* to denote the idea of a strip of land that formed the border region of a country, and *limites* that gradually became the dominant term for the idea of the line of demarcation between (the *fins* of) two countries. However, the word *frontières* gradually absorbed both meanings. During the sixteenth century, the military power and prestige of the fighting men of the frontier was translated into diplomatic language and cartographic representation, and so *frontières* evolved from being the front line of the army to the defensive border region of a country. Furthermore, by the late seventeenth century, although lawyers were still using the term *limites* to settle boundary disputes, in military and political usages *frontières* was increasingly signifying the demarcation line of sovereignty and political jurisdiction. Thus, by the late eighteenth century, the term *limites* was still in use, but *frontières* had absorbed its meaning without losing the meaning of *fins* or strip of defensive territory that formed the border of the country.

---

[3] For example, as in John Hope Franklin, *The Color Line: Legacy for the Twenty-first Century* (Columbia: University of Missouri Press, 1993).

[4] For example, Ann H. Morrison, Carol T. Schreiber, and Karl F. Price, *A Glass Ceiling Survey: Benchmarking Barriers and Practices* (Greensboro, NC: Center for Creative Leadership, 1995).

[5] Lucien Febvre, "Frontière: The Word and the Concept," *Revue de synthèse historique* 45 (1928), repr. in Lucien Febvre, *Pour une histoire à part entière* (Paris, 1962), transl. in Peter Burke, ed., *A New Kind of History: From the Writings of Febvre* (London: Routledge and Kegan Paul, 1973), 208-218.

[6] Febvre, "Frontière," 209-210, illustrates this with a 1558 quotation from French Ambassador Sieur de la Vigne: "the true and surest way of expanding and living in peace and tranquility in the realm is to continue to push the *frontières* as far forward as we can and continue to drive the enemy far away before us!"

In Febvre's interpretation, the increasing tendency of states to demand, define and defend continuous demarcation lines, that could be accurately identified and mapped, reflected the emergence of self-conscious nations. These internationally recognized frontiers of demarcation served not only as a measure of self-protection, but as an expression of national power. He theorizes too that after the Revolution of 1789, new concepts of citizenship, state sovereignty, and nationality were accompanied by the "militarization of the nation," and that these developments gave a much greater value to national boundaries, which were expressed in political and diplomatic terms as territorial frontiers. This process, in turn, gave greater weight to geography and discourses on the "natural frontiers" of nations, but Febvre quickly demolished the concept of natural frontiers, which in his view has been totally irrelevant as a criterion for determining political frontiers. All political frontiers reflect historical facts and processes, but national and ethnic myths claiming "natural frontiers" have been powerful and persistant because, in Febvre's opinion, they have seemed easier to deal with and easier to represent cartographically than the confusion and intractable complications of geographical and social reality. In short, during the process of European colonization of North America, and as the newly independent United States began its century-long expansion westward to the Pacific, the concept of the frontier was already heavily loaded with multiple meanings.

Early modern English and Angloamerican usage of the word "frontier," as reflected in dictionary definitions, always applied the political criterion, referring to boundaries, limits or borders of a country (and sometimes of a province).[7] Nonetheless, Fulmer Mood recounted an opinion published in 1781 by John Witherspoon, the president of Princeton College, that nicely illustrated a specifically Anglo-North American perspective, and the fact that definitions often depend on one's point of view. "I would prefer *frontier* to *back settlements*," he declared, evidently because he wished to reject the idea that the vital center of American society was in the east, and was patriotically inclined to link a forward-looking attitude (in both the senses of the phrase) with a westward direction.[8] For his part, Noah Webster hinted at the first "dim" suggestion of an internal, domestic frontier in his 1806 definition of "frontier" as "furthest settlements," but this idea was totally absent from his later celebrated lexicographical work.[9] In 1874, U.S. census officials originated a definition of the concept of a settlement frontier in terms of density of population per square mile.[10] However, this did not make its way into dictionary

---

[7] Fulmer Mood, "Notes on the History of the Word 'Frontier,'" *Agricultural History* 22.2 (April 1948): 78-83.

[8] Mood, "Notes on the History of the Word 'Frontier,'" 79.

[9] Noah Webster, *A Compendious Dictionary of the English Language* (Hartford: From Sidneys' Press for Hudson and Goodwin, Booksellers; and New Haven: Increase Cooke and Co., Booksellers, 1806); Noah Webster, *An American Dictionary of the English Language* (New York: S. Converse, 1828), cit. in Mood, "Notes on the History of the Word 'Frontier,'" 79.

[10] Fulmer Mood, "The Concept of the Frontier, 1871-1898: Comments on a Select List of Source Documents," *Agricultural History* 19 (January 1945): 24-30, discusses the development of the use of the term frontier in relation to the density of population within the United States.

definitions until 1935, when an English work included it for the benefit of English readers.[11] In short, nineteenth-century dictionaries do not record any specifically American usages of the term until the 1890s, when a number of dictionaries added new ideas to their standard political-international definition. It was at this time when they gave formal acceptance to a concept that had long been in use, indicating that a frontier could also be the border or limits of a "settled" or "inhabited" or "civilized" part of a country, or be "the frontier of civilization", and that such a definition was exemplified by the western frontier in the United States.[12] It was during that same period when Frederick Jackson Turner published his so-called "frontier thesis," confirming that a peculiarly American concept of the term "frontier" had at last received recognition.[13]

In 1893, the annual conference of the American Historical Association coincided with the Columbian Exposition held in Chicago to celebrate the four hundredth anniversary of the European "discovery" of America. It was a fitting forum for Turner to present the paper that was to become an unavoidable reference point in American historiography of the frontier.[14] The historiographical record on Turner and his famous "thesis" is immense, and this is not the place to attempt a detailed analysis.[15] Its association with national mythology makes it particularly

---

[11] H[erbert] W[illiam] Horwill, *A Dictionary of Modern American Usage* (Oxford: Clarendon Press, 1935), cit. in Mood, "Notes on the History of the Word 'Frontier,'" 82.

[12] Mood, "Notes on the History of the Word 'Frontier,'" 80-81, cites William Dwight Whitney, dir., *The Century Dictionary: An Encyclopedic Lexicon of the English Language*, 6 vols. (New York: Century Co., 1889-1891); *Webster's International Dictionary of the English Language* (New York and London: Bell, 1890); Isaac K. Funk and Francis A. March, eds., *A Standard Dictionary of the English Language* (New York and London: Funk and Wagnalls Company, 1893); Sir James A.H. Murray, *A New English Dictionary on Historical Principles* (Oxford: Clarendon Press, 1897); *Webster's New International Dictionary of the English Language* (Springfield, MA: G.&C. Merriam Co., 1909).

[13] For examples of American usage of the word "frontier" from 1700 to 1918, see Sir William A. Craigie and James R. Hulbert, eds., *A Dictionary of American English on Historical Principles* (Chicago: University of Chicago Press, 1940), who defines "frontier" as: "A region in what is now the United States newly or sparsely settled and immediately adjoining the wilderness or unoccupied territory." See also Herman C. Nixon, "Precursors of Turner in the Interpretation of the American Frontier," *South Atlantic Quarterly* 28.1 (January 1929): 83-90, and John T. Juricek, "American Usage of the Word 'Frontier' from Colonial Times to Frederick Jackson Turner," *Proceedings of the American Philosophical Society* 110 (18 February 1966): 10-34.

[14] Frederick Jackson Turner, "The Significance of the Frontier in American History," *Annual Report of the American Historical Association for the Year 1893* (Washington, DC: G.P.O., 1894), 199-227, repr. with other important essays in F.J. Turner, *The Frontier in American History* (New York: H. Holt and Company, 1920), 1-38.

[15] Useful bibliographical aids are Vernon E. Mattson and William E. Marion, eds., *Frederick Jackson Turner: A Reference Guide* (Boston: G.K. Hall, 1985), and John Mack Faragher, ed., *Rereading Frederick Jackson Turner: "The Significance of the Frontier in American History" and Other Essays* (1994; reprint, New Haven and London: Yale University Press, 1998), and in particular his "Afterword: The

difficult to analyze. As one author wrote: "The frontier thesis is America's most popular explanation of herself and it has held this place from 1893 through John F. Kennedy's call of a New Frontier and on to our explorations into space. Turner is America's historian."[16] The enduring fascination of scholars with Turner's "frontier thesis" lies in the fact that it is not, in fact, a single argument which the author duly substantiated with historical evidence, but is an impressionistic composite of multiple threads, a wide-ranging, multi-faceted, highly suggestive but largely unproven hypothesis that, like the mythical Greek hydra, has reacted to having its head chopped off by growing many new ones.

One must first consider the importance of two major historiographical interpretations that Turner explicitly rejected: the "germ theory" regarding the European origins of American culture, values and institutions; and the idea that slavery and its abolition explained the core issues of American history. Turner did not discount these factors entirely but, in his preference for an explanatory theme that would better satisfy his nationalistic ideology, he did relegate them to secondary significance.

Turner found an alternative causal explanation for American historical development in western frontier expansion and the environment this created, which, he argued, were unique to North America. His central idea was that American culture and the United States as a nation-state developed over generations, out of the historical experience of constantly struggling to master the natural, untamed wilderness on successive frontiers that moved further and further westwards across the continent. This recurring struggle, according to Turner, was the single most

---

Significance of the Frontier in American Historiography. A Guide to Further Reading," 225-254. But see especially, Ray A. Billington, *The Frontier Thesis: Valid Interpretation of American History?* (New York: Holt, Rinehart and Winston, 1966); *The Genesis of the Frontier Thesis: A Study in Historical Creativity* (San Marino, CA: Huntington Library, 1971), and *Frederick Jackson Turner: Historian, Scholar, Teacher* (New York: Oxford University Press, 1973); David W. Noble, *Historians Against History: The Frontier Thesis and the National Covenant in American Historical Writing Since 1830* (Minneapolis: University of Minnesota Press, 1965); Wilbur R. Jacobs, John W. Caughey, and Joe B. Franz, *Turner, Bolton, and Webb: Three Historians of the American Frontier* (Seattle: University of Washington Press, 1965); Richard Hofstadter, *The Progressive Historians: Turner, Beard, Parrington* (New York: Knopf, 1968); Howard R. Lamar, "Frederick Jackson Turner," in Marcus Cunliffe and Robin W. Winks, eds., *Past-masters: Some Essays on American Historians* (New York: Harper and Row, 1969), 74-109; George Rogers Taylor, ed., *The Turner Thesis: Concerning the Role of the Frontier in American History* (Lexington, MA: D.C. Heath, 1972); Lee Benson, *Turner and Beard: American Historical Writing Reconsidered* (Westport, CT: Greenwood Press, 1980); Margaret Walsh, *The American Frontier Revisited* (Atlantic Highlands, NJ: Humanities Press, 1981); Jan Willem Schulte Nordholt, "The Turner Thesis Revisited," in David K. Adams and Cornelis A. van Minnen, eds., *Reflections on American Exceptionalism* (Staffordshire: Ryburn Publishing, 1994), 9-18; Allan G. Bogue, *Frederick Jackson Turner: Strange Roads Going Down* (Norman: University of Oklahoma Press, 1998).

[16] Richard L. Rapson, *Major Interpretations of the American Past* (New York: Appleton-Century-Crofts, 1971), 38.

important factor in the nation's history. But it was not a simple proposition. In fact, Turner blended into his hypothesis evaluations of the importance of space and place, man's relation with nature, the physical and socio-economic mobility of populations, different types of frontiers defined by diverse ecosystems and economic activities, interethnic cultural conflict as well as internal cultural evolution, the military character and political significance of frontiers of settlement, and even some of the less desirable effects resulting from the exercise of individual freedom in the absence or weakness of governmental and social constraints in frontier environments. It is in this blending and blurring of many different factors that the historiographical interest of Turner's hypothesis resides.

Turner's point of view was fundamentally nationalistic. As such, his ethnocentrically celebratory narrative of American history strongly espoused the idea of the moving frontier as the forge of the nation in several interconnected ways. He linked the frontier experience, on the one hand, to the territorial expansion of the United States, at the expense of Indians, European colonial powers and Mexico; and on the other, to the internal development of American nationalism and culture. Underlying his entire arsenal of arguments were the notions of progress and U.S. exceptionalism.

Although most of his own studies focused on trans-Appalachian expansion, Turner's main theme was not the history of a particular frontier region or even "the West" in general, but the ways in which processes occurring on the frontiers affected the overall political and cultural development of the nation. The recurring struggle of pioneers with wilderness conditions on successive settlement frontiers led him to envision American history as a process of adaptation and transformation, during which settlers became increasingly Americanized. ("The frontier is the line of most rapid and effective Americanization.") The result of this process was the formation of the supposedly quintessential American national values and character traits: democracy, liberty, egalitarianism, individualism, self-reliance, pragmatism, inventiveness, ingenuity, thrift, optimism, belief in the reality of social mobility, and so on. At the same time, his much cited definition of the frontier as "the meeting point between savagery and civilization" clearly expressed his conviction that Native American cultures were inferior and were therefore destined to lose the culture war as well as their political power, as a result of their increasing economic dependency.

One of the keys to Turner's thought is undoubtedly his recognition of the importance of mobility in the development of American society ("movement has been its dominant fact," and of American nationalism ("The mobility of population is death to localism.") Many eighteenth and nineteenth-century observers of the United States, and many scholars before Turner, were struck by the apparently uncontrollable character and the volume of migrations within the North American republic, and many had linked those demographic movements to the opportunities (real and imagined) for personal economic improvement that existed on the western frontiers of North America. Some chose to stress factors of expulsion from Europe and/or the eastern states, while others emphasized the migrants' belief in the existence of social, economic, and political opportunities in the West. In the 1820s, for example, the German philosopher Georg Wilhelm Friedrich Hegel described the empty agricultural frontier as a social and political safety valve in North America. William S. Holt pointed out that Hegel formulated one of the earliest statements of the "safety valve" theory. Holt did not affirm that this was the origin of Turner's hypothesis, but he did think that it might have planted the seed, since Turner probably read Hegel's work, inspired by the prestige enjoyed by German scholarship at that time.[17] The modern debate over myth and reality of factors of expulsion/attraction, or combinations thereof, is irrelevant to the basic premise that the Western frontiers did represent an opportunity for migrants, regardless of their motives for moving or their subsequent success or failure. The chief initial magnet was the availability of land, not just for subsistence farming and commercial cultivation, but also for speculation, and as the basis of prospects of gaining political power while evading existing government authority. In stressing the physical movement of population within North America as well as its connection with individual hopes of social and economic advancement, Turner was giving historiographical expression to a popular idea.[18]

One of the most contested parts of Turner's construct is that the era of the Western frontier had ended in the 1890s, and with it, the formative period of the United States. He was echoing the official declaration based on the census findings of 1890, to the effect that the North American continental frontier no longer existed, although he did suggest, in his 1893 paper and more forcefully in later writings, that frontier conditions did still exist in places like Alaska, and that there were and would be other frontiers that would pose new challenges to the American nation.

The frontier idea offered a powerful interpretive image. It inspired Walter Prescott Webb to expand Turner's hypothesis, arguing that frontier expansion had conditioned not only U.S. history but more broadly Euro-American, Western, or Atlantic and world history in general, so that the development of colonialism, capitalism, individualism, and democratic ideas and institutions in the European "metropolis" was equally linked to the influence of its frontiers, which were expanding overseas for four centuries from the 1490s until about 1930.[19]

Many other historians, as well as politicians, literary authors, film-makers, song-writers, and myth-mongers generally, have been inspired by Turner's take on

---

[17] Georg Wilhelm Friedrich Hegel, lectures given in 1822-1823 and 1830-1831, published in *Philosophie der Geschichte* (Berlin: Verlag von Duncker und Humblot, 1837-1840), and in *Werke* (Berlin, 1848), 9:106-107, cit. in W[illiam] Stull Holt, "Hegel, the Turner Hypothesis, and the Safety-Valve Theory," *Agricultural History* 22.3 (July 1948): 175-176.

[18] On this theme, see for example Everett S. Lee, "The Turner Thesis Re-examined," *American Quarterly* 13 (1961): 77-83; George W. Pierson, "The M-Factor in American History," *American Quarterly* 14 (1962): 275-289, and "'A Restless Temper' ...," *American Historical Review* 69 (1964): 969-989; Robert F. Berkhofer, Jr., "Space, Time, Culture and the New Frontier," *Agricultural History* 38 (January 1964): 21-30, and abridged repr. in Allan G. Bogue et al., eds., *The West of the American People* (Itasca, IL: F.E. Peacock Publishers, 1970), 30-35; and more generally Cornelis van Minnen and Sylvia L. Hilton, eds., *Nation on the Move: Mobility in U.S. History* (Amsterdam: VU University Press, 2002).

[19] Walter Prescott Webb, *The Great Frontier* (Boston: Houghton Mifflin, 1952).

the frontier theme. Nevertheless, modern social conflict, racism, economic injustices, uncontrolled capitalism, wars and aggressive foreign policies, have produced many doubts about the American historical development and value system. Modern historiographical scholarship reflects the ongoing American struggle for social justice, and consequently Turner's ethnocentrism and chauvinistic nationalism have largely and justifiably fallen from grace, even among more traditionally conservative historians. Anti-Turnerian criticism emerged in the late 1920s, gathering momentum in the 1930s, as radical intellectuals rejected individual aspects of his celebratory portrayal of Western pioneering and its influence on the national character, and as the Depression deepened concern about social and economic tensions. Critics have been inspired to different degrees by ideological disagreement, thematic fashions in historiography, and generational opposition.[20] In particular, scholars writing from Socialist, Marxist, and New Left ideological positions have rejected Turner's frontier hypothesis mainly because of its connection with conservative American nationalism, liberal individualism, and unbridled capitalist exploitation. Nonetheless, much criticism has been based unfairly on oversimplifications of Turner's ideas, and on the false supposition that he did not develop or modify his ideas after 1893.

Historians have countered Turner's rejection of the "germ theory," arguing instead that the European roots of American culture are fundamental and cannot be ignored.[21] Similarly, countless others have disagreed with his dismissal of the slavery issue as a central theme of national (and frontier) history. His defense of U.S. exceptionalism and explanation of its origins have also come under fire in recent times.[22] The troubled historical record of American foreign policies, and particularly those instances of interventionism for motives or in ways that have been judged unacceptable by sizable sectors of American society, have also led many historians of U.S. international relations to stress the themes of failure, tragedy, or selfish opportunism as characteristics of U.S. actions abroad. The Turnerian notion

---

[20] This last is the chief thesis of Gerald D. Nash in *Creating the West: Historical Interpretations, 1890-1990* (Albuquerque: University of New Mexico Press, 1991), *passim*.

[21] For example, Berkhofer, "Space, Time, Culture and the New Frontier," using a concept of culture as "a normative system ... the blueprint or design for behavior," and not the total social heritage of the behavior and cultural artifacts themselves.

[22] See for example, David Mogen, Mark Busby, and Paul Bryant, eds., *The Frontier Experience and the American Dream: Essays on American Literature* (College Station: Texas A&M University Press, 1989); Ian Tyrell, "American Exceptionalism in an Age of International History," *American Historical Review* 96 (October 1991): 1031-1055; Joyce Appleby, "Recovering America's Historic Diversity: Beyond Exceptionalism," *Journal of American History* 79.2 (September 1992): 419-431; David Wrobel, *The End of American Exceptionalism: Frontier Anxiety from the Old West to the New Deal* (Lawrence: University Press of Kansas, 1993); Daniel T. Rodgers, "Exceptionalism," in Anthony Molho and Gordon S. Wood, eds., *Imagined Histories: American Historians Interpret the Past* (Princeton, NJ: Princeton University Press, 1998), 21-40; Deborah L. Madsen, *American Exceptionalism* (Jackson: University of Mississippi Press, 1998); Richard W. Etulain, ed., *Does the Frontier Experience Make America Exceptional?* (Boston: Bedford/St. Martin's, 1999).

that frontier expansionism fostered and spread liberty and democracy, with scarce reference to the values and interests of other peoples' cultures and sovereignties, has been countered by an interpretation that sees it much more in terms of aggressive imperialism.[23]

The popular mythical and historiographical links that have been established, in the case of the United States, between historical frontier experiences associated with the territorial expansion of the nation, on the one hand, and national exceptionalism, on the other, have led to considerations of the usefulness of adopting comparative approaches. Historians frequently stress the need for comparative studies in order to test or refine interpretive frameworks. The frontier theme clearly lends itself to such studies. One need only look within North America itself to find Indian cultures, Spanish, French and Dutch colonies, as well as the later nation-states of Canada and Mexico, all of which fought to defend their own frontiers. Moreover, a hemispheric perspective demands comparisons with frontiers and boundaries in Latin America, and chronological, thematic, or other special approaches might suggest comparing frontier expansion and environments anywhere else in the world.[24] Calling for comparisons of the United States with Canada, Australia, South Africa, Brazil, Argentina, and other places, Walter Nugent, for example, suggests that special importance should be given to immigration as a criterion for differentiating a true frontier from mere imperial outposts.[25]

According to Turner, the availability of vast expanses of open, "free" land on the western frontier was the determining factor in the development of American character traits and national values. One of the major questions posed by comparative approaches asks whether the same circumstance affected other frontier

---

[23] See for example, Lawrence S. Kaplan, "Frederick Jackson Turner and Imperialism," *Social Science* 27 (1952): 12-16; William Appleman Williams, "The Frontier Thesis and American Foreign Policy," in *History as a Way of Learning: Articles, Excerpts, and Essays by William Appleman Williams* (New York: New Viewpoints, 1973), 135-157.

[24] See for example, T[homas] M[atthews] Pearce, "The 'Other' Frontiers of the American West," *Arizona and the West* 4 (1962): 105-112; David H. Miller et al., *The Frontier: Comparative Studies* (Norman: University of Oklahoma Press, 1977); Jerome O. Steffen, *Comparative Frontiers, a Proposal for Studying the American West* (Norman: University of Oklahoma Press, 1980); George Wolfskill and Stanley Palmer, eds., *Essays on Frontiers in World History* (Austin: University of Texas Press, 1981); William H. McNeill, *The Great Frontier: Freedom and Hierarchy in Modern Times* (Princeton, NJ: Princeton University Press, 1983); Howard Lamar and Leonard Thompson, "Comparative Frontier History," in Howard Lamar and Leonard Thompson, eds., *The Frontier in History: North America and Southern Africa Compared* (New Haven: Yale University Press, 1981); John Mack Faragher, "Americans, Mexicans, Métis: A Community Approach to the Comparative Study of North American Frontiers," in William Cronon, George Miles, and Jay Gitlin, eds., *Under an Open Sky: Rethinking America's Western Past* (New York: W.W. Norton, 1992), 90-109; Michael Baud and Willem van Schendel, "Toward a Comparative History of Borderlands," *Journal of World History* 8 (1997): 211-242.

[25] Walter Nugent, "Comparing Wests and Frontiers," in Clyde A. Milner, II, Carol A. O'Connor, and Martha A. Sandweiss, eds., *The Oxford History of the American West* (New York: Oxford University Press, 1994), 803-833.

societies (in the Americas or elsewhere) in the same way, and if not, why not. Mark Bassin, for example found that while both Turner and Russian polymath Sergei Mikhailovich Solov'ev sought to explain national development as a function of frontier expansion, what for the American was a positive, creative influence, for Solov'ev was a negative factor that hindered the progressive evolution of the Russian nation.[26] Even within North America, Jack D. Forbes made the simple point that rarely if ever has there been one single frontier, arguing instead that the historical evidence reveals the existence of "a frontier complex, a multiplicity of frontiers in dynamic interaction." He proposed a definition of frontier which would contain the ideas of "meeting point" and "an inter-group contact situation," involving at least two but possibly more racial, ethnic, cultural or national groups, *that think of themselves as being different from each other*, over a period of time.[27]

Just as the United States evolved from English colonies, the Spanish and Portuguese colonies gave way to independent republican nation-states. That general historical similarity means that Latin America, in particular, clearly offers ample scope for comparative studies of life on political and cultural frontiers, and of their impact on national development and international relations. The founder of Spanish borderlands historiography in the United States, Herbert Eugene Bolton, was the first scholar to affirm repeatedly (from the 1920s) that U.S. history cannot be fully understood without reference to Spanish colonialism, Latin America, and inter-American relations. He called for a broad hemispheric approach which would set the history of the United States in the context of the Americas.[28] Many scholars since have echoed this necessity, but very few have attempted to embrace such a daunting task.[29] In particular, the Northern frontiers of Spain's American empire, the so-called Spanish borderlands, offer sharp contrasts with Angloamerican frontier experiences, giving rise to important propositions and debates that both question and support different elements of the Turnerian interpretive model, as well as offering others.[30]

---

[26] Mark Bassin, "Turner, Solov'ev, and the 'Frontier Hypothesis': The Nationalist Signification of Open Spaces," *Journal of Modern History* 65.3 (September 1993): 473-511. Bassin points out (on page 473) that in 1906 Turner himself called for "a comparative study of the process of settlement."

[27] Jack D. Forbes, "Frontiers in American History," *Journal of the West* 1.1 (July 1962): 63-73, quotes at 69, 65, 67. We have added emphasis to a point that in our view is of special relevance for the understanding of the formation of collective identities.

[28] See for example, Herbert Eugene Bolton, "The Epic of Greater America," *American Historical Review* 38 (1932-1933): 448-474, repr. in *Wider Horizons of American History* (New York: Appleton-Century Co., 1939), and in John Francis Bannon, ed., *Bolton and the Spanish Borderlands* (Norman: University of Oklahoma Press, 1964).

[29] Two comparative, interpretive works are [Charles] Alistair [M.] Hennessy, *The Frontier in Latin American History* (London: Edward Arnold, 1978); and up to 1810, Hebe Clementi, *La frontera en América. 1, Una clave interpretativa de la historia americana* (Buenos Aires: Leviatan, 1985).

[30] On this subject, see Donald E. Worcester, "The Significance of the Spanish Borderlands to the United States," *The Western Historical Review* 7 (1976): 5-18; and in particular the illuminating essay by David J. Weber, "Turner, the Boltonians, and the Borderlands," *American Historical Review* 91.1 (February 1986): 66-81, together with

The comparative approach seems particularly intriguing when comparing white-Indian relations on Angloamerican frontiers with those on other European colonial frontiers or on the national frontiers of Mexico and Canada. Most Spanish historiography and some comparative studies have underscored, for example, that in contrast with Angloamerican frontiers that tended to dispossess and displace indigenous peoples, Spanish frontiers in North America attempted to assimilate them. This difference has led a number of scholars to contrast the Spanish "frontiers of inclusion" with the Angloamerican "frontiers of exclusion."[31] The Turnerian idea of the frontier as a struggle between civilization and savagery necessarily portrays Indians as obstacles in the path of progress, destined to decline and disappear. However, since the 1960s the general celebration of cultural diversity, and a much greater scholarly cognizance of the rights and different perspectives of minorities, have had a huge impact on the way historians, and particularly ethnohistorians, study Native Americans and Western frontiers. There is a strong tendency now to define the frontier concept with such phrases as meeting place, contact point, and middle ground, in sum, peripheral and/or contested territory in which cultural interaction takes place. It is understood that the concept of cultural interaction contemplates both conflictive and cooperative relations, as well as ambivalences, cultural persistence, and cultural (ex)change, not forgetting the possible emergence of new cultural forms resulting from hybridization or more polygenetic mixture. Different authors choose to focus upon different aspects of cultural interaction, and of course, personal and ideological factors lead some to express strong opinions, whether in condemnation or in celebration of the historical processes they study.

Turner used the notion of the official "closure" of the frontier in 1890 as the motive and justification of his interpretation of its significance in American history.

---

his *The Idea of the Spanish Borderlands* (New York: Garland, 1991), and *The Spanish Frontier in North America* (New Haven and London: Yale University Press, 1992). James A. Hijiya, "Why the West Is Lost," *William and Mary Quarterly* 51.2 (April 1994): 275-292, gives eight reasons that explain the continuing tendency to ignore non-Anglo peoples and cultures in North American history textbooks, despite repeated calls for broader, more inclusive vision since the 1960s. Albert L. Hurtado, "Parkmanizing the Spanish Borderlands: Bolton, Turner, and the Historians' World," *Western Historical Quarterly* 26 (Summer 1995): 149-167; Alfredo Jiménez, "El Lejano Norte español: cómo escapar del 'American West' y de las 'Spanish Borderlands,'" *Colonial Latin American Historical Review* 5.4 (1996): 381-412; Robert E. Jackson, ed., *New Views of Borderlands History* (Albuquerque: University of New Mexico Press, 1998); Jeremy Adelman and Stephen Aron, "From Borderlands to Borders: Empires, Nation-States, and the Peoples in Between in North American History," *American Historical Review* 104.3 (June 1999): 814-841, and useful critiques of this article in the following issue of the *American Historical Review* by Evan Haefeli, Christopher Ebert Schmidt-Nowara, and John R. Wunder and Pekka Hämäläinen, with Adelman and Aron's response, *American Historical Review* 104.4 (October 1999): 1221-1239.

[31] For example, Marvin Mikesell, "Comparative Studies in Frontier History," *Annals of the Association of American Geographers* 50 (March 1960): 62-74. John H. Elliott, "España e Inglaterra en las Indias," in Richard Hitchcock and Ralph Penny, eds., *Actas del Primer Congreso Anglo-Hispano. Tomo III. Historia* (Madrid: Editorial Castalia, 1994), 3-19, extended the comparison to Spain and England in the Americas generally.

As seen from the national perspective, his successive frontiers of settlement necessarily advanced in a general sense towards the West, and this led to a degree of confusion between the concept of the frontier process and its Western location. Modern scholars, and particularly New Western historians, dispute this splitting of U.S. history into two phases (before and after 1890), stressing instead that frontier conditions and processes have continued to exist and develop in the United States throughout the twentieth century. Their arguments are varied and persuasive. Migrations to Western metropolitan areas in otherwise sparsely populated areas seem to throw new light on the relations of the West with the East, and on the center-periphery tensions within the West itself. Moreover, "the West" might identify its own regional "vital centers" and its own "fringes" and "frontiers." Working at the same time as Turner, Adna Weber had showed the importance of cities as "centers" of Western settlement and development, and New Western historians have begun to explore this urban theme.[32] Ethnic diversity still fuels cultural resistance and many forms of interaction. There are ongoing battles for land, natural resources and other sources of power, certainly in the trans-Mississippian West but also elsewhere. The role of the federal government in Western development continues to be surprisingly significant.[33]

---

[32] Adna F. Weber, *The Growth of Cities in the Nineteenth Century* (New York: Columbia University, 1899). For a comparative study of urban centers on frontiers of settlement in the United States and Canada, Australia and New Zealand, see David Hamer, *New Towns in the New World: Images and Perceptions of the Nineteenth-Century Urban Frontier* (New York: Columbia University Press, 1990).

[33] For insightful discussions on the evolution of frontier historiography, and of the New Western History, see for example, Rodman W. Paul and Richard W. Etulain, eds., *The Frontier and the American West* (Arlington Heights, IL: AHM Pub. Corp., 1977); Roger L. Nichols, ed., *American Frontier and Western Issues: A Historiographical Review* (Westport, CT: Greenwood Press, 1986); Gerald Thompson, "Frontier West: Place or Process?" *Journal of the Southwest* 29 (1987): 364-375; Donald Worster, "New West, True West: Interpreting the Region's History," *Western Historical Quarterly* 18 (April 1987): 141-156; William Cronon, "Revisiting the Vanishing Frontier: The Legacy of Frederick Jackson Turner," *Western Historical Quarterly* 18 (April 1987): 157-176; Michael P. Malone, "Beyond the Last Frontier: Toward a New Approach to Western American History," *Western Historical Quarterly* 20.4 (November 1989) 409-427; Donald Worster et al., "*The Legacy of Conquest*, by Patricia Nelson Limerick: A Panel of Appraisal," *The Western Historical Quarterly* 20.3 (1989); Robert Young, *White Mythologies: Writing History and the West* (New York: Routledge, 1990); Nash, *Creating the West*, cit.; Patricia Nelson Limerick, Clyde A. Milner, and Charles E. Rankin, eds., *Trails toward a New Western History* (Lawrence: University Press of Kansas, 1991); Richard W. Etulain, ed., *Writing Western History: Essays on Major Western Historians* (1991; reprint, Reno: University of Nevada Press, 2002); Allan G. Bogue, "The Significance of the History of the American West: Postscripts and Prospects," *The Western Historical Quarterly* 24 (1993): 45-68; the review essay by John Mack Faragher, "The Frontier Trail: Rethinking Turner and Re-imagining the American West," *American Historical Review* 98.1 (February 1993): 106-117; Wilbur R. Jacobs, *On Turner's Trail: 100 Years of Writing Western History* (Lawrence: University Press of Kansas, 1994); Stephen Aron, "Lessons in Conquest: Towards a Greater Western History," *Pacific Historical Review* 63 (May 1994): 125-147; Mary

Building on work published in the 1950s and 1960s, and applying climatic and topographical factors that can be expressed cartographically, New Western historians of the 1980s and 1990s have tried to free the West from the Turnerian grip, not only by rejecting Turner's exulting narrative and ethnocentric insensitivity, and by focusing on environmental issues, on cultural diversity and interaction, and on the negative consequences of Angloamerican hegemonic attitudes, but also by defining the West more precisely as a geographical region; as a place, more than as a Turnerian frontier process.[34] This approach has obvious advantages. The Western region gains its own identity (or identities) and continuity, as a place that has always existed and has always been inhabited by many different, interacting peoples. The historical realities and the historiographical potential of such a regional topic provide a more neutral focus than a methodological and interpretive approach that is centered on the frontier theme, however broadly one defines that framework.

As a leading promoter of New Western history, Patricia Limerick has been influential in debunking Turner and questioning the validity of frontier historiography. Her rejection of ethnocentric nationalism and of the tendency to equate the "West" with the "frontier" is understandable. However, it seems that her insistence on separating these two historical subjects has led her to needlessly reject the frontier theme entirely. In essence, Limerick rejects the frontier concept because it has been applied ethnocentrically. "The term *frontier*," she writes, "requires a

---

Ellen Jones, *The American Frontier: Opposing Viewpoints* (San Diego, CA: Greenhaven Press, 1994); Patricia Nelson Limerick, "Turnerians All: The Dream of a Helpful History in an Intelligible World," *American Historical Review* 100.3 (June 1995): 697-716; Kerwin Lee Klein, "Reclaiming the 'F' Word, Or Being and Becoming Postwestern," *Pacific Historical Review* 65 (May 1996): 179-215; Richard White, "Western History," in Eric Foner, ed., *The New American History* (Philadelphia: Temple University Press, 1997); Gregory H. Nobles, *American Frontiers: Cultural Encounters and Continental Conquest* (New York: Hill and Wang, 1999).

[34] Some examples are Richard Slotkin, *The Fatal Environment: The Myth of the Frontier in the Age of Industrialization, 1800-1890* (1985; reprint, Norman: University of Oklahoma Press, 1998); Patricia Nelson Limerick, *The Legacy of Conquest: The Unbroken Past of the American West* (New York: Norton, 1987), and *Something in the Soil: Legacies and Reckonings in the New West* (New York: W.W. Norton, 2000); Richard White, *"It's Your Misfortune and None of My Own": A New History of the American West* (Norman: University of Oklahoma Press, 1991); Donald Worster, *Rivers of Empire: Water, Aridity, and the Growth of the American West* (New York: Pantheon Books, 1985); *Under Western Skies: Nature and History in the American West* (New York: Oxford University Press, 1992), and *An Unsettled Country: Changing Landscapes of the American West* (Albuquerque: University of New Mexico Press, 1994); William Robbins, *Colony and Empire: The Capitalist Transformation of the American West* (Lawrence: University Press of Kansas, 1994), and *Landscapes of Promise: The Oregon Story, 1800-1940* (Seattle: University of Washington Press, 1997); John Mack Faragher, *Daniel Boone: The Life and Legend of an American Pioneer* (New York: Holt, 1992), and *Women and Men on the Overland Trail* (New Haven: Yale University Press, 2001); William C. Davis, *The American Frontier: Pioneers, Settlers and Cowboys, 1800-1899* (Norman: University of Oklahoma Press, 1999).

point of view stationed at the English settlements on the Atlantic coast."[35] Of course, peripheries do not exist except in relation to centers, and vice versa; and of course, one can look at a periphery from a particular center; but the point that modern historiography is trying to make, surely, is that one can also look at that same periphery from the other, neighboring center(s). The very identification of any frontier requires in fact not one but two or more points of view (unless one falls into the Turnerian trap of considering that American frontiers advanced into uninhabited wildernesses). In other words, the modern concept of frontier rises above single national or regional points of view perfectly well. All that is now required is that historians take into account all sides. In addition, one might argue that Patricia Limerick and other New Western historians, far from demolishing the Turnerian approach, have in a certain sense reinforced one aspect of it, insomuch as their central contention—that westward expansion was not the triumphant advance of civilization but the progression of conquest, colonization, and capitalist consolidation (that is, struggles for power, with all their attendant dark motives and methods)—maintains Turner's essential link between what was happening on the nation's frontiers and the development of the national psyche. In short, they have replaced Turner's ethnocentric celebration with general condemnation and national guilt, but the judgemental difference does not of itself invalidate the Turnerian idea of a significant link between the nation's vital center and its frontiers.

On the other hand, the regional criterion that defines New Western history could be considered simply as geographical "downsizing" from the national approach, allowing all the different thematic and interpretive range of scholarship that exists on the national level, with regional peculiarities, but it does not really continue or offer a substitute for national (much less Atlantic) "frontier" history. In fact, New Western historians are not primarily concerned with redefining the concept of "frontier" as an analytical tool for the study of the history of national culture formation. Evidently, the geographical "West," however one draws its boundaries, is not the same thing as the "frontier," which David J. Weber defined as "the edges where people and places meet." The author of the magisterial *The Spanish Frontier in North America* was defending the interest of maintaining the concept of the "frontier" as a useful way of studying the national history of the United States (Turner's purpose), as well as the broader history of the Americas and the Atlantic world.[36] Stephen Aron agrees with New Western historians that the shortcomings of Turner's application of the frontier concept must be recognized and corrected, but, like David Weber, he has also made a good case for recycling the construct. The frontier, Aron feels, "still holds the key to a 'Greater Western

---

[35] Patricia Nelson Limerick, "The Case of the Premature Departure: The Trans-Mississippi West and American History Textbooks," *Journal of American History* 78.4 (March 1992): 1381.

[36] David J. Weber in Worster, "*The Legacy of Conquest*, by Patricia Nelson Limerick," 317. Limerick, "Turnerians All," cit., classifies David Weber, together with William Cronin, John Mack Faragher, and Walter Nugent, as "neo-Turnerian."

History,' if it is reconfigured as the lands where separate polities converged and competed, and where distinct cultures collided and occasionally coincided."[37]

Moreover, the New Western history has other weaknesses of its own. In the first place, there is not, nor can there be, any consensus about exactly what the geographical boundaries of "the West" might be.[38] Generally speaking, New Western historians are not concerned with other places, notably east of the Mississippi (or the 95th, 98th or 100th meridian), or outside the present political borders of the United States, that can be considered to have been historical "Western" frontiers. But insomuch as the twentieth-century West has become more a region with its own peculiarities than a frontier of national expansion, it has simply taken its place as the last of the "transitory Wests" of American history.[39]

In addition, a geographically defined West within the present political limits of the United States cannot fully contain the larger historical reverberations of the notion of a mythical West, "the West" as symbol and state of mind. Whether reflecting on the successive rise and fall of political powers, since the ancient middle-eastern empires recognized by European nations as their cultural cradle, or on the persistant myth of the existence of a Western paradise, or simply on the perceived westward march of "civilization" generally, early modern Europeans associated "the West" with abundance, progress, and happiness. Christopher Columbus's voyage of 1492 had in itself been part of the westward-looking curiosity that had long inspired European thought and occupied European expansionist energies. American visions of "the West" have continued, adapted and endlessly refashioned this symbolic legacy in myriad forms.[40]

At the same time as the New (Far or trans-Mississippi) Western history was emerging, in the 1980s, another new but related field made a successful bid for academic recognition. Using quite comfortably both neo-Turnerian and New Western ideas and methods, historians of the "backcountry" study the earliest North American frontiers, from the first efforts at European colonization to the settlement of the trans-Appalachian territory up to approximately 1820.[41] One overall

---

[37] Stephen Aron, "Lessons in Conquest: Towards a Greater Western History," *Pacific Historical Review* 63 (May 1994): 128.

[38] See for example, Michael P. Malone, ed., *Historians and the American West* (Lincoln: University of Nebraska Press, 1983), 1-14; and Walter Nugent, "Where Is the American West?: Report on a Survey," *Montana: The Magazine of Western History* 42 (Summer 1992): 1-24.

[39] Nugent, "Comparing Wests and Frontiers," 803.

[40] See the classic work Henry Nash Smith, *Virgin Land: The American West as Symbol and Myth* (1950; reprint, Cambridge, MA: Harvard University Press, 1978); and Ray Allen Billington, *Land of Savagery, Land of Promise: The European Image of the American Frontier* (1981; reprint, Norman: University of Oklahoma Press, 1985).

[41] Good examples are Richard R. Beeman, *The Evolution of the Southern Backcountry: A Case Study of Lunenburg County, Virginia, 1746-1832* (Philadelphia: University of Pennsylvania Press, 1984); Thomas P. Slaughter, *The Whiskey Rebellion: Frontier Epilogue to the American Revolution* (New York: Oxford University Press, 1986); Ronald Hoffman, Thad W. Tate, and Peter J. Albert, eds., *An Uncivil War: The Southern Backcountry during the American Revolution* (Charlottesville, VA: Published for the U.S. Capitol Historical Society by the University Press of Virginia, 1985);

conclusion of recent research seems to be that while there is evidence of a strong sense of connection between backcountry elites and East coast and European cultural centers, it is also clear that a common and distinctive backcountry culture was evolving.[42]

Finally, twentieth-century studies of social and economic history have questioned the Turnerian celebration of American mobility as both cause and characteristic of frontier expansion. It is a commonplace to state that modern American historiography has been greatly enriched by the methodological and conceptual influences of other social sciences;[43] but it is true that the study of mobility in the United States, in all its meanings, has occupied a major part of the efforts of modern social scientists and quantitative historians. Nonetheless, many of those trained after the great depression of the 1930s and World War II have rejected the validity of the "safety-valve" theory, and more specifically, Turner's hypothesis that connects migration to/on western frontiers with the socio-economic progress of migrants. Stephan Thernstrom is probably the author most cited as having rejected that particular American myth.[44] Even so, historical evidence showing that migration often brought no economic success does nothing to disprove that people believed in the connection, or indeed, to invalidate the idea that the "safety valve" theory might be usefully applied to the migration towards western frontiers of people who were discontent in the east for non-economic reasons.

*

Modern historians have made great efforts to go beyond the more confrontational interpretations of frontier history, and the ethnocentric Turnerian concept of the frontier as a process of geographically advancing "Americanization" of and by different kinds of pioneers. The "middle ground" concept has found favor as a new

---

Richard White, *The Middle Ground: Indians, Empires, and Republics in the Great Lakes Region, 1650-1815* (New York: Cambridge University Press, 1991); Daniel H. Usner, Jr., *Indians, Settlers and Slaves in a Frontier Exchange Economy: The Lower Mississippi Valley before 1783* (Chapel Hill: University of North Carolina Press, 1992); and Andrew R.L. Cayton and Fredrika J. Teute, eds., *Contact Points: American Frontiers from the Mohawk Valley to the Mississippi, 1750-1830* (Chapel Hill: University of North Carolina Press, 1998). For a discussion of this historiographical trend, see Gregory H. Nobles, "Breaking into the Backcountry: New Approaches to the Early American Frontier, 1750-1800," *The William and Mary Quarterly*, 3rd ser., 46.4 (October 1989): 641-670; and Albert H. Tillson, Jr., "The Southern Backcountry: A Survey of Current Research," *Virginia Magazine of History and Biography* 98 (1990): 388-397.

[42] Nobles, "Breaking into the Backcountry," 643.

[43] See for example, Daniele Fiorentino, ed., *La storia americana e le scienze sociali in Europa e negli Stati Uniti* (Roma: Istituto della Enciclopedia Italiana, 1996).

[44] Stephan Thernstrom, *Poverty and Progress: Social Mobility in a Nineteenth Century City* (Cambridge, MA: Harvard University Press, 1964). For an earlier critique of the Turnerian "safety valve" idea, see for example, Fred A. Shannon, "The Homestead Act and Labor Surplus," *American Historical Review* 41 (July 1936): 637-651.

way of looking at the frontier. Defined only partly or imprecisely by geographical considerations, the "middle ground" is above all a cultural meeting-place; a place where different peoples and cultures might coexist and interact in many ways. Interaction, of course, includes every kind of relationship, from open and violent conflict to active, voluntary cooperation, and complex combined and qualified responses in between which reveal (or conceal) all sorts of simultaneous ambivalences and evolutionary processes.

Nonetheless, Paul Otto argues that modern intellectual attitudes towards multiculturalism, cultural relativism, and political correctness have tended to downplay the conflictive aspects of frontier encounters and of cultural resistance and continuities, in favor of a greater stress on cooperative aspects and what he considers an anachronistic celebration of cultural blending. This historiographical trend is in part a reaction against older interpretations that did emphasize frontier antagonism, and in part an expression of "culturally-bound scholarship" that projects into the past the values of the present. Consequently, this author calls for a clear definition of culture as an essential starting point for more balanced analyses of cultural interaction. He shows a personal preference for the comprehensive (indeed, all-inclusive) definition of Canadian historian C.T. McIntire, but suggests that it might be useful to distinguish worldviews (ideas and values), on the one hand, and societal structures (the concrete results of human creativity such as institutions, associations, relationships), on the other. The main thrust of Otto's reflections is that all culture is by definition dynamic, and constantly changing. Therefore, the notion that people "lose" their "own" culture as a function of "gaining" aspects of a foreign culture (especially when expressed in terms of diminishment or of increase), contradicts the concept of culture as a non-quantifiable aspect of humanity which is always evolving.

By questioning exactly what is meant by the history of "American literature," Michael Boyden poses the problems involved when present political boundaries and national identities are projected into the past. Contemporary opinions strongly discourage the continued application of criteria for selection which have tended to exclude certain groups, based on their gender, class, race, culture or language. This demand for the inclusion of all ethnic groups, even if their literature is not always written in English, is a characteristic of modern democratic and multicultural views of American society. However, the problem of projecting such views into the past, in order to produce a chronologically extended, ethnically inclusive history of "American literature," clashes immediately with the realities of the historically changing territorial boundaries of the United States of America. All cultures are distinguished from others by the chronological and geographical boundaries within which they develop. Even if one ignores the issue of the restrictive appropriation of the adjective "American" to mean only the United States, the attempt to include all peoples, cultures, languages and literatures that at any time in the past have inhabited the territory which is now within the political boundaries of the United States gives rise to all sorts of questions. Using present territoriality, as opposed to culture, as a criterion of judging what is to be included as "American" may appear to offer a more objective or aseptic yardstick than others, but might also be criticized as creating problems of its own. What is acceptable and even desirable for the present may become seriously warped when applied to that foreign country, the past.

The designers of American literary histories who apply the territorial criterion purport to generously accept as part of their own the literary culture of other peoples, who lived in other historical periods when the United States did not exercise any political jurisdiction over the territory in question, or indeed when the United States did not even exist. Some might say that such an ahistorical definition of what is "American" reveals unbounded cultural greed, in the sense that its "acceptance" of all literary manifestations within the territory could be interpreted as a unilateral "appropriation" of other people's cultural heritage. Conversely, the territorial criterion might exclude the literary production of American authors who worked outside the United States. In short, Boyden's essay provokes deep thought about the notion that territoriality offers a better criterion than culture for defining "American" literature, basically because it seems more politically acceptable.

Carmen de la Guardia seeks explanations and justifications of early American territorial expansion in the political culture of the late 1780s. In her review of historiographical interpretations of the early national period, this author supports the thesis that territorial expansion was seen as a means to overcome internal divisions within the republic and as a source of strength in international relations. Viewed from the perspective of public discourse during the great debate on the ratification of the federal constitution of 1787, the Federalist defense of a large federal republic found a way to counter the widely-held notion that a republic could be truly virtuous and cohesive only if it remained small in territorial extent and population. While Antifederalists mostly followed Locke and Montesquieu, the most persuasive argument put forward by Madison was much influenced by the ideas of Scottish philosopher David Hume. In short, the idea took shape that, far from being a death-knell, it could be an advantage for a republic to have a very large territory and population, because the representative form of government and a system of delegated powers would tend to diminish the importance of individual interests and political factions. In short, Madison argued, a large territory would positively encourage the development of national values rooted in the concept of republican civic virtue, and at the same time promote political stability. In this way, the very early constitutional debates provided the theoretical justification, encouragement even, for the continuous expansion of the continental frontiers of the new nation.

The expeditions promoted by Thomas Jefferson between 1803 and 1807 for the exploration of the trans-Mississippian territory provide Marco Sioli with a particular subject matter from which to analyze diverse aspects of Jeffersonian interest in western frontiers, and Jeffersonian attitudes towards the Native American inhabitants of the land. The author contends that the expeditions captained by Meriwether Lewis and William Clark (1803-1806), William Dunbar and George Hunter (1804-1805), Thomas Freeman and Peter Custis (1806), and Zebulon Pike (1805-1807) shared certain characteristics that clarify the motives and purposes of the president and his collaborators. Sioli concludes that apart from essential mapping of routes, landmarks and locations of strategic value, scientific aims and activities were not of paramount importance in Jefferson's instructions or in the achievements of the successive expeditions. Their aims were fundamentally political and military.

Stripped of the scientific veneer that cloaked Jefferson's instructions to Lewis and Clark, Dunbar and Hunter, Freeman and Custis, Pike's expeditions in particular were bald warnings to British, Spanish and Indian neighbors that the United States would extend the boundaries of the Louisiana territory as far as possible and sustain its claim on the land.

The role of Irish immigrants into Texas between 1829 and 1835 provides Graham Davis with a particular case study to discuss different ways in which myths have lain at the heart of popular and historiographical perceptions of the early settlement of the southwestern frontier. Traditional historiography of Irish emigration has accustomed readers to the idea of a poor and oppressed people forced from their homeland by tyranny and famine. Davis demolishes this mythical view by pointing out that the Irishmen that emigrated to Texas were in fact people of some means, able to pay for their passage out and enough supplies to support their families for at least a year. Rather than being forced into exile, they were opportunists attracted by generous Mexican land grants. Secondly, the image of Texas as a paradise encouraged Irish immigration into this region and some optimistic letter-writers and nostalgic memoirs clung to that version, but historical research has underscored the harsh realities of frontier life on the arid, unprotected Texan plains, citing other testimonies that belied that particular myth. Thirdly, historiographical trends dealing with the frontier, from Turner and Webb to the New Western History, can be usefully applied to the Irish Texan case to test myths and interpretations such as the "Americanizing" effect of the frontier, cultural blending in frontier environments, the achievements of industrious pioneer settlers, and the different perspectives of women regarding frontier life. Finally, in confronting the rags-to-riches legend of Irish immigrant Thomas O'Connor with documented historical reality, Graham Davis is not only pursuing the truth of this particular case, but he uses it to underscore his overall argument: that the hold of certain versions of history on the collective imagination has owed a great deal to the fact that they served romantic and nationalistic purposes.

The antebellum north-south divide would seem to be one of the more generally accepted internal frontiers in United States history. Slavery seems to provide a broad brush with which to draw a dividing line between slave and free states: a line which would find not only geographical and territorial expression along the lines of the political jurisdiction of the states, but would give rise to profound regional differences in economic structures, political ideas and institutions, social life, and cultural features. Nonetheless, by comparing the social history of small farmers living in antebellum northern and southern rural communities, Louis Billington and David Brown argue that there were in fact many similarities in their daily lives, and that the Mason-Dixon line did not separate two distinct cultures. In considering the role of political boundaries, the authors reach the conclusion that the most immediately significant boundary recognized and defended in both north and south was that of the individual household, closely followed by local boundaries of importance for the community, and geographical obstacles that fomented isolation, poverty, and backwardness by restricting communication and commerce.

Another line of inquiry indicates that ordinary white northern and southern farmers shared a very similar economic outlook, and were driven by similar motivations and aspirations, in their reactions to the development of opportunities for trade and the market revolution. Recent historiography has increasingly found that entrepreneurial attitudes, including risk-taking, profit-oriented strategies, and the deliberate renunciation of total self-sufficiency in favor of production for the market, were more evident among both northern and southern farmers than was previously thought. Self-sufficient "safety-first" farming was practised in all areas, but farmers in New England and in Appalachia also showed themselves to be sufficiently flexible and aggressive to seek out and respond to market opportunities. Finally, issues of gender also tend to suggest that northern and southern women's lives may not have been so different as has often been supposed, whether considering their household and farming activities or their opportunities for work outside the home and farm. In sum, Billington and Brown's analysis shows that current historiographical trends have opened up the debate on the differences that once appeared to establish a clear north-south divide, by highlighting similarities between certain groups of people in certain areas of their lives, by simultaneously noting striking differences between local communities within regions, and by contextualizing all in the light of more global or, at least, Atlantic perspectives.

Joseph Smith examines President Rutherford B. Hayes's attitude toward the construction of an interoceanic canal in Central America, as expressed in his message of March 1880. The essential importance of the notion that the United States ought to control such a canal was that, by stating this as American policy, Hayes was unilaterally extending government jurisdiction beyond the internationally recognized territorial limits of U.S. sovereignty. American interest in interoceanic communications had been steadily growing since the British and Mexican treaties of 1846 and 1848 had placed the western American frontier on the Pacific coast. It had been expressed repeatedly in many ways, as possible routes were studied and discussed, and as land concessions and legal rights were negotiated. The French project to build a canal across the Isthmus of Panama, under the direction of Ferdinand de Lesseps, was of grave concern to the U.S. government, although the official attitude was studiously supportive. When Hayes declared that if the canal were completed it would be "virtually a part of the coastline of the United States," he was creating the concept of a virtual frontier. The claim did not provoke a diplomatic dispute because the European powers chose to ignore it, but it did not escape scathing criticism in the periodical press. Meanwhile, Hayes worked behind the scenes to put diplomatic pressure on the Colombian government in order to strengthen the American position based on the treaty of 1846. British officials did not doubt that if any transisthmian canal were to be built, it would be or come under American control. Despite the evident commercial interest of such a canal, the U.S. government was not disappointed when the French enterprise collapsed in 1892.

When, in 1890, the continental frontier of the United States was declared to be in existence no longer, this message together with Frederick Jackson Turner's 1893 thesis on its importance in the formation of the American nation became influential in several very different historical processes examined by Frank Schumacher. On the one hand, the closing of the frontier provoked misgivings about the possible consequences of the loss of the frontier experience for future generations of Americans, and contributed to the drive for overseas expansion. However, the ensuing debate led to doubts about the validity of the frontier thesis when applied to tropical possessions. According to Turner's interpretation, the frontier had played a vital role in the historical development of the American nation and of its values, so, as the economic depression of 1893 deepened, so too did the sense of anxious foreboding about the national future.

The acquisition of possessions in the Caribbean and Pacific after 1898 led some to argue that these territories would provide the United States with a useful new frontier. However, Schumacher argues that difficulties connected with adaptation to the physical environment (in particular, the tropical climate of the islands), and the cultural resistance of the native inhabitants, soon persuaded many that conditions on such tropical islands would not strengthen the American virtues and values thought to have been forged on the continental frontier, and indeed might even lead to their degeneration. The notion of American exceptionalism was also challenged by the fact that the government sought information about European, and especially British, colonial ideas and practices, with a view to learning how to deal with the innumerable problems involved in governing tropical colonies. Tropical medicine, urban planning, public sanitation measures, and the like, all formed part of a larger story of transatlantic exchange of knowledge and experience. American imperialism of this period not only destroyed a key element of the exceptionalist paradigm in a general sense for liberal thinkers worldwide, but it brought the United States very actively into the European fold of imperial powers, as well as providing further evidence of the turn-of-the-century Anglo-American rapprochement.

Robert Lewis explores the historiographical potential of characterizing Acadiana or Cajun country as a "French borderland" between the 1890s and 1968. The multiple geographical and historical origins of people of French cultural heritage who now inhabit parts of southern Louisiana greatly complicated in the past their sense of sharing an ethnic identity. That complex shared identity was to a large degree inspired by their resistance against "the voracious Anglo-Saxon maw of assimilation." The French language spoken in Louisiana included many local dialects, both archaic and anglicized, with distinct Acadian and African inflections, as well as the forms used by the French-speaking elite in and around New Orleans, but the gradual loss of proficiency in the language throughout the twentieth century has clearly broken down one important cultural characteristic that contributed to the notion of a francophone community. Despite the traumatic Acadian experience of tragic exile and the once derogatory meaning attached to the term "Cajun," Acadian and Cajun labels have been successfully exploited for local commercial and related "theme-park" purposes.

Nonetheless, a vague invented memory of a shared "French" past seems to be the present form of ethnic consciousness among Louisiana's inhabitants who choose to claim it as an important ingredient of their identity. Lewis argues that the Acadian case offers evidence in support of the idea that ethnogenesis is not so much a product of "objective" traits and "real" characteristics, such as religion, race, ancestry, language, place of birth, history, and so on, but people's belief or perception that they form a distinct ethnic group, or their desire to do so, even if the component elements of that belief or perception are only imagined or invented. As their geographical isolation and economic backwardness have gradually been overcome, the descendants of Acadian settlers seem to have realized that the Acadian or Cajun heritage has become a somewhat flimsy basis for a separate ethnicity, and they have increasingly turned to their self-perception as being "French." This provides a much more inclusive ethnic label that also embraces other white, black and mixed-blood Louisiana natives who claim a French ancestral or cultural connection, as well as offering historical links with France, Canada and the Caribbean. This process of ethnogenesis is largely the expression of a reaction against "Angloamericanization," but commerce has been a much stronger driving force than culture in determining its characteristics.

David K. Adams brings a lifetime of study of the New Deal to these reflections on the frontier theme in the era of Franklin D. Roosevelt. South Dakota is depicted as a geographical and economic borderland deeply marked by deprivation and depression. To be sure, the author shows that individual mobility and the mythical attraction of the west continued to exert their influence on American society throughout the 1930s, and that New Dealers were inspired by powerful old frontier images and mythology as they shaped their discourse of the "new frontier" for their own political ends. However, David Adams's chief argument is not so much about geographical frontiers and socio-economic opportunities as about the fact that New Deal measures provoked administrative difficulties and political infighting, which in turn led to the redefinition of the jurisdictional boundaries of the different branches and agencies of government. In sum, Rooseveltian reformism, by radically changing the extent of what were considered necessary and legitimate areas of government intervention, and by transforming old administrative departments and creating new ones, posed serious problems regarding the general delimitation and internal partition of government authority. This expanding New Deal frontier of federal government action would have far-reaching repercussions on American political life and on notions of the role of government in the struggle for social justice.

John Steinbeck's story of the Joad family's westward trek from Oklahoma to California in search of work was almost a parody of Turnerian celebration of American mobility and opportunity on western frontiers. When Darryl F. Zanuck, vice-president at Twentieth-Century Fox, and film director John Ford decided to turn the novel into a film, they were working within, although simultaneously testing, several other kinds of boundaries. *The Grapes of Wrath* (1940) depicted the family's experience of migrating to the "new" Pacific West, but Melvyn Stokes does not dwell on its demythologizing effect on Turner's frontier hypothesis or on popular notions of westering. Instead, he examines the significance of this film in terms of the invisible but effective frontiers and boundaries which restricted film makers' freedom of expression. The censorship exercised by the Production Code Administration set legal limits on the morally and politically permissible content of the film. Ford recreated and shot several of Steinbeck's more provocative scenes, but was not allowed to include them in the final product. Zanuck, who was in charge of production, had a real interest in making "social consciousness" movies, partly for idealistic reasons and partly because he believed they would be profitable, but worries about negative reactions led Zanuck to alter Ford's radical ending, producing a film that seriously warped Steinbeck's original novel.

Nevertheless, Stokes contends that *The Grapes of Wrath* pushed at the existing boundaries of "free" speech on social issues such as poverty, labor exploitation, workers' rights, and radical politics. It also expanded the frontiers of the film industry itself, in the sense that it was clearly at the cutting edge of the art of movie production in both technical and aesthetic terms. *The Grapes of Wrath* was a box-office success but received mixed criticisms. Within a very few years, financial and other difficulties within the film industry reinforced the effects of cold war attitudes such as that expressed by Eric Johnston, president of the Motion Picture Association of America, in March 1947: "We'll have no more films that show the seamy side of American life." As a result, the boundaries of permissible movie subjects were severely retracted for a long time.

Like the concept of the frontier, that of the "middle ground" can be usefully applied to enhance our understanding of historiographical divides spawned by political ideology. James Ryan explains that most American historians writing about the communist party in the United States (CPUSA 1919-1957) have tended to be either strongly for or against the party's activities for ideological reasons. Both sides, he contends, have systematically ignored historical evidence that contradicted their own sympathetic or adverse analyses. In particular, he argues that the supra-national ties and global aims of communism and socialism have harmed their historiography in the United States. Nonetheless, this author feels that it would not only be more professional and sensible to identify common ground, or to seek what he calls a "middle path," but that this is now a viable proposition. Such a historiographical meeting place could be more geared to cooperative efforts in truth-seeking than to confrontation, since there are aspects of communist party history, especially regarding the history of the indigenous American members of the communist party, that both sides can accept without renouncing the essence of their own interpretations. The author draws attention to the pioneering efforts of the CPUSA to widen the boundaries of public discourse, spotlighting social injustices, racism, and political corruption. However, at the same time their international aims and activities raised legitimate national security concerns, with the result that the political left was discredited in the United States, and progress in civil rights was severely retarded.

After World War II and for most of the 1950s there was no public funding for the arts in the United States. This policy was supported by the conservative right but criticized by pragmatic liberals. David Howard argues that among the many effects of the launching of the Soviet Sputnik in 1957, one unlikely American response was the increase in public funding of the arts. The news about Sputnik of course had a huge and many-faceted impact on public opinion and political discourse, creating a general sense of alarm about American scientific and technological prowess, about standards in basic skills taught in schools, about national defense, and so on. David Howard's chief thesis is that John F. Kennedy and other ambitious "New Frontiersmen" exploited the anxiety caused by what was called the "missile gap," suggesting that there was an equally alarming "culture gap," and that a responsible federal government should actively strive to close both. Among the radical measures they suggested to "save" the national body and mind was the proposal that federal funds should be made available to support the arts. Their main concern was the "gap" which was perceived to separate avant-garde creativity—which inspired only a peripheral minority of bohemians—and the popular culture of the middle class or kitsch, which delighted the masses. Thus, pragmatic liberals such as Jacob Javits, Arthur Schlesinger, Jr., August Heckscher, Jr., and Sebastian De Grazia strove to redefine the role in American society of avant-garde artists as modern cultural "frontiersmen." Avant-garde creations, although perceived by the majority to be on the remote artistic periphery, represented the continued vitality of the idea of individual freedom being expressed and strengthened on the frontier, and they therefore formed an integral part of American culture. The establishment of the National Endowment for the Arts in 1965 would be the culmination of this idea.

The battle for Hawaiian statehood was drawn out over many years. Partisan politics was initially to blame, as republicans and democrats worried about the Hawaiian vote. The matter was further complicated when the statehood negotiations became inextricably bound up with the Alaskan case. Southern opposition to citizenship for the Asian and mixed-blood population of the islands was caused by fears about the effects of the Hawaiian social model, in which interracial marriages were increasingly common, on racial and civil rights issues in the United States, and this was by far the biggest obstacle to acceptance of Hawaiian statehood. Giles Scott-Smith explains these and other factors, as a prologue to his examination of the roles of Dwight D. Eisenhower and Lyndon B. Johnson in this matter. Both presidents were strongly in favor of the admission of Hawaii as a state of the Union, but Johnson's interest proved to be definitive in making it possible. The story of Johnson's political manoevering in the late 1950s in favor of Hawaiian statehood makes fascinating reading, but the author argues that his aims were much more ambitious than solving this long-delayed statehood issue. His strong support for the establishment of the East-West Center for Technical and Cultural Exchange show rather that he had a vision of Hawaii as a meeting point of different cultural worlds, and of the new Center as a bridge between the United States and Asia, which would enhance the power of American propaganda in the Cold War. Johnson's vision embraced Hawaiian statehood and the creation of the East-West Center as political triumphs for himself and his party, as a means of extending the frontiers of American influence into the Pacific and Asia, and ultimately as a contributing factor to the breakdown of racial frontiers within the United States.

Ingrid Eumann's essay examines multiple strands of the perception of Las Vegas as a new western frontier of the late twentieth century. On the surface, the separation of the "real" city from the tourist areas, together with the substitution of "Old West" styles and themes in the city's architecture, decorative arts, and entertainment, in favor of other popular, grandiose and exotic urban landscaping, would seem to suggest that Las Vegas wants to distance itself from its very real heritage as a western frontier town. However, the author argues that the publicity claim of Las Vegas to be the "entertainment capital of the world" places the city squarely in the vanguard of entertainment design and technology, thereby converting it into a new frontier in a metaphoric sense. In addition, as the fastest-growing metropolitan area in the United States, Las Vegas fully complies with traditional images of the western frontier, where newcomers flocked, where opportunities of all sorts abounded, and newness prevailed. Furthermore, on a more psychological level, references to the western frontier heritage are even more palpable through the constant appeals to the darker side of individual freedom. Both fiction and film have tended to insistently stress and develop themes in which Las Vegas subjects individuals to moral tests that might lead either to the reinforcement of traditional notions regarding the beneficial effects of the frontier on human character, or to personal corruption and tragedy. Thus, the images of unrestrained personal liberty in the old Wild West frontiers are echoed in the continued use of such provocative descriptions as "Sin City" and "The City of Freedom," while the ultimate hedonistic experience of modern "fun" interfaces with equally compelling hints of hovering dangers.

The image of Alaska as "the last frontier" of the United States forms part of the state's history, its popular culture and daily life, its touristic propaganda, and its state policy. From the spate of gold rushes that began in the late nineteenth-century to the late twentieth-century clashes of economic and ecological interests, as "advancing civilization" penetrated the Alaskan wilderness, this vast northern region identifies very closely with the historical experiences of the western territories of the contiguous United States, but at the same time claims its right to construct its own separate identity. Tity de Vries points out that, although in 1926 Frederick Jackson Turner himself recognized Alaska as the last frontier, historians of the western frontiers generally did not begin to include it as a part of their field until the 1970s, but, even in the New Western history which arose in the 1980s and 1990s, Alaska continued to appear only as a marginal subject.[45] Nonetheless, historical themes and interpretations play a large part in modern representations of Alaska as the last frontier state. The image of the frontier as a place of opportunity and progress, excitement and romance, is deployed by those who claim that this gives Alaska its authentically American identity and its attraction for investors, businessmen, immigrants and tourists; in a word, development. This would be what Peter A. Coates described as the "booster" interpretation of the frontier image. The association of the frontier with unspoiled wilderness lends itself to other more conservationist and environmentalist discourses which claim that Alaska is different, even unique, and should learn from and avoid the mistakes that caused irreparable damage on earlier western American frontiers.

Tity de Vries analyzes the different interpretations and uses of the frontier concept as it has been applied in the history theme park which was launched in 1967 in Fairbanks under the name of Alaskaland (and which was renamed Pioneer Park in 2003). Boosterism underscored Alaska's heroic past and dynamic future, although taking care to suggest that development would not spoil or destroy the natural and cultural heritage of the state. The park has not been a commercial success, and a large part of the problem has been a lack of focus regarding its aims and potential. The author suggests that the change of focus in the 1990s towards historic preservation, without abandoning more commercial touristic attractions, is a

---

[45] Interestingly enough, *Webster's New International Dictionary of the English Language* (New York, 1909), cited in Mood, "The Concept of the Frontier," 81, had given as one definition of "frontier": "2. The border or advance region of settlement and civilization; as, the Alaskan frontier. Chiefly U.S."

reflection of current ideological and historiographical trends and is also more in accord with the sentiments of the local community, who see the park as a representation of their own past and identity. Nevertheless, taking examples from trains and boats, village buildings, shops, entertainment, and exhibits of mining equipment and techniques, Tity de Vries reveals that the influences of historical boosterism continue to dominate over historical conservation and environmentalism in the presentation of the frontier image of Alaska.

In sum, the essays in this volume offer a mosaic of the many interpretive angles from which the fascinating concepts of frontiers and boundaries can be studied. The authors by no means exhaust the possibilities of this key theme in the history of the United States, but they do aim to contribute to on-going discussions, by bringing together some of the applications that this useful analytical framework has had in American historiography.

REASSESSING AMERICAN FRONTIER THEORY: CULTURE, CULTURAL RELATIVISM, AND THE MIDDLE GROUND IN EARLY AMERICA[1]

Paul Otto

Since the end of the nineteenth century, when Frederick Jackson Turner first pronounced his thesis concerning the significance of the frontier in U.S. history, many American historians have questioned its importance. In the past twenty five or thirty years, frontier theory has experienced a remarkable renaissance, especially in early American studies. Yet the new emphasis on the frontier differs markedly from Turner's thesis. Unlike Turner's approach, which understood the frontier as a line of advancing (western) civilization, modern frontier historians see it as a meeting place of cultures and societies. Many of the new frontier historians go even further and describe the frontier as a "middle ground" or a "place in between" where it is emphasized that representatives of distinct cultures not only meet and interact, but they temporarily or permanently create new cultural patterns and practices.[2] Borrowing heavily from ethnohistory, the new frontier historians also seek to understand historical peoples on their own cultural terms.

The new approach has done much to aid our understanding of relations between Europeans or Euro-Americans and indigenous peoples throughout the history of North America. Being open to the possibility that the frontier was a cultural meeting place of peoples and not a line of advancing European or Euro-American civilization has opened historians' eyes to a whole range of human interactions previously obscured by earlier notions of the frontier as a rigid boundary between races and cultures. But as widespread and useful as the new frontier approach is, a number of weaknesses attend it. First of all, the middle ground interpretation has tended to predominate in studies of the colonial northeast, and as a result, it no longer provides the interpretive power which it first held. Middle ground advocates seem to assume that the frontier entails acculturation and tend to ignore cases of cultural persistence, aiming always (and often exclusively it seems) to identify cases of cultural change and accommodation. Second, in seeking out cases of acculturation and mixing, scholars focus their attentions on increasingly narrow topics producing a wide array of microstudies which are quite interesting but may not tell us much about broader patterns of cultural interaction on the frontier. Third, while this approach focuses upon the extent and nature of cultural change on the

---

[1] The following individuals have read earlier versions of this essay and graciously commented on it: Brad Birzer, Hubert Krygsman, James LaGrand, Lynn Otto, Amy Schutt, Mark Tazelaar, students in my 2001 senior seminar at Dordt College, and participants of a Dordt College Faculty Forum in October 2001. Thanks also goes to participants of the Sixth Middelburg Conference on "Frontiers and Boundaries in U.S. History" who asked important questions and offered insightful comments during and after my paper session, and to the editors of this volume.

[2] The phrase "middle ground" comes from Richard White's well-known work, *The Middle Ground: Indians, Empires, and Republics in the Great Lakes Region, 1650-1815* (New York: Cambridge University Press, 1991) which will be discussed further below.

frontier, those scholars who utilize this theory often only vaguely or too broadly define culture itself, thus having no framework or standard by which to measure the cultural change and degree of acculturation they set out to identify. Finally, middle ground proponents subscribe to cultural relativism, a laudable approach when seeking to understand groups on all sides of the frontier, but a practice which has been inconsistently and unequally applied. This partly results from the difficulty in finding a vantage point from which to examine all cultures equally.

This essay summarizes the central idea of the new frontier theory—especially as it has been applied to the study of the early American frontier in the colonial northeast, elaborates on the weaknesses just noted, and suggests ways of defining and understanding the idea of culture so that historians of Native American-European relations can better delineate patterns of cultural change and development on the frontier.

Frontier as a Region of Cultural Mixing

In today's American frontier theory, U.S. scholars use the term *frontier* to refer to a zone of cross-cultural interaction. They are not alone in using this definition. Over twenty years ago, a group of historians from Canada, Great Britain, the Netherlands, South Africa, and the United States, with common interests in the history of European-indigenous relations in North America and South Africa gathered in a seminar to comparatively explore these relations. They produced a volume, *The Frontier in History: North America and Southern Africa Compared*, edited by Howard Lamar and Leonard Thompson, who gave voice to this newly evolving, broader frontier perspective. In their introduction to the volume, the editors declared that the frontier should be seen "not as a boundary or line, but as a territory or zone of interpenetration between two previously distinct societies."[3] Even before the publication of this volume, James Axtell wrote in his essay "The Ethnohistory of Early America," that "the frontiers where [Europeans, Africans, and Indians] met were thus human spaces, not geographical spaces accidentally occupied by the people. Wherever diverse cultures came together, whether for trade, war, or love, there was the frontier."[4]

This definition of the frontier and its importance to the study of early America has been widely adopted and reiterated by historians of the colonial period. In his 1989 work, *The Formation of a Planter Elite*, Alan Gallay stated that "on the ...

---

[3] Howard Lamar and Leonard Thompson, ed., *The Frontier in History: North America and Southern Africa Compared* (New Haven: Yale University Press, 1981), 5, 7-8. For an insightful discussion on the evolution the frontier thesis since its promotion by Frederick Jackson Turner, see Kerwin Lee Klein, "Reclaiming the 'F' Word, Or Being and Becoming Postwestern," *Pacific Historical Review* 65 (May 1996): 179-215; and Kerwin Lee Klein, *Frontiers of Historical Imagination: Narrating the European Conquest of Native America, 1890-1990* (Berkeley: University of California Press, 1997).

[4] James Axtell, "The Ethnohistory of Early America: A Review Essay," *William and Mary Quarterly* 35.1 (January 1978): 110.

frontier people of different races, religions, and ethnic groups lived in close proximity and greatly influenced each other's lives", adding: "Peoples of the ... frontier ... had to learn from each other and adapt themselves and their institutions to an environment undergoing vast demographic, social, economic, and political changes." More recently, in his survey of American frontiers from the colonial period through the late nineteenth century, Gregory Nobles has claimed that "the real significance of the North American frontier lies not only in the single-minded conquest eventually achieved by one people over others, but also in the complex roles played by all the peoples that took part in the struggle."[5] In recent years, it seems that most historians of early America agree that a complete understanding of the colonial experience must include a discussion of the frontier as defined by Lamar and Thompson. As Colin Calloway has recently argued in *New Worlds for All*, Europeans and Native Americans shared a vast geographic, cultural, material, and linguistic landscape in early America. Andrew Cayton and Fredrika Teute offer some of the most recent expressions of the central role of the frontier in their edited volume *Contact Points*: "Historians may dismiss eighteenth-century assumptions about development as ethnocentric—even racist—but they cannot deny that the European conquest of North America, and the frontiers it created, must be at the center of any analysis of the history of this continent."[6]

The new historiography that has emerged during the past quarter century has not disappointed in revealing the dynamics of intercultural contact along the frontier. Nineteenth-century histories told stories of frontier conquest where uncivilized natives gave way before the advances of civilized Europe and the United States. In those works, sympathy lay with whites and the authors portrayed the Indians as savages. Early correctives to such a vision empathized with the native people, highlighting the injustice of the conquest and their victimization.[7] In both cases, however, native people were seen as objects of the imperial conquest. Beginning in the 1970s, however, works began to appear which gave attention to Native

---

[5] Alan Gallay, *The Formation of a Planter Elite: Jonathan Bryan and the Southern Colonial Frontier* (Athens: University of Georgia Press, 1989), xv-xvi; Gregory Nobles, *American Frontiers: Cultural Encounters and Continental Conquest* (New York: Hill and Wang, 1997), 24. In their recent essay, "From Borderlands to Borders: Empires, Nation-States, and the Peoples in Between in North American History," Jeremy Adelman and Stephen Aron explore the meaning of the frontier in relation to the concept of borderlands, bringing greater clarity to the definitions of both. See also the useful critiques in the following issue of the *American Historical Review* by Evan Haefeli, Christopher Ebert Schmidt-Nowara, and John R. Wunder and Pekka Hämäläinen, and Adelman and Aron's response, *American Historical Review* 104.4 (October 1999): 1221-1239.

[6] Colin G. Calloway, *New Worlds for All: Indians, Europeans, and the Remaking of Early America* (Baltimore, MD: Johns Hopkins University Press, 1997), *passim*; Andrew R.L. Cayton and Fredrika J. Teute, ed., *Contact Points: American Frontiers from the Mohawk Valley to the Mississippi, 1750-1830* (Chapel Hill: University of North Carolina Press, 1998), 2.

[7] Helen Hunt Jackson's *Century of Dishonor* (New York: Harper, 1881) exemplifies this approach.

Americans themselves.[8] The first such studies sought to reveal the rationality of native people, restoring human dignity to the choices they made and the ideas and interests which motivated their actions. By the 1980s, such attention to Indians evolved into an examination of the interaction of people from diverse cultures.[9] The focus soon centered on the worlds created by Europeans and Native Americans together. The history of colonial America, these works suggested, could not be properly understood without hearing both sides of the story. For example, Neal Salisbury brought together the stories of Puritanism and Algonquian rivalries in *Manitou and Providence: Indians, Europeans, and the Making of New England, 1500-1643*.[10] This book retold the history of New England, arguing for the importance of contact between Europeans and Native Americans in the shaping of the New England colonies. Many other works explored cultural interaction and change.[11]

In 1991, this new frontier history seemed to culminate in the publication of Richard White's *The Middle Ground: Indians, Empires, and Republics in the Great Lakes Region, 1650-1815*. In this volume, White dramatically portrayed a world "in between" where French traders and various bands of Algonquian peoples created common meanings and experiences in the *pays d'en haut* of New France. Many other works followed, closely scrutinizing the frontier in early America and the nineteenth-century American West. These demonstrated that where stories of cultural division and conquest had once predominated, scholars could also find stories of cultural confluence and mixing.[12] No longer could historians describe cultures and societies in monolithic terms, assuming the predominance of conflict

---

[8] See for example the the following works by Francis Jennings: *The Invasion of America: Indians, Colonialism, and the Cant of Conquest* (Chapel Hill: University of North Carolina Press, 1975); *The Ambiguous Iroquois Empire: The Covenant Chain Confederation of Indian Tribes with English Colonies* (New York: Norton, 1984); *Empire of Fortune: Crowns, Colonies, and Tribes in the Seven Years War in America* (New York: Norton, 1988).

[9] For example, James Axtell, *The European and the Indian: Essays in the Ethnohistory of Colonial North America* (New York: Oxford University Press, 1981); James Axtell, *The Invasion Within: The Contest of Cultures in Colonial North America* (New York: Oxford University Press, 1985).

[10] Neal Salisbury, *Manitou and Providence: Indians, Europeans, and the Making of New England, 1500-1643* (New York: Oxford University Press, 1982).

[11] Some of these include James H. Merrell, *The Indians' New World: Catawbas and Their Neighbors from European Contact though the Era of Removal* (Chapel Hill: University of North Carolina Press for the Institute of Early American History and Culture, 1989); Daniel K. Richter, *The Ordeal of the Longhouse: The Peoples of the Iroquois League in the Era of European Colonization* (Chapel Hill: University of North Carolina Press for the Institute of Early American History and Culture, 1992).

[12] Notable examples include Kathleen M. Brown, *Good Wives, Nasty Wenches, & Anxious Patriarchs: Gender, Race, and Power in Colonial Virginia* (Chapel Hill: University of North Carolina Press for the Omohundro Institute for Early American History and Culture, 1996); Calloway, *New Worlds for All*; Cayton and Teute, *Contact Points*; Daniel K. Richter, *Facing East from Indian Country: A Native History of Early America* (Cambridge, MA: Harvard University Press, 2001).

when representatives of their respective societies came into contact. Much like Salisbury's history of early New England, these new interpretations often emphasized not only how the frontier and European-Native American relations needed to be reappraised, but how developments on the frontier shaped the broader history of early America. Perhaps this is no better seen than in Fred Anderson's history of the Seven Years War. In *Crucible of War: The Seven Years' War and the Fate of Empire in British North America, 1754-1766*, Anderson tells the story from both sides of the frontier as well as both sides of the Atlantic, weaving together British politics and Indian politics, European rivalries and frontier rivalries. While various participants of this military engagement may have understood the war from their vantage point as either the Seven Years' War or the French and Indian War or perhaps something else, as Anderson demonstrates, all events of that war were interrelated. He claims that the Seven Years' War was "above all ... a theater of intercultural interaction."[13]

The Middle Ground and Cultural Relativism

While the new frontier theory has much to commend it and holds much popularity with historians of early America and the American West, it is not without weaknesses. These lie not so much in the theory itself, as in its application.

In the first place, I believe that something one could call the "middle ground syndrome" has prevailed in frontier studies. As with all seminal works, Richard White's *The Middle Ground* has had great influence, and rightly so. However, I believe that many historians of the frontier since his publication have overemphasized this approach, tending to stress not simply that the frontier was a place of cultural interaction, but that it was above all a place of cultural mixing, change, and adaptation. Cultural confluence, or the blending of cultures on the frontier, has thus become a predominating ideal, while attention to cultural continuities has greatly diminished. As some of the most recent exemplars of that approach, the editors of *Contact Points*, Andrew Cayton and Frederika Teute, write

> in this book, the *essence* of a frontier is the kinetic interactions among many peoples, which created new cultural matrices distinctively American in their eclecticism, fluidity, individual determination, and differentiation. Attention centers, not on the ultimate domination by white Americans of the frontier, but on the multi-sided negotiations of power involved in forming that most distinctive of American landscapes, frontiers.[14]

Admittedly, *The Middle Ground* and the essays within *Contact Points* offer a more nuanced understanding of what happens on the frontier, than the summary statement just cited might indicate. In fact, many of the authors included in *Contact Points*

---

[13] Fred Anderson, *Crucible of War: The Seven Years' War and the Fate of Empire in British North America, 1754-1766* (New York: Alfred A. Knopf, 2000), xx.
[14] Emphasis mine. Cayton and Teute, *Contact Points*, 2; see also 5 and 14.

focus not just upon cultural fluidities, but upon sharpening cultural distinctions and demarcations. Thus the frontier is as much about cultural persistence and the resistance of many of the frontier's participants as it is about accommodation. This is all the more to the point. If historians identify evidence of both cultural mixing and cultural rigidity, then it seems important to explore more deeply the nature of the cultural changes, the ways in which the changes took place, and under what circumstances. The frontier may be a middle ground where much cultural interaction and change takes place, but that is only one piece of the picture. The middle ground experience needs to be seen as part of a larger frontier process in which the confluence of cultures occurs alongside the conflict of cultures, a place where cultural change and cultural persistence coexist.

The middle ground syndrome has also shaped the scope of historical inquiry. As historians search for cases of cultural mixing and acculturation, they have focused their attention more and more narrowly. Instead of frontiers which include broad territories of cultural interaction between colonies and particular tribal groups, the micro-frontier studies reveal the inner-workings of trade posts, villages, and refugee camps.[15] At this level, the studies seem little more than investigations into inter-personal interaction and communication. Granted that such analyses can reveal much about the dynamics of cultural exchange, but such insight to be gleaned from this approach is severely limited since interaction on such a micro-scale must be conditioned at least as much by the personal nature of the interaction as by the cultures represented by those persons. Micro-level analysis helps us see particularly how individuals can act contrary to their cultural mores, but their behavior reveals little about how their broader society or the interaction of multiple groups operates on a larger scale. Thus micro studies have their place, but cannot take the place of broader frontier approaches, especially insofar as one seeks to explore the nature and degree of cultural change on the frontier.

Behind all of these concerns lies a more foundational issue. The new frontier historians often speak too loosely of culture and cultural change without always clearly defining what is meant by those terms. Granted that the culture concept has figured significantly in historical interpretation since the 1960s, and in the broader historiography much has been written about culture, but few of the new frontier historians who emphasize the dynamics of cultural interaction and exchange have adequately defined what they mean by "culture" and "cultural." In *The Middle Ground*, for example, Richard White writes that "different peoples ... remained identifiable, but they shaded into each other." Here and elsewhere in the volume, it is unclear how White defines and determines cultural identity and change. He uses the terms "values," "practices," and "meanings" when referring to culture, but does not detail what he means by these. In fact, White seems to downplay the importance of cultural outlook and worldview, suggesting that native people were free from cultural moorings and identity: "The Indian people I describe in this book have no essential Indianness. They are people who for a long time resolutely fought the European tendency to create them as the other. They asserted a separate identity, but they also claimed a common humanity in a shared world." The contributors to

---

[15] See for example many of the case studies in Cayton and Teute, *Contact Points*.

Contact Points likewise fail to define culture and the process of cultural change.[16] This is not to say that such an undertaking is easy or one's definition would be met by general approbation, but before one can emphasize cultural accommodation, one needs to define what is meant by culture. Only then can historians measure and assess the degree of cultural change and acculturation that has taken place on the frontier.

Last, most scholars of the frontier claim to approach their studies from a stance of cultural relativism, but have no framework for doing so. In 1978, James Axtell wrote that ethnohistory (closely related to the study of frontiers) emphasized "that each culture must be understood in its own terms, and that we must not only see the ethnocentric biases in each culture, but understand the reasons for them."[17] But I believe that many scholars fail to maintain such a stance. Part of the difficulty lies in knowing how to apply cultural relativism. On the one hand, scholars need to treat the subjects of their historical inquiry with evenhandedness. On the other hand, it is impossible to transcend one's own system of values. Fearing to acknowledge any cultural standpoint, scholars lack an independent standard or framework by which to understand culture. Instead, they tend to absolutize a particular culture at a particular moment in time. That is, they establish one society's culture at a certain historical moment as the standard by which to evaluate later cultural development and change. This is most often applied to native people that historians see as "Indians" at the time of first contact with Europeans, but who see them as something else after years of contact and varying degrees of acculturation and accommodation, since they no longer seem to reflect what Indians were at the point of contact. Allen Trelease, in his classic study, *Indian Affairs in Colonial New York*, demonstrated such an attitude when he wrote:

> Within a generation of the original contact, therefore, Indian civilization was on the road to extinction. It was a bitter pill to swallow, and many tribes fought back blindly to avoid it. Others sought refuge in flight, often losing their separate identity in the process, but the pursuit was remorseless. The two cultures were incompatible, and that of the Indian, being the weaker, had eventually to succumb.[18]

When such assumptions are made, cultural change resulting from contact with another society is often judged as an unfortunate and undesired outcome of the frontier. In this regard, many historians today highlight the persistence of "traditional" indigenous culture much in the same way that older scholarship tended to make European cultural traditions the standard by which to evaluate other

---

[16] White, *The Middle Ground*, x-xiv; Cayton and Teute, *Contact Points, passim.*
[17] Axtell, "The Ethnohistory of Early America," 116.
[18] Allen Trelease, *Indian Affairs in Colonial New York: The Seventeenth Century* (Ithaca, NY: Cornell University Press, 1960), 180 and 184. Bernard W. Sheehan offers important insight into the romanticization of Indian culture in *Savagism and Civility: Indians and Englishmen in Colonial Virginia* (New York: Cambridge University Press, 1980) and "The American Indian as Victim," *The Alternative: An American Spectator* 8 (1975): 5-8.

societies. For example, in summarizing his history of the Iroquois people in the seventeenth century, Daniel Richter writes "and in the late twentieth century, when mass media culture and government bureaucracy would wage an assault on all peoples' traditional ways of life, a new generation of militant leaders would again reinvigorate the Great League as a controversial rallying point for native self-determination. Today, the ordeal of the Longhouse is no nearer an end than it was in the 1730s. Neither is the story of the Iroquois peoples." In his study of the Catawba people, James Merrill makes the point about Indian persistence even more forcefully than Richter in the final chapter, "Indians Still: The Nation Endures." Even James Axtell, who in principle argues for cultural relativity, in practice celebrates the Indian cause. Through his rhetoric in *The Invasion Within*, Axtell consistently passes judgement on the Europeans while praising Native Americans. When speaking of the relative success of English evangelism, for example, he states that "Christ's conquests in Anglo-America were made only after pagan resistance had been smashed by microscopic shock troops, waves of covetous plowmen, and an intolerant government of occupation." In contrast, he claims that native culture was attractive to large numbers of Europeans because "they found Indian life to possess a strong sense of community, abundant love, and uncommon integrity—values that the European colonists also honored, if less successfully."[19]

Culture and Cultural Change

One of the first steps in effectively using a framework which approaches the frontier as a place of cultural mixing is to develop a clearcut definition of "culture." Given the extensive debates among historians, anthropologists, and social scientists in the twentieth century about the meaning and definition of culture, it should not be assumed that this essay resolves those debates. What it does offer is a description of the understanding of culture that I have adopted for my own research on European-Native American relations and how it might be applied to avoid some of the weaknesses of the new frontier history.[20]

My approach borrows from the work of C.T. McIntire, a Canadian historian and philosopher of history. McIntire associates culture

> with literally everything brought into existence by humans, the whole way of life of a people and all its ingredients—not just our indicators of meaning, our arts, or our manners—and with all aspects of our humanity, not just our suprabiophysical characteristics. Culture is the outcome of the creative process as well as the condition of the ongoing process of human creativity. We might say that culture represents the ongoing results of our creative acts.

---

[19] Richter, *Ordeal of the Longhouse*, 280; Merrell, *The Indians' New World*, 226-275; Axtell, *The Invasion Within*, 242, 325.

[20] Paul Otto, *The Dutch-Munsee Encounter in America: The Struggle for Sovereignty in the Hudson Valley* (New York and Oxford: Berghahn Books, forthcoming in 2005).

Culture, then, is not a static thing, but a dynamic entity, and, as such, represents the basic expression of human experience, the thing that sets humans apart from other forms of life. "Human acts are how we express our humanity," states McIntire. The products of culture or the results of human culture-making are many. They range from biological functions such as procreation to the "totality results, like societies, peoples, humanity ... and civilizations." Among these many products "are the societal results, the institutions, associations, and relationships, and their features, like churches, families and friendships, governments, states and city-states, factories and markets, feudal relationships, patron-artist relationships, social classes, tribes, communes, cities, and farms."[21]

Since culture encompasses all those activities and their products which distinguish humans from the rest of living things, it is necessary to distil from this definition of culture two distinct and integral elements: *worldview*, which influences human behavior, and *societal structures*, the results or products of that behavior. Worldview, cultural outlook, cultural ideals, societal values all relate to the same basic notion: that at the heart of human motivation lies fundamental religious belief. This is not to say that religious practices, as associated with a particular church or other recognized religious structure, guides human behavior. Instead this understanding of worldview emphasizes the collection of ideas, thoughts, and impulses which lie behind all human activity. Societal structures, in contrast, are the various tangible and intangible ways in which those core beliefs and ideas are manifested. By societal structures I mean various aspects of society—economic systems, political structures, social arrangements, religious activities, aesthetic products, and so forth.[22]

But one must be careful not to over-simplify. Worldview, in particular, should not be confused with a particular ideology. Ideologies are more-or-less uniform collections of ideas with inner-coherence. Worldviews, on the other hand may comprise more than one ideology. Worldviews reflect the composite of ideas, mores, values, and commitments which guide an individual's or society's pattern of living. Particular ideologies may predominate within a worldview, but generally human beings, being complex and existing in the flux of historical experience, experience worldviews in more complicated ways than simply pursuing a particular ideology.

---

[21] C.T. McIntire, "Historical Study and the Historical Dimension of Our World," in C.T. McIntire and Ronald A. Wells, eds., *History and Historical Understanding* (Grand Rapids, MI: Eerdmans, 1984), 34-37.

[22] This simplification is consistent with McIntire's other work: *The Ongoing Task of Christian Historiography* (Toronto: Institute for Christian Studies, 1974), 16-19; and "The Focus of Historical Study," (unpublished essay), 7-10. Similar ideas are shared by other scholars of the same school. See, for example, Sander Griffioen, "The Relevance of Dooyeweerd's Theory of Social Institutions," in Sander Griffioen and Bert M. Balk, ed., *Christian Philosophy at the Close of the Twentieth Century: Assessment and Perspective* (Kampen: Kok, 1995), 140; Bob Goudzwaard, *Capitalism and Progress: A Diagnosis of Western Society*, trans. and ed. Josina Van Nuis Zylstra (Toronto: Wedge and Grand Rapids, MI: Eerdmans, 1979), xix-xxi; and B.J. Van der Walt, *Afrocentric or Eurocentric? Our Task in a Multicultural South Africa* (Potchefstroom: Potchefstroomse Universiteit, 1997), 7-20.

For example, the Puritans who established New England maintained certain traditional, medieval values, but at the same time pursued values which anticipated the modernity of the eighteenth century and beyond. These values in turn were reflected in the various structures they erected in their society; for example, the open field system as a throwback to the middle ages which existed side by side with more modern commercial and economic practices emerging during their time.

History is always linked to culture—to worldviews and societal structures—since history is the story of ongoing cultural development: the creation and development of various structures and evolving cultural outlooks or worldviews. Historical development takes place in a complex environment in which worldviews shape society, but also changes in societal structures in turn shape a people's cultural outlook. In addition, worldviews and societal structures overlap and interact in myriad ways. Forces outside one's culture can also significantly shape the process of history. As one example, environment and geography can shape the structure and value system of a particular society. Furthermore, historians cannot simply generalize about groups of people in terms of worldview and related societal structures since individuals within those groups often exercise human agency in such a way as to transcend the boundaries of worldview and societal structures. Nevertheless, historians who attune themselves to both worldview and societal structures as a framework or context for analyzing historical development and cultural change have a greater advantage when investigating frontier processes.

With this understanding of culture as a basis for historical analysis, many of the difficulties arising in the new frontier theory can be addressed. The most important step has been taken by defining more clearly what one means by culture. Even if frontier historians do not define culture as I do, any effort to work with a concrete definition of culture provides a useful framework for tracing cultural change on the frontier. But I believe the distinction between worldviews and societal structures is particularly helpful. For example, adopting such a framework leads historians to ask and answer questions such as: Where did changes take place—in value systems or the structures of society? What was the nature of that change?

Considering culture in this way avoids the difficulty which arises when scholars begin to speak of the "loss" of culture. In this regard, historians need to be careful not to define any one society or "culture" in such a fixed manner as to assume that historical people simply fall into categories such as "Native American" or "European." While culture is dynamic and changing, it cannot be diminished or increased. Culture is a dimension of human experience and the expression of human behavior. It is the context in which human beings exist. Thus a society or group of people cannot have more or less culture, they can only have a changing and developing culture. True, one can identify certain characteristics of European society at a particular point in time and trace the changes from that point, but to assess cultural change as the loss of culture implies that culture is a quantifiable substance. The same is also true for Native Americans. Historians may be able to identify a number of aspects of Native American culture at the point of contact with Europeans and call it Native American culture. But five hundred years before or hundred years later, that same ethnic group may look very different culturally from the practices and beliefs of those people which came into contact with Europeans. It is useful for historians to distinguish between *ethnicity* and *culture* and keep in mind the ever-changing nature of culture.[23]

Nor is it possible to simply point to certain changes in the culture of a person or group and pronounce that they have become less Native American and more European, or vice versa. Culture changes on multiple levels; historians are safer tracing specific changes and developments in worldview or societal structure and avoiding labeling those changes in terms of becoming more like one group or the other as though culture and ethnicity were necessarily connected. This seems particularly true with regard to structural developments. People can choose or be forced to wear different clothing, eat different food, even speak a different language, but that does not mean that they have adopted an entirely new or different worldview. They may even be compelled or volunteer to participate in different economic, political, and legal systems, perhaps even new religious practices, but this does not necessarily reflect a fundamental change in cultural outlook. Examining cultural change in terms of changing societal structures and worldviews will avoid some of the ambiguity when one speaks loosely and vaguely of "cultural change."

Such ambiguity can be found in *The Invasion Within* where James Axtell analyzes the cultural transformation of some English, French, and Indians, but confuses worldviews and structures. When speaking of Indians "converting" to European ways, particularly to the French, his focus is on the religious structure of Catholicism. When speaking of Europeans converting to Indian ways, then he speaks more broadly of adopting the wide range of Native American culture. His work would be more valuable if he made clear comparisons between the breadth of European culture and Indian culture, or between specific structures such as religious practice among the Indians versus religious practice among Europeans.[24]

Furthermore, historians can make distinctions between more permanent changes—acculturation—, and more temporary measures better defined as accommodation. These terms have been used interchangeably by historians leading to some confusion. I have adopted these terms and their definitions as used by Alden Vaughan and Daniel Richter in their analysis of European captives among Native Americans.[25] Whatever terms are used, a distinction between temporary or short-term changes and permanent ones is particularly useful when used in conjunction with a concrete definition of culture. If historians observe economic changes among native people which copy European practices, for example, did these represent a permanent adoption of such practices, or a tactical or pragmatic short-term move? When European traders chose to live among native people and take Indian brides,

---

[23] There is much talk today of diversity, but little distinction seems to be made between race or ethnicity and culture and religious values. Sander Griffioen offers some insight into these distinctions in essays such as the one noted and "Is a Pluralist Ethos Possible?" *Philosophia Reformata* 59 (1994): 11-25. See also his book co-authored with Richard Mouw, *Pluralisms and Horizons: An Essay in Christian Public Philosophy* (Grand Rapids, MI: Eerdmans, 1993).

[24] Axtell, *The Invasion Within, passim.*

[25] Alden T. Vaughan and Daniel K. Richter, "Crossing the Cultural Divide: Indians and New Englanders, 1605-1763," *Proceedings of the American Antiquarian Society* 90.1 (April 1980): 24 n. 5.

was this a step on the road to becoming a native person, or did this simply represent accommodation to Indian ways to achieve some other end?

Obviously, this approach to the frontier takes a broader view than the microhistories mentioned above. Microhistories can identify important encounters between representatives of two societies, but they can only point to the possibility of more general cultural change and interaction. What insight can be gleaned from microstudies should be tested in the broader contact between different societies, and with clear ideas of where change is taking place—in worldviews or societal structures—, and what kinds of changes are taking place, accommodation or acculturation or both.

Finally, such an approach as I am suggesting can facilitate historical analysis rooted in cultural relativism. As noted above, the difficulty of approaching the past from a position of cultural relativism is that scholars can never transcend their own cultures. We exist in culture and can never see or observe without our vision being conditioned by the various values and systems by which we organize our thought, undertake our research, and construct our words. Does this mean that the ideal of cultural relativism is too elusive to try to attain? Certainly some scholars have given up the attempt. The very recognition of our culturally-bound scholarship, however, is the most important step in trying to achieve a culturally-relativistic study of the frontier. Once scholars identify their own framework for understanding the past, their own perspective out of which their research and writing stems, they can distance themselves from past peoples in their efforts to study and understand those peoples and their interactions on the frontier. Scholars cannot and should not take sides with historical Europeans or Native Americans, since neither group from the past represents the values of any of us today. Both groups followed practices which, when considered by twenty-first century standards, are either commendable or worthy of criticism. Instead, we should honestly admit our own cultural moorings and seek to understand past peoples as much as possible in terms of their own cultural values and societal structures. Rather than taking sides in the contest of cultures or emphasizing cultural confluence in an anachronistic celebration of cultural mixing and cooperation, scholars should make it their goal to study the encounter of diverse groups on the frontier, to consider their points of contact, to analyze the patterns of their interaction, and to trace the ways in which they accommodated or acculturated to one another's societies.[26] Understanding the complexity of culture in terms of worldview and societal structures provides a guide to do so.

---

[26] Such an approach has been called for by both Bernard Sheehan and James Axtell in review essays appearing a decade apart in the *William and Mary Quarterly*. But as these two essays and their other publications demonstrate, they do not agree with one another on how to do so. A study of their monographic works seems to demonstrate that each chooses to sympathize with a different cultural and ethnic group and thus neither succeeds in providing the balanced approach for which they appear to be calling. In addition to Axtell's works cited in notes 5 and 9, see "A Moral History of Indian-White Relations Revisited," *History Teacher* 16.2 (1983): 169-190. For Bernard Sheehan, see his works cited in note 18 as well as "The Problem of Moral Judgments in History," *South Atlantic Quarterly* 84.1 (1985): 37-50.

FOREGROUNDING THE BOUNDARIES OF AMERICAN LITERARY HISTORY

Michael Boyden

> *"If you are a Kiowa,*
> *you will understand what I am saying*
> *and you will speak your name."*
> (Kiowa story of the arrowmaker—anonymous)

Border Matters

The relationship between literature and territory remains a complex one. On the one hand, no-one would deny that there is a certain connection between the two. It is virtually impossible to talk about literature without reference to places. The German romantics entertained the idea of a world literature, and introductory survey courses sometimes carry this label. But this is not how academic literature departments tend to be organized. Significantly, the concept of world literature was developed to legitimate a "German" literary tradition that could rival with France. Often, though not always, literature is sanctioned politically, as in the case of national literatures. This can also be said to work the other way around when literature is mobilized to shape the national consciousness. Things get more fuzzy, however, when dealing with regional, continental or even hemispheric literary variants. Not all states necessarily have a literature of their own (but, of course, who is entitled to make such a verdict?), such as those partaking in a larger cultural unit; and vice versa, not all literatures are perceived as national literatures, for example the literatures of socially minoritized groups that can be situated below or across officially recognized state borders. And to make things even more complex, it is not inconceivable that these conditions apply all at once.[1]

On the other hand, therefore, if territorial and literary boundaries are to some extent isomorphic, they are seldom completely identical. In other words, literature is not simply a matter of getting your geography right. Territoriality can be a necessary, but hardly a sufficient criterion of literary membership. As Stephen Greenblatt and Giles Gunn state in their introduction to *Redrawing the Boundaries*, literature constitutes an "imagined territory," by which they mean that its boundaries are not stable and natural (although they tend to be naturalized), but historical and

---

[1] As I will indicate, the question of territoriality, nationality and literature is also closely interlinked with that of language, since particularly in the Western world the existence of a standard national language is often seen as a criterion for the legitimacy of the nation. For the question of language in relation to national literatures, see in particular José Lambert, "L'éternelle question des frontières: littératures nationales et systèmes littéraires," in Christian Angelet, ed., *Langue, dialecte, littérature: Etudes romanes à la mémoire de Hugo Plomteux* (Leuven: Leuven University Press, 1983).

changing.[2] Greenblatt and Gunn's collection is in itself a good illustration of this historicity and changeability of (the study of) literature.[3] As the title suggests, the work not only charts some of the far-reaching transformations that literary studies has undergone in the past couple of decades, but also aims at a programmatic redefinition or "remapping" of the field. Many Americanists and English literature scholars now share the conviction that, given the globalization of society, it is no longer sufficient to study literature within the limits of a given national framework. Rather, literature should be approached as a global phenomenon that to a large extent defies and elides geographical divisions.

This article addresses the problem of territoriality in relation to the discipline of American literary history as it has evolved since the 1960s. In particular, I want to ask whether and in what way American literary history has changed in view of the growing internationality of literature and the rise of multiculturalism. Is it still possible to write national literary histories? And if so, what form would they have to take? How would the nation have to be defined? Can it (still) be approached as a more or less homogeneous entity, composed of a single people sharing a common culture and language? Or do several cultures coexist within one and the same nation? Do nations stretch across states? Are alternative forms of literary history thinkable? Do geographical borders still matter or have they become entirely irrelevant? If they no longer matter, which borders do? Such and other questions are currently at the center of many theoretical debates in literary and historical studies of the United States. As yet, however, not much corpus research has been done in that direction. In what follows, I will look at two standard literary histories of the United States and see how they have defined themselves and their object of study.

A Discipline Formerly Called American Literary History

National literary histories, one could say, function as border crossing points that manage the relations between literature as a functional domain and its social environment, i.e. the nation-state of which literature is (supposedly) an expression. Precisely because this link between literature and the nation-state is not self-evident, one could argue, national literary histories are "useful": they help to open up a

---

[2] Stephen Greenblatt and Giles Gunn, "Introduction," in *Redrawing the Boundaries: The Transformation of English and American Literary Studies* (New York: Modern Language Association of America, 1992), 6.

[3] See also recently *Globalizing Literary Studies*, a special issue of *PMLA* (2001) coordinated by Giles Gunn (containing some of the papers from a forum of the same name at the 1998 MLA Convention). Influential recent studies on the development of English and American literary scholarship are Gerald Graff, *Professing Literature: An Institutional History* (Chicago: Chicago University Press, 1987), Russell J. Reising, *The Unusable Past: Theory and the Study of American Literature* (New York: Methuen, 1986), Peter Carafiol, *The American Ideal: Literary History As a Worldly Activity* (New York: Oxford University Press, 1991), and David Shumway, *Creating American Civilization: A Genealogy of American Literature As an Academic Discipline* (Minneapolis: University of Minnesota Press, 1994).

cultural space, an "imagined territory" with which people can identify. But the question is, of course, to what extent the nation can (still) be defined by one literary tradition that would somehow organically capture the experience of its people in an age of increasing globalization.[4]

It should be stressed beforehand that American literature scholarship is a fairly recent phenomenon. The first university courses in American literature were organized about a century after the political independence of the United States. Well into the first decades of the twentieth century, the status of American literature remained heavily contested. Of course, literary histories, anthologies and the like had been appearing ever since the beginning of the nineteenth century, but the first concerted effort to institutionalize American literature as a field of scholarly research took shape only in the 1910s (a period of patriotic zeal), when the first *Cambridge History of American Literature* came out.[5] Around mid-century, the discipline then reached what has been called its phase of "maturity" with the publication of Spiller's monumental *Literary History of the United States*.[6] During the 1960s and 1970s, however, this upward trend was discontinued. While Spiller's history went through its second (1953) and third editions (1963) without significant changes to the original design, no new comprehensive histories of American literature saw the light. As a matter of fact, a lot of works were produced that addressed specific ethnicities or literary groupings, or regional and popular traditions. But no new, all-inclusive synthesis of American literature "from the beginnings to the present" was attempted.

For this, one had to wait till 1988, when the *Columbia Literary History of the United States* by Elliott et al. was published, exactly forty years after the *Literary History of the United States* (henceforth abbreviated as CLHUS and LHUS respectively).[7] The preface of CLHUS explains this time lag by the political turmoil

---

[4] A number of social scientists have stated that in a complex world society like ours today territorial boundaries have exhausted their evolutionary potential. That is, they remain useful for the political system, as a means of securing democratic decision making. But when it comes to matters of economics, art or science, they would be "quite meaningless." Niklas Luhmann, "Territorial Boundaries as System Boundaries," in Raimondo Strassoldo and Giovanni Delli Zotti, eds., *Cooperation and Conflict in Border Areas* (Milano: Franco Angeli, 1982), 241. As a consequence of recent political events, however, this point of view has repeatedly been called into question. At present, issues of place, identity and power even seem to be experiencing a sort of "renaissance" in the field (e.g. Rudolf Maresch and Niels Werber, eds., *Raum, Wissen, Macht* (Frankfurt am Main: Suhrkamp, 2002).

[5] William Peterfield Trent, ed., *Cambridge History of American Literature* (New York: Macmillan, 1917-1921). The last volume of the new *Cambridge History of American Literature* by Sacvan Bercovitch et al., eds. (8 vols.), will appear in the fall of 2004. Because of limitations of space, these works will not be discussed here.

[6] Robert E. Spiller, ed., *Literary History of the United States*, 3 vols. (New York: Macmillan, 1948). The publication history of this work is extensively discussed in Kermit Vanderbilt, *American Literature and the Academy* (Philadelphia: University of Pennsylvania Press, 1986).

[7] Emory Elliott et al., eds., *Columbia Literary History of the United States* (New York: Columbia University Press, 1988). In the past couple of decades, there seems to have

of the period (the Cold War, Vietnam, the civil rights movement, etc.) on the one hand, and the new critical approaches to American literature that have emerged in the meantime (especially in European theory) on the other hand. All of this would have created an atmosphere "unconducive" to the writing of a new national literary history.[8] It would no longer be clear what exactly American literature is or in what way it can be made expressive of the national identity.

At least apparently, CLHUS does not reclaim this lost consensus: "There is today no unifying vision of a national identity like that shared by many scholars at the closings of the two world wars."[9] CLHUS sees itself as "modestly postmodern": it "acknowledges diversity, complexity, and contradiction by making them structural principles, and it forgoes closure as well as consensus."[10] Because all criteria to define or categorize American literature are acknowledged as relative, the decision to determine what counts as American literature is delegated to the individual contributors. On the other hand, however, there is clearly the overriding intention to "reconstruct" American literary history by incorporating those works that until recently did not fit into the mainstream. In what follows, I would like to zoom in on this underlying tension.

"America" and Its Others

How different, then, is CLHUS from LHUS? Does it really go beyond the traditional, national model of literary history or is the emphasis on postmodern pluralism and openness, as Hans-Joachim Lang suggests, merely a rhetorical "smokescreen" to hide the ideological or commercial interests of the authors?[11] The "General Introduction" to CLHUS clearly takes pains to distance the work from its predecessor: "In external respects, of course, this volume has the appearance of a traditional literary history, but in many instances the essays challenge established concepts."[12] And a little further on in the text: "While the distinction of its publisher and its imposing title may suggest authority, its editors and contributors know that perspectives and interpretations of every topic treated here do exist."[13] Although the

---

been a "renaissance" of American (literary) history. This is noticeable from the number of programmatic and theoretical works that have accompanied the new national histories. Some titles are: Paul Lauter, ed., *Reconstructing American Literature: Courses, Syllabi, Issues* (Old Westbury: Feminist Press, 1983), Günter H. Lenz, ed., *Reconstructing American Literary and Historical Studies* (Frankfurt am Main: Campus, 1990), David Perkins, *Is Literary History Possible?* (Baltimore and London: Johns Hopkins University Press, 1992), and Sacvan Bercovitch, ed., *Reconstructing American Literary History*, Harvard English Studies 13 (New York: toExcel, 1999).

[8] CLHUS, xi.
[9] Ibid., xii.
[10] Ibid., xiii.
[11] Hans-Joachim Lang, "From the Old Cambridge History of American Literature to the New Columbia Literary History of the United States," in Lenz, *Reconstructing American Literary and Historical Studies*, 111.
[12] CLHUS, xix.
[13] Ibid., xxiii.

title refers back to Spiller, the editors argue that there is now less critical agreement about the meanings of the title words. "To place the stress upon the United States is to acknowledge that for many people in the world the term 'American' is not synonymous with 'United States' but refers to all of the countries on the North American continent."[14] However, they hasten to add that the stress on territoriality does not exclude colonial or pre-Columbian writings or literatures in non-English languages from the history. "For the sake of clarity and consistency," therefore, they have decided to define the "literature of the United States" as "all written and oral literary works produced in that part of the world *that has become* the United States of America."[15]

The first thing to note about this definition is that it seems to be no definition at all. According to the editors, it is not supposed to reflect a consensus in the field about the nature or status of American literature, but rather functions as a provisional yardstick for the contributors to start from. In contradistinction to LHUS's definition of literature as "any writing in which aesthetic, emotional, or intellectual values are made articulate by excellent expression," there are no qualifications about what counts as (oral/written, beautiful/ugly, good/bad, etc.) literature.[16] All that the CLHUS editors seem to do is to define literature as a rhetorical battleground, an "imagined territory" that can be imagined in many different ways. At the same time, however, territory is elevated as a more or less objective marker of literary membership, as a means to go beyond the national

---

[14] Ibid., xix. Elliott wanted the volume to be called the CLHUS because he believed that the name "American" should only be used if the book included the whole North American continent as its subject, but the director of Columbia University Press and his associate editors disagreed. It was only after he presented the plans to the members of the Salzburg Seminar in 1985 where there was a heated debate about the title that he was able to persuade the other editors and the press director to change the title to CLHUS. (Oral communication by Elliott at the 2003 Salzburg Seminar Session 408/ASC 31, quoted with his permission). The 1985 Salzburg Seminar Session 242 was titled "Contemporary American Literature: New Perspectives" and was attended by, among others and apart from Elliott, Sacvan Bercovitch (who was then working on the new *Cambridge History* and the *American Library* Series) and Walton Litz (who has collaborated with Elliott on the *Prentice Hall Anthology of American Literature*).

[15] CLHUS, xix (italics added). Interestingly, the *Columbia History of the American Novel*, Elliott's next big collaborative project which was published in 1991, makes no scruple about the qualification "American" in its title. In the introduction, Elliott motivates this change of approach as follows: "With the present work focusing upon only one genre, there was room to broaden the geographic scope and include chapters on Canadian, Carribean, and Latin American fiction." Emory Elliott et al., eds., *Columbia History of the American Novel* (New York: Columbia University Press, 1991), xiii (abbreviated as CHAN). However, these chapters occupy only a small section of the volume's total of thirty-five chapters, so that one cannot say that American literature outside of the United States receives its due. Also, the focus on "America" as a hemispheric unit does not justify the presence of the chapter on "Colonialism, Imperialism, and Imagined Homes" that deals with important authors of the English speaking world "who were neither born in nor lived in the Americas but whose works and experiences as novelists and public figures are a vital part of our larger literary culture." CHAN, xiv.

[16] LHUS, xvi.

model of literary history. That is, territory is used to stretch the meaning of the literature of the United States to include (both oral and written) literature that was produced before the country existed or that for a long time and for various reasons did not conform to the nation's self-image.

Territory in this sense escapes ideological strife, it offers a way to go beyond the nation-state. As I will try to show, however, it is precisely the intention to be as inclusive and open as possible that to some extent reveals the continued effect of the national model on CLHUS. The history's definition of the literature of the United States thus both confirms and denies the intimate connection between territory and ideology. If the CLHUS definition should be approached as provisional, the question remains: how provisional? Is what is said in the "General Introduction" also borne out by the individual essays of the history?[17]

The overall organization of CLHUS appears rather straightforward. It consists of five chronological parts without further thematic qualifications ("Beginnings to 1810," "1810-1865," "1865-1910," "1910-1945," and "1945 to the Present"). As the preface explains, these parts should "represent organizational convenience and do not imply watersheds in literary development."[18] In this way, CLHUS reacts against Spiller's cyclical view of literary history as a process of "organic growth." According to Spiller's cyclical theory, the literary history of the United States is not merely a chronology of dates and names, but undergoes curves or cycles of cultural development. Up to now, American literature would have experienced two great movements. The first "renaissance" was constituted by the romantic writers of the mid-nineteenth century. A second such high point took place a century later around the time of LHUS's publication (the so-called "continental" phase).[19] As we have noted, CLHUS rejects such a "master plan" to which all the individual essays would have to conform. "No longer is it possible, or desirable, to formulate an image of continuity when diversity of literary materials and a wide variety of critical voices are, in fact, the distinctive features of national literature."[20]

LHUS begins each of its sections with two background chapters (since the second edition, these are graphically separated from the other chapters in the table of contents by means of italics). CLHUS, by contrast, devotes a whole section of each part to background information, although the division between contextual and

---

[17] If taken at face value, the stress on territoriality would exclude many works that are included in CLHUS, e.g. those produced by the "lost generation" in Paris. Conversely, it would have to include many authors who have lived in the United States but who were born and raised elsewhere, such as Marguerite Yourcenar.

[18] CLHUS, xii. CLHUS here seems to follows the design of *The Norton Anthology of American Literature* which equally opts for a purely chronological approach. The preface to the sixth edition of the *Norton* motivates this policy by the desire on the part of the editors to give students of American literature all the information they need "without imposing an interpretation." Nina Baym, ed., *The Norton Anthology of American Literature*, 6th ed. (New York and London: Norton, 2003), xix.

[19] In *The Cycle of American Literature: An Essay in Historical Criticism* (New York: Macmillan, 1955), which Robert E. Spiller published as a kind of "by-product" of LHUS, he talks about these movements in terms of the first and second "frontier."

[20] CLHUS, xxi.

properly literary chapters is less clear-cut. CLHUS also devotes some attention to those minorities that have most forcefully profiled themselves since the 1960s: African-Americans, Mexican Americans, Asian Americans and women. "Part Four" contains a section titled "Regionalism, Ethnicity, and Gender: Comparative Literary Cultures" that is exclusively devoted to these groups. The seclusion of minority voices in a separate section in a sense exemplifies the point I want to make about the (unspoken) boundaries of CLHUS. On the one hand, there is clearly a desire to make these voices heard, to get a hearing for them. On the other hand, this ambition also confronts them with enormous problems of assimilation. In the essay on "Afro-American Literature," for example, Robert Stepto says that most histories of Afro-American writings "are scarcely histories at all. Although they meld fact and chronology, they do not risk the acts of narration and fictionalization that necessarily figure in the larger business of *writing* (as opposed to *assembling*) *history*."[21] Ironically, this criticism is to some extent applicable to his own essay, which is for a large part devoted to sociological rather than literary issues. In a *New York Times* review of CLHUS, significantly titled "66 Ways of Looking at Our literature," Robert M. Adams remarks about the ghettoization of minorities in separate sections that "if a special place weren't made for them programmatically, they might fall out of the history altogether."[22] Their presence in CLHUS would thus in a way underwrite their segregation from the mainstream of American culture.

Nevertheless, CLHUS clearly wants to challenge LHUS's emphasis "upon men rather than upon movements and institutions" by limiting the number of single-author chapters (eleven as opposed to seventeen for LHUS).[23] Some chapters juxtapose two canonical figures, for example "From Cotton Mather to Benjamin Franklin." In others, a major author is contextualized in relation to lesser gods of the period, as in "Edgar Allan Poe and the Writers of the Old South." Nevertheless, traces of Spiller's ground plan remain visible. Like in LHUS, the five big names of "The American Renaissance" (Emerson, Thoreau, Hawthorne, Melville and Whitman) retain their own chapter and stand unchallenged. In total, 82 out of 1,200 pages (excluding mentions in other chapters) are devoted to them, or about 7 percent of the whole history (as opposed to 10 percent in LHUS). As to the number of references in other chapters, a gradual levelling out is noticeable: whereas in LHUS Emerson and Whitman get the most hits (32 percent and 25 percent of the total number of hits assembled by the five classics respectively), CLHUS evenly spreads out the number of hits over the five authors. Proportionately, Melville remains the least popular, with about 16 percent. Emerson gets 20 percent, Whitman 19 percent and Thoreau and Hawthorne both have 22 percent. This tendency seems to indicate the continued relevance of the classics for CLHUS.

---

[21] Ibid., 785.
[22] Robert M. Adams, "66 Ways of Looking at Our Literature," *The New York Times*, 24 January 1988. In reaction to this kind of criticism, Elliott chose to integrate the ethnic authors in the chapters dealing with the mainstream in his *Columbia History of the American Novel*. However, the procedure of "ghettoization," if that is what it is, is copied in the chapters on Canadian, Carribean and Latin American fiction.
[23] LHUS, xvii.

Although CLHUS claims to be many stories, it also tries to be no story at all. The editors, however, do not deny that CLHUS establishes certain continuities, but they maintain that these connections are different from those of traditional literary histories and anthologies: "Our emphasis is upon the varied voices within the one nation."[24] Thus, instead of one beginning, CLHUS has "four parallel departure points": apart from the New England puritans, the Native American cultures, the explorers in the Southwest and the Anglicans in England are mentioned as equally important origins. The editors also encourage the readers to make creative use of the index to determine the influence or importance of a writer. In this way, they can also discover different perspectives on a particular author. For example, the chapters about Melville and Emerson *"might best be read* in conjunction with the piece that opens Part Two, 'Idealism and Independence.'"[25] Or, someone who wants to know more about Twain's career as a humorist before 1865 *"would probably find it useful* to consult the essay 'Forms of Regional Humor' in Part Two." And so on. The use of the conditional mode indicates that in the final instance it is up to the reader to establish such connections: "In important ways, then, the reader of this work will always be involved in an act of creating his or her own interpretations of the literary history of the United States by combining related essays."[26]

But how real is the freedom of the reader to write his or her own literary history? And how different is CLHUS's attempt to represent all "the varied voices in the one nation" from LHUS's cultivation of the idea of the United States as "an articulate racial mixture"?[27] The key question is, as should be clear by now, what "articulacy" can mean in such a context.

In the Beginning Was the Word

In fact, some of the changes that the discipline of American literary history has undergone in forty years can already be inferred from the first sentence of the "General Introduction": "The literary history of this nation began when the first human living in what has since become the United States used language creatively."[28] This sentence contrasts sharply with the first sentence of LHUS's "Address to the Reader" which goes as follows: "The literary history of this nation began when the first settler from abroad of sensitive mind paused in his adventure long enough to feel that he was under a different sky, breathing new air, and that a New World was all before him with only his strength and Providence for guides."[29] The 1948 account can be interpreted in two ways. The most obvious interpretation is that it locates the beginnings of American literature around 1600, at the time of the first permanent English settlements in what was to become the United States. This

---

[24] CLHUS, xxii.
[25] Ibid., xx (italics added).
[26] Ibid., xxi.
[27] LHUS, xiii.
[28] CLHUS, xv.
[29] LHUS, xiii.

is, of course, the standard view as it is still held by many scholars in the field.[30] However, the following lines of the LHUS "Address" also hint at an alternative interpretation (not necessarily incompatible with the first). It continues by stating that during the first three centuries of settlement, the European immigrants were more concerned with preserving their original culture than with exploring the possibilities that the new continent offered: "They encouraged nostalgia, even while spreading civilization, and they were often *insensitive* to the effect upon the imagination of the novel experiences developing upon this continent with extraordinary rapidity and force."[31] The marked use of the word "insensitive" might suggest that the first settler "of sensitive mind" arrived (not literally, of course, but figuratively) in the nineteenth century, the "real" beginning of American literature. This second interpretation would also underscore the centrality that LHUS accords to the mid-nineteenth century as the first high peak of American literature (when American literature was no longer considered English literature written on the other side of the Atlantic).

Whichever interpretation one prefers, the important thing to note here is the difference from the 1988 version. To CLHUS, the oldest record of American literature is the prehistoric Indian cave art in the Southwest, painted more than two thousand years ago. The actual (but unrecorded) beginnings go even further back to include the first oral traditions on the North American continent. There should be no doubt that the purpose of this rewriting of the origins of American literature is to rectify the neglect of (and the harm inflicted upon) the indigenous peoples populating the North American continent at the time of the advent of the English immigrants. By drawing attention to the oral culture of the Indians in the Southwest (as opposed to, for example, the puritan writings in the East), the CLHUS editors also want to correct the overemphasis of the European, and more particularly the New England point of view as foundational for the whole of American culture. By 1988, the unselfconscious reference to European "civilization" as the source of the "native" literature of the United States and the keeping in the dark of the Native American cultures (as they are currently called) as part of the environmental "conditions" in the New World have become a matter of serious debate.

But it is certainly too simple to suggest that LHUS represents a narrow-minded, racist perspective on American literature as opposed to the open, multicultural perspective of CLHUS. The title of the first section of CLHUS ("A Key into the Languages of America") is clearly an allusion to Roger Williams's *A Key into the Language of America*, a seventeenth century work that mockingly inverts the opposition between English "civilization" and Indian "barbarity" by projecting the first as an ideal alternative to the second. This inversion, however, if less harmful, is to a certain extent also a mythologization of Native American cultures. By choosing this title, the CLHUS editors want to call into question the

---

[30] It is the standard view in many anthologies and high school textbooks. For example, the first sentence of *An Outline of American Literature* by Peter B. High reads: "The story of American literature begins in the early 1600s, long before there were any 'Americans.'" Peter B. High, *An Outline of American Literature* (London and New York: Longman, 1986), 5.

[31] LHUS, xiii (italics added).

widespread idea of American society as the exclusive product of European values transposed to and transformed by a New World environment. The pluralization of the title underwrites this concern and shows that the literature of the United States has not one, but several origins. But in this way, the editors at the same time establish certain connections that in some cases can be as doubtful as the ones they attempt to subvert. The first chapter on "The Native Voice" by Scott Momaday brings out the complexity of this issue. Momaday's chapter mirrors Stith Thompson's "The Native Heritage" in LHUS. The "place" of the chapters in the two histories is already telling: Momaday comes literally first, whereas Thompson is tucked away somewhere in the first section of the second volume.[32]

The titles of the two chapters are significant as well: for Momaday the Indian "voice" is alive; for Thompson it is more of a lost culture (of which only traces are preserved) than a living tradition. Significantly, Momaday (ironically?) begins his essay with an entry from Webster's (the voice of authority!), a definition of the verb "write": "to draw or form by or as by scoring or incising a surface."[33] This very broad definition (which could even comprise painting) immediately challenges Thompson's assertion that there is "really no such thing as a written literature among the Indians of the United States" because their pictograms would be more like mnemonic devices than a real language.[34] Although Momaday agrees with Thompson that Indian literature is principally an oral tradition, he does not focus on problems of translation or transmission.[35] This makes it profoundly ironical, perhaps, that the Kiowa story of the arrowmaker, whose fate is tied to his language, is rendered in English, a language that, perhaps, nor the arrowmaker himself, nor the enemy spying on him outside of his tipi would have understood. To Momaday, however, the native voice is "indispensable," even though (or precisely because?) in some cases it is "almost impossible to recall."[36] It is both "unheard" and "pervasive," and it has had an undeniable influence on American literature even if there is no conscious relation, because it is present everywhere in the landscape of the New World.[37] For Momaday, therefore, American literature "begins with the first human perception of the American landscape expressed and preserved in language."[38]

---

[32] Thompson's chapter comes after "The American Language" by H.L. Mencken and "The Mingling of Tongues" (on non-English literature in the United States) by Henry Pochmann. In contemporary debates, the question of what constitutes an "American" language is much less central. This could be a sign of the growing monolingualism within the United States. In this respect, see Werner Sollors, ed., *Multilingual America: Transnationalism, Ethnicity, and the Languages of American Literature* (New York and London: New York University Press, 1998).

[33] CLHUS, 5.

[34] LHUS, 694.

[35] To Thompson, Indian songs and poems are "almost never ... pleasant to the unaccustomed ear unless profoundly modified by some professional composer": they contain "excessive" repetitions and are "likely to tire the listener from outside the group." LHUS, 700.

[36] CLHUS, 5-6.

[37] Ibid., 14.

[38] Ibid., 6.

Momaday's account is certainly not more accurate or comprehensive than Thompson's. The latter gives a better sense of the "continental" nature of the Indian traditions, ranging from British Columbia into Mexico. Strangely, perhaps, Momaday does not even mention the *Walam Olum*, the "most ambitious 'literary' production of the Indians of the United States" as Thompson typifies it.[39] The important thing to note here, though, is not Momaday's omission of the *Walam Olum*, but rather the presence of the inverted commas in Thompson's characterization, which make clear that to him its value is "entirely linguistic and historical, not actually literary." The most striking difference between the two essays, therefore, lies in their view of the relation between the oral and written traditions. Against Mary Austin (who wrote the strikingly "modern" final chapter on "Aboriginal" literature of the *Cambridge History of American Literature*), Thompson asserts that it is unlikely that Indian poetry ever exerted "any profound influence on the rhythm of American poetry."[40] The adjective "American" here qualifies the written literature of the European "civilization" as opposed to the oral traditions of the Indians. These traditions, Thompson concludes, "have largely remained unassimilated and even unknown by the dominant group."[41] Momaday, by contrast, concludes his essay with a discussion of contemporary Native American writings. Although he acknowledges that there is a dichotomy between the oral tradition and modern American Indian poets and novelists, he asserts that "the voice is the same": "The continuity is unbroken. It extends from prehistoric times to the present, and it is the very integrity of American literature."[42]

The other three chapters of CLHUS's first section complement, modify and contradict Momaday's point of view. In the essay on "Literature of Discovery and Exploration," although at the beginning he asserts that the first "classics" of American literature were written in French and Spanish, Wayne Franklin concludes with the standard view that John Smith is "our first American author" because of his "intimate engagement with geography" through which he defined the New World as "his own domain": "In him we may perceive for the first time that felt mixture of self and world, personality and place, which has made the role of space in American art as much an affair of the spirit as of topography pure and simple."[43] In "English Literature at the American Moment," Lewalski looks at the ways in which America has been imagined in English literature and asserts that "American literature is as

---

[39] LHUS, 695.
[40] Ibid., 700.
[41] Ibid., 702.
[42] CLHUS, 15. The problems inherent in this "doctrine of continuity" as Lang would call it, are already apparent when one considers how oral literature is to be indexed (Lang, 119). The reader of CLHUS in search of the Kiowa story of the arrowmaker will not find it in the index. The closest entry is "Native Americans," which gets no more hits than "Mather, Cotton" (who, in relation to LHUS, seems to have become even more popular).
[43] CLHUS, 21. In his 1878 *History of American Literature 1607-1765* (Ithaca, NY: Cornell University Press, 1949) Moses Coit Tyler already expressed the view that John Smith was the first author in American literature.

much a product of continuities as an indigenous creation."[44] In "The Puritan Vision of the New World," finally, Bercovitch tells us in his characteristic style how the puritans' "spiritual use of geography" helped to create "America" as the "single, most potent cultural symbol of the modern world."[45]

Conclusion

What this means is that American literature meets many borders: aesthetic, linguistic, political, geographical, racial, etc. As my short comparison of CLHUS and LHUS has shown, these boundaries can be differently "used," they are intimately entwined with rhetoric. To proclaim the prehistoric rock art at Barrier Canyon (rather than the writings of a wandering Englishman) as the "origin" of American literature, is to historically justify a way of life that attaches itself to a specific locale and lays claim to the label "American." This, of course, does not mean that such a way of life has no reason for existence. Borders of this kind are both historical and real. As Greenblatt and Gunn remark in *Redrawing the Boundaries*: "These boundaries can be crossed, confused, consolidated, and collapsed; they can also be revised, reconceived, redesigned, or replaced. The one thing they cannot be in literary studies is entirely abolished."[46] To my mind, therefore, the changes in the discipline of American literary history in the past couple of decades reveal at least two things. On the one hand, there seems to be a growing irritability in relation to issues of identity, ethnicity and diversity, a growing awareness also of the political dimension of literary classifications. On the other hand, however, there is clearly a tendency to, as it were, "reconnect" to American culture in all its pluriformity.

This tendency is in no way new. On the contrary, precisely the drive to "speak for" the lost voices (if they are "lost," how can they be recovered?) in American society by "evaluating cultural expression in ways that are fair and just to all" reveals the continuing relevance of the national model of literary history that has come under so much fire since the 1960s.[47] This is because, almost inevitably, being "fair and just to all" also means: writing in a language that everybody can understand (and "everybody" is mostly a synonym of the dominant group). The very rhetoric of openness and diversity that confronts the traditional approach to literary history, therefore, also to some extent reproduces the ethnolinguistic nationalism that unifies U.S. society by creating or propagating a common culture and identity. I do not wish to suggest that this paradox is not at all problematized in current debates about globalization and multiculturalism or that the (sub- or neo-?)national paradigm is necessarily bad. But the fact remains, and this is my point, that the (for that matter, entirely justifiable) desire to be representative towards all the various

---

[44] CLHUS, 24.
[45] Ibid., 43-44.
[46] Greenblatt and Gunn, *Redrawing the Boundaries*, 4.
[47] Emory Elliott, "Cultural Diversity and the Problem of Aesthetics," in Emory Elliott, Louis Freitas Caton, and Jeffrey Rhyne, eds., *Aesthetics in a Multicultural Age* (Oxford and New York: Oxford University Press, 2002), 9.

cultures on U.S. territory shows that, as Lang observes, "[l]iterary history ... is still a story about time, place, books and people."[48] At least in this sense, then, CLHUS is not all that different from its forerunners.

In spite of its persistence, however, it cannot be denied that the national model of literary history and what it entails has been severely problematized during the past twenty years or so. Most literary scholars no longer think that the nation-state can encompass or express the lives of the people living on its territory. Paradoxically, perhaps, the concept of territory has become an important tool for questioning the national model. By using territoriality as a primary criterion of demarcation, a number of recent literary histories have attempted to open up the concept of American literature so as to include "foreign" or forgotten and suppressed peoples, their languages and cultures. This, however, does not necessarily mean that the new literary histories completely do away with the national model. On the contrary, in many respects they are rewriting or refashioning the traditional narrative of continuity and growth in terms of the current social situation in the United States. Brook Thomas claims that these histories still express a strong need for communal identities, "but not at the level of the nation."[49] Different social groups within the United States thus continue to use a version of the national model to articulate their own identities and histories, but they no longer necessarily believe in the nation as a category that can subsume all the rest. Thomas adds that the meaning of the nation as a concept has considerably changed over time and that, for this reason, it is "flexible enough to remain an important, if not exclusive, way of organizing the study of literature."[50] What other ways will emerge to imagine literature, and whether they will eventually supersede the national model, remains at this point guesswork.

---

[48] Lang, "From the Old Cambridge History of American History," 112.

[49] Brook Thomas, "National Literary Histories: Imagined Communities or Imagined Societies," *Modern Language Quarterly* 64 (Summer 2003): 149.

[50] Ibid., 152.

REPUBLICANISM, FEDERALISM AND TERRITORIAL EXPANSION IN THE UNITED STATES[1]

Carmen de la Guardia Herrero

In recent years there has been a renewed interest in the study of the American West from many different historiographical perspectives. A great many authors have been particularly interested in the *"space*—physical, cultural, economic, social, and political—in which people would create the West."[2] Other research has emphasized the *process* of settlement on different frontiers.[3] Furthermore, in the past few years, historians focusing on the political history of the revolutionary period have analized the political culture which made possible the emergence of the ideas that justified the expansionist course of action adopted by Americans in the early national period.[4]

This essay will try to make a contribution to this latter historiographical trend which is revising the connections between early U.S. political culture and territorial expansionism. We will start by exploring the historiographical debate which arose from divergent approaches to frontier studies, to reflect subsequently on the arguments put forward by those leaders of the late 1780s who justified the territorial expansion of the United States. As we shall see, it was during the great debates between those who favored ratification of the 1787 Constitution—the Federalists—and those who criticized the new text—the Antifederalists—when a theoretical

---

[1] This essay is part of a broader research project financed by the Spanish Ministry of Science and Technology, ref. BHA2000-0709.

[2] Richard White, "Western History," in Eric Foner, ed., *The New American History* (Philadelphia: Temple University Press, 1997), 205. Patricia Limerick, William Robbins, Elliot West, Richard White, and Donald Worster were key members of the group of New Western Historians. See also Patricia Nelson Limerick, "Turnerians All: The Dream of a Helpful History in an Intelligible World," *American Historical Review* 100.3 (June 1995): 697-716.

[3] In this group of "neo-Turnerians" the works of William Cronin, John Mack Faragher, Walter Nugent and David Weber; White, "Western History," 204; see also Jeremy Adelman and Stephen Aron, "From Borderlands to Borders: Empires, Nation-States, and the Peoples in Between in North American History," *American Historical Review* 104.3 (June 1999): 815-841; John R. Wunder and Pekka Hämäläinen, "Of Lethal Places and Lethal Essays," *American Historical Review* 104.4 (October 1999): 1229-1239; and John Mack Faragher, "Afterword: The Significance of the Frontier in American Historiography," in John Mack Faragher, *Re-reading Frederick Jackson Turner: The Significance of the Frontier in American History and Other Essays* (New York: Henry Holt, 1994), 237-241.

[4] See for example, Peter S. Onuf, "Liberty, Development, and Union: Visions of the West in the 1780s," *The William and Mary Quarterly* 43.2 (April 1986): 179-213; Peter S. Onuf, *Jefferson's Empire: The Language of American Nationhood* (Charlottesville: University of Virginia Press, 2000); Karl Friedrich Walling, *Republican Empire, Alexander Hamilton on War and Free Government* (Lawrence: University Press of Kansas, 1999); Stanley Elkins and Eric McKitrick, *The Age of Federalism* (Oxford: Oxford University Press, 1993).

justification for the territorial expansion of the young nation was formulated as a possible and even necessary means of achieving political stability.

"Histories" of the United States

As has been the case with all other disciplines, historiography has gone through the same vicissitudes as human perception of reality itself. Benedetto Croce's claim that "all true history is Contemporary History" was not just an attempt to distinguish our discipline from mere chronicling but, more significantly, a way of stressing that no other historiography was possible except that which reflected in its study of the past the issues and problems of the present.[5] Each historical generation distinguishes itself from the previous ones not only by the things that it considers worth remembering, but also by its way of approaching and analyzing the "traces" of its own past. To a certain extent, then, exploring the historiographical output of any political community amounts to exploring its sense of itself.[6]

Since Frederick Jackson Turner put forward his thesis on the frontier in 1893, ways of making history in the United States have undergone many changes. Turner, together with Charles A. Beard and Vernon L. Parrington, led the group of historians known as the Progressive or New Historians. These members of the second generation of professional historians were soon inspired by subjects and methods which differed from those of their predecessors.[7] Of middle-class origins and heavily influenced by the Progressive movement, these graduates and doctors from the newly founded history departments of American universities were to show a deep concern for the smooth running of democratic societies. In fact, they believed that, as historians, they had an important social role to play. As they understood it, historical research, besides being relevant to the present, should contribute to a deepening of the democratization of both the social and political life of the United

---

[5] Quoted by Gerald N. Grob and George Athan Billias, *Interpretations of American History: Patterns and Perspectives* (New York: Free Press, 1992), 1.

[6] For arguments in favor of the existence of different "paradigms" in the history of American historiography, see John Higham, "Changing Paradigms: The Collapse of Consensus History," *The Journal of American History* 76.2 (September 1989): 460-466, and Daniel T. Rodgers, "Republicanism: The Career of a Concept," *The Journal of American History* 79.1 (June 1992): 11-38.

[7] For the process of professionalization of historical studies in the United States, see John Higham, *History: Professional Scholarship in America* (Baltimore: John Hopkins University Press, 1986); Peter Novick, *That Noble Dream: The Objectivity Question and the American Historical Profession* (Cambridge: Cambridge University Press, 1988); Dorothy Ross, "Historical Consciousness in Nineteenth-Century America," *The American Historical Review* 89.4 (October 1984): 909-927; David D. Van Tassel, "From Learned Society to Professional Organization: The American Historical Association, 1884-1900," *American Historical Review* 89.4 (October 1984): 929-956; Gordon S. Wood, "A Century of Writing Early American History: Then and Now Compared; Or How Henry Adams Got it Wrong," *American Historical Review* 100.3 (June 1995): 678-696.

States.[8] In addition, Progressive or New Historians argued that the historical course followed by the United States differed from that of European history. While their professors, all of them linked to the first generation of scientific historians, were mainly concerned with political history, and regarded American institutions merely as a sequel of medieval German institutions, Progressive Historians insisted that there had been a breach with the institutional past of premodern Europe. In the opinion of this second generation of professional historians, America was a country which, because of its peculiarities, had given rise to a "frontier" society in the West and to an original urban society in both the Northeast and the Midwest. These New Historians thought that history of an exclusively political kind, based on political, legal and diplomatic sources, did not suffice, and advocated establishing closer links with those sciences which studied modern society, in particular, with economics and sociology.[9]

There is implicit in both the works of Frederick Jackson Turner and those of Beard and Parrington a dialectical conception of history. To them, the singularity that set America apart from old Europe was the result of clashes between conflicting sides. In his studies of the frontier, Turner aimed at accounting for such particularity. He tried to show that the frontier—"the meeting point between savagery and civilization"—had been instrumental to the peculiar historical development of the United States. Rebelling against his own teachers, whose main concern was analyzing institutional and legal history in search of conclusive evidence of the similarities between America's constitutional framework and the European Anglo-Saxon model, Turner advocated the study of those "vital forces" which had shaped America's exceptionalism, forces that, in his view, were brought about by the existence of a moving frontier. "Behind institutions, behind constitutional forms and modifications, lie the vital forces that call these organs into life and shape them to meet changing conditions," Turner claimed. "The peculiarity of American institutions is the fact that they have been compelled to adapt themselves to the changes of an expanding people—to the changes involved in crossing a continent, in winning a wilderness, and in developing at each area of this progress out of the primitive economic and political conditions of the frontier into the complexity of city life."[10]

Just as Progressive Historians had criticized their predecessors for fashioning a static history and exaggerating the similarities between America and Europe, while suggesting as an alternative a dynamic history which vindicated the singularity of

---

[8] For Progressive Historians, see Richard Hofstadter, *The Progressive Historians: Turner, Beard, Parrington* (New York: Vintage Books, 1970) and Ray Allen Billington, *Frederick Jackson Turner: Historian, Scholar, Teacher* (New York: Oxford University Press, 1973); also John Higham, *Writing American History: Essays on Modern Scholarship* (Bloomington: Indiana University Press, 1972) and Ellen Nore, *Charles A. Beard: An Intellectual History* (Carbondale: Southern Illinois University Press, 1983).

[9] Georg Iggers, *La ciencia histórica en el siglo XX: Las tendencias actuales* (Barcelona: Idea Book, 1998), 44.

[10] Frederick Jackson Turner, "The Significance of the Frontier in American History," *Annual Report of the American Historical Association for 1893* (Washington, DC, 1894), 199-227.

thirteen colonies throughout the eighteenth century.[17] Such a statement was to have two significant consequences. On the one hand, by defending the influence exerted by these authors—all of them advocates of communal rather than individualistic values—he broke with a long-standing tradition of American exceptionalism. The thirteen colonies and Britain had shared the same cultural background and, what is more, no feature in the history of the United States anticipated the triumph of individual initiative, a point of view which bluntly contradicted those of his predecessors, the Progressive and Consensus Historians.

On the other hand, Bernard Bailyn held a highly critical view of the treatment that had been given to the frontier in American historiography. If it was true that, far from being exceptional, the history of the United States shared many characteristics with European history, then the moving frontier could not have had such an important effect on the historical development of the early United States. Bernard Bailyn believed that historians had contributed to distort the real history of the United States by "viewing the colonial world as a frontier—that is, as an advance, as a forward- and outward-looking, future anticipating progress toward what we know eventuated." In his opinion, first the thirteen colonies and then the United States were "a marchland ... a periphery, a ragged outer margin of a central world, a regressive, backward-looking diminishment of metropolitan accomplishment."[18]

Republicanism

Such a radical break with the thesis of American exceptionalism, together with his endeavor to understand the political culture that lay behind revolutionary action, signaled the beginning of one of the greatest debates in American historiography. Although such key terms of republican ideology as "republicanism" or "civic virtue" were not employed by Bernard Bailyn in his work *Ideological Origins*, he vigorously defended the idea that the roots of the American revolution were to be found in Anglo-American republican politics.[19] He pointed out that ideas such as corruption, virtue and common good, which were central to English republican culture, pervaded the language of pamphleteers, who used them to justify revolutionary action.

---

[17] Bernard Bailyn, *The Ideological Origins of the American Revolution* (Cambridge: Belknap Press of Harvard University Press, 1967).

[18] Bernard Bailyn, *The Peopling of British North America: An Introduction* (New York: Vintage Books, 1987), 112-113, quoted by Gregory H. Nobles, "Breaking into the Backcountry: New Approaches to the Early American Frontier, 1750-1800," *The William and Mary Quarterly* 46 (October 1989): 641-670. In this article Gregory H. Nobles is critical of Turner's exceptionalism but also of Bailyn's excessive stress of the continuities between Europe and America. "His (Bailyn's) emphasis on cultural connection underlines an important point that other historians have discussed in more balanced terms," he writes on page 642.

[19] Bernard Bailyn, *The Origins of American Politics* (New York: Vintage Books, 1968. 1970), 21.

It was Gordon S. Wood, in his 1969 work *The Creation of the American Republic*, who first applied the term "republican ideology" to define the conceptual framework of early American patriots.[20] Wood depicted American leaders in the early stages of the revolution as a group of idealists. Those patriots were men who wanted to create a new commonwealth by following the guidelines that had been set by English republican tradition. They wished to establish a classical republic which would be based on the virtue of its own citizens and leaders, thus ridding America both of materialism and the corruption of the English monarchy. Wood regarded republicanism as a radical ideology with ethical implications. Republican leaders claimed that there was a direct connection between the system of government adopted by a nation and the character of its citizens. The revolutionaries hoped that their republicanism would regenerate American society by establishing a republican nation that would be founded solely on civic virtue.

Not only was such an interpretation a fierce attack on the Consensus Historians defense of American "liberal tradition," but it also demolished the arguments put forward by both Progressive and Consensus Historians regarding the exceptionalism of American political ideology: an exceptionalism which, as we have seen, was partly explained by the existence of a constantly moving frontier.

We still have to consider a study published in 1975 by J.G.A. Pocock, *The Machiavellian Moment: Florentine Political Thought and the Atlantic Republican Tradition*, to complete what Robert E. Shalhope called the "Republican Synthesis."[21] Shalhope, together with many other historians, came to see the works of Bailyn, Wood and Pocock as complementary, and by bringing together some of the most relevant ideas of these three authors—the so-called "Republican Synthesis"—they achieved a more accurate appraisal of the role played by republican ideology in the political and social shaping of the United States.[22] Pocock, in particular, showed that there had been a continuous flow of republican influence, which sprang from the Greek and Roman philosophers, pervaded the ideology of theorists of the Italian renaissance republics such as Machiavelli, was also present in the libertarian thought of the English commonwealthmen and, of course, impregnated the political culture of England's thirteen colonies.[23]

According to the "Republican Synthesis" interpretation, republicanism dominated American political culture for a very long time. From the revolutionary

---

[20] Gordon S. Wood, *The Creation of the American Republic, 1776-1787* (Chapel Hill: University of North Carolina Press, 1969).
[21] J.G.A. Pocock, *The Machiavellian Moment: Florentine Political Thought and the Atlantic Republican Tradition* (Princeton, NJ: Princeton University Press, 1975).
[22] Robert Shalhope was the first to bring together the works of these three historians and to apply the term "republican synthesis" to the material taken out of their work. Robert E. Shalhope, "Toward a Republican Synthesis: The Emergence of an Understanding of Republicanism in American Historiography," *William and Mary Quarterly* 29.1 (1972): 49-80; see also Robert E. Shalhope, "Republicanism and Early American Historiography," *William and Mary Quarterly* 39.2 (April 1982): 334-356.
[23] Ana Marta González, "Republicanismo: orígenes historiográficos y relevancia de un debate," *Revista de Occidente* 247 (2001): 121-145; also Ruth H. Bloch, "The Constitution and Culture," *The William and Mary Quarterly* 44.3 (July 1987): 550-555.

era, through the constitutional period and—in Pocock's view—down to the Civil War, republican ideology was to remain the most important influence. The conclusions reached by these three historians were very similar even though there were some new nuances in J.G.A. Pocock's outlook, both in his approach to the sources and in the way he tackled political discourse, which was closer to the "linguistic turn" than to the "cultural turn." Bearing in mind that throughout history there had been a conflict between the sphere of liberty and the sphere of power, "the American Revolutionaries quickly formed a consensus in which the concept of republicanism epitomized the new social and political world."[24] The republican way of life aimed at preserving liberty from the aggressions of power. In addition to this, the prosperity and stability of a republic rested on the values of its citizens. No other quality was given a higher value than civic virtue, which was understood as the willingness to put the common good before personal interest. Constitutional stability and freedom could only be achieved by exercising civic virtue. Life in the *polis* would allow men to fully develop their human faculties, while all other human beings—young people, women and those who were economically dependant— would benefit from the civic humanism of the governing elite, which would protect them against the horrors of historical experience: epidemics, famines, tyranny and wars.[25]

Soon after J.G.A. Pocock's work was published in 1975, a great debate erupted among American historians.[26] During the celebration of the Bicentennial of the American Revolution in 1976, historical congresses discussed the "Republican Synthesis." The attack against the importance given to civic republicanism in the American Revolution was launched from very different flanks. Traditional historians insisted on the significance of the liberal tradition in American political culture; New Left historians criticized them for having left aside the social and economic background and some cultural historians, mostly those of feminist persuasion, protested against the place allotted to social outsiders in the republican scheme of things, while poststructuralists simply dismissed Pocock's discourse analysis.[27] Of all this criticism, probably the most persistent was that expressed by Joyce Appleby.[28] An expert on the influence of Locke's work on American political tradition, Appleby did not agree with the architects of the republican synthesis, which holds that republicanism was the only visible influence during the revolutionary era. She admitted that there had been other influences besides liberal

---

[24] Shalhope, "Republicanism and Early American Historiography," 334.
[25] Shalhope, "Toward a Republican Synthesis," 49-80.
[26] Grob and Billias, *Interpretations of American History*, 159-202.
[27] For the historiography of the first debates on American republicanism, see Peter Onuf, "Reflections on the Founding Constitutional Historiography in Bicentennial Perspective," *William and Mary Quarterly* 46 (1989): 341-375 and Gary Wills, "The Creation of the American Republic, 1776-1787: A Symposium of Views and Reviews," *William and Mary Quarterly* 44 (1987): 550-657. For a summary of all criticism, see Rogers, "Republicanism," 23.
[28] A compilation of her essays on republicanism can be found in Joyce Appleby, *Liberalism and Republicanism in the Historical Imagination* (Cambridge, MA: Harvard University Press, 1992).

ideas, but she insisted that all of them had existed side by side in the political culture of the American revolutionaries. "The chaste and venerable classical republicanism distilled by Harrington for English needs and updated by Montesquieu for eighteenth-century readers, or the liberal republicanism that contemporaries traced to the inquires of Bacon, Newton, Locke, and Smith. My answer," stated Joyce Appleby, "is that both were present."[29]

This attempt to find a historiographical middle ground, which was promoted by several American scholars, would finally gain the upper hand. During the 1970s and 1980s, a reconciliation among the diverging views of American historians was hampered by the influence of Geertz's concept of ideology—which was so prominent in the work of both Bailyn and Wood—and by Khun's concept of paradigm—a decisive influence in Pocock's first works—, but halfway through the 1990s, the different stances started to converge, as Joyce Appleby had wished.[30] For those historians that held that there existed a republican ideology or paradigm it was very difficult to accept other influences besides republicanism. As opposed to the liberal definition of ideas as small units which people could adopt or leave aside depending on their needs or interests, the historians who favored the republican thesis saw ideas as forming part of a whole—paradigms in Kuhn's parlance—and it was precisely that whole which made understanding of reality possible. All those contemporaries who shared the same paradigm were to be considered members of an ideological community.[31]

By the late 1980s, however, the main contributors to this debate had already detached themselves from their own conceptual principles and were favoring more open positions. Although Pocock stuck to the concept of paradigm, his main interest now was the difference between language and discourse. In his view, while political language might have rules, political discourse "is typically polyglot, the speech of Plato's cave or the confusion of tongues."[32] Gordon S. Wood, in his new preface to a reissue of *The Creation of the American Republic*, also adopted a more conciliatory stance. "Like any young historian, I hoped my book would have some effect on the profession and on our understanding of constitution making in the Revolutionary era," Wood stated. "But I had little sense that I was participating in what Daniel Rodgers has called a 'conceptual transformation' in American History Writing ... Although I was aware of the importance of the communal values of republicanism to the Revolutionary generation and realized that Hartz had been wrong in his exclusive emphasis on American liberalism, I was still not at all prepared for the

---

[29] Joyce Appleby, "Republicanism in Old and New Contexts," *The William and Mary Quarterly* 43 (1986): 20-34.

[30] Clifford Geertz's work, *Interpretations of Culture* (New York: Basic Books, 1973) had a great influence on Bailyn's work, while Thomas S. Khun's work, *The Structure of Scientific Revolutions* (Chicago: University of Chicago Press, 1970) decisively influenced Pocock's first works.

[31] Appleby, *Liberalism and Republicanism in the Historical Imagination*, 285.

[32] J.G.A. Pocock, "Virtues, Rights and Manners," in J.G.A. Pocock, *Virtue, Commerce and History: Essays on Political Thought and History, Chiefly in the Eighteenth Century* (Cambridge: Cambridge University Press, 1985), 37-50, quoted by Rodgers, "Republicanism," 35.

emergence of what Robert Shalhope in 1972 labeled the 'Republican Synthesis.' My book was linked with Bernard Bailyn's *Ideological Origins* ... and with J.G.A. Pocock's *Machiavellian Moment*, published in 1975, for better or for worse, in the 1970s and 1980s our three works were picked up and cited by an increasing number of scholars who had all sorts of interpretative needs and political agendas." But in that same preface Wood nevertheless acknowledged that "If I wrote it now, one subject I probably would treat differently would be republicanism. Since republicanism has come to seem to many scholars to be a more distinct and palpable body of thought than it was in fact, perhaps it needs to be better set in its eighteenth-century context."[33]

Federalism and Expansion

The conciliatory ending of the historiographical debate about the influence of liberalism and republicanism on the American Revolution has proved to be one of its most outstanding contributions, insofar as it has allowed us to catch a glimpse of the immense richness of the political culture of the revolutionary era. Undoubtedly, a wide variety of influences was instrumental in building up that novel and rich theoretical construction which made the emergence and smooth running of the institutional framework of the Federal Republic possible.

One of the reasons that lay behind the 1787 attempt to establish a "more perfect Union" resided in the difficulties that the Confederation had met, from 1783 onwards, when trying to solve the serious problems posed by those European powers which shared political borders with the United States. As both Great Britain and Spain had interests in North America, neither of them wished the young nation to have a stable future. And they certainly employed all their diplomatic resources to emphasize and exploit the differences among the member states of the Confederation.[34]

Nevertheless, the strategies that these two powers adopted to weaken the United States were different. Both England and Spain signed alliances with the Indian Nations living near the borders of the United States, in order to stop the

---

[33] Gordon S. Wood, *The Creation of the American Republic, 1776-1787* (Repr. Chapel Hill: University of North Carolina Press, 1998), v-vii.

[34] For the difficulties posed by foreign policy as one of the reasons for the calling of the 1787 Constitutional Convention, see Walter LaFeber, "The Constitution and United States Foreign Policy: An Interpretation," *The Journal of American History* 74.3 (December 1987): 695-717; John Allphin Moore, Jr., "Empire, Republicanism, and Reason: Foreign Affairs as Viewed by the Founders of the Constitution," *The History Teacher* 29.3 (May 1993): 297-315; also such classic works as Frederick W. Marks III, *Independence on Trial: Foreign Affairs and the Making of the Constitution* (Baton Rouge: Louisiana State University Press, 1973) and Merrill Jensen, *The New Nation: A History of the United States during the Confederation, 1781-1789* (New York: Knopf, 1950); and more recently, James E. Lewis, Jr., *The American Union and the Problem of Neighborhood: The United States and the Collapse of the Spanish Empire, 1783-1829* (Chapel Hill and London: University of North Carolina Press, 1998).

American colonisers from advancing, but only Spain offered to negotiate a treaty with the United States. While offering commercial advantages that clearly satisfied the Northern mercantile states, Spain continued to ban the Americans from navigating the Mississippi to its mouth and refused to clarify the southern border with the United States, an attitude which was naturally a severe blow for the states with territories in the West. In spite of this, in his address to the Congress of 3 August 1786, John Jay, who was then Foreign Affairs secretary of the Congress of the Confederation, made a strong defense of the need to sign the treaty: "The situation of the United States appears to me to be seriously delicate, and to call for great circumstance in our bonduel, both at home and abroad," Jay stated, "nor in my opinion will it cease ... until a vigorous national government be formed and public credit and confidence established."[35] However, as was to be expected, during the debate on the treaty with Spain, all five southern states, whose interests were seriously damaged by the Spanish prohibition to sail the lower Mississippi, rejected its terms, thus defeating the treaty which, under the Articles of Confederation, needed the votes of nine states. The divergent interests of the members of the Confederation—a point which both British and Spanish diplomacy never failed to highlight—led to continual confrontation and drove to despair those American politicians who saw in the reinforcement of the common power of the states the only way of overcoming internal conflict and developing a successful foreign policy.

"To be respectable abroad it is necessary to be so at home," wrote John Jay to Thomas Jefferson, "and that will not be the case until our republic acquires more confidence, and our government more strength."[36] Establishing a link between foreign and domestic policy was common practice among the Founding Fathers. Many others, apart from John Jay, made remarks about the connections. When it came to co-operating in their international policy, during the 1780s, the difficulties that arose among the states often led to political crises. On the other hand, the Confederation government's failure to protect either international trade or the western settlements also caused a great deal of internal discontent. "What is to be done? Must we remain passive victims to foreign politics, or shall we exert the lawful means that our independence has put into our hands of extorting redress?" James Madison wrote to his friend James Monroe in 1785, saying "The very question would be an affront to every citizen who loves his country. What then, are these means? Retaliating regulations of trade only. How are these to be effectuated? Only by harmony in the measures of the States."[37]

The feeling that only by achieving a more perfect union would it be possible to put an end to external threats, together with the conviction that more international respect would result in a tighter union of the thirteen states, were the two underlying causes for the call of what, in the event, would be the Constitutional Convention of 1787.

---

[35] Jay Speech to Congress, New York, 3 August 1786, John Jay Papers, National Archives, Washington, DC.

[36] John Jay to Thomas Jefferson, New York, 14 July 1786, John Jay Papers, Rare Book and Manuscript Library, Columbia University, New York.

[37] James Madison to Monroe, 7 August 1785, *Letters and Other Writings of James Madison*, Congressional Edition (Philadelphia: J.B. Lippincott & Co., 1865), 1:169-170.

The multiple ideas influencing the American legislators became apparent during the constitutional debates, a point recently agreed upon by historians who had earlier stressed either liberal or republican influences. Even more evident, however, was the fact that, by turning to texts of both classical and contemporary thinkers, they were able to frame not only a set of novel political concepts for domestic purposes but also novel solutions to their international problems. The discussions prompted by the reading of classical political texts, or by the writings of the Scottish, English and French Enlightenment, allowed revolutionaries to work out original solutions which would bring them huge international respect, while helping them to reinforce the union of the states.[38]

Chief among the concerns of American legislators during the revolutionary era was the need to achieve a balance between power and liberty. They were aware that in order to check the ambitions of the great colonial powers it was necessary to reinforce the power of the Congress of the Confederation, but they feared that this might lead to a curtailment of American liberties. "The means of defence against foreign danger, have been always the instrument of tyranny at home" claimed James Madison.[39] Such fear was reflected in the functions that the Constitution bestowed on the executive power. The presidency was not granted sole prerogative to declare war or sign peace, for it would have amounted to "Throwing into his hands the influence of a monarch, having the opportunity of involving his country in a war," as one of Philadelphia's delegates stated.[40] Nonetheless, the executive had to be reinforced if it was to face the threat posed by the great colonial empires, which might jeopardize not just the internal stability of the Union but its very existence.

It was during the debates on how to work out an effective solution to the dilemma between power and liberty that one of the most original and epoch-making solutions for the future of the United States was found. James Wilson, Philadelphia's representative in the Constitutional Convention expressed it in this way: "We must consider two points of Importance existing in our country: the extent and manners of the United States. The former seems to require the vigour of a monarchy, the manners are against a king and are purely republican," and he concluded "Montesquieu is in favor of Confederated Republicks, I am for such a confederation if we can take for its basis liberty, and can ensure a vigorous execution of the Laws."[41] This address, which was delivered on 1 June 1787, marked the beginning of one the most important debates of the constitutional period: The discussion of whether it was possible or not for a large republic to preserve liberty while

---

[38] Moore, "Empire, Republicanism, and Reason," 300.

[39] James Madison, Notes of Debates in the Federal Convention, Entry for Friday, 29 June 1787, "In Convention", in Winton U. Solberg, ed., *The Federal Convention and the Formation of the Union of the American States* (1958; reprint, Indianapolis: Bobbs-Merrill Company, 1979), 190.

[40] Quoted by LaFeber, "The Constitution and United States Foreign Policy," 697.

[41] Madison Notes, 1 June, 1787, Max Ferrand, ed., *The Records of the Federal Convention* (New Haven: Yale University, 1911), 70-71; partly quoted by Moore, "Empire, Republicanism and Reason," 301; quoted in full by LaFeber, "The Constitution and United States Foreign Policy," 697.

reinforcing power at the same time. It was in this context that the issues connected with an expanding frontier were hotly debated.

It was a widely held view during the eighteenth century that a republican government would only succeed if it was established over a small territory with a similarly small population. "It is natural to a republic to have only a small territory, otherwise it cannot long subsist. In a large one there are men of large fortunes, and consequently of less moderation," Montesquieu had claimed in *The Spirit of the Laws*, one of the most frequently quoted works of the revolutionary era. "In a large republic the public good is sacrificed to a thousand views, in a small one, the interest of the public is easily perceived, better understood, and more within the reach of every citizen." The triumph of personal interest over public good would mean the end of civic virtue and bring about the most feared invasion that a republic could suffer, that of corruption. The belief, shared by many Americans in the eighteenth century, that republican virtue would not survive in a large republic was to be one of the bones of contention between Federalists, who supported ratification of the 1787 Constitution, and Antifederalists, who feared that the new political order would put an end to the virtues of the republican system.[42]

As soon as the results of the 1787 Philadelphia Convention were known, a fierce contest started between those in favor of the new constitutional text and those who opposed it. As it had been established that, in order to come into effect, the Constitution should be ratified by nine out of the thirteen states, both Federalists and Antifederalists embarked on a tough media campaign to further their positions.

Notwithstanding the differences that existed within the group of revolutionaries who objected to the new constitutional text, they all shared a distinct fear that an increase in national power might jeopardize citizens' active participation. The Antifederalists had a clear conception of what they were for, "which was an active and open public sphere." While their conception of politics paid little heed to institutional organization, they advocated the existence of an active public discourse "requiring free speech, a free press, and freedom to assemble at the local level, where juries and militia units" would provide a firm defence of civic virtues.[43] To many Antifederalists, broadening those powers that were to be delegated in common institutions—powers that were now divided into three branches—would mean that the former thirteen states had become a single state; a fact that they equated with the annihilation of the republic. "Let us now proceed to enquire, as I first proposed, whether it be the best the Thirteen United States should be reduced to one great republic or not?" wondered "Brutus" in the first of sixteen articles, fiercely critical of the Constitution, which were published under that pseudonym by a judge from New York called Robert Yates, in *The New York Journal*. "If respect is to be paid to the opinion of the greatest and wisest men who have ever thought or wrote on the

---

[42] James D. Savage, "Corruption and Virtue at the Constitutional Convention," *The Journal of Politics* 56.1 (1994): 174-186.

[43] Saul Cornell, *The Other Founders: Anti-Federalism and the Dissenting Tradition in America 1788-1828* (Chapel Hill: University of North Carolina Press, 1999); see also Michael Lienesh's review of this book in *The William and Mary Quarterly* 57.3 (July 2000): 713 and James H. Hutson, "Country, Court, and Constitution: Antifederalism and the Historians," *The William and Mary Quarterly* 38.3 (July 1981): 337-368.

science of government that a free republic cannot succeed over a country of such immense extent." Once again, of course, it was Montesquieu's statements that "Brutus" had in mind. "History furnishes no example of a free republic anything like the extent of the United States. The Grecian Republics were of small extent, so was that of the Romans. Both of these extended their conquests over large territories of country and the consequence was that their governments were changed from that of a free government to those of the most tyrannical that ever existed in the world," "Brutus" stated at the end of his article. Very similar arguments were put forward by "Cato" possibly George Clinton, the governor of New York and by Richard Henry Lee and Melancton Smith, who wrote together under the pseudonym "The Federal Farmer." "It was the extensive territory of the Roman republic that produced a Sylla, a Marius, a Caligula, a Nero and a Elagabalus," "The Farmer" claimed.[44]

As soon as Antifederalist articles started appearing in the New York press, those who backed the Constitution rushed to its defence. Alexander Hamilton, one of the leaders who favored ratification in the state of New York, centered his efforts on persuading his state to vote for the new constitutional text. He sought and found support among such political experts as James Madison and John Jay. Altogether they wrote eighty-five articles, which appeared in several New York journals under the common pseudonym "Publius."[45]

Their main aim was to demolish the most solid of all Antifederalist arguments, according to which, the lessons of history showed that a large republic would necessarily turn into a tyrannical regime. Quite obviously, in this case, they could not turn to the baron of Montesquieu to perform the task. Madison started with an article, published in number 9 of *The Federalist* series, where he pointed out that the size of any of the thirteen states of the Union exceeded by far that of all classical and renaissance republics. But the most comprehensive and significant argument for the future expansion of the United States was put forward by Madison in essay number 10. While Montesquieu was the most pervasive influence in Antifederalist texts, the work of the Scottish philosopher David Hume can be discerned in all of Madison's writings. In his attempt to find a solution to the tricky question which posed the conflict between liberty and power, James Madison set forth an argument to prove that only by accepting territorial expansion would the United States be able to secure civic virtue. Following Hume's arguments very closely, he stated that one of the most serious risks that small republics had to face was the emergence of factions.[46]

---

[44] Morton Borden, ed., *The Antifederalist Papers* (East Lansing: Michigan State University Press, 1965); see also Bernard Bailyn, *The Debate on the Constitution: Federalist and Antifederalist Speeches, Articles, and Letters During the Struggle over Ratification* (New York: Library of America, 1993).

[45] Karl Friedrich Walling, *Alexander Hamilton on War and Free Government* (Lawrence: University Press of Kansas, 1999), 95-122.

[46] For Hume's influence on Madison, see Douglas A. Adair, "The Tenth Federalist Revisited," *The William and Mary Quarterly*, James Madison, 1751-1836: Bicentennial Number 8.1 (1951): 48-67 and "That Politics Must Be Reduced to a Science: David Hume, James Madison and the Tenth Federalist," *The Huntington Library Quarterly* 20 (1957): 343-360; also John M. Werner, "David Hume and America," *Journal of the History of Ideas* 33.3 (1972): 439-456; Gordon D. Ross, "The Federalist and the

"By a faction I understand a number of citizens ... that are united and actuated by some common impulse of passion, or of interest adverse to the writs of other citizens or to the permanent and aggregate interests of the community," Madison explained.[47] Since passions were inherent to human nature, the only way to check them would be to devise a system that might control their effects. As long as factions were a minority, regular vote might do the job of keeping them within democracy, but if they became a majority, as might often be the case, then it would be necessary to frame a system to prevent them from succeeding and destroying the common good.

As opposed to pure democracy—which Madison defined as a society composed of a small number of citizens who participate directly in the administration of the *res publica* through different assemblies—a republic was the system in which the scheme of representation takes place. The fact that republics delegated power to "a chosen body of citizens whose wisdom may best discern the true interest of their country" was one of the reasons that made it desirable "to enlarge the sphere." The bigger the republic, claimed Madison, the higher the number of citizens that would be needed in order to elect each representative, so that it "will be more difficult for unworthy candidates to practise with success the vicious arts" of politics. Furthermore, "to extend the sphere, you take in a greater variety of parties and interests," thus making it less likely that factions or groups inspired by a common passion would be able to get their own way. For Madison, the diversity of power first and then its fragmentation between federal institutions and the individual states, as was advocated by the federal system, would prevent the feared triumph of factions, with its corresponding danger for the stability of the nation. "In the extent and proper structure of the Union ... we behold a republican remedy for the deseases most incident to republican government," James Madison concluded.[48]

By the time the Constitution was ratified, those Federalist positions which linked territorial expansion to civic virtue and, therefore, to political stability, were already a reality. For those Founding Fathers, the frontier of the United States could be and should be an expansive frontier.

Conclusion

During the eighteenth century, England's thirteen colonies bubbled with political ideas of the most varied origins. Twentieth-century American historians would spend more than two decades debating whether the political ideology of the revolutionary era had been liberal or republican. Only when more flexible conceptual categories were introduced was it possible to achieve a rapprochement of

---

Experience of Small Republics," *Eighteenth Century Studies* 5.4 (Summer 1972): 559-568 and Stanley Elkins and Eric McKirtick, *The Age of Federalism* (Oxford: Oxford University Press, 1993).

[47] James Madison, "The Federalist Number 10," in Clinton Rossiter, ed., *The Federalist Papers* (New York: A Mentor Book, 1961), 78.
[48] Idem, 84.

the different positions and, above all, to comprehend more fully the theoretical propositions of the Founding Fathers. One of those theories, the defense of territorial expansion as the only means of preventing the corruptive effect of factions and of achieving both civic virtue and political stability, not only enabled the colonization of the frontier to continue apace but actually made frontier expansion a most desirable political aim for the United States.

BREAKING INTO THE TRANS-MISSISSIPPIAN FRONTIERS: THOMAS JEFFERSON'S EXPEDITIONS TO THE WEST

Marco Sioli

The expedition of Meriwether Lewis and William Clark to explore the Missouri River and to find a commercially viable overland route to the Pacific was planned well before any expectation that the United States might soon acquire the trans-Mississippi territory. The treaty between the United States of America and the French Republic was signed on 30 April 1803. But Jefferson began discussing an expedition to the western territories with Meriwether Lewis, his private secretary and an army captain, months earlier. In January 1803, he began a low key effort to build support in the Congress. In a message focusing on Indian affairs east of the Mississippi frontier, he noted that the country along the Missouri river was "inhabited by numerous Indian tribes" and he speculated that "an intelligent officer with ten or twelve chosen men ... might explore the whole line, even to the Western ocean."[1]

However, when the news of the Louisiana Purchase reached Washington in July of 1803, the character of the expedition was fundamentally changed. Thomas Jefferson had invested heavily in that transaction and he naturally wished to know what sort of a bargain he had made with Napoleon. Consequently, the mission to explore the trans-Mississippi frontier became much more urgent by the summer of 1803, when Captain Lewis and his friend Lieutenant William Clark were hard at work planning for the expedition with Jefferson's keen support. During the fall, they continued recruiting men and gathering equipment, reaching St. Louis in December. They spent the rest of the winter and spring making the necessary preparations until the day of departure on 14 May 1804. After a year and a half ascending the Missouri River, crossing the Lolo Pass, and descending the Columbia River they arrived at the Pacific Coast at the end of November 1805. One of the members of the expedition wrote in his diary that they had traveled through "a country possessed by numerous, powerful and warlike nations of savages, of gigantic stature, fierce, treacherous and cruel; and particularly hostile to white men."[2]

By reaching the Pacific Ocean and coming back victoriously to St. Louis, Lewis and Clark led the first American transcontinental exploration, and their journey became one of the most celebrated events in American history. Painters and sculptors, biographers and journalists imagined their own vision of the expedition and many tourists today are re-living the adventure following an easier bicentennial

---

[1] "Jefferson to the Congress, 18 January 1803," in Donald T. Jackson, ed., *Letters of the Lewis and Clark Expedition, with Related Documents, 1783-1854*, 2 vols. (Urbana: University of Illinois Press, 1978), 1:13. Also on the web at <http://memory.loc.gov/ammem/mtjhtml/mtjser1.html>. On the relation between the expedition and the purchase see in particular James E. Lewis, Jr., "The Geopolitical Context of the Expedition" in Alan Taylor, ed., *Lewis and Clark: Journey to Another America* (St. Louis: Missouri Historical Society Press, 2003), 88-103.

[2] Patrick Gass, *A Journal of the Voyages and Travels of a Corps of Discovery* (Pittsburgh: David M'Keehan, 1807), 12.

trail, and stopping in the many interpretive centers placed along the way.[3] From a passage through the trans-Mississippi frontier territory, Lewis and Clark's trail has become both a representation of regional identity and a fictional memory of the American West: "a repository for a national frontier past" and "a key element in the mythology and ideology of American nationalism."[4]

To commemorate the bicentennial of the Lewis and Clark exploration many books have been published or reprinted.[5] The long trek has been analyzed from different angles: from the traditional study of the narrative of the journey, to the perspectives of the men and women who accompanied the explorers, and those of the Indians who met them along the way. The results show a multi-faceted historiographical picture: on the one hand, there are still heroes in the tradition of an American odyssey filled with national epic, vision, adventure and triumph: a condensation of Frederick Jackson Turner's frontier thesis;[6] and on the other hand, historians have portrayed men who were doubtless brave but also bound by cultural prejudice and obsessed by achieving their goal. In the middle, there are attempts to comprehend the different experiences of the multi-ethnicity and the confluence of cultures that characterized the early far western frontier.[7]

But although Lewis and Clark's expedition to explore the Missouri River was the most successful and famous, it was only one of the four expeditions promoted by Jefferson. The other three expeditions—to the Ouachita River led by William Dunbar and George Hunter (1804-1805), to the Red River carried out by Thomas Freeman and Peter Custis (1806), and to the sources of Mississippi River and then to the Southwest frontier undertaken by Zebulon Pike (1805-1807)—were not so successful and famous, but they revealed similar strategies, methods and purposes.[8]

The aim of this essay is to discuss some of the evidence concerning the connections among these expeditions, in relation to Jeffersonian attitudes towards the western frontier. Of special interest were the roles of the explorers in defining the geographical borders of U.S. sovereignty; Jefferson's instructions for the lands to be surveyed for eventual sale to American farmers; and in particular, his interest in the Indian nations that inhabited the frontier lands. His requests for the gathering

---

[3] See in this context the web site <www.lewisandclarktrail.com>.

[4] William Cronon, George Miles, and Jay Gitlin, "Becoming West: Toward a New Meaning for Western History," in William Cronon, George Miles, and Jay Gitlin, *Under an Open Sky: Rethinking America's Western Past* (New York: W.W. Norton, 1992), 25.

[5] See, in particular, Alan Taylor, ed., *Lewis and Clark*; Thomas P. Slaughter, *Exploring Lewis and Clark: Reflections on Men and Wilderness* (New York: Alfred A. Knopf, 2003) and James P. Ronda, *Lewis and Clark Among the Indians* (Lincoln: University of Nebraska Press, 2002).

[6] For example, Stephen E. Ambrose, *Undaunted Courage: Meriwether Lewis, Thomas Jefferson, and the Opening of the American West* (New York: Simon and Schuster, 1996).

[7] See for example, *A Confluence of Cultures: Native Americans and the Expedition of Lewis and Clark, 2003 Symposium Proceedings* (Missoula: University of Montana, 2003).

[8] Gregory Nobles, *American Frontiers: Cultural Encounter and Continental Conquest* (New York: Hill and Wang, 1999), 118-120.

of information about their names, their numbers, the limits of their possessions, their relations with other tribes, their commerce, languages, traditions, food, clothing, laws and customs were not for the purpose of defending or conserving their ethnicity, but in order to better "civilize and instruct them,"[9] with a view to rendering the Indians much more adaptable to the idea of closed territories. Jefferson's ethnographic interest was in essence a mere application of his agrarian *mentalité*, that he introduced by means of two complementary strategies—the acquisition of Indian lands for sale to white settlers, and the creation of boundaries for the confinement of the Indians inside reservations—which, in the space of a few decades, would transform the open trans-Mississippi frontier into a closed territory.[10]

Dunbar and Hunter

In a letter to William Dunbar of Natchez, Mississippi, in March of 1804, Jefferson wrote about the need to prepare "a map of Louisiana, which in it's [sic] contour and main waters will be perfectly correct, and will give us a skeleton to be filled up with details hereafter" and, especially, the need to explore the southwestern frontier following the Arkansas and Red Rivers. In the same letter he offered Dunbar the leadership of such an "enterprise."[11]

Dunbar shared with Jefferson the passion for science and agriculture, together with his intellectual curiosity, as well as his interest in land and slave properties. Born in Scotland in 1749 into an aristocratic family, he arrived in America in 1771. After trading with the Ohio Valley Indians, and traveling to Jamaica to purchase slaves, he finally settled near Natchez, where he built an elaborate mansion, known as "The Forest," similar to Jefferson's home at Monticello in Virginia. Dunbar was introduced to Jefferson through a letter from the U.S. consul in New Orleans and the two men began a correspondence on different matters, from botany to geography,

---

[9] "Jefferson's Instruction to Lewis and Clark Regarding Indians, June 1803," quoted in Anthony F.C. Wallace, *Jefferson and the Indians: The Tragic Fate of the First Americans* (Cambridge, MA: Belknap Press of Harvard University Press, 1999), 97.

[10] For an excellent general overview of the ambivalent early American attitudes towards Native inhabitants of the western frontiers, see the classic work by Reginald Horsman, *Expansion and American Indian Policy, 1783-1812* (East Lansing: Michigan State University Press, 1967). See also Francis Paul Prucha, *American Indian Policy in the Formative Years: The Indian Trade and Intercourse Acts, 1790-1834* (Cambridge, MA: Harvard University Press, 1962); Thomas D. Clark and John D.W. Guice, *The Old Southwest, 1795-1830: Frontiers in Conflict*, new edition (Norman and London: University of Oklahoma Press, 1996), and Robert M. Owens, "Jeffersonian Benevolence on the Ground: The Indian Land Cession Treaties of William Henry Harrison," *Journal of the Early Republic* 22.3 (Fall 2002): 405-435.

[11] "Jefferson to Dunbar, 13 March 1804," Thomas Jefferson Papers on the web at <http://memory.loc.gov/ammem/mtjhtml/mtjser1.html>, series 1: General Correspondence, 1651-1827, from 4 March 1804 to 20 August 1804, image 35. See also John Francis McDermott, ed., *The Western Journals of Dr. George Hunter, 1796-1805* (Philadelphia: American Philosophical Society, 1963), 8-9.

from philosophy to the life-style of the Indians. Jefferson supported Dunbar's request for membership of the American Philosophical Society in Philadelphia, as they began to think of an expedition to the Red and Arkansas Rivers.[12]

Like Dunbar, George Hunter was born in Scotland but into a lower class family. Arriving in Philadelphia in 1774, Hunter obtained employment as a druggist. During the War of Independence he enlisted as a soldier, but quickly transferred to the Hospital Department as an apothecary. In the following years Hunter developed a reputation as a chemist and druggist, and he began a series of explorations in Kentucky in the search for mineral deposits.[13] Jefferson thought that he was the right person to accompany Dunbar. In a letter to Dunbar dated 15 April 1804, the president communicated the decision for what he called the "Grand Expedition".[14] It should aim to reach the sources of both the Red and Arkansas Rivers, rivalling Lewis and Clark's mission on the Missouri.[15] The grand expedition was intended by Jefferson to "delineate with correctness the great arteries" of U.S. territory.[16] It was clear to Jefferson that the Lewis and Clark expedition would leave a large part of the Louisiana Purchase territory unexamined, and that the Red River was the best "artery" for the exploration of the Southwest.[17]

More than any other southwestern river, the Red River had originated disputes for colonial control in that part of the New World. It had been the scene of a number of early European ventures into western North America. Spanish expeditions of the 1530s and 1540s reached Caddo territory but failed to find easily recoverable natural resources and so did not immediately colonize. Much later the Caddo were visited by the French explorer La Salle, before he was assassinated by his own men in 1687. Realizing the strategic value of this fluvial artery, Spain and France vied for its control. Louis Jouchereau de Saint Denis founded Natchitoches in 1714, securing French dominion over the Red River valley. The Indian tribes preferred to trade with the French rather than be converted to Catholicism by Spanish missionaries. French settlers thus established an active trade with the Comanche and Wichita Indians, receiving buffalo hides, horses and mules in exchange for whisky, clothes and metal objects, but especially firearms with which they fought neighboring tribes such as the Osage and the Apache. France ceded western Louisiana to Spain in 1762, but

---

[12] Trey Berry, "The Forgotten Expedition: The Journey of Dunbar and Hunter Along the Ouachita River in Arkansas and Louisiana, 1804-1805," unpublished essay presented at the conference "Lewis and Clark: The Unheard Voices," State College, Pennsylvania State University, 14-16 November 2002, cited with the author's permission.

[13] Ibid.

[14] "Jefferson to Dunbar, 15 April 1804," Thomas Jefferson Papers on the web at <http://memory.loc.gov/ammem/mtjhtml/mtjser1.html>, series 1: General Correspondence, 1651-1827, from 4 March 1804 to 20 August 1804, image 375.

[15] "Dunbar to Jefferson, 13 May 1804," ibid., series 1: General Correspondence, 1651-1827, from 4 March 1804 to 20 August 1804, image 565.

[16] "Jefferson to Dunbar, 25 May 1805," ibid., series 1: General Correspondence, 1651-1827, from 19 March 1805 to 29 June 1805, image 554.

[17] See Donald Jackson, *Thomas Jefferson and the Stony Mountains: Exploring the West from Monticello* (Urbana: University of Illinois Press, 1981), 223.

during the next forty years of Spanish rule, relations with the territory's tribes followed the French model.[18]

Despite Spanish and French military and commercial activities in the trans-Mississippian territory, information on its geography and natural history was poor. Jean-Baptiste Bénard de La Harpe's journal had reported the existence of unicorns along the Red River.[19] Its shores were reputed to be populated by bison, tigers, wolves, deer, turkeys and alligators, and many unknown species of plants and fruits were supposed to grow along its course. American scientists were extremely curious about this area and the Red River got more discussion in the press than any other

---

[18] On the rivalry between Spain and France, and their relations with trans-Mississippian tribes, see for example David J. Weber, *The Spanish Frontier in North America* (New Haven and London: Yale University Press, 1992), especially 147-235; Abraham P. Nasatir, ed., *Before Lewis and Clark: Documents Illustrating the History of the Missouri, 1785-1804* (St. Louis: St. Louis Historical Documents Foundation, 1952), 2 vols. (reprint, Lincoln: University of Nebraska Press, 1990); John C. Ewers, "Symbols of Chiefly Authority in Spanish Louisiana," in John Francis McDermott, ed., *The Spanish in the Mississippi Valley, 1762-1804* (Urbana: University of Illinois Press, 1974), 272-286; Lawrence Kinnaird, "Spanish Treaties with Indian Tribes," *Western Historical Quarterly* 10 (January 1979): 39-48, and with Lucia B. Kinnaird, "Choctaws West of the Mississippi, 1766-1800," *Southwestern Historical Quarterly* 63 (1980): 349-470; Elizabeth A.H. John, *Storms Brewed in Other Men's Worlds: The Confrontation of Indians, Spanish and French in the Southwest, 1540-1795* (1981; reprint, Norman: University of Oklahoma Press, 1996); William E. Foley and C. David Rice, *The First Chouteaus: River Barons of Early St. Louis* (Urbana and Chicago: University of Illinois Press, 1983); Daniel H. Usner, Jr., *Indians, Settlers and Slaves in a Frontier Exchange Economy: The Lower Mississippi Valley before 1783* (Chapel Hill: University of North Carolina Press, 1992); Gilbert C. Din, "Between a Rock and a Hard Place: The Indian Trade in Spanish Arkansas," in Jeannie Whayne, comp., *Cultural Encounters in the Early South: Indians and Europeans in Arkansas* (Fayetteville: University of Arkansas Press, 1995), 112-130; F. Todd Smith, *The Caddo Indians: Tribes at the Convergence of Empires, 1542-1854* (College Station: Texas A&M University Press, 1995); "A Native Response to the Transfer of Louisiana: The Red River Caddos and Spain, 1762-1803," *Louisiana History* 37.2 (Spring 1996): 163-185; and "Spanish Indian Policy in Louisiana: The Natchitoches District, 1763-1803," in *The Louisiana Purchase Bicentennial Series in Louisiana History. Vol. II: The Spanish Presence in Louisiana, 1763-1803* (Lafayette: Center for Louisiana Studies, University of Southwestern Louisiana, 1996), 284-295; Morris S. Arnold, *The Rumble of a Distant Drum: The Quapaws and Old World Newcomers, 1673-1804* (Fayetteville: University of Arkansas Press, 2000); Carl J. Ekberg, *François Vallé and His World: Upper Louisiana before Lewis and Clark* (Columbia: University of Missouri Press, 2003); Susan Allison Miller, "Those Homelands You Call the 'Louisiana Purchase,'" in Paul Hoffman, ed., *The Louisiana Purchase and Its Peoples: Perspectives from the New Orleans Conference* (Lafayette: Louisiana Historical Association and Center for Louisiana Studies, University of Louisiana, 2004), 75-87.

[19] Ralph Smith, "Account of the Journey of Bernard [sic] de La Harpe: Discovery Made by Him of Several Indian Nations Situated in the West," *Southwestern Historical Quarterly* 62 (1959): 18-49.

river except the Missouri.[20] But during the preparation of the trip, both Jefferson and Dunbar expressed misgivings about the plan to ascend the Red River, since the Osage Indians, who constantly raided this territory, might attack the expedition. An Osage delegation led by the great chief White Hair arrived in Washington on 16 July 1804: the first Western Indians most east-coast Americans had ever seen. Dunbar convinced Jefferson to postpone the expedition, warning of the danger posed by the Osage faction led by Great Track. Instead he requested permission to explore a small river called Ouachita, where he could avoid trouble with the Indians.[21]

On 16 October 1804 the expedition left St. Catherine's Landing on the Mississippi River with thirteen soldiers, Hunter's teenage son and one of Dunbar's slaves, in a "Chinese-style vessel" designed and constructed by Hunter in Pittsburgh several months earlier. They were not the first to explore the river, but unlike other European trappers, traders and hunters, they hoped to complete a precise map of the Ouachita River. To create the most accurate map possible Dunbar used a pocket chronometer, and a surveying compass. Their journals were full of descriptions of the soils, water levels, flora and fauna, and daily astronomical and thermometer readings.[22] The journals also recorded the human dramas that occurred during this exploration: from the capture of a runaway slave to the continuous complaining of the soldiers with no officer to lead them, ending with an accident to Hunter. On 22 November, when he was cleaning his pistol on the boat, the gun fired and Hunter was seriously wounded in one thumb and two fingers. He remained in serious pain and danger of infection for over two weeks.[23] It was clear that, despite his experience as a soldier in the revolutionary war, he was not well trained in gun handling and military practices. On 8 January 1805, after a brief snowstorm and in view of the continuously falling temperatures, the corps decided to begin the return journey, without having reached the source of the Ouachita River. They arrived in Natchez on 27 January.[24]

During the following weeks Dunbar and Hunter prepared their accounts of the expedition for Jefferson. In an interview for the *New Orleans Gazette* that was published on 14 February 1805, Hunter "presented a more grandiose view of the Louisiana Purchase."[25] Upon his return to "The Forest," Dunbar began diligently to

---

[20] John L. Allen, "Geographical Knowledge and American Images of the Louisiana Territory," *Western Historical Quarterly* 1 (1971): 151-170; and more recently, John L. Allen, *Lewis and Clark and the Image of the American Northwest* (New York: Dover Publishing, 1991), and John L. Allen "'So Fine a Country': The Early Exploration of Louisiana Territory, 1714-1820," in Hoffman, ed., *The Louisiana Purchase and Its Peoples*, 231-247.

[21] "Dunbar to Jefferson, 9 June 1804" and "Jefferson to Dunbar, July 1804," Dunbar Papers, Special Collections, Ouachita Baptist University, Arkadelphia, AR, cited in Berry, "The Forgotten Expedition."

[22] Berry, "The Forgotten Expedition."

[23] "George Hunter Journals, 1796-1805," American Philosophical Society, Philadelphia, cited in Berry, "The Forgotten Expedition."

[24] "Dunbar Journal," Special Collections, Ouachita Baptist University, cited in Berry, "The Forgotten Expedition."

[25] Quoted in ibid.

prepare his report and by the time of his death five years later he had published twelve papers in the American Philosophical Society's journal discussing his natural history and astronomic observations.

Nevertheless, the failure of the Dunbar and Hunter expedition showed the necessity for Jefferson to include more soldiers than scientists on these expeditions, or better still, soldiers trained as scientists who would be able to carry out the scientific endeavors but at the same time maintain a strong control over their subordinates and ensure that the political target would be reached. In the end, the need to explore the Arkansas and Red Rivers remained an unsolved problem in Jefferson's strategies.

Freeman and Custis

It was not easy for Jefferson to find leaders for the Red River expedition because of fear of the Spanish reaction and of the Indian danger. Many young men of talent seemed reluctant to go. At last Jefferson settled on Thomas Freeman, a young Irish-American surveyor and a civil engineer on the Washington city project. He was not the best choice. Dunbar spoke well of Freeman but he confused young Thomas with Colonel Constant Freeman of the American garrison at New Orleans. Andrew Ellicott, the mathematician who schooled Meriwether Lewis in the taking of astronomical observations, defined Freeman as "an idle, lying, troublesome, discontented, mischief-making man" and again: "Mr. Freeman is one of the greatest rascals and liars in existence."[26] But Freeman's friendly association with James Wilkinson was an intriguing factor that poses many questions.

James Wilkinson was an ambiguous figure in American history. He served under General Anthony Wayne, leading raids against the Indians of the Ohio Valley in the last decade of the eighteenth century. In 1798 he was transferred to the southern frontier. He was for three years Jefferson's personal representative as commissioner to treat with the southern Indians to secure permission for building military posts and to obtain cession of land in strategic locations. During this mission Wilkinson noted the reluctance of the southern Indians to sell their lands, but continued his efforts to pacify the tribes, and to prepare them for removal from the east, in accordance with Jefferson's plan to move both Indian and white population around in his "yeoman empire." When Congress formally created the Territory of Louisiana in 1805, Jefferson appointed Wilkinson as governor.[27]

But Wilkinson was also "Secret agent 13" in the pay of the king of Spain. He had been a Spanish agent since 1787 when he suggested to the Spanish crown that he might be able to detach Kentucky from the Union. Jefferson was probably happy to use him as an informal channel of communication with Spain, taking advantage of his role as a double-dealer. Jefferson never withdrew his support of Wilkinson,

---

[26] "Andrew Ellicott to Sarah Ellicott, November 8, 1798 and January 10, 1799," in Catherine Van Cortlandt Mathews, *Andrew Ellicott: His Life and Letters* (New York: Grafton Press, 1908), 160-164.
[27] Wallace, *Jefferson and the Indians*, 253-258.

exonerating his complicity in Aaron Burr's separatist scheme and appointing him as an emissary to Cuba. In the end Wilkinson retired to Mexico where he died in 1825.[28]

Thomas Freeman arrived in Natchez in 1797 with Andrew Ellicott. He came as one of the American surveyors to chart the new boundary between Spanish Florida and the United States. When Ellicott dismissed him in November 1798, he was hired by Wilkinson to be the supervising civil engineer in the construction of Fort Adams, a new American outpost on the lower Mississippi. Wilkinson and Freeman shared many ideas and dreams about Texas that four decades later would be almost universally accepted as "Manifest Destiny," but which, at that time, "were clearly perceived as imperialistic."[29]

If Jefferson's choice in appointing Freeman as the leader of the Red River expedition was not the best, his efforts to find a naturalist scientifically trained and physically able to undertake the trip were even less fortunate. The first refusal came from Constantine Samuel Rafinesque-Schmaltz who preferred to return to Europe.[30] The famous Pennsylvania naturalist William Bartram was sixty-six and Jefferson did not really expect him to accept. But when Bartram declined he suggested Alexander Wilson, the Scottish-American poet and naturalist who would later become the editor of *American Ornitology*. Wilson wrote to President Jefferson, hoping to be appointed to the expedition to the Red River. His collection of some five hundred bird species was a true representation of westward expansion and exploration, but despite this record Jefferson rejected Wilson—who was terribly disappointed—

---

[28] For a biography, see James R. Jacobs, *Tarnished Warrior: Major General James Wilkinson* (New York: Macmillan Company, 1938), and more recently, John Thornton Posey, "Rascality Revisited: In Defense of General James Wilkinson," *Filson Club History Quarterly* 74.4 (Fall 2000): 309-351. On Burr's western intrigues, see Isaac Joslin Cox, "The Louisiana-Texas Frontier during the Burr Conspiracy," *Mississippi Valley Historical Review* 10.3 (December 1923): 274-284; Thomas Perkins Abernethy, *The Burr Conspiracy* (New York: Oxford University Press, 1954); Clarence E. Carter, "Burr-Wilkinson Intrigues in St. Louis," *Missouri Historical Society Bulletin* 10 (July 1954): 447-464; Walter Flavius McCaleb, *The Aaron Burr Conspiracy; and, A New Light on Aaron Burr*, expanded edition with introduction by Charles A. Beard (New York: Argosy-Antiquarian, 1966); Donald Barr Chidsey, *The Great Conspiracy: Aaron Burr and His Strange Doings in the West* (New York: Crown Publishers, 1967); James E. Lewis, Jr., "The Burr Conspiracy and the Problem of Western Loyalty," in Peter J. Kastor, ed., *The Louisiana Purchase: Emergence of an American Nation* (Washington, DC: Congressional Quarterly Press, 2002), 64-73; Buckner F. Melton, *Aaron Burr: Conspiracy to Treason* (New York: Wiley, 2002).

[29] Dan Flores, ed., *Southern Counterpart to Lewis and Clark: The Freeman and Custis Expedition of 1806* (Norman: University of Oklahoma Press, 2002), 51.

[30] "Rafinesque to Jefferson, 27 November 1804," in Donald T. Jackson, ed., *Letters of the Lewis and Clark Expedition*, 2:217-218, and "Jefferson to Rafinesque, 15 December 1804," Thomas Jefferson Papers on the web at <http://memory.loc.gov/ammem/mtjhtml/mtjser1.html>, series 1: General Correspondence, 1651-1827, from 21 August 1804 to 29 December 1804, image 864.

accepting instead Freeman's suggestion and offering the position to the young Peter Custis.[31]

Custis was only twenty-five, but he was a Virginia native and moreover related to the late President Washington. Although Custis was pursuing a solid medical education at the University of Pennsylvania, which he entered in 1804, he did not appear to have had enough experience in the field. Jefferson could only hope to have "procured a good botanist." Custis did not hesitate to postpone the completion of his medical degree in order to join the Red River expedition, during which he received three dollars a day plus expenses from the day he left Philadelphia for Natchez in January 1806.[32]

In April 1806, the Red River expedition finally got under way. In the same month Don Francisco Viana, adjutant inspector of the troops for the *Provincias Internas* of New Spain sent a garrison of 134 soldiers to Nacogdoches. The Spanish Governor Antonio Cordero had heard from an "American emigrant" that fifteen hundred men where preparing for an invasion of Texas.[33] For the Spaniards, the "scientific mission" was clearly an excuse.

Custis and Freeman's Journal tells us that the expedition left Fort Adams on the afternoon of 19 April, with "two flat bottomed barges and a pirogue." The scientific limitations of the expedition were clear at their departure because of the elevated banks of the river, which meant, as Freeman wrote: "the remarks of the survey will be confined to the width, depth and course it pursues."[34] Custis was clear about these limitations, affirming that:

> Owing to Mr. Freeman's great anxiety to proceed ... I have not had so complete opportunity of examining the country and its productions as I could have wished: I shall therefore be able to give you only a rapid and imperfect sketch.[35]

The only excursions Custis was allowed to have were caused by the necessity of portaging the rapids of the Red River. But even with these restrictions, Custis did his best to describe the landscape: rocks and trees, waters and underwater plants.

---

[31] "Bartram to Jefferson, 6 February 1806," Thomas Jefferson Papers on the web at <http://memory.loc.gov/ammem/mtjhtml/mtjser1.html>, series 1: General Correspondence, 1651-1827, from 24 December 1805 to 12 May 1806, image 500. See also Thomas Slaughter, *The Nature of John and William Bartram* (New York: Vintage Books, 1996), xvii. Alexander Wilson's accompanying letter is missing from Jefferson's collection, and the suspected reasons were explained in Flores, *Southern Counterpart to Lewis and Clark*, 58.

[32] "Jefferson to Dunbar, 12 January 1806," Thomas Jefferson Papers on the web at <http://memory.loc.gov/ammem/mtjhtml/mtjser1.html>, series 1: General Correspondence, 1651-1827, from 24 December 1805 to 12 May 1806, image 238, and "Dearborn to Custis (letter of appointment), 14 January 1806," in Rowland, *Life, Letters and Papers of William Dunbar*, 189-190.

[33] "Cordero to Viana, 21 April 1806," Bexar Archives, University of Texas at Austin, quoted in Flores, *Southern Counterpart to Lewis and Clark*, 77.

[34] Flores, *Southern Counterpart to Lewis and Clark*, 101

[35] Ibid., 103.

The banks along the lower Red River, with plenty of cottonwood trees, presented a series of small plantations with a mixture of inhabitants: French, Spanish, Indian, and "Negro blood, the latter often predominating," living in "small cottages on the banks and near the river."[36] The party arrived in Natchitoches on 19 May, remaining in the last American outpost until the first days of June. At the departure, the expedition was augmented by twenty soldiers "for the purpose of assisting the exploring party ... to repel by force any opposition they might meet with."[37] In this way the expedition became much more military and ready for an armed confrontation with the Spanish.

Freeman and Custis passed the Great Rafts on the river—one of the amazing natural phenomena of North America—without giving any particular explanation of the reasons for the gigantic log-jam "composed of the trunks of trees, brought down by the floods, and lodged on sand bars; forming an impenetrable mass."[38] The Red River's course continued with a series of bayous, where numerous dead trees frequently meant difficulties and danger for the small party. Noticing the presence of Spanish troops, the party was forced to stop at a small Caddo Indian village. Freeman asked the chief to display "the American instead of the Spanish flag" and the "flag of the U.S. was hoisted on a pole in the middle of the square in the village, where it was kept constantly flying."[39]

Three Caddo Indians accompanied the expedition, when it left the village on 11 July, "to act as guides, and spies."[40] The expedition crossed a beautiful prairie that "was the site of an Old Caddo Village deserted by that nation after the massacre of the greatest part of the inhabitants, by the Osage Indians." The Caddo Indians expressed a wish to visit this place "with a bottle of liquor, that they might take a drink and talk to the great spirit."[41] Around and near this place lay their cultivated fields. Following the river they came upon the ruins of other Old Caddo villages, at that time ghost towns, but which had been considerable settlements at the time of La Salle's expeditions in the 1680s.[42]

On 26 July three Caddo runners reached the expedition with the following information: "the Spanish troops upward of 1,000 in number entered it [the village] and cut down the staff on which the American Flag was flying, and carried the Flag with them. They insulted the Chief, said they were going after the Americans on Red River."[43] Continuing along the river during the following days the expedition met Spanish sentinels and "Piquet guards" and when they encamped to dine on 29 July, they were reached by a large detachment of Spanish dragoons. The Spanish officer

---

[36] Ibid., 118.
[37] Ibid., 123.
[38] Ibid., 133.
[39] Ibid., 157.
[40] Ibid., 176.
[41] Ibid., 184.
[42] La Salle's expedition passed this place in July 1687. See Henry Reed Stiles, ed., *Joutel's Journal of La Salle's Last Voyage* (Albany, NY: Joseph McDonough, 1906), 165-169. The Europeans carried the seed of destruction. A smallpox epidemic in 1690 caused the death of three thousand Caddo.
[43] Flores, *Southern Counterpart to Lewis and Clark*, 193.

stated that "his orders were not to suffer any body of armed troops to march through the territory of the Spanish government." Freeman asked the officer "to state in writing his objections to the progress of the party" but this was refused by the Spaniard. The expedition was forced to stop and the following day they "began to descend the river."[44]

Freeman and Custis's expedition had no clear scientific goals. Freeman's haste and his "great anxiety to proceed" was linked to the necessity of defining the boundaries of the area, drawing maps, and initiating friendly relations with the Indians, as Jefferson clearly stipulated. This southern counterpart to the Lewis and Clark expedition lost the classical appeal linked to natural history or anthropology. Furthermore, Freeman and Custis revealed a territory where the Indians and the Spaniards were equally determined to maintain control of their lands.

Zebulon Pike

If the first three expeditions—Lewis and Clark, Dunbar and Hunter, Freeman and Custis—showed a veneer of scientific exploration, in the fourth, Jefferson and Wilkinson revealed more clearly another intent. Zebulon Pike was a simple lieutenant, twenty-six years old, without any scientific training. According to Elliott Coues:

> "Pike was the simon-pure and simple soldier, who had been ordered by his general to carry our flag among British traders and Sioux, Ojibwa, and other Indians of the Northwest, in the first instance; in the second place, to display that emblem of authority among Osage, Pawnee, and Comanche, and plant a standard of the republic on the still disputed boundary of New Spain and the Southwest. All else that he accomplished was incidental."[45]

In particular, the aims of his first mission to the source of the Mississippi River were to announce the sovereignty of the United States to the Native inhabitants of that northern frontier, to buy from them the sites for army posts if possible, and to escort an Indian delegation back to St. Louis to negotiate and sign a treaty.[46]

Lieutenant Pike left St. Louis with his twenty soldiers on 9 August 1805. The expedition set out in a boat of the same type used by Lewis and Clark. Immediately above the confluence of the *Riviere des Moines* with the Mississippi River, Pike saw and described a Sac Indian village. A few miles higher up Pike found the first village of the Fox. The Sac and Fox tribes spoke the same language and were culturally very similar; they had been close allies since 1733, when they fought the Europeans together, and consequently were forced to move south of the Great

---

[44] Ibid., 205-206.
[45] Elliott Coues, ed., *The Expeditions of Zebulon Montgomery Pike, to the Head Waters of the Mississippi River, through the Louisiana Territory, and in New Spain, during the Years 1805-6-7*, 3 vols. (New York: Francis P. Harper, 1895), 1:vi.
[46] Jackson, *Thomas Jefferson and the Stony Mountains*, 242-267.

Lakes. Traditionally hunters and trappers, they were forced to become farmers. "Here the United States have an agent (Mr. William Ewing) appointed to instruct this nation in agriculture," wrote Pike.[47]

Near the mouth of the Turkey River, Pike met "a war party of Indians" that "appeared anxious to avoid the Americans," as they were considered "a vindicative, ferocious and warlike people."[48] On 5 September, the expedition reached a big Indian village at *Prairie du Chien*, at the confluence of the Wisconsin River with the Mississippi. This place was at that time the real leading edge of the frontier and an active trading center. Here Pike "made a choice for an eligible site of a fort" and his recommendation was considered, but Fort Crawford was built only in 1816. At the village, Pike chose to change "their large boat for others better adapted to the prosecution of their voyage." From this point on, the Mississippi was no longer an easy river to ascend in big boats. Here also "the party received in addition two interpreters," and were joined by Mr. Frazer, "an American who was going on a trading expedition, to winter with some of the bands of the Sioux."

All together they held a council with Le Feuille, a chief of the lower band of the Sioux, the Indians who controlled the western part of the Upper Mississippi River.[49] The Sioux chief gave his permission for the soldiers to proceed and prepared a pipe. After smoking, Le Feuille gave the pipe to Pike saying: "I have never been at war with the new father; and I hope always to preserve the same good understanding with him that now exists. I now present you with a pipe, to show to the upper bands, in token of our good understanding, that they may see my work, and imitate my conduct to you." On returning to the boat, Pike sent the chief "two carrots of tobacco, four knives, half a pound of vermillion, and a quart of salt," to which Mr. Frazer added eight gallons of rum.[50] Giving the Indians goods, tobacco, and alcoholic beverages, Pike followed the common European tradition for governing the frontier. Tools, tobacco—and especially alcohol—were to be given to the Indians to make them economically and psychologically dependent upon whites.[51]

The expedition continued the trip toward the source of the Mississippi, meeting other Sioux warriors and camps. On 22 September, at the mouth of St. Peter's River, they met Sioux chief Petit Corbeau with about 150 warriors. "They honoured Pike with a salute, in the Indian manner, with ball!" and organized a council with six Sioux chiefs for the next day at the Falls of St. Anthony, where Pike addressed them in a rather direct speech: "the principal subject of which was the desire of obtaining

---

[47] *An Account of a Voyage up the Mississippi River, from St. Louis to Its Source Compiled from Mr. Pike's Journal* (hereafter *An Account*) (Washington, DC: n.p., 1807), 4-5. See in this context my previous work "When the Mississippi Was an Indian River: Zebulon Pike's Trip from St. Louis to Its Sources, 1805-1806," in *Revue Française d'Études Américaines,* 98 (2003): 9-19.
[48] *An Account*, 6.
[49] Ibid., 7.
[50] Ibid., 10-11.
[51] For these politics of "benevolence,", see in particular Richard White, *The Middle Ground: Indians, Empires, and Republics in the Great Lakes Region, 1650-1815* (Cambridge: Cambridge University Press, 1991), 469-516.

lands at this place ... and making peace between them and the Chipeway." In this first treaty between the Sioux and the United States, the Sioux chiefs gave Pike the land he desired, a hundred thousand acres of it, and "a safe passport for him", in exchange for "presents to the value of 200 dollars and 60 gallons of liquors." But future problems were clearly foreshadowed: "It was somewhat difficult to obtain their signature to the grant," wrote Pike, "as they conceived their word of honour sufficient." They also "spoke doubtfully respecting the peace."[52]

After much trouble in getting their boat through the St. Anthony rapids, they continued the journey, but at that time six of the twenty-two men were sick. Above the falls, things were still not easy for the expedition. Navigation was made difficult by shoals and cross currents, and the river "would be considered impracticable by a person not determined to proceed," wrote Pike. Settlers would not be able to use it easily.[53] In mid-October Pike ordered the soldiers to erect a stockade shelter south of Little Falls. Only a few soldiers continued the exploration on foot in the snow until, in mid-January 1806, they reached Sandy Lake and the North West Company palisade camp, a trading post established by the British twelve years earlier. On leaving the stockade with the superintendent of the North West Company settlement for a trip to the lake, they met an Indian who expressed great astonishment when told that Pike was an American. The Indian expressed the greatest veneration for the American character, which he associated "with warlike achievements." The Indian said "the American is neither a Frenchman nor an Englishman, but a white Indian."[54]

Pike was determined to proceed on to the head of the river, but it was not easy to find. He left the North West Company camp on the morning of 29 January when it was snowing very hard, and arrived at the Pakagama Falls. Other days were spent traveling on the frozen meadows along the river, and often losing track of the river itself. In the end they reached Sangsue Lake, deciding erroneously that it was "the main source of the Mississippi."[55] In 1823 the Italian explorer Giacomo Costantino Beltrami discovered that the real source is instead at Itaska Lake "which receives no tributary stream, and seems to draw its waters from the bosom of the earth."[56]

Then the explorers reached another establishment of the North West Company and on 10 February Pike put the American flag on the staff on which the English flag was flying. Some Ojibwa Indians shot at it with rifles and "broke the iron pin to

---

[52] *An Account*, 15-17.
[53] Ibid., 23.
[54] Ibid., 36. For reflections on the idea of "White Indians," see Alan Taylor, "Regulator and White Indians. Forms of Agrarian Resistance in Post-Revolutionary New England," in Robert A. Gross, ed., *In Debt to Shays: The Bicentennial of an Agrarian Rebellion* (Charlottesville: University Press of Virginia, 1993), 145-160; and my "When the Mississippi Was an Indian River," 14-15.
[55] *An Account*, 39.
[56] Giacomo Costantino Beltrami, *La Découverte des Sources du Mississippi et de la Rivière Sanglante* (New Orleans: B. Levy, 1824), letter 8. Quotation from Giacomo Costantino Beltrami, *Pilgrimage in Europe and America: Leading to the Discovery of the Sources of the Mississippi and Bloody River*, 2 vols. (London: Hunt and Clarke, 1828), 2:434.

which it was fastened, and brought it to the ground."[57] On 16 February Pike organized a council with the Ojibwa Indians: he asked them to make peace with the Sioux and that "some of the chiefs should accompany him to St. Louis." However, the chiefs did not think it useful to follow Pike to St. Louis in "a journey of such extent and through hostile tribes."[58] An Indian chief also informed Pike that "a string of wampum had been sent to the Chipeway from the British commanding officer of the area." The pro-British feeling among the Ojibwa was evident, and would continue later during the War of 1812. On 28 February the party started on their return to St. Louis, arriving on 30 April, after "an absence of eight months and twenty two days."[59]

After a two months stay in St. Louis, Pike set out on a second exploring expedition to the Southwest, during which time he was promoted to captain. Leaving St. Louis on 15 July 1806, he ascended the Missouri River to the Osage land and villages. Thence he continued southwestward overland until he reached the Arkansas River. In the present state of Colorado, on 23 November, he sighted and attempted without success to scale the peak which now bears his name. He then ventured southward toward the Rio Grande, reaching one of its tributaries in February 1807. Along the way Pike returned some prisoners released by the Osage, made peace between the Kansas and the Pawnee Indians and established friendly relations with the Comanche. Finally he wandered onto the Rio Grande, where he was taken into custody by Spanish troops and escorted to Santa Fe and then to Chihuahua for questioning by General Antonio Salcedo, before being allowed to return east under military guard. On his return trip, Pike crossed Texas by way of the Old San Antonio Road to Natchitoches, Louisiana.[60]

Pike published his account of the expedition in Philadelphia in 1810.[61] In its simplicity, this account shows the cultural diversities on the American frontiers, the different Indian languages, (which were as foreign to one another among the various tribes of the area as they were to the Europeans), as well as the disputes and suspicions among the Indian nations, and their fear and hostility toward the white settlers and the U.S. Army. But especially, it describes the permanent state of war among the Indians, and in particular the traditional enmities between the Sioux nation and the several tribes of the Ojibwa, between the Osage and the Caddo, and between the Kansas and the Pawnee Indians.

Despite the travelogue tone of Pike's account, the venture was a military expedition. Pike was first of all a soldier, a military man trained in arms and not a scientist wedded to compass, chronometer and other scientific instruments. Both of Pike's expeditions originated with the governor of the Louisiana Territory, General James Wilkinson; and both were strictly military in method and in purpose.

---

[57] *An Account*, 41.
[58] Ibid., 43.
[59] Ibid., 67. Ojibwa and Chipeway were just two of a number of Europeanized versions of this tribe's name.
[60] Wallace, *Jefferson and the Indians*, 247.
[61] Zebulon Montgomery Pike, *An Account of Expeditions to the Sources of the Mississippi and through the Western Part of Louisiana, to the Source of the Arkansaw, Kans, La Platte, and Pierre Jaun Rivers* (Philadelphia: C. e A. Conrad, 1810).

Lieutenant Pike was promoted first to captain and then to general as a result of these missions. The success and the moral effect of his account were enormous, but clouds remained on his scientific observations. Pike was accused of plagiarism by Alexander von Humboldt. The famous European explorer caught Pike red-handed and Pike's silence in this matter aggravates the offence.[62] Humboldt's direct charge of plagiarism against Pike was reiterated in the English translation of his work where he affirmed:

> Mr. Pike displayed admirable courage in an important undertaking for the investigation of western Louisiana; but unprovided with instruments, and strictly watched on the road from Santa Fe to Natchitoches, he could do nothing towards the progress of the geography of the *Provincias Internas*. The maps of Mexico, which are annexed to the narratives of his journey, are reduced from my great map of New Spain, of which I left a copy, in 1804, at the secretary of state's office at Washington.[63]

From Frontier to Boundaries

With Pike's expeditions things become much clearer. The Jeffersonian expeditions were less engaged in scientific discovery than in defining the political boundaries of the new frontier territory. Their chief aims were to draw maps or check the accuracy of existing maps; to identify potential difficulties for the government of the vast territory, as well as the opportunities it offered for commerce; and to render the Indians sensible of the authority of the new imperial power that was extending its frontier into the trans-Mississippian West. If scientific—including ethnological and linguistic—information could be gathered along the way, that would be welcome; but the diplomatic, military and commercial aspects of the expeditions were preeminent.[64]

Pike's expeditions did not provide a huge store of information. No plants or animals were sent back to satisfy Jefferson's intellectual curiosity. It was a military expedition to reconnoiter the territory and make a claim of sovereignty, much in the same way as European imperial powers would continue to do throughout the nineteenth century in areas where they wanted to establish their presence, and where they would dispossess the native peoples, expropriate the lands, and destroy not only the pre-existing cultures of the native inhabitants but often their very physical existence. Pike proudly hoisted the fifteen-star, fifteen-stripe American flag: the first to fly over the upper course of the Mississippi and in the far Southwest.[65] It was a small but relevant sign of the presence of the new geopolitical power in the area.[66]

---

[62] Ibid., xii.
[63] Alexander von Humboldt, *Personal Narrative of Travels to the Equinoctial Regions of the New Continent during the Years 1799-1804, Written in French by, and translated into English by Helen Maria Williams* (Philadelphia: M.Carey, 1815), xxii.
[64] Wallace, *Jefferson and the Indians*, 247.
[65] The fifteen-star, fifteen-stripe flag was authorized by the Flag Act of 13 January 1794, which added two stars and two stripes to the original thirteen star flag to represent the

The publication of Pike's *Account* was immediately a great success, and American interest in the Southwest increased. But the editor of the *Louisiana Gazette* became extremely suspicious about the motives of the expeditions led by Freeman and Custis, and by Pike. He denounced "those secret expeditions, secret orders, and secret plans", and concluded that the rumors of war with Spain in 1806 had not been grounded in the Burr Conspiracy but in Jefferson's "philosophic mind" that "has long wished to emancipate the people of Old and New Mexico."[67]

Jefferson needed to show the Federalists that the fifteen million dollars paid for the Louisiana territory were not too high a price but, in fact, a bargain. But, to be the best bargain the territory must be the largest possible. This could be obtained by enlarging the boundaries of Louisiana. For this purpose Jefferson convinced himself that the Rio Grande was the Southwest boundary. In doing so, he ignored Spanish sovereignty in Texas. Spanish Secretary of State Pedro Cevallos was very clear. Not only did Spain not relinquish West Florida, but any American claim on Texas was "absurd reasoning! Which does not merit to be refuted."[68] For Spanish officials, Jeffersonian exploration in the southwest was merely a pretext to enlarge American boundaries. In their view, despite or because of its libertarian principles, the American republic was an expansionist power.[69] Dan Flores, the historian of the Freeman and Custis expedition, concurs: "Jefferson's claim of Texas was ill-founded, at best; at worst it was undisguised imperialism."[70]

Jefferson's model of an agrarian state, which would cultivate and consume its own production while exporting its surplus, was designed to counter commercial

---

admission of Vermont (the fourteenth state on 4 March 1791) and Kentucky (the fifteenth state on 1 June 1792).

[66] Pike's account supports Sheehan's historical analysis concerning American policy toward the Indians in these years. See Bernard W. Sheehan, *Seeds of Extinction: Jefferson Philanthropy and the American Indian* (Chapel Hill: University of North Carolina Press, 1973).

[67] *Louisiana Gazette*, 16 May 1811. For a concise history of Spanish-American frontier disputes during these tumultuous years see Weber, *The Spanish Frontier in North America,* 296-299. On Burr's western intrigues, see note 28. Thomas Jefferson's prejudice toward Spanish Colonists is discussed in Patricia Nelson Limerick, "Explaining Ourselves: Jefferson, History, and the Changing West," in James P. Ronda, ed., *Thomas Jefferson and the Changing West* (Albuquerque: University of New Mexico Press, 1997), 185-194.

[68] "His Excellency Don Pedro Cevallos to Messrs. Monroe and Pinckney, Aranjuez [Spain], 24 February 1805," *Annals of Congress*, 8th Cong., 2d sess., 1391. Also on the web at <http://memory.loc.gov/cgi-bin/ampage?collId=llac&fileName=014/llac014.db&recNum=692>.

[69] Sylvia L. Hilton, "Movilidad y expansión en la construcción política de los Estados Unidos: 'estos errantes colonos' en las fronteras españolas del Misisipí (1776-1803)," *Revista Complutense de Historia de América* (Madrid) 28 (2002): 63-96. This is a detailed interpretive analysis, based on primary sources, of Spanish views on American expansionism between 1776 and 1804.

[70] Flores, *Southern Counterpart to Lewis and Clark*, 26.

luxury on the one hand and the growth of an urban working class on the other.[71] His "yeoman empire" was opposed to the British model which used commerce and manufacturing as vehicles of empire. In theory and practice, an agrarian republic was necessarily expansionist. As its population grew, its agricultural character could be preserved only by continual access to new land. Jefferson provided this land with the Louisiana Purchase, his "scientific" expeditions, and especially the dispossession of Indian lands.

Jefferson's Legacy to Frontier Tribes

After the return of Pike's second expedition in the summer of 1807, Jefferson's projects for the exploration of the Louisiana territory came to an end. Spanish diplomatic and military opposition was fierce and the capture of Pike was a clear message to the sixty-four-year-old American president, who was coming close to the end of his second term, that the Spanish would not tolerate expeditions into areas they considered their own.[72] The political boundaries of the territory were not much clearer, but nonetheless white settlers started migrating into these lands. The "vindictive, ferocious, and warlike people" would eventually transform the landscape with new settlements and Indian reservations. At St. Louis a number of treaties would be signed. The advancing white frontier would mean the demarcation of boundaries for western tribes.

The Black Hawk War of 1832 grew out of Sac and Fox grievances created by the treaty of 1804. These tribes were defeated by the U.S. Army and required to cede a substantial territory as indemnity for the expenses of the U.S. military, even though the Sac nation as a whole had not supported Black Hawk.[73] They moved from the Mississippi River to Kansas in 1837 and 1842. Many of the Fox returned to Iowa during the 1850s where they bought land that was later recognized as a reservation. After the Civil War, the other Fox in Kansas joined the Sac and moved with most of them to Indian territories—now Oklahoma—in 1869.

The Sioux, too, after the first cession of land to Pike, went to war against the United States, assaulting Fort Meigs, in support of the English during the War of 1812. On 15 July 1815, at the close of the war, the various Sioux tribes made peace with the United States, finally acknowledging U.S. sovereignty, and signing five treaties near St. Louis. In 1837, with the example of Sac and Fox before them, the Sioux sold all of their territory east of the Mississippi and in 1851 they sold all their remaining land in Iowa and Minnesota as well. After a century of domination and conquest the Sioux had accepted a very definite conception of the boundaries of

---

[71] Laura Rigal, *The American Manufactory: Art, Labor, and the World of Things* (Princeton, NJ: Princeton University Press, 1998), 92.
[72] Dan L. Flores, "Rendezvous at Spanish Bluffs: Jefferson's Red River Exploration," *Red River Valley Historical Review* 4 (Spring 1979): 4-26.
[73] Wallace, *Jefferson and the Indians*, 337.

their tribal territory.[74] The treaty of Fort Laramie in 1868 established a Great Sioux Reservation equivalent to contemporary South Dakota.[75] Even here, illegal trespassing by miners onto Indian lands in the Black Hills triggered the last of the Sioux wars, which ended with the death of chief Sitting Bull and the Wounded Knee massacre on 29 December 1890.[76]

Another tribe encountered by Pike, the Osage, signed their first treaty with the United States in 1808, ceding to the federal government all the lands between the Arkansas and Missouri Rivers, including their old village located on the Little Osage River. William Clark, in those years the superintendent of Indian affairs, estimated the area to amount to "near 50,000 square miles of excellent country." In return, the Osage were promised the protection of the American fort at Fire Prairie and the chance to trade at the fort store. Clark made them a present of guns, powder, ball, and blankets to a value of $317.74 and also promised to provide within a year $1,200 in merchandise, as well as a blacksmith, a mill, plows, and two log houses. All together, the compensations to the Indians came to approximately $5,000, about ten cents per square mile of land.[77]

Some years later, after the approval of this treaty, the Great Osage and the Little Osage moved west to the valley of the Neosho River in Kansas. Pawhuska, a descendant of the old Chief Pawhuska, established the Great Osage Village near the present town of Shaw in Neosho County, while the Little Osage made their village just west of Chanute, Kansas. The Osage settled here for nearly half a century. Their reservation in Kansas was fifty miles wide, on the northern border of present-day Oklahoma.[78] When the Civil War started, members of the Great Osage Band served in the Confederate army, while many warriors from the Little Osage fought with the Union army, although provision had been made by treaty for the Little Osage men to fight for the Confederacy. This division caused great distress within the tribe, and they suffered great property loss when their reservation was overrun by guerilla bands of white soldiers in the Kansas border fighting. When the war was over, the government secured the cession of a large portion of the Osage land in Kansas. The tribe soon faced intolerable conditions because the white settlers were clamoring for more of the Indian land. An act of Congress on 15 July 1870 provided that the

---

[74] Richard White, "The Winning of the West: The Expansion of the Western Sioux in the Eighteenth and Nineteenth Centuries," *Journal of American History* 65 (1978): 319-343.

[75] The Fort Laramie treaty is on the web at <http://www.yale.edu/lawweb/avalon/ntreaty/nt001.htm>.

[76] Dee Brown, *Bury My Heart at Wounded Knee: An Indian History of the American West* (New York: Holt, Rinehart and Winston, 1970), 289-326.

[77] Wallace, *Jefferson and the Indians*, 272. See also "An Act Making Appropriations for Carrying into Effect a Treaty Between the United States and the Great and Little Osage Nation of Indians, Concluded at Fort Clark, on 10 November 1808" on the web at <http://www.yale.edu/lawweb/avalon/statutes/native/na020.htm>. For the history of the Osage Nation from its origins to its forced departure from Missouri see Gilbert C. Din and Abraham P. Nasatir, *The Imperial Osages: A Study of Spanish-Indian Diplomacy in the Mississippi Valley* (Norman: University of Oklahoma Press, 1983), and Kristie C. Wolferman, *The Osage in Missouri* (Columbia: University of Missouri Press, 1997).

[78] Terry P. Wilson, *The Osage* (New York: Chelsea House Publishers, 1988).

remainder of the Osage land in Kansas be sold for the benefit of the tribe. From the proceeds of this sale, a new reservation was purchased in the Indian Territory, the tract lying in the eastern end of the Cherokee Outlet and which became the present-day Osage County. By 1872, they were settled on their new reservation in Oklahoma.[79]

There are many more examples, but it was clear that the dispossession of the Indian lands and the creation of Indian reservations meant the transformation of the American frontiers into boundaries for the first Americans. Cession of land, removal policies, diseases, alcohol, and wars transformed the wide frontier territory, once belonging to the Indians, into reservations that might be only fifty miles wide. By the late nineteenth century, the entire Indian population had been concentrated within increasingly restrictive boundaries.[80]

---

[79] Ibid.
[80] William T. Hagan, "How the West Was Lost," in Frederick E. Hoxie, ed., *Indians in American History* (Arlington Heights: Harlan Davidson, 1988), 179-202.

MYTHS AND LEGENDS OF THE IRISH PIONEERS IN TEXAS

Graham Davis

There is a scene in John Ford's classic western, *The Man Who Shot Liberty Valance,* in which the James Stewart character tells a newspaperman that he did not kill the outlaw Liberty Valance, as everybody thought. The newspaperman puts him right. His paper from back east worked on the basis that "when the legend becomes fact, print the legend." There is probably as much legend associated with the American West as anywhere, propagated by the press, dime novels, and Hollywood films. What the "new western history" seeks to do is to demythologize much of what has been accepted.[1] The myths discussed in this essay refer to the subject of Irish emigration and the Great Irish Famine, the notion of Texas as a Garden of Eden, Frederick Jackson Turner's frontier thesis, and the legend of the rags-to-riches story of "cattle king," Thomas O'Connor.

Irish Emigration

An enduring myth about Irish emigration, given force by the association of famine and a mass exodus from Ireland in the 1840s, is the image of oppressed Irish men and women driven out of their country as part of a sinister plan to rid the country of its "surplus" population.[2] This central idea of the Great Famine (1845-1852) was established by the Young Ireland journalist-historian, John Mitchel. His enduring influence may be traced to two works; *Jail Journal or Five Years in British Prisons* (1854) and *The Last Conquest of Ireland (Perhaps)* (1860). Most emigrants ended up forced into exile in the United States, where for at least a generation they suffered poverty and discrimination in the slums of Boston, New York and Philadelphia. What is left out of the story is pre-famine emigration. Between 1815 and 1845 around one million emigrants left Ireland, with mass emigration established by 1835. This was dominated by relatively prosperous farmers who could afford the cost of the Atlantic crossing by selling stock and leases on their holdings and who were setting out for a better life in the New World. Before 1835, most emigrants were farmers from the north and south-east, the most prosperous parts of Ireland, and they remained part of the outflow in the decade 1835-1845.[3] The Irish who set out for Texas in 1834 were from Co. Wexford and Waterford. They were farmers prosperous enough to afford £60 for passage for their families and the cost of a

---

[1] Patricia Nelson Limerick, "Making the Most of Words: Verbal Activity and Western America," in Walter Cronon, George Miles, and Jay Gitlin, eds., *Under an Open Sky: Rethinking America's Western Past* (New York and London: W.W. Norton, 1992), 167-184.

[2] Graham Davis, "Making History: John Mitchel and the Great Famine," in Neil Sammells and Paul Hyland, eds., *Irish Writing: Exile and Subversion* (Basingstoke and London: Macmillan, 1991), 98-115.

[3] James H. Johnstone, "The Distribution of Irish Emigration in the Decade before the Great Famine," *Irish Geography* 21 (1988): 78-87.

year's supplies and farming implements. Emigration from Ireland before 1835 was a voluntary and premeditated decision taken in the main by prosperous farmers. Emigrants as victims suited an Irish nationalist perspective; emigrants as opportunists did not.

The evidence of Irish colonists reinforces the pull factor with the opportunity to acquire land in Mexican Texas. William St. John, a Refugio colonist, testified in old age in reply to the question: "What induced your father and mother to leave Ireland to come to America?" "Just to better our situation and get more land."[4] Fellow Refugio colonist, Martin Power, resisted pressure to return home in a letter to his father: "I have for my time at least 80 pound a year since I left Ballinhash to present date … I know that you would not at this time insist on me to go home … and not only that but see the door open to make an independent fortune in a short time."[5] Land was the key to securing an independent fortune.

The Irish colonists had endured a cholera epidemic in New Orleans, shipwreck off the Gulf Coast of Texas, the threat of hostile Indians and the devastation caused to their homesteads by the Mexican army led by President Santa Anna. This caused much grief back in Ireland. Yet Martin Power was right in seeing the potential wealth to be gained from settlement in Texas. Each adult colonist received 4,428 acres of pasture and 177 acres of arable land, a far more generous settlement than the 640 acres given to Stephen F. Austin's American colonists. If they could withstand the hazards of frontier life, they would have a fair chance of success as independent farmers and ranchers.

Texas as Paradise

Apart from the obvious attraction of generous land entitlement, what induced Irish tenant farmers to emigrate to Texas? It is clear from the language of the emigrant guides of the time and the letters and reminiscences of the emigrants themselves that Texas was sold to would-be emigrants as a paradise. The word, paradise, is repeated by Mexican government officials to encourage their own people to settle on their northern frontier, in the travelers' guides that boosted the prospect of settlement in Texas, and it features in memoirs of Irish settlers. The idea of Texas as a paradise became part of the mindset of the colonists.

Texas was "so fertile, of such benign climate, so rich in metals and natural resources that when descriptions of it were read out, instantly, one came to believe that they were talking of Paradise."[6] John J. Linn, Refugio colonist and Victoria merchant, recalled his early days in Texas: "Texas was then a terrestrial paradise. Health, Plenty, and Good-Will teemed throughout the land. A live mastodon would

---

[4] Deposition of William St. John, in *Welder vs. Lambert*, 10 September 1892, District Court, Refugio County, Texas.

[5] Martin Power to his father in Ireland, 23 June 1839, *Power Papers*, Library of the Institute of Texan Cultures, University of Texas, San Antonio; author's emphasis.

[6] The Committee on Foreign Relations Report to the Mexican Government (1821-1822), quoted in Nettie Lee Benson, "Texas Viewed from Mexico, 1820-1834," *Southwestern Historical Quarterly* 90.3 (1987): 225.

not have been a greater curiosity than a tax collector."[7] Another Refugio colonist, Rosalie Hart Priour, proclaimed in her memoirs on seeing the location of her new home: "The situation is one of the finest in Texas. The house was built on the bank of the creek and shaded by live-oaks with tops in the shape of umbrellas. The wild grapevines covered the trees and formed a nice, cool arbor the sun could never penetrate. Wild flowers of every variety and in the greatest profusion covered the plains as far as the eye could reach. To me it seemed like a miniature paradise."[8]

The most revealing comment in terms of motivation came in an emigrant letter from Jemima and Mary Toll, who had settled in New York before migrating to San Patricio, Texas:

> I found this country equal to what was said in the hand bills and better again ... really I was astonished when I came amongst the colonists to see them all full of comfort, plenty of Corn, bread, Mush Butter Milk and beef.... As for pigs and fowls they are as numerous as flees ... do not be daunted by the prospect here is good ... you'll have no work, your daughters can milk 50 cows for you, and make butter which is 25 cents a lb here, in Matamoros 50 cents. A cow has 2 calfes in 10 months a sheep and a goat 3 yearlings in 15 months. The healthiest country in the world. <u>The richest land will show like Gentlemens domains in Ireland.</u> Fine wood and water as in any part of the world. As for fowl and fish of every kind no man can believe, but those that see.[9]

Not only was there food in abundance, but the climate encouraged stock to reproduce all year round, and most pertinent of all, Irish colonists could be the new elite, like gentlemen in Ireland. However, frontier life did not suit all the colonists. Thomas Gunning, an Irishman from County Sligo, having settled in New York, was persuaded to undertake a second-stage migration to San Patricio. He claimed to have been misled by "a notorious pair of scoundrels," the empresarios McMullen and McGloin. Gunning expressed his disillusionment with the San Patricio colony in a series of letters to correspondents in Ireland:

> everything wild & of course uncultivated, not a single house on it. Woods & prairie or land that never grew timber in abundance, we set about building huts & prepared for tilling, we provided ourselves with grain + seeds of every description, from appearances were not discouraged, vegetation went on luxuriantly in the month of November, the labor of our hands showed uncommonly well till the corn was going into ear, when to our mortification it literally got burn'd up for eleven weeks together we w'd not see a drop of rain,

---

[7] John J. Linn, *Reminiscences of Fifty Years in Texas* (1883; reprint, Austin: State House Press, 1986), 23.

[8] Rosalie Hart Priour, "The Adventures of a Family of Emmigrants Who Emmigrated to Texas in 1834," Corpus Christi Museum, Corpus Christi, Texas, 49.

[9] Letter from Jemima and Mary Toll, New York, [n.d.] reprinted in David Woodman, Jr., *Guide to Texas Emigrants* (1835; reprint, Waco: Texian Press, 1974), 168-169.

we could have land at a shilling an acre without limit, if we could grow anything we could do well enough.[10]

Gunning was not put off Texas merely by the climate. He had claimed to be a Catholic to obtain the land grant from the Mexican government, but as a Protestant, he found it uncongenial among his Catholic neighbors, both Mexican and Irish, who had a common bond in their religious faith. At the same time, he hardly relished the prospect of an attack from the warlike Comanches.

Frederick Jackson Turner's Frontier Thesis

The rigors of pioneer life did not suit those like Gunning who were used to the amenities and civilization that New York provided. Pioneer is another key word in defining American identity, evoking the wholesome values of the frontier. These were articulated famously by Frederick Jackson Turner in 1893 and qualified by the Texan historian, Walter Prescott Webb, and Ray Billington, a leading historian of the American West.

Turner claimed that the frontier experience explained the nature of American democracy and forged the values of American citizens. The availability of "free land" and the frontier influence on the pioneer-hero were seen as central to the development of American institutions:

> The frontier is the line of most rapid and effective Americanisation. The wilderness masters the colonist. It finds him in European dress, industries, tools, modes of travel and thought. It takes him from the railroad car and pits him in the birch canoe. It strips off the garments of civilisation and arrays him in the hunting shirt and the moccasin, it puts him in the log cabin of the Cherokee and Iraquois.... In short, at the frontier the environment is at first too strong for the man. He must accept the conditions which it furnishes, or perish. Little by little he transforms the wilderness, but the outcome is not the old Europe.... The fact is, here is a new product that is American.... Thus the advance of the frontier has meant a steady movement away from the influence of Europe, a steady growth of independence on American lines.[11]

Expanding on the Turner thesis, Webb developed the theory of the frontier, defining it as a force for the disintegration of the cultural baggage that Europeans brought with them to the New World. In a characteristic phrase, he argued that "European institutions and practices wore themselves out against the abrasive frontier grindstone." Webb believed that the individual, finding himself alone in the presence of nature

---

[10] Thomas Gunning to Major O'Hara, 26 January 1832, Gunning Letters, MS20328, 1831-1836, National Library of Ireland, Dublin.

[11] F.J. Turner, "The Significance of the Frontier in American History," in *The Frontier in American History* (1920; reprint, New York: Holt, Rinehart and Winston, 1962), 3-4.

could do in this new environment anything he wanted to do and as much of it as he wanted to do without human opposition. For example, if he wanted to cut down trees, kill game, or navigate streams, he could, cut, kill, and navigate without seeking a permit or running afoul of a policeman. The hazard that the tree might fall on him, the game tear him to pieces, or the stream drown him was his own lookout, he was neither prohibited nor rescued from his own acts. Nature viewed anything he did with a cold and impersonal, though sometimes a kindly eye. He found his own rewards and his own punishments, a double responsibility which in the first instance developed his boldness, initiative, and aggressiveness, and in the second fostered wariness, caution and circumspection—acknowledged frontier traits.[12]

Webb's defence of the frontier was driven paradoxically by important influences drawn from European thinkers: a Wordsworthian belief in nature as a benign force for good, at the same time as it operated as a theater for a Darwinian survival of the fittest. So the frontier was both egalitarian in shedding Old World obsessions of rank and social hierarchy, and individualistic and competitive in allowing the strongest to come out on top.

At this point it is worth considering who the pioneers were. Western travelers sometimes depicted frontiersmen as fugitives from justice—debtors, delinquents, and malefactors who fled from the laws of civilized society and became squatters on frontier lands.[13] Texas acquired a reputation for attracting more than its fair share of such characters in the period 1821 to 1846. "GTT" (gone to Texas) became a familiar sign for abandoned wives and homes as such men escaped from a run-in with the sheriff when leaving the southern states to settle on cheap land available in Texas.[14] By contrast, other travel writers, still retaining the prejudices of European civilization, were more prone to emphasize the barbaric features of frontier life. Ray Billington argued that the frontier legend of lawlessness was propagated by a few centers—the Mississippi river towns where the mountain men made their annual rendezvous, the cattle towns, mining camps, and the "hells on wheels" of the railway crews. While the hell-raising of these places was endlessly reported for their sensational newspaper copy, the numbers involved represented only a small proportion of pioneer settlers. Billington claims that the true pioneers were, in fact, the thousands of small farmers, ranchers, and entrepreneurs who formed the bulk of those who moved west. Unlike their more colorful fellow pioneers, the reprobates or indolent backwoodsmen, these sober and industrious frontiersmen were the founders of a western culture. Inevitably it was a culture that included much that was imported from the civilized eastern states.

---

[12] Walter Prescott Webb, *The Great Frontier* (Austin: University of Texas Press, 1964), 34-35.

[13] Ray Billington, *America's Frontier Culture: Three Essays* (College Station: Texas A&M University Press, 1977), 52-54.

[14] Mark E. Nackman, "Anglo-American Migrants to the West: Men of Broken Fortunes? The Case of Texas, 1821-1846," *Western Historical Quarterly* (October 1974): 442-455.

In the case of the Irish colonists in Texas, there were two broadly distinctive groups. Most of those who settled in San Patricio (1829-1835) were recruited from Irish immigrants already residing in the United States. They were, in effect, second-stage migrants who had already become used to American ways picked up in New York, Philadelphia and New Orleans. A few like Gunning found frontier life in Texas so uncomfortable that they returned to the United States. Those who settled in Refugio (1834-1835) were mostly farmers recruited directly from south-east Ireland. Both groups of Irish colonists were overwhelmingly Catholic, possessed some capital, were literate, and had a taste for adventure in exploring new horizons. They were attracted to Mexican Texas by the prospect of owning their own land. It represented a significant economic advance from cultivating thirty acres or so as tenant farmers in Ireland to becoming farmers and ranchers in Texas with over four thousand acres per family. To survive the rigors of frontier life they needed to adapt to harsh conditions, supported by their Mexican neighbors. That many were able to succeed as merchants, lawyers, and ranchers in Texas suggests they were able to adapt to new conditions and opportunities by building on the cultural capital they brought with them from Ireland and the United States. In becoming Texan pioneers they retained their Catholic faith and their Irish identity and culture.

By the 1960s traditional ways of depicting the frontier story came to be regarded by historians as "racist, sexist and imperialist."[15] There was discomfort over the violent conquest of the Indians; the notion of free land on the frontier was discredited; and the archetypal Anglo-Saxon frontiersman was found to be unrepresentative of western settlers. Meanwhile, among the general public the appeal of western myths and folklore remained unabated. What followed was the new western history that not only incorporated contemporary issues but also returned to Turner's key ideas. Turner had argued that the process of invasion, settlement, and community formation repeated itself in a wave of sequential frontiers. So successive frontiers could be studied in a comparative way. Conflict gave way to the formation of new structures and to more stable regions across America.

The general characteristics identifed by new western historians are applicable to the Irish pioneers who settled in South Texas. So a broader framework of reference can rescue their experience from the merely parochial and connect it to a fuller version of the American West. Four general characteristics of frontier life are applicable:

1. The frontier, often seen as isolated, was in fact connected to other parts of the world.
2. The frontier was a place where displaced migrants brought the familiar world of European values with them and looked to change with the opportunities that opened up for them.

---

[15] Walter Cronon, George Miles, and Jay Gitlin, "Becoming West: Toward a New Meaning for Western History," in Cronon, Miles and Gitlin, *Under an Open Sky*, 3-27.

3. Frontier communities were peripheral to imperial, metropolitan centers. They were perennially short of labor and capital, and frontier economies were extractive, transferring non-industrial resources to more populous areas.
4. The remoteness of frontier life undermined social and political hierarchies. State power was weak; economic activity was poorly regulated; and cultural innovation faced few barriers.

European economies and merchants (including the Irish empresarios all of whom had merchant backgrounds) were central to the creation of colonies in the New World, and European expansion involved the movement of people looking for new opportunities. This included the Irish migrants who settled in Texas. European values, including Irish and Catholic values, were retained, but new opportunities to acquire land, to enter professions and the business world, were seized on by the Irish settlers in Texas. It is clear that the Irish settlements in Texas, while being geographically isolated, were dependent on New Orleans for trade and for access to capital. With the development of ranching, beefs were exported by sea to New Orleans before the northern markets opened up. The remoteness of frontier life contributed to a lack of political and economic controls by the Mexican government. This was a factor in the Texas Revolution (1835-1836). The coexistence of European and native traditions allowed for a genuine mixture of cultures. This was especially evident in the intermarriage of Irish and Mexican families, the more easily facilitated by the common bond of the Catholic religion. There was also an important transfer of ranching culture from the Mexicans to the Irish.

A contemporary rationale and defence of the colonists was advanced during the Texas Revolution by the political figure W.H. Wharton in an address to the nation in April 1836. His words contain foretastes of Turner's frontier thesis of 1893 and of the Doctrine of Manifest Destiny first enunciated in 1845:

> The donation of 4428 acres, sounds hugely at a distance. Considering, however, the difficulty and danger necessarily encountered in taking possesion of those lands it will not be deemed an entire gratuity nor a magnificent bounty.... The lands granted were in the occupancy of savages, and situated in a wilderness of which the government had never taken possession, and they were not sufficiently explored to obtain that knowledge of their character and situation necessary to a sale of them. They were shut out from all commercial intercourse with the rest of the world, and inaccessible to the commonest of comforts of life; nor were they brought into possession and cultivation by the colonists without much toil and privation, and patience and enterprise, and suffering and blood, and loss of lives from Indian hostilites, and other causes. Under the smiles of a benignant heaven, however, the untiring perseverance of the colonists triumphed over all natural obstacles, expelled the savages by

whom the country was infested, reduced the forest into cultivation and made the desert smile.[16]

Wharton argued that not only was there justification for the war for Texan independence against Mexico, but that heaven had rewarded and encouraged the colonists in expelling the "savages" and taming the wilderness. Beyond the hardship experiences common to all parts of the American frontier, the Irish colonists, located in the heart of the war zone during the Texas Revolution and on the disputed border territory between the Nueces River and the Rio Grande, suffered a notable "blood sacrifice" in contributing to the independence of Texas. The annexation of Texas that followed the war between the Unites States and Mexico in 1846 formed part of American territorial expansion that culminated in the closing of the frontier in 1890.

What has been celebrated repeatedly is the image of the frontiersman, armed with an axe and a rifle, a rugged individual who tamed a wilderness, subjugated native Indians, and built settled communities. In Texas, the pioneer settlers were not only part of what became the American frontier, but they also took on the sanctified role of archetypal figures who helped to establish an independent republic against the tyranny of the Mexican President Santa Anna. The creation of frontier values was overwhelmingly depicted as the construction of a male world. Yet the isolation of frontier life meant that within the structure of the family it was often the women who maintained some rudiments of civilized standards. Food, medicine, care of the children, and the preservation of some form of worship were the natural and enduring concern of women pioneers. Herein lies one of the paradoxes of frontier life. In fact, most of the surviving contemporary accounts of pioneer life, apart from the reports of military campaigns, were written by women.[17]

Most of these accounts were memoirs, written or dictated in old age. Inevitably, some distortion and selectivity are part of the long-remembered past. Other surviving accounts are the stories and anecdotes handed down through the generations within families. These have sometimes been written up in newspaper and magazine articles by journalists with an eye for good copy for the general public. Old Texas tales, especially those that recall the pioneer frontier days, form part of a literary genre that perpetuates popular myths. One obvious difference between male and female accounts is that where men delighted in describing the teeming wildlife to be killed at will, women were more sensitive to the dangers of wandering unprotected through a wilderness. Women were also as able as men in cultivating their own myths. In this case an idealized form of domestic perfection redolent of nineteenth-century ideals that was to be reinforced in the America of the 1950s and to be seriously challenged by modern women in the 1960s.

---

[16] Address of Wm. H. Wharton, 16 April 1836, in Charles Adams Gulick, ed., *Papers of Mirabeau Buonaparte Lamar*, 6 vols. (1921-1927; reprint, Austin and New York: Pemberton Press, 1968), vol. 1, no. 357.

[17] Fane Downs, "Tryals and Troubles: Women in Early 19th Century Texas," *Southwestern Historical Quarterly* 90 (1986): 35-56.

The pioneer woman arose early and milked eight or ten long-horned cows, that had to be hobbled or tied to a post, to get as much milk as one Jersey cow gives now. She parched and ground her coffee, made her bread, cured her meat, tended her poultry and garden, moulded her candles, made the soap—and with water carried from the well the clothes were kept as white as snow. There were no sewing machines and her family was clothed by the stitch-stitch of her nimble fingers. Her husband's suits rivaled the tailor made. Her shirts were ornate, unlike those today. Her own clothes reflected her artistic hand. Her children, likewise, wore clothes adorned by her mother's deft fingers. We marvel that these women had time for church and social duties, and for neighborly kindness....[18]

The sentimental tone of the above account owes something to fond memories of childhood relived in old age. This may also have been an idealized standard of domestic virtue to which most could only aspire. A contrasting contemporary account by Jack Duval, a Kentucky soldier in the Texan army, suggests as much. Duval was passing in the vicinity of Refugio and asked for milk from an Irishwoman. She led him to an outhouse where there were a number of pans filled with milk. He was dismayed by the lack of hygiene when "she rolled up her sleeve and deliberately proceeded to skim it with her open hand, which looked to me to have been unacquainted with soap and water for some time past. When she had finished skimming the milk in this primitive fashion, she poured the contents of the pan into my camp kettle, at the same time saying: 'There, my little mon, there's a pan of milk for yez that's fit for the Pope of Room, Heaven protect his Holiness.'"[19] Duval paid for the milk, took it back to camp but preferred to drink coffee to such "nice new milk" while his companions were much less squeamish about it.

Thomas O'Connor

The greatest legend that grew up out of the Irish pioneers in Texas was the remarkable story of Thomas O'Connor.[20] The story contains the classic ingredients of Texas history: pioneer settler, soldier in the Texas Revolution, Indian fighter, and successful cattle rancher. It also represents the culmination of the adventures of the Irish pioneers who settled in Refugio and San Patricio between 1829 and 1834. A

---

[18] Mrs. Kate Dougherty Bluntzer, "Biographies and Memoirs of Pioneers," 1958, 3-4, Kilgore Collection, Texas A&M University, Corpus Christi State University. Kate Dougherty Bluntzer was the daughter of Roberty Dougherty, schoolmaster and San Patricio County judge who immigrated to the United States from his native Donegal in 1847. He moved to Texas in 1860, married in 1864. Kate's memoirs recalled in her eighties in an unpublished collection refer back to her childhood in the 1860s and 1870s.

[19] J.C. Duval, *Early Times in Texas* (Austin: Gammell, 1892), 25.

[20] Graham Davis, "Ranching Culture and the Texas Cattle King: Thomas O'Connor of Refugio County," chapter 6 in *Land!:Irish Pioneers in Mexican and Revolutionary Texas* (College Station: Texas A&M University Press, 2002), 194-240.

great part of the land granted originally to colonists by the Mexican government through the Irish empresarios Power and Hewetson was ultimately to form part of the immense estate left by Thomas O'Connor at his death in 1887.

Thomas O'Connor was baptized (within a few days of his birth) in County Wexford, Ireland, on 11 February 1817. Legend, reproduced on a Texas historical marker at the old O'Connor ranch, records that he was an orphan, but he was, in fact, the younger son of a tenant farmer. The obituaries in the San Antonio newspapers that reported his death on 16 October 1887 proclaimed the qualities of the man and the scale of his achievement, but also gave credence to a frontier legend. The *San Antonio Daily Express* described Thomas O'Connor as "probably the wealthiest man in Texas" and reported that he was without a penny when he landed in this country, "but by enterprise and economy amassed a very large fortune, and at the time of his death, was the largest individual land and cattle owner in Texas."[21] In another piece in the same issue, it was claimed that "during his long life he is reputed to have amassed $6,000,000, and that he possessed the respect of all for his unimpeachable integrity."[22] The legend of rags to riches was further strengthened with the account that the deceased "began life a good many years ago as a poor man, earning a scanty living by making saddletrees for ranchmen and cowboys. His spare money he invested in lands and cattle, until in a few years he became one of the richest men in the entire state, numbering his cattle by the thousands and his acres by the million. Three or four years ago, Mr. O'Connor was offered $4,000,000 in cash for his Refugio County cattle ranch, but refused it."[23]

The romance of a poor Irish orphan immigrant creating a fabulous fortune by displaying the best frontier qualities of rugged individualism, determination, foresight and frugality has an obvious appeal. "Print the legend" was dutifully done. The true story explains more realistically how Thomas O'Connor was able to build a great estate within his lifetime. As the younger brother, he had no prospect of inheriting the lease on the family mill farm. However, he was more fortunate than most in having James Power, the Irish empresario, as his uncle. It was through his offices as empresario that Thomas O'Connor was able to claim a family "composed of domestic servants" and receive a full league of land (4,428 acres) rather than the quarter of a league to which he was entitled as a single man.[24] James Power was O'Connor's early guide and mentor. He probably encouraged his nephew to work breaking in horses for ten head of cattle and twenty-five cents a day, which he invested in buying cattle. Power, as colonel of the Refugio militia, rallied the young colonists behind the Texan cause. Thomas O'Connor enlisted for three periods of army service, thus qualifying for three grants of bounty land, totalling 1,280 acres. He was also one of the youngest soldiers at the decisive battle of San Jacinto in April 1836. His army service not only converted him from a Mexican citizen into a Texan, but provided material benefits that contributed to his financial independence.

---

[21] *San Antonio Daily Express*, 18 October 1887.
[22] Ibid.
[23] Ibid.
[24] The Petition of Thomas O'Connor, 1834, Title Book no. 17, Spanish Archives, General Land Office, Austin, Texas.

Between 1836 and 1842, O'Connor earned at least $4,000 from supplying the military, contracts that Colonel Power must have helped secure.[25] He was also helped financially by his future father-in-law, Nicholas Fagan, who lent him money to buy more land, and at the time of his marriage to Mary Fagan in 1838, he acquired additional land and cattle. At the age of twenty-one, he had acquired 7,735 acres. His mentors, Power and Fagan, and his army contracts enabled him to buy land and begin the process of building his fortune. Selling saddletrees made a frontier fable but did not found a ranching empire.

Space prohibits a detailed version of the O'Connor story, but the main outlines can be clearly laid down. Thomas O'Connor took full advantage of opportunities to procure land from hard-pressed veterans selling bounty land, farmers struggling to pay tax debts, and colonists who had no taste for pioneer life. Each new small-scale purchase added to his burgeoning estate. At each stage of the development of Texas ranching, O'Connor anticipated events. In 1848, he was one of the first cattlemen to send beefs via Indianola to New Orleans. After the Civil War, he sent his herds on the long trails north. He diversified his business with the tallow and hide business in Rockport in the 1860s, and in the 1870s began fencing his land and shocked his contemporaries by selling his herd to buy more land. With his son Thomas Marion, he went into the meatpacking business and with other ranchers invested in the new refrigerated railway cars that allowed the transportation of freshly slaughtered beef to New Orleans. In the 1880s he used the O'Connor and Sullivan Bank to extend loans to fellow ranchers and acquired substantial estates when borrowers defaulted on their loans. He also initiated drilling for artesian wells to provide a constant water supply of water for the O'Connor ranches. Finally he was an early proponent of importing foreign breeds of cattle, a practice that was fully developed after his death.

Conclusion

The O'Connor story, along with the myths already discussed, represents the sobering realization that the truth is often more interesting than the legend. Myths and legends have had an important narrative function in the formative development and expansion of the United States during the nineteenth century but, as our examples show, do not reflect historical reality. Behind legends lie interpretations of the past that ought to be challenged. In complementary ways, the oppressive view of Irish emigration, the attractive fable of Texas as a paradise, the character-forming nature of frontier life, and the rags-to-riches story of an Irish immigrant establishing a ranching empire, all served in their day to project the idea of the American dream.

---

[25] Thomas O'Connor's Military Contracts, 1836-1842, all in Public Debt Claims, Genealogy Library, Texas State Library and Archives, Austin, Texas.

YEOMEN AND YANKEES ACROSS THE MASON-DIXON LINE: A DIFFERENT PERSPECTIVE ON THE ANTEBELLUM NORTH/SOUTH DIVIDE?

Louis Billington and David Brown

Richard Arnold, a Yankee businessman of Quaker origins, was also a Georgia slaveholder who owned large rice and cotton plantations visited by Frederick Law Olmsted. Until the 1840s, Arnold returned to his native state of Rhode Island every summer, bringing with him his family and key household slaves, and took his place in the business and social life of Providence and Newport. Arnold's "two lives" illustrate that the notion of demarcating borders between the antebellum North and South has always been problematic in practice.[1] Nonetheless, the importance of the Mason-Dixon demarcation as a line of separation has been taken for granted by most American historians. Periodically, there have been heated debates concerning the salience of different features between the regions—income, land holding, urbanization, religious culture, and educational levels, for example—and just how far they mark each as separate from the other.[2] While such arguments have qualified more crass generalizations, they have hardly questioned the fundamental notion that the antebellum North and South were distinct. The emphasis placed upon globalization and transnationalism in the past few years might impact upon this assumption. Thomas Bender has recently called for the greater internationalization of American history—a recognition that historical development within the United States occurred within a global context often without regard to the units and borders created by nation states. "If historians have often treated the nation as self-contained and undifferentiated," he wrote, "it is increasingly clear that this assumption is true neither in the present nor the past." If external lines of demarcation are somewhat blurred, however, might internal divisions within the developing United States, such as the Mason-Dixon line, also be somewhat less precise and more permeable than generally recognized?[3]

---

[1] Charles Hoffmann and Tess Hoffmann, *North by South: The Two Lives of Richard James Arnold* (Athens: University of Georgia Press, 1988); Frederick Law Olmsted, *The Cotton Kingdom: A Traveller's Observations on Cotton and Slavery in the American Slave State*, ed. Arthur M. Schlesinger (New York: Alfred A. Knopf, 1962), 176-202.

[2] See especially a round table in the *American Historical Review*. Forrest McDonald and Grady McWhiney, "The South from Self Sufficiency to Peonage: An Interpretation," Edward Pessen, "How Different From Each Other Were the Antebellum North and South?" plus comments by Thomas Alexander and Stanley Engerman, *American Historical Review* 85 (December 1980): 1095-1166. More recent literature is discussed in John W. Quist, *Restless Visionaries: The Social Roots of Antebellum Reform in Alabama and Michigan* (Baton Rouge: Louisiana State University Press, 1998), 1-17.

[3] Thomas Bender, *La Pietra Report: Project on Internationalizing the Study of American History* (New York, 2000), 5. This Report was written on behalf of the Organization of American Historians. Its arguments were expanded upon in Thomas Bender, ed.,

This essay considers the construction and significance of borders in the lives of non-elite men and women, both North and South, in the antebellum United States. It examines the flourishing social history that has emerged in the past twenty years, and that has so greatly enriched our understanding of "ordinary" people, in order to identify the different kinds of boundaries that existed at the lower levels of society. We compare the socio-economic development of rural communities in New England from the early nineteenth-century to the Civil War, with southern communities where nonslaveholding farmers predominated. In particular, we examine the material circumstances of farmers, their reactions to the market revolution, and gender relations across the sectional divide. Our analysis of recent literature on northern and southern yeomen suggests fewer significant differences than commonly assumed. The most significant border in nineteenth-century America, the Mason-Dixon line, did not sharply divide yeomen into two distinct and separate groups, but was more an ideological and political construction.[4] New Englanders as archetypal northerners came from widely differing backgrounds and experiences, many of which would have been familiar to southerners. A few, like Richard Arnold, were actually Cavaliers *and* Yankees, southern planters *and* New England businessmen. More importantly, large numbers of northerners and southerners shared broadly similar lifestyles, being family farmers and small businessmen looking for ways to make a living and stay ahead. They attended evangelical churches, supporting or rejecting the new evangelical missionary agencies, and many joined the nation-wide movement to challenge excessive drinking in an alcoholic Republic where the abuse of liquor recognized no boundaries. For decades, northerners and especially New Englanders had moved South as farmers, teachers, clergymen, peddlers, artisans, and businessmen. The 1860 census reported 360,000 northerners living in the South, and a smaller, but not insignificant number of southerners went north for recreation, education, or business opportunities.[5]

Limitations of space preclude an extended discussion of slavery. Our conclusions apply more generally to southern communities away from the plantation belt, in the mountains and upcountry regions, where numbers of slaves were minimal and most farms were reliant upon family members, supplemented by the

---

Rethinking American History in a Global Age (Berkeley: California University Press, 2002).

[4] The idea of sectionalism was primarily a political construction. Politicians in Congress spoke of two sections within the antebellum United States long before it became common to do so in everyday life. See Fulmer Mood, "The Origin, Evolution, and Application of the Sectional Concept, 1750-1900," in Merrill Jensen, ed., *Regionalism in America* (Madison: University of Wisconsin Press, 1952). Undeniably, though, a sense of sectionalism, fuelled by political debate and major political incidents such as Kansas-Nebraska, Dred Scott, and John Brown's raid, was apparent by 1860 at all levels of American society. Our concern is not to dispute that sense of distinctiveness, but to see if it actually reflected significant differences in the daily lives of rural northerners and southerners.

[5] Hoffmann and Hoffmann, *North By South*, xii-xxi; Quist, *Restless Visionaries*, 1-17; W.J. Rorabaugh, *The Alcoholic Republic: An American Tradition* (New York: Oxford University Press, 1979).

occasional use of casual labor. Approximately three-quarters of southern white families owned no slaves in 1860. As many historians have shown, however, there were significant areas of mutual interest between slaveholders and nonslaveholding whites. Planters displayed a paternalistic concern for their neighbors in the processing, transportation, and sale of their crops and would also allow their less affluent neighbors to hire slaves.[6] Southern farmers undoubtedly had more contacts with African Americans, both slave and free, than their New England counterparts, and some yeomen were planters in the making, harboring, and sometimes fulfilling, ambitions to enter the planter class. However, the chance of yeomen buying land, let alone slaves, diminished significantly during the 1850s.[7] The reality was that slavery had little direct influence upon the day-to-day activities of many farmers and the latest estimate suggests that only half the southern white population actually had "an economic stake in slavery."[8] This essay is primarily concerned with those outside of the plantation economy, focusing upon yeomen farmers who "worked their own land and relied on family labor and primarily local networks of exchange to maintain and reproduce largely self-sufficient households."[9]

Geographical and Political Boundaries

Boundaries may be personal, cultural, spatial, temporal, or symbolic. They can be politically constructed, such as the border between the United States and Canada, or might reflect the physical landscape, as great rivers and mountain ranges form natural barriers. At the opposite extreme from great national, regional, and geographical divides, boundaries mark out much smaller and more intimate areas such as a community, a neighborhood, or a household. Anthropologists explore all these types of boundaries to describe ways in which people define their social identities, "those boundaries of their social lives which demarcate most powerfully and meaningfully their sense of similarity to and differences from other people."[10] We will consider some of these definitions when exploring communities within New England and the South and when making comparisons between them.

---

[6] Eugene Genovese and Elizabeth Fox-Genovese, "Yeoman Farmers in a Slaveholder's Democracy," in *Fruits of Merchant Capital: Slavery and Bourgeois Property in the Rise and Expansion of Capitalism* (New York and Oxford: Oxford University Press, 1983), 249-264; Bruce Collins, *White Society in the Antebellum South* (London: Longman, 1985), 17, 37-40; J. William Harris, *Plain Folk and Gentry in a Slave Society* (Middletown, CT: Wesleyan University Press, 1985), 94-122.

[7] Gavin Wright, *The Political Economy of the Cotton South: Households, Markets and Wealth in the Nineteenth Century* (New York and London: Norton, 1978), 24-42.

[8] Peter Kolchin, *American Slavery, 1619-1877* (London: Penguin, 1993), 180-181.

[9] Charles Bolton, *Poor Whites of the Antebellum South: Tenants and Laborers in Central North Carolina and Northeast Mississippi* (Durham and London: Duke University Press, 1994), 11.

[10] Anthony P. Cohen, ed., *Symbolising Boundaries: Identity and Diversity in British Cultures* (Manchester: Manchester University Press, 1986), 1.

Lifestyles of rural northerners and southerners were intimately connected to the land and the physical environment, and their mobility was constrained by the hills, mountains, marshes, forests, and rivers around them. The parameters of community life—the physical spaces appropriated by specific settlements—were defined and limited by the local environment and the challenges and restrictions which it presented. Indeed, recent historiography has shown that the quest to become better connected was a central concern of many, if not all, rural communities during the antebellum era.[17] By the 1850s, and sometimes much earlier, physical barriers which had been taken for granted began to be challenged as pressure mounted to overcome geographic isolation and gain access to wider markets for trade. Local elites made great efforts to build railroads and make bigger markets accessible, even when their less affluent neighbors remained sceptical of the benefits railroads might bring. Despite rapid communication improvements, both contemporaries and later historians noted the existence of distinct subregions within the sections. The Appalachian mountains, for example, presented an imposing physical barrier to westward expansion and fostered a distinctive culture which has recently been the focus of great attention by southern historians. Following in the immediate wake of Frederick Jackson Turner, George Vincent described Appalachia as "the retarded frontier" in 1898, signifying its supposedly backward and stagnant state. This view was apparent in antebellum stereotypes of mountain trash and extreme poverty that persisted in some quarters into the 1990s.[18] Contemporary New Englanders also

---

the city to the Mississippi state line. Work Projects Administration, *Portland City Guide* (Portland, ME: Forest City Printing Company, 1940), 42-43.

[17] This generalization applies to virtually all works considered in this essay. Only Steven Hahn, *The Roots of Southern Populism: Yeoman Farmers and the Transformation of the Georgia Upcountry, 1850-1880* (New York: Oxford University Press, 1983), and, to a lesser extent, J. Mills Thornton, III, *Politics and Power in a Slave Society: Alabama, 1800-1860* (Baton Rouge: Louisiana State University Press, 1978), present non-slaveholding southerners as resistant to economic development.

[18] George E. Vincent, "The Retarded Frontier," *American Journal of Sociology* 4 (1898): 1-20. On stereotyping and Appalachia, see Dwight Billings, Gurney Norman, and Katherine Ledford, eds., *Confronting Appalachian Stereotypes: Back Talk from an American Region* (Lexington: University Press of Kentucky, 1999) esp. 3-20, and David C. Hsiung, *Two Worlds in the Tennessee Mountains: Exploring the Origins of Appalachian Stereotypes* (Lexington: University Press of Kentucky, 1997). See also H. Tyler Blethen and Curtis M. Wood, "The Appalachian Frontier and the Southern Frontier: A Comparative Perspective," *Journal of the Appalachian Studies Association* 3 (1991): 36-47. There has been a virtual renaissance of Appalachian studies in the past decade. Some of the more important works include: Allen Batteau, *The Invention of Appalachia* (Tucson: University of Arizona Press, 1990); Martin Crawford, *Ashe County's Civil War: Community and Society in the Appalachian South* (Charlottesville: University Press of Virginia, 2001); Wilma A. Dunaway, *The First American Frontier: Transition to Capitalism in Southern Appalachia, 1700-1860* (Chapel Hill: University of North Carolina Press, 1996); Durwood Dunn, *Cade's Cove: The Life and Death of a Southern Mountain Community, 1818-1937* (Knoxville: University of Tennessee Press, 1988); Inscoe, *Mountain Masters*; John C. Inscoe and Gordon B. McKinney, *The Heart of Confederate Appalachia: Western North Carolina in the Civil War* (Chapel Hill: University of North Carolina Press, 2000); Robert D. Mitchell, ed., *Appalachian*

worried about rural poverty and isolation, as individuals perceived as being more intelligent and energetic migrated to the West or the cities. Social commentators like Josiah Strong identified many similar depravities in comparing the lifestyles of southern mountain whites with poor farmers in the remoter hill country of New England, an extension of Appalachia. Both groups shared the "same illiteracy, the same ignorance of the Christian religion, the same vices, the same 'marriage' and 'divorce' without reference to the laws of God or man." Most writers took a less extreme view but popular magazines published in the cities produced numerous articles expressing anxiety about rural decline in northern New England.[19]

The Market Revolution and Mentalité across the Mason-Dixon Line

Interpreting the sectional divide within the nineteenth-century United States can often be reduced to a set of general dichotomies: free versus slave, urban versus rural, industrial versus agrarian, progressive versus conservative and so on. To what extent, though, did these considerations actually separate northern and southern farmers? What was the *mentalité* of the antebellum yeoman? The social and economic values of New England farmers, and their relationships to the market have long been debated. In the 1970s, historians such as James Henretta and Michael Merrill emphasized that the pre-industrial New England farm family was not motivated by a drive for profit, but by the need for family security and the affirmation of community values and co-operation. A "moral economy" rooted in mutuality and a network of face to face relationships with kin and neighbors was at the center of farm family values. Conceptually, this interpretation drew heavily on the work of E.P. Thompson focusing on eighteenth-century English society. It also drew selectively on older New England town histories to stress, if not individual family self-sufficiency, a great degree of community self-sufficiency rooted in a complex exchange network of goods, labor, and credit. By contrast, in their concentration upon slaves and planters, southern historians virtually ignored ordinary farmers up to the 1980s. With the notable exception of the work of Frank Owsley, when yeomen and poor whites were mentioned, it was almost as an

---

Frontiers: Settlement, Society, and Development in the Preindustrial Era (Lexington: University Press of Kentucky, 1990); Kenneth W. Noe, *Southwest Virginia's Railroad: Modernization and the Sectional Crisis* (Knoxville: University of Tennessee Press, 1994); Mary Beth Pudep, Dwight Billings, and Altina L. Waller, eds., *Appalachia in the Making: The Mountain South in the Nineteenth Century* (Chapel Hill: University of North Carolina Press, 1996). For an evaluation of some of this literature, see Ronald Lewis and Dwight Billings, "Appalachian Culture and Economic Development: A Retrospective View on the Theory and Literature," *Journal of Appalachian Studies* 3 (Spring 1997): 3-42.

[19] Josiah Strong, cited in Hal S. Barron, *Those Who Stayed Behind: Rural Society in Nineteenth-Century New England* (Cambridge: Cambridge University Press, 1984), 37-39. See also David Emblidge, ed., *The Appalachian Trail Reader* (New York: Oxford University Press, 1996). Emblidge's introduction stresses the common historical experiences of Appalachian peoples in the North and the South.

afterthought.[20] The past two decades, however, have witnessed a shift in the social history of the South away from slaves and planters towards nonslaveholding whites.[21] As in the historiography of New England farmers, the notion of the market revolution has been the most important feature of this literature, framing the way in which historians have interpreted community. On one level, the idea of a southern market revolution challenges the long held conception of the "dual economy." Morton Rothstein's classic formulation depicted two distinct economies, one the domain of slaveholders relying upon slave labor and selling cash crops on the world stage, the other rooted in the geographical isolation of the yeoman farmer who had little market orientation.[22] Bradley Bond has done most to dispute the latter image, suggesting that southern yeomen were far more aggressively market-orientated than hitherto appreciated. Looking at the piney-woods of Mississippi, very much a frontier region even by the late antebellum period, he found farmers who were rarely self-sufficient in grain, but eager to produce and sell surplus meat on markets "of their own choosing." The ultimate aim of what he calls their "strategy of accumulation," deliberately juxtaposed against the more familiar concept of self sufficiency, was to be in a position to produce cotton, the classic market crop. Household needs were not entirely neglected, but were a secondary priority, which

---

[20] Michael Merrill, "Cash Is Good to Eat: Self-Sufficiency and Exchange in the Rural Economy of the United States," *Radical History Review* 3 (1977): 42-71; James A. Henretta, "Families and Farms: Mentalité in Pre-Industrial America," *William and Mary Quarterly* 35 (January 1978): 3-32. See also Christopher Clark, "Household Economy, Market Exchange, and the Rise of Capitalism in the Connecticut Valley, 1800-1860," *Journal of Social History* 13 (Winter 1979): 169-189. Frank L. Owsley, *Plain Folk of the South* (Baton Rouge: Louisiana State University Press, 1949).

[21] Works considering nonslaveholding whites directly include: Bolton, *Poor Whites of the Antebellum South*; Victoria Bynum, *Unruly Women: The Politics of Social and Sexual Control in the Old South* (Chapel Hill: University of North Carolina Press, 1992); Bill Cecil-Fronsman, *Common Whites: Class and Culture in Antebellum North Carolina* (Lexington: University Press of Kentucky, 1992); Samuel C. Hyde, ed., *Plain Folk of the South Revisited* (Baton Rouge: Louisana State University Press, 1997); Scott P. Culclasure and Charles C. Bolton, eds., *The Confessions of Edward Isham: A Poor White Life of the Old South* (Athens: University of Georgia Press, 1998). Recent community studies, in which nonslaveholder/slaveholder relations are considered in detail, include: Samuel C. Hyde, Jr., *Pistols and Politics: The Dilemma of Democracy in Louisiana's Florida Parishes, 1810-1899* (Baton Rouge: Louisiana State University Press, 1996); Harris, *Plain Folk and Gentry in a Slave Society*; Timothy James Lockley, *Lines in the Sand: Race and Class in Lowcountry Georgia, 1750-1860* (Athens: University of Georgia Press, 2001); Robert Tracy McKenzie, *One South or Many? Plantation Belt and Upcountry in Civil-War Era Tennessee* (Cambridge: Cambridge University Press, 1994); Donald L. Winters, *Tennessee Farming, Tennessee Farmers: Antebellum Agriculture in the Upper South* (Knoxville: University of Tennessee Press, 1994), in addition to other studies listed elsewhere in the notes. See Samuel C. Hyde, Jr., "Plain Folk Yeomanry in the Antebellum South," in John B. Boles, ed., *A Companion to the American South* (Oxford: Blackwell, 2002), 139-155, for a recent overview of literature.

[22] Morton Rothstein, "The Antebellum South as a Dual Economy: A Tentative Hypothesis," *Agricultural History* 41 (October 1967): 373-383.

did not impinge upon "their ability to produce for the market." Thus, rather than following a safety-first, self-sufficient, strategy, Bond depicted southern yeomen as risk takers whose decision to migrate West was often the result of frustration at the lack of opportunity in the upcountry areas of their birth in the Upper South.[23] Several historians have found a similar acquisitive and commercial situation in Appalachia, of all places, stressing market participation almost from first settlement.[24] While not going quite as far as this, most recent community studies note the increased production of cotton, the leading cash crop, by southern farmers in the 1850s.[25]

Similarly, more recent historians of rural New England have also emphasized different values and identified a greater concern with profit and enterprise than was recognized by earlier scholars. From the outset, some argue, many New England towns were developed by money-making entrepreneurs, land speculators, or fur traders. Winifred Rothenberg in particular has looked at hundreds of farm and store account books and suggests that, at least in Massachusetts, there was a complex market for farm products with prices fluctuating in regular cycles in both Boston and the hinterlands. Farmers participated actively in this market and consciously pursued profit. Many other scholars have added to what has sometimes become a rather sterile and poorly focused debate.[26] Clearly, New England farmers had never been self-sufficient, and throughout the colonial period, they produced a surplus of

---

[23] Bradley G. Bond, "Herders, Farmers and Markets on the Inner Frontier: The Mississippi Piney Woods, 1850-1860," in Hyde, *Plain Folk of the South Revisited*, 73-99 (on 74 first quotation, on 99 second and third quotations). See also Bradley B. Bond, *Political Culture in the Nineteenth Century South: Mississippi, 1830-1900* (Baton Rouge: Louisiana State University Press, 1995), 43-70.

[24] Dunaway, *The First American Frontier*; David C. Hsiung, "How Isolated Was Appalachia? Upper East Tennessee, 1780-1835," *Appalachian Journal* 14 (Summer 1989): 336-349; Robert D. Mitchell, *Commercialism and Frontier: Perspectives on the Early Shenandoah Valley* (Charlottesville: University Press of Virginia, 1977).

[25] See, for example, Lacy K. Ford, *The Origins of Southern Radicalism: The South Carolina Upcountry 1800-1860* (New York: Oxford University Press, 1988), 244-258. Harry L. Watson, "Slavery and Development in a Dual Economy: The South and the Market Revolution," in Melvyn Stokes and Steven Conway, eds., *The Market Revolution in America: Social, Political, and Religious Expressions, 1800-1860* (Charlottesville: University of Virginia Press, 1996), 43-73, discusses economic development in the South in detail, but tends to perpetuate the idea that yeomen were anti-commercial, and is much better in discussing the plantation economy.

[26] John Frederick Martin, *Profits in the Wilderness: Entrepreneurship and the Founding of New England Towns in the Seventeenth Century* (Chapel Hill: University of North Carolina Press, 1991); Stephen Innes, *Labor in a New Land: Economy and Society in Seventeenth-Century Springfield* (Princeton, NJ: Princeton University Press, 1983); Winifred B. Rothenberg, *From Market-Places to a Market Economy: The Transformation of Rural Massachusetts, 1750-1850* (Chicago: University of Chicago Press, 1992). See also Christopher Clark, *The Roots of Rural Capitalism: Western Massachusetts, 1780-1860* (Ithaca, NY: Cornell University Press, 1990), 3-17, and Allan Kulikoff, "The Transition to Capitalism in Rural America," *William and Mary Quarterly* 46 (January 1989): 120-144, which provides citations in the debate too numerous to list here.

livestock, food and timber products, some of which were exported from Boston, Newport, and other coastal cities to the West Indies and elsewhere. More was produced in areas better suited to commercial farming like the Connecticut River valley and southern Rhode Island, but most farms had some marketable surpluses from time to time. As Jonathan Prude has suggested in examining the economies of the towns of Dudley and Oxford in central Massachusetts, the imperatives of commercial capitalism were not yet entirely dominant by the first decade of the nineteenth century. Prude sees the towns as essentially "semicommercial" with an advancing market economy constrained by widely held, traditional, community norms. In Oxford and Dudley, as in many other towns, people used more store-bought clothing, but the bulk of their dress was largely home-made by family members or itinerant artisans. Similarly with food, a growing range of spices, sweets, liquors, as well as imported flour and meat was widely available, but the bulk of a family's diet was produced on their farm or at least in the local community. Cash transactions and the use of a growing number of banks increased, but the old world of mutuality, barter, and the exchange of goods and services did not disappear.[27]

North and South, then, scholars have depicted a dynamic and fluid rural economy in flux by the late antebellum period, and probably earlier, in which ordinary farmers were as prominent as elites. It seems that a more commercial orientation was apparent across the sections. Does this negate the longstanding belief in the economic and cultural divergence between southern yeomen in plantation areas and those in the upcountry? Upcountry yeomen were thought to have concentrated their efforts towards self-sufficiency, or at least "safety-first" agriculture, where the production of cotton, and consequent participation in the market, was viewed with caution. In contrast, yeomen within the Black Belt, who lived side-by-side with planters, supposedly concentrated their efforts upon the production of cash crops for the market.[28] What might appear as oppositional interpretations are not irreconcilable. Regardless of specific location, yeomen in South Carolina were mostly committed to a safety-first, or pragmatic, approach, but were willing to enter the market once their immediate needs had been satisfied.[29] Community studies across the South show wide variations in approach, within regions, within specific communities, within local neighborhoods, even within families. They point to the false dichotomy of interpreting agricultural production as either solely for the market, as Bond suggests, or primarily against it, as Steven Hahn posits. This realization does not negate important differences between the low and upcountry, particularly with regard to market access, or suggest that the self-sufficient/commercial model has no value at all, but reflects a more complicated situation. Gavin Wright, who pioneered the safety-first thesis, emphasized the flexibility with which most southern farmers operated. "What is argued here,"

---

[27] Gloria L. Main, *Peoples of a Spacious Land: Families and Cultures in Colonial New England* (Cambridge, MA: Harvard University Press, 2001), 203-237; Jonathan Prude, *The Coming of Industrial Order: Town and Factory Life in Rural Massachusetts, 1810-1860* (Cambridge: Cambridge University Press, 1983), 13-15.
[28] Hahn, *Roots of Southern Populism*, 50-85.
[29] Ford, *Origins of Southern Radicalism*, 73; McCurry, *Masters of Small Worlds*, 63.

Wright stated, "is that the standard characterizations are too rigid: it was not a matter of choosing between a 'home' and a 'fortune,' but a question of priorities." Moreover, what is clearly emerging in the current literature is the realization that in order to achieve self-sufficiency, most farmers had to engage with the market in some form by the late antebellum period.[30]

On balance, southern historians have tended to agree implicitly with John Majewski's contention that a market "revolution" is too strong a term to describe economic changes which had roots in the Revolutionary and early national periods. Majewski uses the term "market development." Christopher Clark has made a similar point about northern economic growth. "Most farm households depended to some degree on exchanging goods and services," he wrote, and it was very rare to have little or no contact with the market. Clark rightly argued that "the debate is rather about the character and significance of this exchange, and about the strategic relationships between farmers and markets in different regions and at different times."[31] These relationships have now been well explored, not least by Clark himself and there is a general acceptance that by the mid-nineteenth-century major economic changes had taken place in the New England countryside. How these changes came about is complex, and the literature is as varied as that on the southern yeoman. Some scholars have focused on major regions such as western Massachusetts, others have studied counties or individual communities. Many have explored within tighter boundaries, examining the adjustment of individual farm families to agricultural change or the impact of those changes on gender roles.[32]

---

[30] Wright, *Political Economy of the Cotton South*, 62-74 (quotation on 70). Martin Crawford, looking at the extreme north-west of North Carolina found that "subsistence and market production were not contradictory activities but mutually sustainable ones, the balance of which might vary from area to area, from farm to farm, and from season to season." Martin Crawford, "Mountain Farmers and the Market Economy: Ashe County during the 1850s," *North Carolina Historical Review* 71 (October 1994): 430-450 (quotation on 445). However, it has also been recently stated that "farmers in many highland areas moved against the national trend by reverting from commercial to more subsistent farming during the century's middle decades," emphasizing how difficult it is to make sweeping judgments with any accuracy; Inscoe and McKinney, *Heart of Confederate Appalachia*, 21.

[31] Majewski, *House Dividing*, 7; Christopher Clark, "Economics and Culture: Opening up the Rural History of the Early American Northeast," *American Quarterly* 43 (June 1991): 279-301 (quotation on 282). See also Allan Kulikoff, *The Agrarian Origins of American Capitalism* (Charlottesville: University Press of Virginia, 1992).

[32] The following are only a sample of a large and growing literature: Clark, *Roots of Rural Capitalism*; Garrison, *Landscape and Material Life*; Daniel Vickers, *Farmers and Fishermen: Two Centuries of Work in Essex County, Massachusetts, 1630-1850* (Chapel Hill: University of North Carolina Press, 1994); Jack Larkin, *The Reshaping of Everyday Life, 1790-1840* (New York: Harper and Row, 1988); Daniel P. Jones, *The Economic and Social Transformation of Rural Rhode Island, 1780-1850* (Boston: Northeastern University Press, 1992); Peter Benes, ed., *The Farm* (Boston: Boston University Press, 1988); P. Jeffrey Potash, *Vermont's Burned-Over District: Patterns of Community Development and Religious Activity, 1761-1850* (Brooklyn, NY: Carlson, 1991); David Jaffee, *People of the Wachusett: Greater New England in History and Memory, 1630-1860* (Ithaca, NY: Cornell University Press, 1999); Joseph S. Wood, *The*

Migration within and beyond New England has long been the subject of studies, but they have become more sharply focused on individual farm families or particular communities as more and more young men and women sought "careers" outside farming. The consequences for farm families of new sources of credit, industrialization, urban growth, transport improvements, and the expansion of educational institutions have also been considered. To educational institutions in the sense of schools and colleges might be added the impact of a growing agricultural press and state and local agricultural societies dedicated to improving farmers and farming. Finally, the impact of competition from western agricultural products in New England, though long familiar worked itself out in complex ways at a regional, community, and family level.[33] Thus, recent historiography suggests that it is very difficult to establish significant differences in the economic outlook, aspirations, and daily concerns of the northern and southern farmer.[34]

Gender

Political boundaries and borders were constructed by men, who were also primarily behind economic changes. Yet women were an essential part of the family and farm economy, and the boundaries between male and female worlds were complex and sometimes fluid. A sectional comparison shows many similarities between the lives of rural women, suggesting that gender was far more important than region in determining daily routines, roles, and responsibilities. In New England, farmers' wives generally took charge of the home, preparing and cooking food, cleaning, cultivating the garden, as well as taking care of children. They made clothes and participated in much outwork for the textile industry, shoemaking, straw hat manufacture, and other local enterprises.[35] They had control of their own space with

---

New England Village (Baltimore, MD: Johns Hopkins University Press, 1997); Jerald E. Brown, *The Years of the Life of Samuel Lane, 1718-1806: A New Hampshire Man and His World* (Hanover, NH: University Press of New England, 2000).

[33] Key works on women's roles will be cited below. For education and literacy, see William Gilmore, *Reading Becomes a Necessity of Life: Material and Cultural Life in Rural New England, 1780-1835* (Knoxville: University of Tennessee Press, 1989). Agricultural societies and the agricultural press are the subject of a large literature see, for example, Clark, *Roots of Rural Capitalism*, 93-96, 276-311; Tamara Plakins Thornton, *Cultivating Gentlemen: The Meaning of Country Life among the Boston Elite, 1785-1860* (New Haven, CT: Yale University Press, 1989), 57-106; Randolph A. Roth, *The Democratic Dilemma: Religion, Reform and the Social Order in the Connecticut River Valley of Vermont, 1791-1850* (Cambridge: Cambridge University Press, 1987), 119, 228-229, 261-268.

[34] The shift to a more commercial agriculture also threw up much debate and heart searching in both sections, while many farmers continued to straddle the worlds of commerce and self-sufficiency down to the Civil War, regardless of specific location.

[35] Jane C. Nylander, *Our Own Snug Fireside: Images of the New England Home, 1760–1860* (New York: Alfred A, Knopf, 1993); Laurel Thatcher Ulrich, *A Midwife's Tale: The Life of Martha Ballard Based on Her Diary, 1785-1812* (New York: Alfred A. Knopf, 1990); Thomas Dublin, "Women and Outwork in a Nineteenth-Century New

its distinct boundaries and borders though space was often at a premium, and a husband's duty as a selectman or other local official might fill the house with men. Most married women worked with, and supervised, their own female children and the daughters of neighbors and kin, who came in and out of the household on a regular basis. Older daughters might work for more prosperous neighbors or travel some distance to help a family member cope with illness or a new-born child.[36] At the beginning of the nineteenth century, some New England women took part in the outdoor work of the farm, especially at busy times of the year, and elsewhere in the North this was common practice. In time, however, ideology and technological change resulted in fewer northern women working in the fields. The shift is most marked in New England, where influential social commentators such as Timothy Dwight and popular agricultural journalists both inveighed against the "uncivilized" custom of women undertaking field work, which they identified with the labor of slaves or European peasants. By comparison, it is evident that down to the Civil War and beyond, southern yeomen farmers often depended upon the labor of wives and daughters in the fields. In general, less research has been undertaken into the lives of southern farm women than their New England counterparts, but it is clear that southern women also had responsibilities for a wide range of domestic and garden tasks including the production of household essentials, most importantly family clothing.[37]

England Town: Fitzwilliam, New Hampshire, 1830-50," in Steven Hahn and Jonathan Prude, eds., *The Countryside in the Age of Capitalist Transformation: Essays in the Social History of Rural America* (Chapel Hill: University of North Carolina Press, 1985), 51-69.

[36] Laurel Thatcher Ulrich, "Martha Ballard and Her Girls: Women's Work in Eighteenth-Century Maine," in Stephen Innes, ed., *Work and Labor in Early America* (Chapel Hill: University of North Carolina Press, 1978), 70-105; Lynn A. Bonfield and Mary C. Morrison, *Roxana's Children: The Biography of a Nineteenth-Century Vermont Family* (Amherst: University of Massachusetts Press, 1995), 3-19; Ann Taves, ed., *Religion and Domestic Violence in Early New England: The Memoirs of Abigail Abbot Bailey* (Bloomington: Indiana University Press, 1989). Many women's diaries complain of the house being full of men. See, for example, Blanche Brown Bryant and Gertrude Elaine Baker, eds., *The Diaries of Sally and Pamela Brown* (Springfield, VT: William L. Bryant Foundation, 1970), 68-69. Southern women also held primary responsibility for raising children, of course. See Sally G. McMillen, *Motherhood in the Old South: Pregnancy, Childbirth, and Infant Rearing, 1800-1860* (Chapel Hill: University of North Carolina Press, 1990).

[37] McCurry makes the important point that southern "women's work in the fields, although customary, was customarily ignored and even denied." She suggests that historians have been unwittingly complicit in sustaining the idea that only slaves worked in the field, which was in fact a myth promulgated by antebellum southerners to ease class tensions. McCurry, *Masters of Small Worlds*, 72-85 (quotation on 80). Timothy Dwight, *Travels in New England and New York*, ed. Barbara Miller Solomon (Cambridge, MA: Harvard University Press, 1969), 4:334-335; Joan M. Jensen, *Loosening the Bonds: Mid-Atlantic Farm Women, 1750-1850* (New Haven, CT: Yale University Press, 1986), 36-67; George Lyman Kittredge, *The Old Farmer and His Almanack* (Boston: William Ware, 1904), 182-183; Margaret Jones Bosterli, ed.,

A growing literature also explores New England women's activities beyond the home. Some were midwives and traveled regularly within their own and adjacent towns. Others traveled as specialist weavers or tailors working in their neighbors' homes. Women went to stores and traded on their husband's and their own accounts. Other activities which took them beyond the boundaries of their home and farm were quilting and singing parties, dances, and for many, the regular visit to church. Some radical sects allowed women greater freedom in the church, and as itinerant preachers, they pushed back symbolic boundaries regarding women's proper roles.[38] On the other hand, many aspects of New England women's lives remained constant down to the Civil War, but the shift to a more commercial agriculture, industrialization, and the growth of towns and cities produced major changes. Successful farmers' wives saw many physical improvements in their homes, but for some, the shift to new standards of middle class respectability and the cult of domesticity may have seen the boundaries of appropriate female behavior narrow.[39] Poorer married women in remote localities with limited connections to the commercial economy saw fewer changes. Their homes had no modern conveniences, and their sons and daughters still went away to seek employment as laborers or servants. By comparison, there is some evidence that the daughters of more middling sorts of farmers slowly turned their back on work as servants, preferring the economic and social opportunities provided by short-term employment in textile mills, a range of other urban occupations, or as school teachers. This employment often took them beyond the borders of their own state or even their own region, but they remained part of a network of young women from their home and adjacent towns, who provided mutual support. Visits and letters enabled families to keep in touch with daughters across New England, the Midwest, and much further afield.[40]

The impact of market development on nonslaveholding southern women has yet to be fully explored, but work in progress suggests that some new opportunities were apparent. A recent collection of essays shows that working women of the Old South "participated in the developing marketplace in an impressive variety of ways,

---

Vinegar Pie and Chicken Bread: A Woman's Diary of Life in the Rural South, 1890-1891 (Fayetteville: University of Arkansas Press, 1982), 19-21.

[38] Thatcher Ulrich, *A Midwife's Tale*; Nylander, *Our Own Snug Fireside*, 228-230; Louis Billington, "'Female Laborers in the Church': Women Preachers in the Northeastern United States, 1790-1840," *Journal of American Studies* 19 (1985): 369-394; Catherine A. Brekus, *Strangers and Pilgrims: Female Preaching in America, 1740-1845* (Chapel Hill: University of North Carolina Press, 1998), 117-336.

[39] Sally McMurray, *Families and Farmhouse in Nineteenth-Century America: Vernacular Design and Social Change* (New York: Oxford University Press, 1988), 3-86; Brekus, *Strangers and Pilgrims*, 284-287.

[40] Roth, *Democratic Dilemma*, 244-246; Holly V. Izard, "The Ward Family and Their Helps: Domestic Work, Workers and Relationships on a New England Farm, 1787-1866," *American Antiquarian Society* 103 (1993): 181-185; Bonfield and Morison, *Roxana's Children*, 39-51, 62-95; Thomas Dublin, ed., *Farm to Factory: Women's Letters, 1830-1860* (New York: Columbia University Press, 1981); Polly Welts Kaufman, *Women Teachers on the Frontier* (New Haven, CT: Yale University Press), 153-224.

as wage earners and as entrepreneurs, regardless of traditional social expectations about gender and race." Participation in the market, however, was very much dependent upon specific circumstances and was far more likely for women in southern towns and cities. In rural areas, wives and daughters carried out more routine fieldwork than their northern counterparts. By the 1850s, there were clearly many more non-agricultural avenues of employment open to women in New England.[41] Indeed, some scholars have recently suggested that opportunities for work and social activities outside the home became increasingly restricted for southern women of all classes in the later antebellum years. In a very real sense, the home constituted a permanent barrier only occasionally breached to visit friends and family or attend church. Stephanie McCurry's *Masters of Small Worlds* identifies an increasingly restrictive patriarchal system in South Carolina that underpinned the position of yeomen farmers as the dominant, and sometimes despotic, heads of households. All dependents, she argues, were viewed as subordinate, uniting southern males whether they owned slaves or not. Other southern historians have noted the ways in which masculinity and independence were fundamentally linked in a complex honor system that excluded women.[42] By comparison, while many Yankee women from farm families were increasingly constrained by notions of "woman's sphere" and "appropriate behaviour," they also used such concepts to build up supportive networks which enabled some to take advantage of widening educational and employment opportunities. These opportunities remained limited, but New England women enjoyed a greater degree of freedom than their counterparts in the South where "the home was women's sphere, but man's dominion."[43]

---

[41] Susanna Delfino and Michele Gillespie, eds., *Neither Lady nor Slave: Working Women of the Old South* (Chapel Hill: University of North Carolina Press, 2002), 2. Other works have emphasized the gap between rural and urban southern women. Suzanne Lebsock, *The Free Women of Petersburg: Status and Culture in a Southern Town, 1784-1860* (New York: W.W. Norton, 1984) depicts female networks within Petersburg remarkably similar to those developed in New England, based upon charity work and the upkeep of moral standards. Jean E. Friedman's *The Enclosed Garden: Women and Community in the Evangelical South, 1830-1900* (Chapel Hill: University of North Carolina Press, 1985) argues that the experience of rural southern women was confined and limited, which contrasted greatly with women in the North.

[42] McCurry, *Masters of Small Worlds*, passim. Steven M. Stowe, *Intimacy and Power in the Old South: Ritual in the Lives of the Planters* (Baltimore, MD: Johns Hopkins University Press, 1987); Bertram Wyatt-Brown, *Southern Honor: Ethics and Behavior in the Old South* (New York: Oxford University Press, 1982).

[43] Brenda E. Stevenson, *Life in Black and White: Family and Community in the Slave South* (New York: Oxford University Press, 1996), 39. As suggested in a recent essay, "we need to know more about poor and farm women who comprised the majority of the South's female population; this may require the use of more innovative sources to uncover their lives." Sally G. McMillen, "Women in the Old South," in Boles, *A Companion to the American South*, 207.

Conclusion

For more than two decades, scholars have examined the development of rural communities in antebellum New England and the South. They have frequently posed similar questions and looked at the same themes but, strangely, seem remarkably reluctant to cross the sectional divide in their approach. This pioneering comparative investigation of the current literature points towards the similar worlds of northern and southern farmers. Indeed, it is very difficult to establish salient characteristics that place rural communities either side of the Mason-Dixon line in contradistinction to one another. A full discussion of the ways in which New England farmers and southern yeomen perceived slavery at mid-century is the subject of a very different essay from the one offered here, but our examination of daily concerns and activities shows more similarities than differences. Sectional identity is often taken as a given, but we hope that this essay will encourage historians to make more use of a comparative perspective and have a greater awareness of the process of constructing a northern and southern identity.[44] By 1860, some commentators portrayed New England as a hive of factories, schools, colleges, hospitals, and progressive welfare institutions, but others were also alarmed by the growth of towns and cities, increased ethnic diversity, and sharper divisions between rich and poor. Such doubters often took refuge in a nostalgic quest for an "Old New England" rooted in an imagined experience of the past—virtuous simplicity, rural independence, and class harmony. Abolitionists contributed to this romantic image, contrasting a free, independent yeomen-based New England with a diseased and rotten plantation-centered South. Proslavery advocates projected a very different but equally idealized South and contrasted it with the chaotic and unstable North. This article suggests that for many antebellum farmers these oppositional "imagined communities" contradicted the reality of many common and shared experiences.[45]

---

[44] A very recent thrust in southern historiography has problematized the notion of "Southernness," as indicated by titles such as *Creating an Old South* and *Becoming Southern*. Edward E. Baptist, *Creating an Old South: Middle Florida's Plantation Frontier Before the Civil War* (Chapel Hill: University of North Carolina Press, 2002); Christopher Morris, *Becoming Southern: The Evolution of a Way of Life, Warren County and Vicksburg, Mississippi, 1770-1860* (New York: Oxford University Press, 1995).

[45] Susan Mary-Grant, *North Over South: Northern Nationalism and American Identity in the Antebellum Era* (Lawrence: University Press of Kansas, 2000) shows that each section was viewed in an increasingly hostile manner by the other. See also Sarah Burns, *Pastoral Inventions: Rural Life in Nineteenth-Century American Art and Culture* (Philadelphia: Temple University Press, 1989), 84-85.

THE SPECIAL MESSAGE OF RUTHERFORD B. HAYES, 8 MARCH 1880, AND THE "AMERICAN" CANAL POLICY

Joseph Smith

The rise of the United States to a position of pre-eminence in the western hemisphere during the nineteenth century was reflected in and also promoted by the issue of Special Messages by the president to the United States Congress. These statements of policy boldly asserted American rights to exercise authority over neighboring countries but without necessarily incurring any material obligations in return. The foremost occasion in the nineteenth century was President James Monroe's message to Congress in 1823 which announced that his country was taking the newly-independent states of Latin America under its self-appointed protection. President James K. Polk was more precise in 1845 when his message to Congress declared his government's opposition to the establishment of European colonies in any part of the North American continent. In 1876 President Ulysses S. Grant informed Congress that the United States would not recognize the future transfer of Latin American territory to a European power. Although more restricted in terms of the actual geographical area that it covered, President Rutherford B. Hayes took the opportunity to make a similarly robust and proprietary statement in 1880.

"The policy of this country is a canal under American control," declared President Rutherford B. Hayes in the opening sentence of his Special Message to the United States Congress on 8 March 1880.[1] The message was brief and extended to only a few paragraphs, but it was notable because it contained the unilateral claim of the United States to exercise jurisdiction in a particular territory that it did not own and was far beyond its own national borders. Although he did not make a direct reference to the controversial French proposal to construct a sea-level canal across the isthmus of Panama, Hayes had the French scheme very much in mind when he argued that the completed canal directly affected American national security because it would be "virtually a part of the coastline of the United States." The use of "virtually" pointed to an inherent weakness in the president's case in terms of international law. It did not prevent him, however, from asserting "that it is the right and duty of the United States to assert and maintain such supervision and authority over any interoceanic canal across the isthmus that connects North and South America as will protect our national interests."[2]

---

[1] The Special Message is reprinted in Committee on Foreign Relations, United States Senate, *Background Documents Relating to the Panama Canal*, 95th Cong., 1st sess., November 1977, 51.

[2] Ibid. Hayes did acknowledge that "existing treaties" or "rights of sovereignty or property of other nations" might "stand in the way of this policy." He believed, however, that this contingency could be resolved by "just and liberal negotiations." Nevertheless, Hayes had not consulted with any Latin American government before sending his message to Congress and, in this respect, acted in a similar fashion to President James Monroe in November 1823.

Although Hayes was simply issuing a presidential statement which required no implementing action to be taken by Congress, the message was designed to serve as an indication of the government's future intent and also as a prescriptive warning to both the organizers of the French scheme and foreign powers. Historian David Pletcher describes it as "a forceful special message that seemed to commit the nation to unprecedented expansion of its influence in Central America."[3] In the short-term, however, the Special Message had only a limited impact. The foreign threat did not materialize because the French government gave assurances that it had no intention of interfering in isthmian affairs. Consequently, the French canal company was able to proceed with its plans which included the commencement of actual work on the canal just as Hayes's presidential term of office expired in March 1881.

The French scheme collapsed in 1892 and was replaced by an "American" canal that was eventually opened to shipping in 1914. The successful completion of this canal, however, has been more readily attributed to the diplomacy of Theodore Roosevelt than to Rutherford Hayes.[4] But Hayes had paved the way for Roosevelt. Prior to 1880 successive American presidents had generally been reluctant to become involved in canal schemes and had favored a canal funded and built by private capitalists and under an international guaranty agreed to by the great maritime powers of Europe and the United States. Although it never gained the status of a "doctrine" or a celebrated American diplomatic state paper, the 1880 Special Message was historically significant in that for the first time the policy of securing a canal under American ownership and control was sanctioned by the president and articulated in public.[5]

Ever since the Spanish explorer, Vasco Núñez de Balboa, had glimpsed the Pacific Ocean in 1513 the dream of constructing a canal across Central America to link the Atlantic and the Pacific had gone unrealized. The project was too big and daunting in terms of discovering a feasible route through very difficult terrain and attracting sufficient capital for a speculative venture in such a remote part of the world.[6] After the discovery of gold in California in 1848, the increase in demand for faster transit across Central America was partly met by the building of a railroad across the isthmus of Panama between 1851 and 1855. However, the successful

---

[3] David M. Pletcher, *The Diplomacy of Trade and Investment: American Economic Expansion in the Hemisphere, 1865-1900* (Columbia: University of Missouri Press, 1998), 130.

[4] Theodore Roosevelt is credited with the statement: "I took the Canal Zone." See James F. Vivian, "The 'Taking' of the Panama Canal Zone: Myth and Reality," *Diplomatic History* 4 (1980): 95-100.

[5] The message has also been generally neglected by historians who have regarded it as merely a minor event in the rise of the United States to the status of a world power at the close of the nineteenth century. For a recent example, see Frank Ninkovich, *The United States and Imperialism* (Malden MA: Blackwell, 2001), 105.

[6] For a general survey of canal projects see, Gerstle Mack, *The Land Divided: A History of the Panama Canal and Other Canal Projects* (New York: Knopf, 1944) and Miles Du Val, *From Cadiz to Cathay: The Story of the Long Diplomatic Struggle for the Panama Canal* (Palo Alto, CA: Stanford University Press, 1947). A readable study for the period after 1870 is David McCullough, *The Path between the Seas: The Creation of the Panama Canal, 1870-1914* (New York: Simon and Schuster, 1977).

construction and opening of the Suez Canal in 1869 posed the prospect of a "second Suez" and stimulated serious interest in schemes for a Central American canal. In 1872 President Grant appointed an Interoceanic Canal Commission that sent a series of expeditions of surveyors and engineers to the region. The choice was narrowed down to either Panama or Nicaragua.[7] While the actual length of a canal in Panama would be considerably shorter, the existing river system in Nicaragua made a waterway in that country easier to construct and also less expensive. The Commission reported in 1876 and unanimously recommended the adoption of the route via Nicaragua. A group of American canal promoters led by Admiral Daniel Ammen, a former member of the Interoceanic Canal Commission, sought to translate the recommendation into action. In 1879, however, their prospective Nicaraguan scheme was suddenly challenged by the emergence of an ambitious French project that promised to be the biggest single economic venture ever launched in Latin America during the nineteenth century.

The organizers of the French scheme held an "International Geographical Congress" at Paris in May 1879. The congress deliberated over several possible routes and decided in favor of the isthmus of Panama where a sea-level canal would be constructed close to the existing Panama Railroad linking the cities of Colón and Panama. Under the presidency of the French entrepreneur, Ferdinand de Lesseps, the Panama Canal Company (La Compagnie Universelle du Canal Interocéanique de Panamá) was formed. It paid 10 million francs ($2 million) to Lieutenant Lucien Napoleon Bonaparte Wyse to purchase the concession that he had acquired from the Colombian government in 1878 to build the canal.[8] Plans were announced to begin actual construction in 1881 and to complete the work by 1889 to coincide with the centenary of the French Revolution.

News of the proceedings at Paris aroused a critical response in the United States. On 25 June 1879, Senator Ambrose Burnside of Rhode Island introduced the first of several resolutions in Congress stating that any attempt by the European powers to construct an isthmian canal under their protection would be a violation of the Monroe Doctrine. A similar note of alarm was expressed in the American press. "It is certain," remarked the *New York Herald* on 3 July 1879, "that our government will neither recognize nor respect or tolerate any European interference in the matter."[9] In December the House of Representatives created a Select Committee on Interoceanic Canals to investigate the canal issue. The frequent reference to the Monroe Doctrine reflected popular concern in the United States that the de Lesseps project would provide the means by which France would establish a protectorate over the isthmus.[10] Indeed, French designs on Latin American territory had already been illustrated by Louis-Napoleon's attempt to impose a European monarchy on Mexico during the 1860s. Even though that intervention had failed, the potential

---

[7] Tehuantepec in southern Mexico was also considered.
[8] Panama was part of the nation of Colombia, whose official title was the United States of Colombia.
[9] *New York Herald*, 3 July 1879.
[10] The relationship of the canal issue with the Monroe Doctrine is discussed in Dexter Perkins, *The Monroe Doctrine, 1867-1907* (Baltimore, MD: Johns Hopkins Press, 1937), 65-92.

threat from France was not forgotten. The American minister in Bogotá, Ernest Dichman, warned the state department in August 1879 that, "a canal constructed by such a company [Panama Canal Company] will be nothing less than the planting of a French colony on the Isthmus." He considered "that the government of the United States cannot view with indifference, the construction and management thereof by a European Government or by a company subject to the jurisdiction of such government."[11]

The government of the United States headed by President Hayes was far from indifferent. In his diary entry for 7 February 1880, the president deemed the canal issue as "the most important subject now under consideration."[12] At a meeting of the cabinet on 10 February, Hayes stated that the subject was of such national importance that "our principles should be at an early day announced."[13] The following day he wrote in his personal diary that he had informed the cabinet:

> That paramount interests were involved. That the control of the canal was essential to our prosperity and safety. That the ocean highway from that part of our country on the Atlantic to that part of our country on the Pacific must always be under our control; that, if it passed into European control, our security, our peace, our commercial and general prosperity, and our commanding and natural position among the nations would be endangered.[14]

On 20 February Hayes wrote in his diary that "the United States cannot consent that it [the canal] shall be under European control." A straightforward choice, therefore, existed between "either an American canal or no canal."[15] Moreover, the ideas expressed by the president coincided with and reflected the emergence of a political consensus on the issue. The British minister in Washington, Edward Thornton, summed up the state of American public opinion on 23 February 1880: "the feeling that no ship canal should be constructed to connect the Atlantic and Pacific Oceans without it being completely under the control of the United States is daily gaining strength in this country, and seems to be acquiesced in by all political parties."[16] A few days later, on 8 March 1880, Hayes responded to a request from the United States Senate for official correspondence on the canal question. Prominent among the material that he delivered to Congress was his Special Message insisting that the

---

[11] Dichman to Evarts, 17 October 1879, no. 151, Dispatches, Columbia, Record Group [hereafter RG] 59, Records of the Department of State, National Archives, Washington, D.C., 33.

[12] Charles R. Williams, ed., *Diary and Letters of Rutherford Birchard Hayes*, 5 vols. (Columbus: Ohio State Archaeological and Historical Society, 1922-1926), 3:586. Hayes was the winner of the disputed election of 1876 and served as president from 1877 to 1881. For a recent biography, see Ari Hoogenboom, *Rutherford B. Hayes: Warrior and President* (Lawrence: University Press of Kansas, 1995).

[13] Williams, *Diary and Letters*, 3:587.

[14] Ibid., 3:587-588.

[15] Ibid., 3:589.

[16] Thornton to Salisbury, 23 February 1880, no. 53, Foreign Office Records [hereafter cited as FO] 5/1720, Public Record Office, London.

United States would seek to control any future canal that was constructed across the isthmus.

The Special Message was notable because it contained the assertion by Hayes that his government had the right to exercise authority over territory beyond its borders, as if that land were within the United States. European governments acknowledged that, for political, economic and strategic reasons, the United States had a special interest in canal developments. They were also aware that the message referred to future American policy and did not mean that Hayes was about to undertake any imminent action. European governments sensibly chose to ignore the message and thereby avoided making it a matter of diplomatic correspondence. But the claim to exercise authority beyond American borders was noted and severely criticized in the British press. "The Washington protest," remarked an editorial in *The Times*, "is a claim to an indefinite suzerainty from Mexico to Patagonia, though throughout the vast region the government at Washington exercises no power, and to its populations it acknowledges no duty." The British newspaper also considered that the United States was essentially seeking to exercise a veto on all canal-building and added somewhat sarcastically: "Great Britain may congratulate herself that the Caledonian Canal is already dug; it might otherwise have given rise to international complications."[17] The *South American Journal* adopted a similarly critical attitude. While acknowledging that, for commercial and strategic reasons, the United States was justified in showing a close interest in any canal scheme, there was condemnation of what was described as the attempt by the American government to exercise "exclusive protection or control." In the view of the *South American Journal*, "the international pretensions of the United States to exercise exclusive control over the canal are not founded in reason or in justice."[18]

The references in the British press to the "Washington protest" and "the international pretensions of the United States" highlighted the fact that the Special Message to Congress was interpreted as an example of diplomatic posturing by the American president rather than a matter of international law that required compliance. While the message succeeded in its purpose of informing the American people—and the world—of the administration's "principles," it did not specifically call for any direct action or even response from Congress, the American public or foreign governments in either Central America or the rest of the world. Moreover, Hayes not only refrained from criticizing the French scheme by name but he made no mention of seeking to prevent a private commercial company from proceeding with its normal commercial activity. The United States was not, therefore, claiming a veto power on canal-building. On the other hand, by announcing his canal policy publicly, the president seized an opportunity to lobby against de Lesseps and to discourage support in the United States for the French company. This was demonstrated by the timing of the message to coincide with the personal presence of de Lesseps in Washington.

---

[17] *The Times* [London], 20 March 1880. The Caledonian Canal was constructed in Scotland during the 1820s.
[18] *South American Journal*, 18 March 1880.

Despite his emphasis on the danger to American national interests posed by the threat of European intervention, Hayes had good relations with both de Lesseps and the French government. In fact, Edward Thornton had reported to the Foreign Office that the French minister in Washington, Max Outrey, had given private assurances to the state department, as early as September 1879, in which he disavowed any intention on the part of the French government to become involved in the affairs of the isthmus. Moreover, it was public knowledge that the Hayes administration had been kept fully informed of the French scheme from its conception. Lieutenant Wyse had visited the White House in March 1879 to inform Hayes of his plans. The French naval officer mentioned the forthcoming Congress in Paris and expressed the wish that the United States would send delegates. Hayes later asked Admiral Ammen and the Cuban-born engineer, Aniceto G. Menocal, to represent the United States at the conference, though in an unofficial capacity. As confirmed advocates of the Nicaragua route, both delegates returned to the United States, where they complained that the meeting had been fixed in favor of choosing the Panama route. "In fact, so far as the final result is concerned," alleged Menocal, "the vote might have been taken before any discussion took place, as it was evident from first to last that the Wyse party, backed by the Geographical Society and M. de Lesseps, had previously arranged all the details with such skill that success was virtually secured from the start."[19]

The decision at Paris to select the Panama route evidently came as a surprise to the Hayes administration. In July 1879 Thornton reported a conversation with Secretary of State William Evarts who had told him that "the route by the Lake of Nicaragua would be the safest and most economical one," and that it was "his belief that M. Lesseps would be unable to raise any part of the capital in either the United States or England."[20] After their return from France, Ammen and Menocal were active in promoting the superiority of the Nicaragua route. They formed a company known as the Provisional Interoceanic Canal Society and announced their intention of negotiating a canal concession from the Nicaraguan government.[21] In his Annual Message to Congress for December 1879, Hayes referred specifically to the current proposals for a canal "by the Nicaragua route" and stated that sufficient capital "from this country and Europe" would be forthcoming "should the work be undertaken under the protective auspices of the United States."[22] The December message showed that an "American" canal scheme via Nicaragua was being actively pursued, and implied that it was supported by the Hayes administration. But both the Hayes administration and the private promoters of the Nicaraguan route had to reckon with the powerful personality and energy of Ferdinand de Lesseps. At the

---

[19] A.G. Menocal, "Intrigues at the Paris Canal Congress," *North American Review* 129 (1879): 291

[20] Thornton to Salisbury, 21 July 1879, no 169, FO 5/1683. Evarts had also been surprised to learn that the Colombian government had granted the Wyse concession. See Evarts to Dichman, 9 July 1879, no. 57, Instructions, Colombia, RG 59, 17.

[21] The Society was incorporated in 1880 as the Maritime Canal Company of Nicaragua.

[22] See James D. Richardson, ed., *A Compilation of the Messages and Papers of the Presidents, 1789-1897*, 10 vols. (Washington, DC: Government Printing Office, 1896-1899): 7:569.

age of seventy-four, de Lesseps visited Panama towards the end of December 1879 and shortly afterwards set sail for the United States where he embarked on an arduous public relations tour from coast to coast. In speech after speech the celebrated French entrepreneur made a point of refuting charges that the French government was involved in his scheme. Instead, he stressed the private and non-governmental nature of the venture. Moreover, far from being a purely European operation he told his audiences in the United States that, if American investors took up a majority of the subscriptions to fund the project, then the headquarters of the canal company would be located in New York. Though he regarded it as an inferior scheme to Panama, de Lesseps did not oppose the building of a canal via Nicaragua. "Every new highway is a step forward," enthused the charming Frenchman.[23]

While in the United States, de Lesseps was able to have meetings with leading political figures, including the president and the secretary of state. The British minister believed that Hayes and Evarts "will probably endeavour to dissuade him [de Lesseps] from attempting to carry out his vast undertaking except upon the conditions which it may suit this country to dictate and which may give it a controlling power over the canal."[24] De Lesseps visited the White House in February 1880 and returned to Washington in March to meet the president again and to appear before the House Select Committee on Interoceanic Canals. However, despite the numerous public assurances by de Lesseps and the private undertaking of the French government that the Panama Canal Company was and would remain a private enterprise, the House Select Committee chose to reaffirm the Monroe Doctrine on 6 March. Two days later Hayes delivered his uncompromising message to Congress declaring that the United States could not consent to a canal under European control.

The policy outlined by Hayes in his Special Message appealed to American nationalism, but there was also the risk that it might obstruct the building of what promised to be an important means of communication between the east and west coasts of the United States. "Public opinion," reported Thornton, "is apparently changing in this country upon the subject of such an intervention by the United States as it may prevent the construction of the canal owing to the fears entertained by foreign capitalists lest their investments should be unduly interfered with by this Government."[25] Indeed, de Lesseps astutely read the changing mood of American public opinion and cleverly responded to the Special Message with a speech welcoming the president's statement as adding to "the political security of the canal." Referring to the issue of "the supposed opposition of the United States," de Lesseps noted: "It would be a calumny against the great people of the United States to attribute to them sentiments hostile to an enterprise that will promote their material and moral interests, no less than those of the whole world."[26] Although the amount of American financial subscriptions proved disappointing, de Lesseps initially compensated for this by cultivating support in other ways. For example, his

---

[23] Ferdinand de Lesseps, "The Interoceanic Canal," *North American Review* 130 (1880): 8.
[24] Thornton to Salisbury, 16 February 1880, no 45, FO 55/281.
[25] Thornton to Salisbury, 15 March 1880, no 84, FO 55/281.
[26] De Lesseps, "The Interoceanic Canal," 77.

company established an American advisory board of which the presidency, involving an annual salary of $25,000, was first offered to ex-President Grant. Grant refused, and it was then accepted by the secretary of the Navy, Richard Thompson, who resigned from the cabinet in December 1880.[27] De Lesseps also disarmed criticism by making very generous financial terms for the purchase of the American-owned Panama Railroad Company and by indicating that much of the material and machinery for the construction of the canal would be bought from within the United States.

Meanwhile, Hayes and Evarts sought to out-maneuver de Lesseps by putting diplomatic pressure on the Colombian government to reaffirm the terms of the 1846 treaty between the United States and Colombia.[28] According to Article 35 of the treaty, the United States had given a guarantee to preserve the "perfect neutrality" of the isthmus "with the view that the free transit from the one to the other sea, may not be interrupted or embarrassed in any future time while this Treaty exists."[29] The Hayes administration now sought to use this provision to support its claim that the United States possessed a special right and duty to control any canal that was built across the isthmus. The diplomatic task of persuading the Colombian government was assigned to Ernest Dichman. After his period of leave in the United States, the American minister returned to Colombia in May 1880 on board the warship *Tennessee*. Edward Thornton interpreted this as a calculated "demonstration of force."[30] In Colombia, however, the American minister encountered open resentment and hostility from government officials and politicians. "The position of the United States," he wrote, "tends to dispel the fairy vision of happiness and wealth which were confidently expected to flow from the realization of the de Lesseps canal scheme."[31] Not surprisingly, no diplomatic progress was made in Bogotá. A similar diplomatic impasse prevailed in Washington until February 1881, when a protocol was suddenly agreed to by the departing Colombian minister, Santo Domingo Vila, and the state department official, William Trescot. The protocol reaffirmed the American guarantee contained in the 1846 treaty and made any future change in the Wyse concession dependent upon American approval. In this way Evarts believed that American rights over isthmian transit would be both reaffirmed and reserved for the future. But the protocol proved unacceptable to the Colombian government because it gravely undermined Colombian sovereignty over the isthmus of Panama.[32] Santo Domingo Vila was sharply criticized for his error of judgment,

---

[27] On Grant's support for the Nicaragua route, see Ulysses S. Grant, "The Nicaragua Canal," *North American Review* 132 (1881): 107-116.

[28] Colombia was known as New Granada in 1846.

[29] See Committee, *Background Documents*, 9.

[30] Thornton to Salisbury, 26 April 1880, no. 132, FO 5/1721. Hayes also ordered two American warships to look for coaling bases in the Gulf of Chiriquí on the Pacific side of the isthmus.

[31] Dichman to Evarts, 3 July 1880, no. 183, Dispatches, Colombia, RG 59, 33.

[32] While ostensibly claiming to guarantee Colombian sovereignty over the isthmus, the insistence on American control over the canal actually weakened it. See Stephen J. Randall, *Colombia and the United States: Hegemony and Interdependence* (Athens, GA: University of Georgia Press, 1992), 65.

and no further action was taken on the protocol. The fact that no new Colombian diplomatic representative was sent to Washington until 1884 further indicated Colombia's disinclination to negotiate a canal treaty with the United States.

Indeed, as the term of office of the Hayes administration came to an end in March 1881, French survey teams were busy attempting to determine the exact location for their forthcoming canal operations in Panama. Within a year actual construction work was underway. *The Times* jubilantly remarked that the Monroe Doctrine had been unable "to ban M. de Lesseps from wielding his victorious prospectuses."[33] However, in 1889—the centenary of the French Revolution—construction work was far behind the original schedule. A desperate lack of finance brought work to a halt and resulted in the French company going into bankruptcy in 1892. The scheme that had been launched with so much fanfare at Paris in 1879 was ruined just over a decade later by a combination of mismanagement, financial corruption and the inability to overcome major engineering and climatic difficulties. The Special Message played a contributory role. While it had not prevented the French company from proceeding with actual building work, it had achieved its purpose of discouraging American investors from backing de Lesseps.

During the 1880s attempts by American promoters to initiate rival canal schemes in Nicaragua and Tehuantepec also failed. Indeed, the construction of a Central American canal faced so many formidable obstacles that the alarm provoked in the United States by the French scheme proved to have been misplaced. Not only had the French government been quick to reassure Hayes that it had no intention of interfering in isthmian affairs but the world's leading commercial power, Great Britain, had also maintained a detached attitude. Among British Foreign Office officials, there was considerable scepticism as to whether an isthmian canal could actually be built. They regarded the issue of Special Messages as an American conceit and an irritating example of the style in which Brother Jonathan was prone to conduct diplomatic business. Nevertheless, British officials understood the implication in Hayes's Special Message that the United States possessed a preponderating political and military influence in the isthmian region. If an isthmian canal was ever completed, British officials believed that it would fall almost certainly under "American" control. In 1880 the British minister in Colombia, Colonel Mansfield, reckoned that a canal built by an American company:

> would of course take little account of the sovereignty of the Government in whose territory the works would be executed, whether it be Colombia or Nicaragua. Were the decision to be in favour of Panama, the severance of that State from the Colombian Union would be a mere question of time, and ... a small so-called independent state at the isthmus would be simply an outpost of the United States.[34]

---

[33] *The Times* [London], 10 June 1881
[34] Mansfield to Foreign Office, 5 April 1880, no. 13, FO 55/273.

The diplomatic realism of Britain set the tone for the European response to the 1880 Special Message.[35] Indeed, the prediction that Mansfield had made in 1880 was realized in 1903 when the United States recognized the secession of Panama from Colombia and proceeded not just to talk about an 'American' canal but actually to build the waterway as a governmental enterprise. At the same time to avoid any doubts about legal authority, the United States insisted upon acquiring sovereign rights over the territory through which the canal passed. The resulting creation of the Panama Canal Zone represented the extension of the jurisdiction of the United States beyond its borders and thereby the vindication of the Special Message made by Hayes in 1881 affirming that his country would control any future isthmian canal.[37]

---

[35] The British government believed that British interests in the region were safeguarded by the agreement between Britain and the United States, signed in 1850 and known as the Clayton-Bulwer Treaty. After 1881 this treaty became a matter of contentious diplomatic correspondence between Britain and the United States. On diplomatic rivalry between these two countries over the canal issue during the second half of the nineteenth century see Joseph Smith, *Illusions of Conflict: Anglo-American Diplomacy toward Latin America, 1865-1896* (Pittsburgh, PA: University of Pittsburgh Press, 1979), 81-116.

[37] The claim that the Panama Canal Zone was sovereign United States territory was a controversial issue that plagued relations between the United States and Panama for most of the twentieth century. See Walter LaFeber, *The Panama Canal: The Crisis in Historical Perspective* (New York: Oxford University Press, 1989).

ON THE FRONTIER OF CIVILIZATION: DELIBERATIONS OF EXCEPTIONALISM AND ENVIRONMENTAL DETERMINISM IN THE CREATION OF AMERICA'S TROPICAL EMPIRE, 1890-1910

Frank Schumacher

In 1893 Frederick Jackson Turner argued before the Chicago convention of the American Historical Association that the frontier had decisively shaped the contours of the nation's history. Turner's highly influential analysis advanced an environmentalist framework and suggested that the frontier's pioneering spirit and lifestyle had endowed white settlers with a distinct American creed, advanced the nation's democratization, and propelled the United States on a truly exceptional trajectory of national development.

What would soon simply be referred to as the "Turner-Thesis" was motivated in part by the widespread apprehensions about the nation's future after the closure of the frontier in the 1890s. As the continuous process of westward expansion was deemed essential to America's well-being, many commentators anticipated powerful negative consequences for the future development of the United States unless the nation's energy could be redirected.

To those who favored the acquisition of colonial possessions, overseas expansion appeared as a remedy to the social and economic ills associated with the disappearance of a western, continental frontier. The expansionists interpreted the quest for empire as a natural continuation of continental conquest and argued that this new frontier would provide Americans with the "strenuous life," to use one of Theodore Roosevelt's favored terms, deemed necessary to preserve manliness, virility, self-reliance, ingenuity, democratic spirit, and national greatness.

This essay argues that the tropical frontier of America's colonial empire produced ironies and paradoxes which subverted the environmentalist argument advanced by Turner and others in at least two fundamental respects: 1) environmental determinism, colonial medicine, and the daily experience of the colonists questioned the assumption that the new frontier would support the development of human qualities positive to the national development of the American Republic; 2) the multiple emerging links between the American and European colonial projects after 1900 and, in particular, American interest in the application of British colonial ideas and practices to the nation's new colonies undermined the argument that the frontier would continue to foster a uniquely American path of development. In at least two ways then, the hope that the frontier spirit could be kept alive in its original sense was subverted by the creation of a tropical empire.

Frederick Jackson Turner and American Exceptionalism

Frederick Jackson Turner has been rightfully called an American historian *par excellence*.[1] At the core of his work was the desire to develop a sound national explanation for American identity and development.[2] He rejected the dominant theories of American historical scholarship in the late nineteenth century, in particular the "Teutonic germ theory," whose proponents linked the evolution of American democracy to the tradition of ancient Germanic democratic practices.[3] Instead, Turner argued for a unique and exceptional path of national development and credited the frontier environment of the American West, not the German forests of antiquity with the key to understanding the rise of America.

For Turner the frontier as border between wilderness and civilization and its steady westward advance symbolized a repudiation of the European contours of America's national development and created the source for a distinct American identity:

> ... the advance of the frontier has meant a steady movement away from the influence of Europe, a steady growth of independence on American lines. And to study this advance ... is to study the really American part of our history.[4]

In addition to the Americanizing and identity forming impact of the frontier, Turner also credited the westward movement with the development of American character traits.[5] The rugged qualities of the frontiersman were defined by individualism, mobility, innovativeness, self-reliance, distrust of authority, and national pride. In

---

[1] Jan Willem Schulte Nordholt, "The Turner Thesis Revisited," in David K. Adams and Cornelis A. van Minnen, eds., *Reflections on American Exceptionalism* (Staffordshire: Ryburn Publishing, 1994), 9.

[2] For biographical introductions to Turner: Ray Allen Billington, *Frederick Jackson Turner: Historian, Scholar, Teacher* (New York: Oxford University Press, 1973); Allan G. Bogue, *Frederick Jackson Turner: Strange Roads Going Down* (Norman: University of Oklahoma Press, 1998); for Turner's writings: Vernon E. Mattson and William E. Marion, *Frederick Jackson Turner: A Reference Guide* (Boston: G.K. Hall, 1985); for the impact of the Turner thesis on the development of American historiography: Matthias Waechter, *Die Erfindung des amerikanischen Westens: Die Geschichte der Frontier Debatte* (Freiburg: Rombach Verlag, 1996).

[3] For turn-of-the-century American historiography and the impact of the "Teutonic germ" school: Peter Novick, *That Noble Dream: The "Objectivity Question" and the American Historical Profession* (Cambridge: Cambridge University Press, 1988).

[4] Frederick Jackson Turner, *The Frontier in American History*, chapter 1, page 2, <http://xroads.virginia.edu/~HYPER/TURNER/chapter1.html> (13 April 2003).

[5] Turner uses the term "Americanized" as to the impact of the frontier on immigrants: "... the frontier promoted the formation of a composite nationality for the American people. The coast was preponderantly English, but the later tides of continental immigration flowed across to the free lands. ... In the crucible of the frontier the immigrants were Americanized, liberated, and fused into a mixed race, English in neither nationality nor characteristics," ibid., 11.

sum: the frontier experience educated the colonists and shaped them into Americans. Turner emphasized:

> The wilderness masters the colonist. It finds him a European in dress, industries, tools, modes of travel, and thought. It takes him from the railroad car and puts him in the birch canoe. It strips off the garments of civilization and arrays him in the hunting shirt and the moccasin.

On a different occasion Turner even compared the impact of the frontier on Americans to the importance of the Mediterranean Sea to Greek civilization:

> What the Mediterranean Sea was to the Greeks, breaking the bond of custom, offering new experiences, calling out new institutions and activities, that the ever retreating Great West has been to the eastern United States directly, and to the nations of Europe more remotely.[6]

For Turner then, the frontier symbolized the creative power of the environment in the shaping of national history which in turn enabled the exceptional and unique character of American development.

Consequently, the closing of the frontier caused substantial and widespread anxiety about the nation's future course.[7] Turner himself made little prediction about the future development of the United States but his analytical framework was open enough to accommodate an intense discourse on the merits of overseas expansion, and fostered the use of the frontier as a powerful metaphor in national deliberations on the merits and pitfalls of an American overseas empire. Although Turner did make mention of the possibly beneficial nature of overseas colonization, his speeches and writings never amounted to anything like a concerted effort to advocate the projection of continuous expansion.[8]

To be sure, unease about the closed frontier was but one dimension of a multitude of factors contributing to the drive for overseas ventures.[9] Economic interests, strategic concerns, notions of race and manifest destiny, the sense of crisis of the 1890s, and a mental predisposition to participation in the great power game all played their role. But on all of those levels, frontier-related arguments served important functions for the proponents and opponents of empire.

Turner friend, political scientist, and later president, Woodrow Wilson agreed with Turner on the beneficial impact of the continental frontier on democratization and national development and suggested that those benefits could be expected to

---

[6] Frederick Jackson Turner, "Problems in American History," quoted in Richard W. Etulain, ed., *Does the Frontier Experience Make America Exceptional?* (Boston: Bedford/St. Martin's, 1999), 7.

[7] David Wrobel, *The End of American Exceptionalism: Frontier Anxiety from the Old West to the New Deal* (Lawrence: University Press of Kansas, 1993).

[8] Wrobel, *The End of American Exceptionalism*, 57-58.

[9] For a recent introduction to the history of American overseas expansion: Frank A. Ninkovich, *The United States and Imperialism* (Malden, MA: Blackwell Publishers, 2001).

accompany the colonial project in the noncontiguous territories as well.[10] Others, such as the Protestant minister Josiah Strong applied the quasi-religious rhetoric of Manifest Destiny in favor of overseas expansion.[11] Finally, another future president, Theodore Roosevelt echoed many of Turner's convictions and particularly stressed the reinvigorating effect of frontier life on the national community. He anticipated that, just as the western frontier in his understanding had done, colonial state-building would produce a renewed pioneering spirit characterized by manliness and virility.[12]

In sum, widespread agreement on the beneficial influence of the frontier on American national identity was an important element in turn-of-the-century discourses on the future of the United States. In one way or another, many interpretations anticipated that the overseas frontier would prove as valuable in the future as the creation of transcontinental empire had been in the past. Turner never advocated overseas colonization in a coherent fashion, but his arguments were ambivalent enough to allow advocates of expansion to mine his interpretative framework for the advancement of their case.

Environmental Determinism, Climatic Anxiety, and the New Frontier

Many of the deliberations on the perceived benefits of the American frontier in the 1890s rested on environmentalist arguments. Turner and others linked the natural environment and the human struggle for the advancement of civilization on the frontier with the rise of the United States. The identification of natural factors in the history of national development was not new. It was part of the larger theoretical framework of environmental determinism which had been *en vogue* since the early nineteenth century. But while strands of this theory sharpened the frontier argument, others weakened its applicability to overseas expansion, since many American environmental determinists warned of the possibly negative consequences of a tropical frontier for the young republic.

The theory of environmental determinism argued that all human activity, history, and the evolution of civilization were controlled by environmental conditions.[13] This explanatory framework allocated prime importance to the climate

---

[10] Wrobel, *The End of American Exceptionalism*, 58-59.
[11] Anders Stephanson, *Manifest Destiny: American Expansion and the Empire of Right* (New York: Hill and Wang, 1996).
[12] For a comparison of Turner's and Roosevelt's frontier concept: Richard Slotkin, *Gunfighter Nation: The Myth of the Frontier in Twentieth-Century America* (Norman: University of Oklahoma Press, 1998), 29-62.
[13] On environmental determinism: "Environmental Determinism," in R.J. Johnston, Derek Gregory, and David M. Smith, eds., *The Dictionary of Human Geography* (Cambridge, MA: Blackwell Reference, 1994), 162-164; David N. Livingston, *The Geographical Tradition: Episodes in the History of a Contested Enterprise* (Cambridge, MA: Blackwell Publishers, 1992); Clarence J. Glacken, *Traces on the Rhodean Shore: Nature and Culture in Western Thought from Ancient Times to the End of the*

and attached moral categories and considerations of race and virtue to climatic zones. American environmental determinists described peoples in hot climates as casual, promiscuous, lazy, with limited intelligence and thus incapable of self government. Peoples of the temperate zones were described with the opposite attributes as the theorists argued that colder climate had shaped strong, resistant, industrious, intelligent and highly civilized cultures.[14]

The classification of races according to climatic conditions and the idea of a racial hierarchy resulted in the view that the most civilized white races were destined to live in the temperate zones while the "barbaric races" inhabited the tropics. For Americans, tropical climate thus became synonymous with lack of civilization, disease, and weakness. Advocates of environmental determinism warned that permanent white colonization of non-temperate zones was out of the question, as colonists were bound to deteriorate mentally and physically under those conditions. Life under the tropical sun was doomed to follow a path of decay, characterized by alcoholism, sexual promiscuity, and insanity.

These warnings drew much support as they resonated with traditional ambivalences in Euro-American notions of the tropics.[15] Visions of tropical paradise, as popularized by writers such as Herman Melville and James Fenimore Cooper, had enchanted American readers long before the country's imperial expansion confronted the United States with questions of tropical acclimatization.

Eighteenth Century (Berkeley: University of California Press, 1967), chaps. 2, 6, 9, and 12; Gregory Lewthwaite, "Environmentalism and Determinism: A Search for Clarification," *Annual Association of American Geography* 56 (1966): 1-23.

[14] On the American tradition of environmental determinism in the early twentieth century: Frank Schumacher, "'Under the Weather': Climatic Anxiety, Environmental Determinism, and the Creation of the American Empire—A Preliminary Exploration," in Ursula Lehmkuhl and Stefanie Schneider, eds., *Umweltgeschichte—Histoire Totale oder Bindestrich-Geschichte*, Erfurter Beiträge zur Nordamerikanischen Geschichte 4 (Erfurt, 2002), 31-46.

[15] For an introduction to the varying images and perceptions: Nancy Leys Stephan, *Picturing Tropical Nature* (Ithaca, NY: Cornell University Press, 2001); the British author C.R. Enock captured the range of ambivalent images in Euro-American discourses on the tropics nicely: "When we speak familiarly of 'The Tropics' there may arise before us scenes and pictures more or less attractive, visions perhaps of blue skies and feathery, gracile palms, under which the dark-skinned native lives his simple life in a world far removed from that prosaic one of the white man. Memory, or imagination, may revert to fruitful lands beneath a perennial sun, bounded by mountain ranges soft in distance; or to the humid, tangled forests wherein Nature has housed her most varied animal creation and displayed her most gorgeous hues in flower and winged creature. ... Or again we seem to march with that host of intrepid explorers who have pressed onwards through burning deserts and tiger-haunted jungles, or amid fever-stricken swamps and snow-capped precipices, braving all Nature's moods and the treachery of savage man. ... Nor do our eyes range necessarily only over wild man and wild nature in the tropics. We contemplate handsome cities, centres of wealth and civilization, and communities where science, banishing the dreadful fevers and malarias of those delusive spots which have formed the 'White Man's Grave,' has created healthful and habitable homes," C.R. Enock, *The Tropics: Their Resources, People and Future* (New York, 1915), 1-2.

On the other hand, the tropics also provoked fear and insecurity about limits to acclimatization and the increased susceptibility of white colonizers to disease. Long before Americans assumed the role of tropical colonizers, the public had been acutely aware of the health hazards confronted by British troops and colonists in India. After 1898, during the Spanish-American War and the Philippine War, frequent reports about outbreaks of virulent epidemics such as cholera, typhoid, malaria, tuberculosis, leprosy, smallpox, dysentery, and plague increased American perception of the tropics as a hotbed of disease.[16] Highly publicized accounts of the devastating spread of illnesses among U.S. troops startled the public and confirmed longstanding apprehensions about tropical acclimatization.[17] To make matters even worse, three major cholera epidemics swept through the Philippine Islands between 1902 and 1919 and killed more than two hundred thousand Filipinos, Chinese, and Americans.

Despite dramatic advances in tropical medicine in the early years of the twentieth century, and the great emphasis placed by American colonial administration on the improvement of sanitary conditions through hygiene education, systematic vaccinations, and the construction of a health infrastructure in the colonies, the disease ridden images of the overseas possessions persisted in the public mind.[18] Discussion of the overseas empire then, did not focus so much on a

---

[16] For a concise survey of the evolution of those health concerns: Nora Mitchell, *The Indian Hill-Station: Kodaikanal* (Chicago: University of Chicago, Department of Geography, 1972), 13-55.

[17] The U.S. Army was shocked to find out that disease was the main cause of disability and death among colonial troops stationed in the Philippines and the Caribbean. Combat injuries only accounted for 10.6 per cent of disabled soldiers. By 1900/1901 the disease rate among volunteer troops in the Philippine War had reached fifty per cent. The Army Medical Department argued that the climate, with its high humidity and continuous temperatures of well over a hundred degrees, weakened soldiers used to northern environments and made them highly susceptible to tropical diseases. Mary C. Gillett, *The Army Medical Department 1865-1917* (Washington, DC: U.S. Army Historical Series, 1995), 216.

[18] Even the government had serious doubts as to the effectiveness of its measures. The Philippine Commission, America's colonial executive council reported in 1901: "While it may be confidently anticipated that the establishment of a well-organized department of public health in these islands will lead to a general improvement in sanitary conditions, it will doubtless remain true that troops which are forced to campaign in the damp lowlands, or to garrison towns which have sprung up in situations where towns should never have been built, will suffer more or less severely from diarrhea, dysentery, and malaria," U.S. Department of War, *Report of the Philippine Commission, 1901*, 1:63-64; on American public health policies and tropical medicine in the Philippines: Warwick Anderson, "Colonial Pathologies: American Medicine in the Philippines, 1898-1921" (Ph.D. diss., University of Pennsylvania, 1992); Warwick Anderson, "Immunities of Empire: Race, Disease, and the New Tropical Medicine, 1900-1920," *Bulletin of the History of Medicine* 70.1 (1996): 94-118; on American social engineering in the Philippines: Glenn Anthony May, *Social Engineering in the Philippines: The Aims, Execution, and Impact of American Colonial Policy* (Westport,

possibly up-lifting effect of the tropical frontier as on the debilitating impact of the environmental conditions prevalent there.[19]

Doubts about white acclimatization in the tropics also found their way into the substantial outpouring of literature on colonial conditions around the turn-of-the-century. Many handbooks and travel guides, designed for colonial administrators, businessmen, teachers, and missionaries, gave ample space to descriptions of the climatic conditions and informed the readership of the assumed negative impact of the tropics on the nervous systems and organisms of people from colder climates.[20] The muggy and oppressive weather and the grueling heat in particular were considered harmful to men, women and children alike.[21] One of the most popular guides to the Philippines introduced the climate of the islands with the hardly encouraging description:

> The Bible and all history tells us that God made the world, and incidentally, the Philippine Islands must have been thrown in for good measure. There are places in the world that have worse climates, but they can be counted on the fingers of one hand. ... The climate of Manila and of the greater part of the Archipelago is enervating in the extreme ... it is an impossible place for colonization. Five months of the year typhoons are of frequent occurrence, sometimes doing great damage. Earthquakes frequently enliven proceedings. The plague, cholera and all sorts of tropical diseases invariably make their way to Manila....[22]

In addition, reports about American troops engaged in a relentless war against an indigenous independence movement often included evidence of the deterioration of civilized standards. The escalation of violent and brutal behavior and reports about the widespread use of torture against Filipinos were widely interpreted as a

---

CT: Greenwood Press, 1980); Stanley Karnow, *In Our Image: America's Empire in the Philippines* (New York: Ballantine Press, 1989).

[19] One important dimension of this argument, the discourse on manliness and colonial degeneracy is discussed in: Kristin L. Hoganson, *Fighting for American Manhood: How Gender Politics Provoked the Spanish-American and Philippine-American Wars* (New Haven, CT: Yale University Press, 1998), especially 180-199.

[20] Among the most popular were: William S. Bryan, *Our Islands and Their People*, 2 vols. (St. Louis: Thompson Publishing Co., 1899); Trumbull White, *Our New Possessions* (Chicago: Henry Publishing Co., 1901); Thomas Jondrie Vivian and Ruel Perley Smith, *Everything about Our New Possessions: Being a Handy Book on Cuba, Porto Rico, Hawaii and the Philippines* (New York: R.F. Fenno and Co., 1899).

[21] The concern about heat was not new in American discourses on climate. Since the early days of colonial settlement, European colonists in North America had displayed anxieties about climatic conditions: Karen Ordahl Kuppermann, "Fear of Hot Climates in the Anglo-American Colonial Experience," *William and Mary Quarterly* 41.2 (April 1984): 213-240.

[22] Charles Ballentine, *As It Is in The Philippines* (New York: Lewis, Scribner and Co., 1902), 11-13.

breakdown of convention caused by a hostile and debilitating environment.[23] And the substantial number of colonial officials who suffered from nervous breakdowns, or tropical neurasthenia (sometimes called *Philippinitis*) seemed to confirm the destructive influence of the environment on tropical frontier life.[24]

The United States Exceptional? Inter-Imperial Learning on the Tropical Frontier

The colonial experience of the overseas empire not only questioned the beneficial impact of a frontier environment on the nation's development but also complicated the United States' claim to exceptionalism. Turner had argued that the western frontier transformed European settlers into Americans. He interpreted the western "wilderness" as the nation's schoolhouse which stripped the newly arrived Europeans of their old world baggage and replaced it with a truly American character and an exceptional national identity.[25] The experience of the overseas frontier, however, pointed in a different direction. Overwhelmed by the perceived debilitating effect of tropical life, Americans eagerly joined a seasoned and closely knit community of European colonial powers in order to study the responses of their British, Dutch, French, Portuguese, and German neighbors to the challenges of tropical colonization. As Daniel Rodgers, author of an acclaimed study on the transatlantic nature of progressive reform discourses has observed: "From Delhi to London, Leopoldville to Brussels, the imperial world was crisscrossed with appropriations, rivalries, and imitations.... This was a system of exchange in which the Americans were deeply involved."[26]

---

[23] Hoganson, *Fighting for American Manhood*, 180-199; on the Philippine-American War: Brian McAllister Linn, *The Philippine War, 1899-1902* (Lawrence: University of Kansas Press, 2000); Brian McAllister Linn, *The U.S. Army and Counterinsurgency in the Philippine War, 1899-1902* (Chapel Hill: University of North Carolina Press, 1989); Stuart Creighton Miller, *"Benevolent Assimilation": The American Conquest of the Philippines, 1899-1903* (New Haven, CT: Yale University Press, 1982); John M. Gates, *Schoolbooks and Krags: The United States Army in the Philippines, 1898-1902* (Westport, CT: Greenwood Press, 1973).

[24] Warwick Anderson, "The Trespass Speaks: White Masculinity and Colonial Breakdown," in *American Historical Review* 102.5 (December 1997): 1343-1370.

[25] There is a substantial historiography on American exceptionalism. As introduction: Daniel T. Rodgers, "Exceptionalism," in Anthony Molho and Gordon S. Wood, eds., *Imagined Histories: American Historians Interpret the Past* (Princeton: Princeton University Press, 1998), 21-40; Adams and Van Minnen, *Reflections on American Exceptionalism*; Ian Tyrell, "American Exceptionalism in an Age of International History," *American Historical Review* 96 (October 1991): 1031-1055; Ian Tyrell, "Thinking Again about (American) Empire," <www.sscnet.ucla.edu/history/activities/usccpapers/empire.htm> (5 July 2002); Deborah L. Madsen, *American Exceptionalism* (Jackson: University of Mississippi Press, 1998).

[26] Daniel T. Rodgers, "Response" to the Review-Symposium on *Atlantic Crossings*, <http://hsozkult.geschichte.hu-berlin.de/Rezensio/symposiu/rodgers.htm> (8 July 2002).

Americans participated in an intense exchange of ideas with the European powers on colonial rule, health policies, social engineering, law, education, and warfare that belied the claim to frontier-induced exceptionalism made by Turner. The colonial project subverted the idea that the frontier (including the overseas frontier) refined notions of American exceptional identity by distancing the United States from Europe. In the minds of many contemporary observers, Europe and America had never been closer than under the sun of the tropical frontier.

The newcomers to overseas colonization displayed a particular affinity for British modes of colonial rule. By the end of the nineteenth century many Americans still held ambivalent views of Britain's world power status.[27] At the same time, however, a strong sense of admiration and support for the British concept of empire steadily gained ground in the United States. In a surge of Anglo-American rapprochement and Anglo-Saxonism, Americans praised the advantages of British rule, the efficiency of its colonial administration, and its enlightened approach to colonial state building.[28] Consequently, American colonial officials systematically mined the British imperial experience for insights into effective approaches to colonial administration and life on the tropical frontier.

The transfer of ideas and practices of tropical colonization encompassed a wide range of colonial activities, from military organization to health policies to administration to urban planning. Americans sought European, mostly British, know-how to ease the multiple challenges of the new frontier, at the same time as they adapted their own approaches to government and development, derived from the creation of their transcontinental empire, to the new circumstances.

---

[27] Edward P. Crapol, *America for Americans: Economic Nationalism and Anglophobia in the Late Nineteenth Century* (Westport, CT: Greenwood Press, 1973); Edward P. Crapol, "From Anglophobia to Fragile Rapprochement: Anglo-American Relations in the Early Twentieth Century," in Hans-Jürgen Schröder, ed., *Confrontation and Cooperation: Germany and the United States in the Era of World War I, 1900-1924* (Providence, RI: Berg Publishers, 1993), 13-32.

[28] On Anglo-Saxonism and the creation of the American empire: Paul A. Kramer, "Empires, Exceptions, and Anglo-Saxons: Race and Rule between the British and United States Empires, 1880-1910," *Journal of American History* 88.4 (March 2002): 1315-1353; Reginald Horsman, *Race and Manifest Destiny: The Origins of American Racial Anglo-Saxonism* (Cambridge, MA: Harvard University Press, 1981); Anna-Maria Martellone, "In the Name of Anglo-Saxondom, for Empire and for Democracy: The Anglo-American Discourse, 1880-1920," in Adams and Van Minnen, *Reflections on American Exceptionalism*, 83-96; Stuart Anderson, *Race and Rapprochment: Anglo-Saxonism and Anglo-American Relations, 1895-1904* (Rutherford, NJ: Farleigh Dickenson University Press, 1981); on Anglo-American rapprochement: H.C. Allen, *Great Britain and the United States, 1783-1952* (London: Odhams Press, 1954); Kenneth Bourne, *Britain and the Balance of Power in North America, 1815-1908* (London, 1967); Alexander E. Campell, *Great Britain and the United States, 1895-1903* (London: Longmans, 1960); Charles S. Campbell, *Anglo-American Understanding, 1898-1903* (Baltimore: Johns Hopkins University Press, 1957); R.G. Neale, *Britain and American Imperialism, 1898-1900* (Brisbane: University of Queensland Press, 1965); Bradford Perkins, *The Great Rapprochement: England and the United States, 1895-1914* (New York: Atheneum, 1968).

A case in point was the U.S. Army.[29] The military's devastating medical experiences during the Spanish-American War prompted a number of fact-finding commissions into methods and procedures of the tropical acclimatization of British troops. Military surgeons were sent to British tropical colonies to study drill routines, food rations, sanitary measures, equipment, troops rotation, and organization.[30] Their analyses and recommendations sparked extensive professional discussions and had a substantial impact on the structure, outlook, and self-perception of the American empire's new army.[31]

This was also apparent in American discourses on the utility of colonial support troops. Many officers reasoned that indigenous soldiers, used to the climatic and environmental conditions in the tropics, ought to replace troops from the temperate zones which appeared unfit for long-term duty in overseas colonies.[32] To

---

[29] On military lesson-learning: Dennis J. Vetock, *Lessons Learned: A History of US Army Lesson Learning* (Carlisle Barracks, PA: U.S. Army Military History Institute, 1988), especially 26-36.

[30] An important example of such a fact-finding mission was the inspection tour of later Surgeon General Robert Maitland O'Reilly to Jamaica in December 1898. He was sent to the island with directions to prepare recommendations relative to troop hygiene in the tropics with particular attention to occupation, food, and housing. See: John Stewart Kulp's portrait of O'Reilly in *Journal of the Association of Military Surgeons of the United States* 11.3 (September 1902): 199-200. On the impact of that mission, Kulp concludes: "It is not too much to say that a large part of the success attending the American occupation of the tropics is a logical result of these observations."

[31] British approaches to the tropical acclimatization of new troops and their applicability to the American colonial army were discussed at great length: "The Care of Troops in the Tropics," *Journal of the Military Service Institution of the United States* 23.95 (September 1898): 355-359; "Acclimatization in the Tropics," *Journal of the Military Service Institution of the United States* 23.94 (July 1898): 161-163; J. Lane Notter, "On the Sanitary Methods of Dealing with Epidemics," *Journal of the Military Service Institution of the United States* 25.100 (July 1899): 111-124; Charles E. Woodruff, "Hygiene in the Tropics," *Journal of the Military Service Institution of the United States* 25.101 (September 1899): 296-299; "The Problem of the Tropics," *Journal of the Military Service Institution of the United States* 25.102 (November 1899): 446-448; J. Hamilton Stone, "Our Troops in the Tropics-From the Surgeon's Standpoint," *Journal of the Military Service Institution of the United States* 26.105 (May 1900): 358-369; S.J. Rockenbach, "Practice Marches in the Tropics," *Journal of the Military Service Institution of the United States* 41.149 (September/October 1907): 197-201; Charles Edward Belin Flagg, "Military Hygiene in the Tropics," *Journal of the Association of Military Surgeons of the United States* 10.4 (May 1902): 546-571; Charles Francis Mason, "Notes from the Experiences of a Medical Officer in the Tropics," *Journal of the Association of Military Surgeons of the United States* 13.5 (November 1903): 306-314; Henry S.T. Harris, "English, German, and French Conceptions of Colonial Prophylaxis in East Africa," *The Military Surgeon* 20.5 (May 1907): 367-375.

[32] Similar arguments of race, tropical climate and physiological immunity were advanced for the use of African-American troops in the Philippines: Warwick Anderson, "Immunities of Empire: Race, Disease, and the New Tropical Medicine, 1900-1920," *Bulletin of the History of Medicine* 70.1 (1996): 94-118.

contain widespread apprehension about arming large numbers of natives, the American military leadership examined the colonial military policies of the European powers.[33] Americans were particularly pleased with the British approach and applied many features of that system of colonial support troops to the Philippines.[34]

These examples of ideational transfer reflected the U.S. military's strong transatlantic orientation at the turn-of-the-century. The army reforms in the early years of the twentieth century were fueled in part by a close examination of the simultaneous colonial wars in South Africa and the Philippines. Both nation's difficulties in containing native resistance and a strong sense of racial brotherhood resulted in an intensive Anglo-American discourse urging the improvement of the professionalism of the armed forces and reforms necessary to increase their effectiveness in a colonial setting.[35]

On a more general level, this discourse and the shared experience of frontier warfare produced a widely held sense of common destiny beyond national confines

---

[33] Of particular importance was the 1903 inspection tour of General Leonard Wood, military governor of Cuba until 1902 and military governor of the southern Philippines after 1903. He visited British colonies such as Egypt, India, and the Malay Straits for the Department of War and studied British colonial military installations and policies. For information about this inspection tour: Hermann Hagedorn, *Leonard Wood: A Biography* (New York: Harper and Brothers, 1931), 1:393-417; John G. Holme, *The Life of Leonard Wood* (New York: Doubleday, Page, and Co., 1920), 135-152; A.J. Bacevich, *Diplomat in Khaki: Major General Frank Ross McCoy and American Foreign Policy, 1898-1949* (Lawrence: University Press of Kansas, 1989), 21-41.

[34] The *Journal of the Military Service Institution*, for example, devoted its 1901 Seaman essay prize competition to the use of native colonial troops with particular reference to European experiences: Charles D. Rhodes, "The Utilization of Native Troops in our Foreign Possessions," *Journal of the Military Service Institution of the United States* 30 (January 1902): 1-22; for government fact-finding: U.S. Department of War, Adjutant General's Office, Military Information Division, *Colonial Army Systems of the Netherlands, Great Britain, France, Germany, Portugal, Italy, and Belgium* (Washington, DC: Government Printing Office, 1901); on the evolution of colonial support troops in the Philippines: James Richard Woodlard, "The Philippine Scouts: The Development of America's Colonial Army" (Ph.D. diss., Ohio State University 1975); Brian McAllister Linn, "Cerberu's Dilemma: The US Army and Internal Security in the Pacific, 1902-1940," in David Killingray and David Omissi, eds., *Guardians of Empire: The Armed Forces of the Colonial Powers, c. 1700-1964* (Manchester: Manchester University Press, 1999), 114-136; George Y. Coats, "The Philippine Constabulary, 1901-1917" (Ph.D. diss., Ohio State University, 1968).

[35] As one historian has observed: "The weaknesses exposed in the American and British armies in the Spanish-American War and Boer War, produced closer collaboration between the two states on military reform," Ronald J. Barr, *The Progressive Army: US Army Command and Administration, 1870-1914* (New York: St. Martin's Press, 1998), 59; see also: Timothy K. Nenninger, *The Leavenworth Schools and the Old Army: Education, Professionalism, and the Officer Corps of the United States Army, 1881-1918* (Westport, CT: Greenwood Press, 1978).

which left a deep imprint even in popular culture.[36] Not surprisingly, Elbridge Brooks, a famous author of juvenile literature, concluded his popular novel *With Lawton and Roberts* (1900), in which an American boy first volunteers in the Philippine War and then fights for Britain in the Boer War, with the theme of imperial "brotherhood": "... the Stars and Stripes in the Philippines, and the Union Jack in South Africa, are advancing the interests of humanity and civilization...."[37]

Not only the military but also America's colonial administration took many cues from the British experience. The civilian authorities followed a similar strategy and tapped into European approaches to colonial governance. To this end the McKinley and Roosevelt administrations initiated the First Philippine Commission, launched research programs into comparative colonial studies, collaborated with the academic community, and enabled administrators to frequently visit the colonial possessions of the other powers, particularly in South and Southeast Asia.

In December of 1899, Elihu Root, the chief architect of America's colonial policy in the Philippines, wrote to a friend: "The first thing I did after my appointment was to make out a list of a great number of books which cover in detail both the practice and the principles of many forms of colonial government under the English law, and I am giving them all the time I can take from my active duties."[38] The secretary collected a library for reference in his office, mostly with British texts on colonial law and administration and considered the systematic evaluation of the activities of other colonial powers as an essential guide to American decision-making. Secretary Root shared this willingness to learn from the experiences of other colonial powers with virtually all top colonial administrators.[39]

The government also initiated a massive research program through the Library of Congress and a number of government departments to collect all information

---

[36] For the American discourse on the Boer War, most recently: Kramer, "Empires Exceptions, and Anglo-Saxons"; a good starting point for the American perception of British actions in South Africa: Thomas J. Noer, *Briton, Boer, and Yankee: The United States and South Africa, 1870-1914* (Kent: Kent State University Press, 1978); Richard B. Mulanax, *The Boer War in American Politics and Diplomacy* (Lanham, MD: University Press of America, 1994); Stuart E. Knee, "Anglo-American Understanding and the Boer War," *Australian Journal of Politics and History* 30.2 (1984): 196-208; Byron Farewell, "Taking Sides in the Boer War," *American Heritage* 27.3 (1976): 20-25, 92-97; Willard B. Gatewood, "Black Americans and the Boer War, 1899-1902," *South Atlantic Quarterly* 75.2 (1976): 226-244.

[37] Elbridge S. Brooks, *Lawton and Roberts: A Boy's Adventure in the Philippines and the Transvaal* (1900), quoted in Iriye, "Intercultural Relations," 433.

[38] Letter from Root to Samuel L. Parish, 1 December 1899, Elihu Root Papers, Manuscript Division, Library of Congress, Washington, D.C. (hereafter: LC).

[39] See for example the final four-volume report of the Philippine Commission which included much material on the administrative, judicial, social, and military conditions of British rule in India, Burma, Ceylon, the Federated Malay States, and the Straits settlement: U.S. Congress, Senate, *Report of the Philippine Commission to the President*, S. Doc. 138, 56th Cong., 1st sess., 1900.

available on the colonial policies of other nations.[40] The results were impressive. For example, the Department of the Treasury reported on *The Colonial Systems of the World*. Under the directorship of O.P. Austin, the Department's Bureau of Statistics amassed information on the world's 125 colonies, protectorates and dependencies. The widely distributed report (more than ten thousand copies were printed) delivered a comprehensive interpretative framework for the analysis of the "present governmental conditions in the colonies of the world" and enabled Americans to situate their own colonial project within the international context.[41] In conclusion the report emphasized the significance of the British model: "The most acceptable and therefore most successful of the colonial systems are those in which the largest liberty of self-government is given to the people. The British colonial system, which has by far outgrown that of any other nation, gives, wherever practicable, a large degree of self-government to the colonies."[42]

During this period of intense search for colonial models, universities, professional organizations, and scholarly journals placed themselves at the service of empire and helped to chart the nation's course through the analysis of other colonial approaches, most notably through British concepts of colonialism.[43] The nation's universities established courses in comparative colonial administration and

---

[40] The Library of Congress became an initial clearing house for information on other colonial systems and information on America's colonial possessions. On request by Henry Cabot Lodge, chairman of the Senate Committee on the Philippines, it compiled extensive bibliographies on material available to colonial decision-makers. For example: A.P.C. Grifflin, *A List of Books Relating to the Theory of Colonization, Government of Dependencies, Protectorates, and Related Topics* (Washington, DC: Government Printing Office, 1900); A.P.C. Grifflin, *A List of Books Relating to Cuba (with Reference to Collected Works and Periodicals)* (Washington, DC: Government Printing Office, 1898); A.P.C. Grifflin, *A List of Books Relating to Hawaii (with Reference to Collected Works and Periodicals)* (Washington, DC: Government Printing Office, 1898); A.P.C. Grifflin, *A List of Books (with Reference to Periodicals) on the Philippines in the Library of Congress* (Washington, DC: Government Printing Office, 1903); A.P.C. Grifflin, *A List of Books (with Reference to Periodicals) on Porto Rico* (Washington, DC: Government Printing Office, 1901); A.P.C. Grifflin, *A List of Books (with Reference to Periodicals) on Samoa and Guam* (Washington, DC: Government Printing Office, 1901); A.P.C. Grifflin, *A List of Works Relating to the American Occupation of the Philippine Islands, 1898-1903* (Washington, DC: Government Printing Office, 1905).

[41] Department of the Treasury, *Colonial Administration, 1800-1900: Methods of Government and Development Adopted by the Principal Colonizing Nations in Their Control of Tropical and Other Colonies and Dependencies* (Washington, DC: Government Printing Office, 1901), here 1199.

[42] Ibid., 1407.

[43] On the role of academics in the service of empire: Franklin Chew Lun Ng, "Governance of American Empire: American Colonial Administration and Attitudes, 1898-1917" (Ph.D. diss., University of Chicago, 1975); Brian C. Schmidt, *The Political Discourse of Anarchy. A Disciplinary History of International Relations* (Albany: State University of New York Press, 1998), chap. 4.

economy relying heavily on British expertise.[44] But Americans also launched their own research programs. One of the most active proponents of field research in tropical colonies was Alleyne Ireland, the University of Chicago's colonial commissioner. Ireland was a frequent speaker at national and international conferences on colonialism, a prolific writer, and advisor to the government. He was an ardent proponent of transplanting British colonial methods to America's new overseas territories.[45]

In addition to a systematic analysis of international colonial expertise through reports and research projects, U.S. imperial administrators, like U.S. military officials, also relied heavily on visits and inspection tours to the possessions of other colonial powers in Asia. As Paul Kramer has observed: "Soon enough, American colonial officials took their place in a network of imperial policy tours and exchanges with colonial officials from the American Philippines, Dutch Java and the East Indies, and the British Straits Settlements and Federated Malay States."[46]

Visits were not only limited to neighboring colonies but sometimes involved travel halfway around the world. Many of the high-ranking administrators and military governors discussed their concerns with famous British proconsuls such as

---

[44] A number of British authors on colonialism reached fame as standard textbooks and reference works: John R. Seely, *The Expansion of England* (Boston: Roberts Bros., 1898); Charles W. Dilke, *Greater Britain* (New York: Harper and Bros., 1869); Edward Gibbon Wakefield, *A View of the Art of Colonization with Present Reference to the British Empire* (London: J.W. Parker, 1849); Archibald R. Colquhoun, *The Mastery of the Pacific* (New York: Macmillan Co., 1899); highly influential were also works by famous British colonial administrators such as: Evelyn Baring Cromer, *Modern Egypt* (New York: Macmillan Co., 1908); George Nathaniel Curzon, *Lord Curzon in India* (New York: Macmillan Co., 1906).

[45] Ireland's background and career is described in: Chew Lun Ng, "Governance of American Empire," 75-87; for a selection of writings: *Tropical Colonization: An Introduction to the Study of the Subject* (New York: Macmillan, 1899); *The Anglo-Boer Conflict* (Boston: Small, Maynard and Co., 1900); *The Control and Development of Tropical Colonies: Syllabus of a Course of Six Lecture-Studies* (Chicago: University of Chicago Press, 1900); "The Cohesive Elements of British Imperialism," *Outlook* 63 (December 1899): 744-750; "Colonial Policy in the Far East," *Outlook* 79 (25 March 1905): 744-750; "European Experience with Tropical Colonies," *Atlantic Monthly* 82 (December 1898): 729-735; "The Far Eastern Tropics: Studies in Colonial Administration I. Introductory," *Outlook* 72 (22 November 1902): 684-688; "The Far Eastern Tropics: Studies in Colonial Administration II. Hong Kong," *Outlook* 72 (29 November 1902): 741-745; "A Few Facts about the Colonies of the Great Powers," *McClure's Magazine* 14 (February 1900): 334-338; "Growth of the British Colonial Conception," *Atlantic Monthly* 83 (April 1899): 488-498; "India and British Imperialism," *Century Magazine* 105 (November 1922): 147-154; "Studies in Colonial Administration III. British North Borneo," *Outlook* 74 (2 May 1903): 128-132; "Studies in Colonial Administration V. Burma," *Outlook* 75 (25 July 1903): 127-132; "Studies in Colonial Administration VI. The Federated Malay States," *Outlook* 76 (27 February 1904): 502-506; "Studies in Colonial Administration VII. The Straits Settlements," *Outlook* 77 (14 May 1904): 122-126.

[46] Kramer, "Empires, Exceptions, and Anglo-Saxons," 1351.

Lord Cromer, who had represented the empire in Egypt for twenty-eight years, Alfred Milner, who played an important role in Egypt and was later High Commissioner for South Africa, and Sir Harry Johnson, who had administered the Uganda protectorates.[47]

In multiple ways U.S. colonial enterprise was thus profoundly influenced by international and in particular Anglo-American discourses on colonial state-building. The overseas frontier did not foster a unique path of development nor did it complete the separation from Europe, as Turner's analysis of the Americanizing impact of the continental frontier had suggested. In fact, overseas colonial ventures brought Europe and the United States closer together.

The discourse on the colonial project subverted the original frontier thesis in at least two fundamental respects: the perceived health hazards and degenerative effects expected from life in the tropics questioned the environmentalist claim made by Turner and others about the beneficial influence of the frontier experience. Secondly, the emulation of European and particularly British examples in the creation and administration of tropical colonies undermined the claim to an exceptional national development.

Shortly after William Howard Taft arrived in the Philippines to take up the job of top civilian administrator of the colony in 1900, he wrote to a friend that the climate in Manila was much better than he had expected, in fact only slightly different from the hot summer months back home in Cincinnati. All the talk, Taft argued, about the dangers of white acclimatization in the tropics was highly exaggerated. Little did he know at the time that after a while he, his wife, and his children would have to return to the United States for health reasons.[48] His deteriorating health could only be strengthened by frequent visits for rest and relaxation to the city of Baguio in the highlands of northern Luzon, where the American colonial government had taken its cues from the British experience in India, and constructed one of the finest hilltop resorts and seasonal capitals in Asia.[49] Baguio was the colonial urban planner's response to the shared European-American anxiety about tropical degeneracy and other challenges of colonial life. It served as the ultimate architectural symbol of the subversive nature of the overseas frontier.

---

[47] We have for example detailed descriptions of at least five meetings between W. Cameron Forbes, Governor General of the Philippines and Lord Cromer in London. Descriptions are to be found in Forbes' excellent diaries: i.e. Journals of W. Cameron Forbes, 1st Series, vol. 3, January 1909 [there is only one long entry for the month]; 1st Series, vol. 5, 1 June 1912; 1st Series, vol. 5, 17 November 1913; 2nd Series, vol. 1, 17 April 1915, all in Manuscript Division, LC.

[48] Michael Adas describes Taft's reaction in: "Improving on the Civilising Mission? Assumptions of United States Exceptionalism in the Colonisation of the Philippines," *Itinerario: European Journal of Overseas History* 22.4 (1998): 44-66, here 44 and 62.

[49] On Baguio and further literature on the colonial function of the hilltop resorts: Frank Schumacher, "Creating Imperial Urban Spaces: Baguio and the American Empire in the Philippines, 1898-1920," in Christoph Ribbat and Anke Ortlepp, eds., *Taking up Space: New Approaches to American History* (Trier: WVT-Verlag, forthcoming).

CAJUN LOUISIANA:
A "FRENCH" BORDERLAND IN
THE TWENTIETH CENTURY

Robert M. Lewis

Tourist brochures proclaim the Cajuns of southwestern Louisiana to be an ethnic group unique in the United States. In "Acadiana," the area bounded by the Gulf Coast, the Texas border to the west and the Mississippi River to the east, with the city of Lafayette as its center, live a people who have resisted the pressures of modernization and preserved their "French" identity for more than two centuries. The distinguishing characteristics of the culture are promoted as "French" language, "French" music, a "French" cuisine of crawfish, gumbo, rice, *boudin* and beans, and a relaxed attitude to life and leisure—*laisser les bons temps rouler* is the catch-phrase and summons to play. "[T]hese fun-loving people shrugged off their cares in song and dance—a tradition that persists today," one state agency announces. "Cajun Country," the Office of Tourism announces, has "mystic charm," "a land of towering sugar cane, winding bayous, Acadian cottages and crawfish ponds." "If you have any preconceptions, you had best set them aside before you explore these historic towns and cities with vibrant folklife, colorful carefree traditions and their own way of speaking that will make you wonder if you really are in the U.S."[1] "Perhaps the unique 'joie de vivre' attitude of Louisiana's Cajun people is the result of years of suffering ... that allowed them to turn soup into gumbo, the washboard into a musical instrument, and the swamps of Louisiana into a paradise," declares an "authorized" "Virtuoso United States Travel Consultant."[2]

The popular images suggest that southwest Louisiana's "French Triangle" is a borderland that has escaped complete Americanization; it is a region in the South but not wholly of the South. The word "borderland" has several overlapping meanings. It implies a frontier area both of separation and linkage, a zone of cross-cultural interaction, a middle ground where different cultural traditions are blended or mediated or juxtaposed in conflict. While every region has some distinctive attributes that qualify as unique, and all contain subcultures, the encounter between contrasting cultural traditions is characteristic of a borderland, and a primary, if not the primary, source of identity. "Acadiana" has been surrounded by diverse cultural forces. During the nineteenth century, north Louisiana and Texas were dominated by English-speaking migrants; in the cotton-growing Black Belt of the Mississippi Delta were the descendants of African American slaves, the great majority of whom were English-speaking and brought by migrants from the other southern states after the Louisiana Purchase in 1803; New Orleans, with a fifth of the state's population, has always had a multicultural population and as large a proportion of recent

---

[1] *Welcome to Louisiana* (Baton Rouge: State of Louisiana Office of Tourism, n.d. [c. 1990]), 7; Louisiana Office of Tourism, <http://www.cajuntaste.com/Page5.html> (11 October 2003).

[2] Wizardtravel.com, <http://www.unitedstatesvacationguide.com/Louisiana_Overview.html> (11 October 2003).

immigrants as any other Southern city. In the nineteenth century, the boundaries of these cultural zones remained fairly distinct, because contact was limited; after 1900, Acadiana felt the full weight of the forces of modernization. Borders became borderlands.

Are the Louisiana Cajuns unique? Did their distinctive sense of peoplehood survive longer in the Deep South and did their experience differ from other comparable groups elsewhere in the United States? The customary generalization is that ethnicity as a vital force does not survive three generations—faced with nativist prejudice, immigrants preserve the culture of their homeland but their children accommodate and adjust, and their grandchildren assimilate and conform. What remains is "symbolic ethnicity"—expressive, psychologically meaningful, but insubstantial as barrier against pluralistic integration.[3] Did the Acadian diaspora of the 1760s and 1780s retain such deep-felt "French" cultural characteristics that more than a hundred, even two hundred, years later their descendants identified themselves and were identified by others as a people apart? If "Cajun Country" did indeed remain a region separate from the rest of the state, what factors were responsible for that remarkably long-lived sense of group cohesion? Was it awareness of genealogical ancestry and marked by a very high incidence of intermarriage? Did geographical isolation within a morass of swamps and bayous preclude easy contact with the outside world? Did self-sufficient farming and hunting allow them to avoid marketplace conformity? Was it adherence to the Catholic faith in a strongly Protestant state? Did a profound sense of French ethnic heritage keep them separate, both from those of African descent, French- and English-speaking, and from Anglo-Saxon newcomers? Was it loyalty to the French language as the foundation stone of song-style and oral tradition?

This essay considers Acadiana as a borderland from the establishment of racial supremacy in Louisiana in the 1890s to the foundation of CODOFIL, the Council for the Development of French in Louisiana, the primary agency responsible for preserving the French language, in 1968. By the turn of the century, the Supreme Court's decision in *Plessy v. Ferguson* in 1896 had sanctioned the state's legal imposition of "separate but equal" laws that designated public facilities for whites only and excluded Americans of African descent, however light their skin color or diluted their African bloodline. The state legislature attempted to reassure whites that the lengthy political disputes over the rights of citizenship that followed the Civil War and Reconstruction were past. For the next two generations, legally defined caste lines on marriage, schooling, and access to public places created potential unity among whites of different language and ethnic groupings. The Civil Rights Acts of 1964 and 1965 that ended discriminatory practises were one of the factors that forced "French" whites to reconsider and to follow the example of militant African Americans and found CODOFIL as a state-funded agency to foster

---

[3] Herbert J. Gans, "Symbolic Ethnicity: The Future of Ethnic Groups and Cultures in America," in Herbert J. Gans et al., eds., *On the Making of Americans: Essays in Honor of David Riesman* (Philadelphia: University of Pennsylvania Press, 1979), 204.

their distinctive identity.[4] From the 1900s to the 1960s, the Cajuns worried less about federal interference in matters of racial etiquette and much more about the dangers of modernization and "Americanization" that undermined their sense of separate identity.

Ethnogenesis

It has become a truism among scholars of the current generation that ethnicity is "constructed." Immigrants arriving in the United States throughout most of the nineteenth century identified themselves originally by their place of birth or provincial region rather than "nation." The people called by others German or Irish or Italian were divided by religion, folk customs, dialect, class, and political allegiance, and their homogenization was as much a product of new forces of nationalism in the homeland as a defensive consolidation prompted by the hostility of native-born Americans.[5] Although some scholars explore "objective" structural traits, and in particular, what "real" characteristics a group shares in religion, race, ancestry, language, geographical contiguity and economic interests, most sociologists place greater emphasis on perception. What matters in the process of "ethnogenesis" or "ethnicization," they argue, is a sense of peoplehood, and why a group believes it constitutes an "imagined community," with an "invented tradition."[6] Hence, according to one definition, an ethnic group comprises "persons who are perceived by themselves and/or others to have a unique set of cultural and historical commonalities, which may be real or imagined."[7]

Herbert Gans has addressed the paradox of a growing sense of ethnic allegiance and affiliation when most evidence suggests that genuine ethnic traits have faded in modern America. Discrimination in education and employment has declined; intermarriage across ethnic lines has increased; loyalty to traditional religious denominations is less marked; ethnic residential enclaves are less cohesive; ties to the old country are much more tenuous, particularly the use of ancestral languages in everyday communication. And yet respondents indicate a continuing, even a heightened, sense of belonging to their ancestral group. Identification with a sub-group, especially on festive occasions or during rites of passage, fits emotional

---

[4] See Virginia R. Domínguez, *White by Definition: Social Classification in Creole Louisiana* (New Brunswick, NJ: Rutgers University Press, 1986).

[5] Kathleen Neils Conzen, "German-Americans and the Invention of Ethnicity," in Frank Trommler and Joseph McVeigh, eds., *America and the Germans: An Assessment of a Three-Hundred-Year History* (Philadelphia: University of Pennsylvania Press, 1985), 131-147.

[6] Benedict Anderson, *Imagined Communities: Reflections on the Origin and Spread of Nationalism*, rev. ed. (London: Verso, 1991); Eric Hobsbawm and Terence Ranger, eds., *The Invention of Tradition* (Cambridge: Cambridge University Press, 1983); Forum debate, "The Invention of Ethnicity: The Perspective from the U.S.A.," *Journal of American Ethnic History* 12 (Fall 1992): 3-63.

[7] Wilbur Zelinsky, *The Enigma of Ethnicity: Another American Dilemma* (Iowa City: University of Iowa Press, 2001), 44.

and psychological needs perceived by individuals; it is often a matter of personal choice, a symbolic act that serves "an expressive rather than instrumental function."[8]

All the evidence suggests that the present-day Louisiana Cajuns retain an unusually pronounced identification to place and past. Public opinion polls show an expanding sense of Cajun identity among the young.[9] On the surface there are abundant signs of flourishing "cultural tourism." French" folk festivals of music and dance celebrating "French" foodways have increased tenfold since the 1960s. "Cajun" has become a cherished brand name for regional specialities and protected by legislation. Mardi Gras customs have been revived. The newly fashioned "living history" communities of the Village Acadien and Vermilionville showcase "traditional" crafts retailed by commercial sponsors. The Cajun French Music Association, little more than a generation old, hosts an annual award ceremony for recordings that contain at least some French-language lyrics. The acclaimed paintings of Floyd Sonnier dwell nostalgically on the remembered dramas of deportation and travail, while the Acadian Center in St. Martinville erected a commemorative wall in 1998 to recognize the Acadian "Holocaust."[10] But evidence of acculturation is also overwhelming. Most Cajun music has little more than token words of French and few listeners understand them. Supermarkets, fast food outlets, and the mass market have replaced subsistence fishing and farming. Conversational use of the French language has dropped very steadily—fewer than five per cent of teenagers used the "mother tongue" at home in the 1990s—so that most predict that English will be the only living language in the state in 2020.[11] Yet, the more Cajuns resemble other Americans in the ways in which they conduct their lives, the more they cling to the myth of peoplehood.

What explains this apparent contradiction between a continuing loss of genuine French cultural traits and a growing consciousness of "French" identity within the American mainstream? A broader perspective is needed. Although language loss is profound, it is less marked in Louisiana than in other parts of the United States. In the northeast, the great majority of the descendants of European immigrants have no knowledge of their ancestral "mother" language and never use it at home, and these were the offspring of immigrants who came to the United States several generations later than the ancestors of the Cajuns, many more than a century later. The Cajuns also have a remarkably high index of endogamy—most continue to marry other

---

[8] Gans, "Symbolic Ethnicity," 193-220.

[9] Shane K. Bernard, *The Cajuns: Americanization of a People since 1941* (Jackson: University Press of Mississippi, 2003), 145-148; Jacques M. Henry and Carl L. Bankston III, *Blue Collar Bayou: Louisiana Cajuns in the New Economy of Ethnicity* (Westport, CT: Praeger, 2002).

[10] Sara Le Menestrel, *Le voie des Cadiens: Tourisme et identité en Louisiane* (Paris: Belin, 1999); Marjorie R. Esman, "Tourism as Ethnic Preservation: The Cajuns of Louisiana," *Annals of Tourism Research* 11 (1984): 451-467; C. Paige Gutierrez, *Cajun Foodways* (Jackson: University Press of Mississippi, 1992); Henry and Bankston, *Blue Collar Bayou*, 193-205.

[11] Albert Valdman, ed., *French and Creole in Louisiana* (New York: Plenum Press, 1997); Kevin J. Rottet, *Language Shift in the Coastal Marshes of Louisiana* (New York: Peter Lang, 2001).

Cajuns, perhaps because of a "blue-collar" class culture or residential proximity more than genealogical ties.[12] The formation of CODOFIL in 1968 and State assistance for French-language cultural programs is usually taken as the starting-point of Cajun revitalization, but Cajuns had had a pronounced group consciousness long before. History and the remembered past may provide explanations.

The "French" Melting Pot: Acadians and Cajuns

The Cajuns are the product of a fusion of French-language cultures. Louisiana was inhabited by the Spanish and French and their African slaves when it was sold to the United States in 1803. Several thousand refugees, the descendants of the French, mainly from Poitou, who had settled in Canada, in the area of Nova Scotia they called Acadie, arrived in Louisiana between 1765 and 1785 after they had been expelled by the British in 1755. The Acadian settlements they established along the Mississippi and the Atchafalaya and Lafourche rivers then welcomed French settlers, both immigrants from France and some of the French masters, slaves, and free persons of color who had fled to Cuba in 1792 after the revolution in Saint-Domingue, and who subsequently were expelled to New Orleans by the Spanish in 1809-1810.[13]

By the 1880s, this polyglot mix of French-language cultures outside New Orleans was recognized as having a separate identity as "Cajuns." American observers considered the Acadians or 'Cadians a charming but backward peasantry mired in remote swamps in Catholic superstition and idleness; French-speaking writers based in New Orleans seldom mentioned them, except as "acadien" or "'cadien" or occasionally "créole"—"français" they reserved for those born in France—but also in derogatory fashion as lazy and ignorant but hospitable and generous. The "Acadians" lacked a literary tradition but were cited by observers as describing themselves as "les Français," and Anglo-Saxon intruders as "les Américains."[14]

Throughout the nineteenth century, the Cajuns remained insular rather than isolated. Most were small-scale sharecroppers largely self-sufficient but linked to

---

[12] Richard D. Alba, *Ethnic Identity: The Transformation of White America* (New Haven: Yale University Press, 1990), 93-101; Henry and Bankston, *Blue Collar Bayou*, 130-135.

[13] Gwendolyn Midlo Hall, *Africans in Colonial Louisiana: The Development of Afro-Creole Culture in the Eighteenth Century* (Baton Rouge: Louisiana State University Press, 1992); Carl A. Brasseaux, *The Founding of New Acadia: The Beginnings of Acadian Life in Louisiana, 1765-1803* (Baton Rouge: Louisiana State University Press, 1987); Carl A. Brasseaux, *Acadian to Cajun: Transformation of a People, 1803-1877* (Jackson: University Press of Mississippi, 1992); Carl A. Brasseaux and Glenn R. Conrad, eds., *The Road to Louisiana: The Saint-Domingue Refugees, 1792-1809* (Lafayette: Center for Louisiana Studies, University of Southwestern Louisiana, 1992).

[14] Jacques Henry, "From *Acadien* to *Cajun* to *Cadien*: Ethnic Labelization and Construction of Identity," *Journal of American Ethnic History* 17 (Summer 1998): 29-62.

the fringes of market society by navigable waterways. As steamboats replaced sail and pirogue, and Louisiana's four hundred miles of railroad in 1860 expanded to two thousand in 1900 and became part of a transcontinental system, they traded timber, furs, cotton, and rice with greater regularity. In Louisiana under Spanish and French and American rule, the Acadians had embraced slavery, but with the steady advance of American settlers, had moved away from the Mississippi River towards the bayou Teche and were never prominent in the commercial cotton and sugar plantation economy of the delta. Because the port of New Orleans and control of navigation along the Mississippi was the major prize during the Civil War, Acadiana saw little more than skirmishes, but the prolonged conflict, Confederate conscription, and the lengthy process of Reconstruction and Redemption left the entire state impoverished. Northern capitalists investing in railroad construction brought extensive rice cultivation and timber extraction to the southwest in the 1880s but the Cajuns reaped little immediate benefit. By 1900, Cajun communities were amongst the poorest in the nation.[15]

It was in New Orleans that the mixed-race, French-speaking Homer Plessy was party to the landmark legal case of 1896 that sanctioned "Jim Crow" segregation in the state.[16] Separation of the races was never a pressing social or political issue in Acadiana. There were French-speaking mixed-race Creoles of color and the descendants of slaves but, like the Cajuns, most were impoverished sharecroppers and observed a traditional etiquette of separation of the races. Louisiana had one of the least-developed educational systems in the nation—less than a third of those of school age received public instruction in 1900, and a third of the population was unable to read. There was no mandatory school attendance until 1916 and weak enforcement until the 1930s. Because educational provision and public transportation were rudimentary in the small rural hamlets, the key civil rights issues of equal schooling and equal accommodation in railroad carriages had little immediate relevance, and Cajuns acquiesced willingly to the Democratic program of racial domination. Racial divisions were intensified when the Catholic Church gradually introduced segregated parishes between 1915 and 1925 and most French-speaking whites and blacks worshipped apart.[17]

The Americanization movement to assimilate "hyphenated" foreign-born Americans and their children during and after World War I brought further discrimination against minority cultures. Throughout the country, foreign-language instruction in schools lost funding. In Louisiana, the new constitution of 1921

---

[15] Brasseaux, *Acadian to Cajun*; Carl A. Brasseaux, "Four Hundred Years of Acadian Life in North America," *Journal of Popular Culture* 23 (Summer 1989): 8-11; Lawrence E. Estaville, Jr., "Were the Nineteenth-Century Cajuns Geographically Isolated?" *Geoscience and Man* 25 (June 1988): 85-95; Lawrence E. Estaville, Jr., "Changeless Cajuns: Nineteenth-Century Reality or Myth?" *Louisiana History* 28 (1987): 117-140.

[16] See Adam Fairclough, *Race and Democracy: The Civil Rights Struggle in Louisiana* (Athens: University of Georgia Press, 1995).

[17] Virginia R. Domínguez, *White by Definition: Social Classification in Creole Louisiana* (New Brunswick, NJ: Rutgers University Press, 1986); Dolores Egger Labbé, *Jim Crow Comes to Church: The Establishment of Segregated Catholic Parishes in South Louisiana* (Lafayette: University of Southwestern Louisiana, 1971).

confirmed the decision of 1916 and made financial provision for schooling in the English language only. Acadiana had the highest rates of illiteracy in the state and the nation, partly because it was rural and impoverished and partly because of general indifference to education.[18] By the 1920s, there were few examples of written French available: once-flourishing French-language newspapers had declined steadily for two generations, and the last New Orleans daily, *L'Abeille*, ceased publication, even as a bilingual paper, in 1925.

Distance from market forces provided less protection during the twentieth century. Agri-business came relatively late to Louisiana, but between 1930 and 1992 the size of the average farm increased from 58 acres to 306, and the number of independent units dropped from 161,445 to 26,652.[19] Communal practises of harvesting (*ramasserie*) and butchering (*boucherie*), and celebration in *bals de maison* and *veillées*, also declined as tractors replaced the hoe, the horse, and cooperative labor. Some of those displaced from sharecropping and relative self-sufficiency found employment in the booming oil and gas industry, but the Texans who controlled it demanded a working knowledge of English. Only gradually did modern communications reach the southwest. When Huey Long became governor in 1928, there were only 330 miles of paved road in the state, and by doubling the tax on gasoline, he added three thousand miles by 1932. But even the New Deal's rural electrification had little impact: in 1940, only 17 percent of rural homes in Acadiana had electric lighting. Radios were more common—41 percent in rural Lafayette Parish had a radio in 1942—but that too became an agency of acculturation. The most popular radio program of the 1940s was "Cousin Dud" Dudley J. LeBlanc's Sunday hour, yet the astute state senator, conscious of current trends in his constituency, divided his talk into French and English half-hour sections. Music on the radio in the 1930s was increasingly "American." Commercial recordings of Cajun music had begun in 1928 in towns like Ville Platte and Crowley to serve a local market for popular accordion and fiddle dance tunes with French lyrics. Poor farmers were prepared to pay seventy-five cents for two four-minute songs of Joseph and Cleoma Falcon or Amédé Ardoin that they could play repeatedly on a wind-up gramophone at home and preserve dance-hall memories. However, music on the radio by the late 1930s was less often the traditionally inspired "Acadian" songs and increasingly local versions of the popular western-swing string bands performed by the Hackberry Ramblers, often with English lyrics.[20]

Cajuns had relied on myth to preserve their identity. Henry Wadsworth Longfellow's long epic poem *Evangeline* became popular a generation after its publication in English in 1847. The tale of the two lovers Evangeline and Gabriel separated by expulsion from Acadia during the *Grand Dérangement* of 1755 kept memories vivid of the prejudice of the English and English-speaking Louisianians.

---

[18] Bernard, *Americanization*, 18-19.
[19] Henry and Bankston, *Blue Collar Bayou*, 91.
[20] Bernard, *Americanization*, xx-xxi, 20; Barry Jean Ancelet, *Cajun Music: Origins and Development* (Lafayette: University of Southwestern Louisiana Center for Louisiana Studies, 1989).

In the twentieth century, myth creation became more pronounced. Felix Voorhies's *Acadian Reminiscences* (1907) gave the tale local and tangible form in the fictitious Emmeline Labiche and Louis Arceneaux. Evangeline statues, shrines, and parks were created in St. Martinville in the 1920s, with "pilgrimages" to meet Acadian "cousins from the North" in Nova Scotia in 1930, 1936, 1946, 1955, 1963, and 1966. The pioneer was politician Dudley LeBlanc of Abbeville, a highly successful entrepreneur, who had made his fortune promoting his patent medicine Hadacol. It was LeBlanc who wrote the first popular history, in English—*The True History of the Acadians* in 1927, enlarged as *The Acadian Miracle* in 1966—that glorified endurance during and after the expulsion as noble patriotism worthy of true Americans. The Acadians of Nova Scotia had retained a strong sense of tradition, especially of injustice and exile, and contact with them greatly encouraged articulate Cajuns like LeBlanc.[21]

The year of 1955 marked two hundred years since the Acadian deportation. The state appointed an official Acadian Bicentennial Commission whose chairman Thomas J. Arceneaux had been prominent in an elite association, the Société de France-Amérique de la Louisiane Acadienne. The emphasis was on the continuity of "Acadian" tradition, with re-created Acadian costumes, textiles, folksongs, dances and cuisine, and fraternal visits north and south hosted by LeBlanc. Perhaps the highlight was Arceneaux's concoction of a Louisiana Acadian flag. Acadian nationalists in Nova Scotia had devised a fitting symbol in 1884, and Arceneaux adapted that emblem for his state in 1955. With the red, white and blue of France and the United States, he retained the Catholic gold star and *fleur de lys* emblems of French Canada and Quebec, and added a gold tower representing the arms of Castille and the state's Spanish heritage. In 1965 the Louisiana state legislature adopted it as the official flag of "Acadiana." This invented tradition of Acadian bonds fed hopes of solidarity between north and south.

However, even the boosterish *Our Acadian Heritage, Let's Keep It!* pamphlet issued by the state did not disguise a deep sense of failure. There were no French-language versions of the advice literature on cooking and costume. Many of the poems written in celebration expressed frustration and defeatism. One Acadian activist stated the dilemma in the starkest terms—"weep for us who love the past, but hardly find a Cajun!"—and predicted Americanization:

They disappeared from l'Acadie when England's army came,
And now they face a new invader—Progress is its name.

The old traditions of Grandpère are growing hard to keep—
How can a horse and full-topped buggy keep up with a jeep?

It has become almost passé to speak the bayou French;
The pungent smell of fishing has become an oilfield stench.

---

[21] Carl A. Brasseaux, *In Search of Evangeline: Birth and Evolution of the Evangeline Myth* (Thibodaux, LA: Blue Heron Press, 1988).

The young ones—do they care about the weekly fais-do-do?
Mais non! They have a television—or at least a radio!

The good French names—Alcée—Achille—so very few you meet.
The once abounding Jean Pierre's are now plain Jack or Pete.[22]

The main reason for despair was the rapid rate of language loss. In 1900, when more than 85 per cent of the population spoke French as their first language, three-quarters of Cajuns in all but three parishes (St. Martin, Lafayette, and Vermilion) could also speak English.[23] Two generations later, only the very old were likely to be fluent and the everyday language of family interaction was no longer French. When French-language instruction ceased in schools after 1921, anglicization became much more marked. Definitions of language competence vary greatly, but perhaps three-quarters of soldiers from Acadiana serving in World War II could speak French fluently. By the time of the Vietnam War, little more than a third spoke French as their first language. The decline was far more evident in the next generation: only 12 percent of those born between 1966 and 1970 had first-language competence in French, and a mere 8 percent of those born 1971-1975. Surveys found that those who came of age in the 1940s and 1950s had lost confidence and the ability to communicate except in English and that grandparents, rather than parents, were the most likely to speak in French to the children.[24]

The Cajunization of Acadiana

Acadiana, the twenty-two parishes in south Louisiana where the descendants of Acadian exiles were most closely congregated, became an officially designated area, recognized by the state legislature in 1971. It seems that the term was first used by employees of the Acadian Television Corporation in Lafayette in 1963 to define its catchment area.[25] Since the 1920s, the emphasis of cultural nationalists had been on Acadian genealogy and connections with the Nova Scotia "homeland." By the 1950s and 1960s, that campaign had succeeded and local businesses used "Acadian" and "Evangeline" as brand names to establish ties to the locality. However, the narrow

---

[22] Ruth Shaver Means, "Exodus," in *Lyric Louisiana: A Collection of Poems Honoring the Acadian Bicentennial Celebration of 1955. By members of the Louisiana Poetry Society, and the winning poems in the Acadian Bicentennial Contest* (n.p., n.p., 1955), 55.

[23] Lawrence E. Estaville, Jr., "The Louisiana French in 1900," *Journal of Historical Geography* 14 (October 1988): 353.

[24] Bernard, *Americanization*, 66, 83; Rocky Sexton, "Cajun-French Language Maintenance and Shift: A Southwest Louisiana Case Study to 1970," *Journal of American Ethnic History* 19.4 (2000): 22-48; Henry and Bankston, *Blue Collar Bayou*, 159, 174. Estimating the extent of language loss or retention is a very technical field that relies on surveys of actual use more than the vague questions in the decennial censuses. See Valdman, *French and Creole in Louisiana*, and Rottet, *Language Shift*.

[25] <http://www.cajunculture.com/Other/acadiana.htm> (24 March 2004).

genealogical definition of "Acadian" excluded those who could not trace their roots to descendants of the deportation of 1755.

In the 1960s, the word "Cajun" first appeared as a positive indication of identity.[26] For years it had been perceived as a derogatory epithet, a slur denoting low birth and low status; now, it was beginning to be viewed with pride. "Cajun" also was more inclusive and incorporated a broader reference group. It had subsumed other white French identities. Almost all whites who were Louisiana natives of French cultural extraction described themselves as Cajun, even if they had no Acadian roots. Significantly, the ability to speak French was not a necessary qualification.[27]

Neither of the designations "Acadian" or "Cajun" included Louisiana's African American population, irrespective of descent from the slaves of French-speaking planters or their English-speaking successors. Indeed, many African Americans felt excluded by the state's past record in race relations, and after desegregation of college sports, were exceedingly reluctant to be included among the "Ragin' Cajuns" in the University of Southwestern Louisiana's football team. In the 1960s, they called themselves blacks, not Cajuns, or if mixed-race, Creoles of color. However, everyday usage of their Creole French dialect that retained African words, grammar, and inflections fell even more dramatically than that of Cajun French. African Americans of French cultural heritage were left isolated. If they selected race as the more appropriate signifier, then their natural allies were English-speaking African Americans elsewhere in the state.

Conclusion: Towards "French" Louisiana

By the late 1960s, the white inhabitants of southwestern Louisiana had acquired positive attributes of peoplehood as "Cajuns." As a cultural marker, "Acadian" signified ancestral ties and historical associations with Nova Scotia beyond the United States. The "land of the Acadians" of the South, commonly used by cultural nationalists in the 1920s, denoted the borderland, the contested area resisting anglicization. It had negative associations with the past, with forced expulsion two hundred years earlier, with residual loyalties not wholly American. It was a badge of desperation, a rearguard action against complete incorporation. For most of the twentieth century, the steady loss of French-language fluency seemed a premonition of eventual absorption into the voracious Anglo-Saxon maw of assimilation. Geographical isolation, religion, mythology, genealogy and poverty denoted peculiarities but not irreducible differences as market forces lowered barriers. A flag and a label for the territory invented in the 1960s established a border dividing

---

[26] Barry Jean Ancelet, "From Evangeline Hot Sauce to Cajun Ice: Signs of Ethnicity in South Louisiana," http://www.louisianafolklife.org/LT/Articles_Essays/main_misc_hot_sauce.html> (15 October 2003).

[27] Cécyle Trépanier, "The Cajunization of French Louisiana: Forging a Regional Identity," *The Geographical Journal* 157 (July 1991): 161-171; James H. Dormon, *A People Called Cajuns: An Introduction to an Ethnohistory* (Lafayette: Center for Louisiana Studies, University of Southwestern Louisiana, 1983), 71-90.

"Acadians" from the rest of Louisiana but still left the troubling borderland status not completely resolved.

The Acadian connection proved too flimsy to define the boundary against the "Americans" without. "Cajun" was a more inclusive term for those of French cultural descent. In 1956, Revon Reed, an activist from Mamou who wrote the first significant book in Cajun French, defined his ethnicity in terms of consciousness, rather than Acadian ancestry or language fluency—"Ca c'est ça le Cajun qui croit qu'il est un Cajun" ["He's a Cajun who thinks he is one"].[28] CODOFIL's campaign for French language teaching had symbolic rather than real significance: at best, it merely postponed the inevitable decline in conversational fluency, but by injecting a new sense of crisis and militancy, promoted ethnogenesis. The election in 1972 of Edwin Edwards, the first governor of the state of Acadian descent since the 1840s, was recognition of a successful battle for political power. Pride in Cajun music and Cajun foodways had greater facility for integrating cultural minorities. All commentators recognized both as products of French, African, English, Spanish, German, and Native American fusion, as well as mainstream American influences, throughout the nineteenth and twentieth centuries.[29] "Cajun Country" belonged to the present rather than merely the past.

Cajun cultural activism of the 1960s enhanced the status of all whites of French descent, and not merely Acadians, but excluded "Creole" African Americans who were more preoccupied with the struggle for racial justice in the Civil Rights movement. Only myth and an invented past could create cultural unity. Because Cajun French had not been a written language, for a generation, activists tried to find a new phonetic spelling for the adjective, and having toyed with "cadjin," "cadien," and other forms, had to leave the issue unresolved, with two major variants in usage. That lack of definition revealed how self-conscious and deliberate was the effort to reach cultural consensus—and of limited effectiveness.[30]

While "Acadian" and "Cajun" remained positive signifiers of identity, the emphasis in the 1980s and 1990s turned to "French" as the most inclusive term. "French" music encompassed white Cajun and black zydeco strains, French-language lyrics or none.[31] There were now "French" festivals to fit all tastes: an annual Festival International de Louisiane, forging links with the francophone world (although few could comprehend the language); the Congrès Mondiale held every five years for the Acadians north and south; the Francofête of 1999 to celebrate three centuries of French culture in Louisiana; the Louisiana Purchase festival of 2004 to hail progress for all Americans—"the bicentennial of the great American journey of exploration, discovery and cooperation between newcomers and native

---

[28] Revon Reed, *Lache pas la patate: portrait des Acadiens de la Louisiane* (Montreal: Éditions Parti Pris, 1976), 21.
[29] Ann Allen Savoy, ed., *Cajun Music: A Reflection of a People* (Eunice, LA: Bluebird Press, 1985).
[30] Henry, "From 'Acadien' to 'Cajun' to 'Cadien.'"
[31] Robert Lewis, "'L'Acadie Retrouvée': The Re-Making of Cajun Identity in Louisiana, 1968-1994," in Richard H. King and Helen Taylor, eds., *Dixie Debates: Perspectives on Southern Cultures* (London: Pluto Press, 1994), 67-84.

peoples."[32] In all the festivals, the motive force was commerce rather than culture. The Francofête (printed in brochures more often without than with the circumflex accent), held at many locations throughout the state to commemorate Pierre le Moyne's founding of an outpost at the mouth of the Mississippi in 1699, seldom mentioned French art or high culture or France. The emphasis was resolutely commercial, on music and food to sweeten the joys of retail therapy for tourists.

"Acadian" evoked pride in the past but also bitter memories of exile and injustice. "Cajun" was no longer a badge of humiliation. But "French" had a vague mystical charm. For all but a few, French language was no longer a marker of cultural difference, but associations with the past and with the contemporary francophone world established "French" Louisianians as Americans with a difference. "French" Creoles might celebrate links with Africa and the Caribbean, "French" Acadians with Canada, and "French" Cajuns with music and foodways that were distinctive, even from New Orleans. All might embrace a "French" mythical past that linked them to a world without borders as the last best hope to avoid assimilation and acculturation. As "Acadians," they had resisted market forces and modernization; as "Cajuns," they fought for the symbolic preservation of the French language; as "French," they welcomed tourism with a whiff of Old World charm. Affiliation with "French" culture was so deeprooted that during France's quarrel with the United States over the Iraq War, the state legislature of Louisiana, as conservative and patriotic as any region in the country, protested loudly against Congress's call to change the name of French fries to "freedom fries."[33] French is dead; long live the "French."

---

[32] <http://www.explorestlouis.com/pressReleases/2004/SignEvents.htm> (24 March 2004)
[33] In Louisiana, Concerns Over France-Bashing," *Associated Press*, 14 March 2003 <http://www.foxnews.com/story/0,2933,81003,00.html> (24 March 2004).

There was in fact widespread recognition within the United States of the development of social democracy in the United Kingdom and elsewhere in Europe. New Dealers such as Frances Perkins were well cognisant of British welfare, social insurance and labor legislation; and during the 1930s evidence was taken in Washington from European experts. Trans-national openness can also be found in the formulation of agricultural policies. Rexford Tugwell had studied European and Soviet agriculture, and precedents for Shelterbelt were found in the Ukraine.[5] A classic melding of the American progressive tradition and lessons from Europe is found in the TVA. It owed much to Senator George W. Norris of Nebraska, whom Roosevelt called "the very perfect knight of American progressive ideals," but also to Sweden's "Middle Way." Precedents for the subsistence homesteads of the Resettlement Administration are to be found in British Land Settlement policies for returning soldiers at the end of the Great War. Similarly Progressives and New Dealers alike learned from European experience in city planning, public housing and greenbelt suburbs.[6] It was this breaking down of the frontiers of the mind that helped impel the Roosevelt administration into transforming "government into an active instrument of social justice."[7]

Schuster, 1985), 43-44; "Speech to the People's Forum," 3 March 1912, in Basil Rauch, ed., *Franklin D. Roosevelt: Selected Speeches, Messages, Press Conferences, and Letters* (New York: Rinehart and Co., Inc., 1957), 12-16; Nathan Miller, *FDR: An Intimate History* (New York: Doubleday and Company, Inc., 1983), 89-90; Axel R. Schäfer, *American Progressives and German Social Reform, 1875-1920* (Stuttgart: Franz Steiner Verlag, 2000). For reference to "German sanity in the days of Bismarck," see FDR to George H. Earle, 22 December 1933, in Elliot Roosevelt, ed., *FDR: His Personal Letters, 1928-1945* (New York: Duell, Sloan and Pearce, 1950), 1:379.

[5] Frances Perkins, *The Roosevelt I Knew* (New York: Viking Press, 1946), 279-284; George Martin, *Madam Secretary: Frances Perkins* (Boston: Houghton Mifflin Company, 1976), 221-228; Charles McKinley and Robert W. Frase, *Launching Social Security: A Capture-and-Record Account, 1935-1937* (Madison: University of Wisconsin Press, 1970), 20-21, 237-238; Rexford G. Tugwell, *To the Lesser Heights of Morningside* (Philadelphia: University of Pennsylvania Press, 1982); William E. Leuchtenburg, *The FDR Years: On Roosevelt and His Legacy* (New York: Columbia University Press, 1995), 283-305; Paula M. Nelson, *The Prairie Winnows Out Its Own: The West River Country of South Dakota in the Years of Depression and Dust* (Iowa City: University Iowa Press, 1996), 190-191; Donald Worster, *Dust Bowl: The Southern Plains in the 1930s* (New York: Oxford University Press, 1979), 220.

[6] Leuchtenburg, *FDR Years*, 159, 161; W.J. Makin, comp., *Story of Twenty-Five Years* (London: George Newnes Ltd., 1935), 281. The British parliament had devoted considerable time to developing resettlement policies for returning veterans. See *Sailor and Soldier (Gifts for Settlement) Act* of 1916, *Small Holding Colonies Act* of 1916, *Land Settlement (Facilities) Act* of 1919; Joseph L. Arnold, *The New Deal in the Suburbs: A History of the Greenbelt Town Program, 1935-1954* (Columbus: Ohio State University Press, 1971).

[7] William J. vanden Heuvel, "We Have Nothing to Fear But Fear Itself," in Cornelis A. van Minnen, ed., *The Franklin Delano Roosevelt Four Freedoms Awards 2002* (Middelburg: Roosevelt Study Center, 2002), 15. An authoritative and engaging study of the transmission of ideas is Daniel T. Rodgers, *Atlantic Crossings: Social Politics in a Progressive Age* (Cambridge, MA: Harvard University Press, 1998).

An essential ingredient of this was leadership. There was in the New Deal always administrative uncertainty that sometimes bordered on confusion. There were always ambiguities orchestrated by political challenge from both left and right; but equally there was also clarity of conscience and purpose. FDR often spoke of planning, and claimed in July 1933 that the spate of legislation in the early New Deal represented not "just a collection of haphazard schemes but rather the ordered component parts of a connected and logical whole." Many critics have emphasized the apparently unreconcilable elements within the federal programs (which was certainly so according to many blue-prints for socio-economic change), but FDR was aware of and confronted some of these in that same July Fireside Chat, underlining that his policies represented merely the "foundation stones" for recovery in the context of a "rounded leadership by the Federal Government."[8] It was this leadership that made the 1930s *the* defining period of the twentieth century in American history, one with which historians must continue to engage, and of which to take note.

It was a leadership that accepted the challenges presented by the closing of the old western frontier. Roosevelt's New Frontier, that antedated John F. Kennedy's by a generation demanded new skills to master the environment. In a radio address to the Young Democratic Clubs of America in 1935 Roosevelt insisted that, with the old frontier occupied, it had to be realized that "science and invention and economic revolution had opened up a new frontier—one not based on geography but on the resourcefulness of men and women applied to the old frontier." New thinking was required both with regard to the economy and to the political system itself.[9]

There had always been a frontier of settlement since the first European incursions into North America, and the experience of this frontier had always contributed to the American's sense of self. When, following the 1890 census, the superintendent declared that the frontier as an area of free land was closed, Frederick Jackson Turner codified an historic experience and made it the determinant of an American exceptionalism.[10] As such his thesis came to be torn apart but, as with most myths that fall from grace and become heresies, there was some truth to his analysis. There *had* been a moving frontier of settlement and opportunity. There *were* successive waves of migrants into the borderlands of the country, just as there had been a great diaspora into the United States from Europe and Asia. Individualism *and* a sense of common interest *were,* in the borderlands of the United

---

[8] "Radio Address on the Recovery Program," 24 July 1933, in Rauch, *Selected Speeches*, 107-115.

[9] David K. Adams, "Roosevelt and Kennedy," *Bulletin of the British Association for American Studies* 7 (December 1963): 29-39.

[10] Frederick Jackson Turner, "The Significance of the Frontier in American History," *Annual Report of the American Historical Association, 1893* (Washington, DC: American Historical Association, 1894), 199-227. An essential characteristic of the frontier experience has been what George M. Pierson has called the M-Factor in American History, *The Moving American* (New York: Alfred A. Knopf, 1973), 229-257. This mobility has been variously explored in Cornelis A. van Minnen and Sylvia L. Hilton, eds., *Nation on the Move: Mobility in U.S. History* (Amsterdam: VU University Press, 2002).

States, equal characteristics of frontier life; and in the struggles of sodbuster and rancher alike against climate, geography and the vested interests of speculative corporations, there had developed what Roosevelt recognized to be a desire for political leadership that transcended localism. The common interest lay in the articulation of policies to enshrine common goals within a system of democratic government. The nature of this democracy came to be an issue particularly when Roosevelt tried to reconstruct the Democratic Party as a liberal party in 1938,[11] and when the Executive Re-organization Act of 1939 institutionalized the trend towards presidential power that had been explicit in much of the legislation of the hundred days.[12]

The debate about New Deal liberalism has become scholastic in its complexity, but its essence is quite simply contained in the title given by Roosevelt and Rosenman to the 1938 volume of the *Public Papers*, "The Continuing Struggle for Liberalism" and in FDR's introduction to that volume. Reviewing his record he reaffirmed that flexibility was necessary so that government could "meet new social problems with new social controls—to insure to the average person the right to his own economic and political, life, liberty, and the pursuit of happiness. That theory of the role of government was expressed by Abraham Lincoln when he said, 'the legitimate object of government is to do for a community of people whatever they need to have done, but cannot do at all, or cannot do so well, for themselves in their separate and individual capacities.'" Roosevelt accepted that proposed policies might not be perfect, but the liberal "is willing to start with something less than perfect in this imperfect world.[13] He conceived of policy not as a pre-determined program but as process and, as he wrote to a correspondent in 1932, "Ideals do not change, but methods do change with every generation and world circumstances."[14] This remained true to the end. One did what one had to do in order to confront immediate problems in the context of objectives already and continuously defined. This may indeed be the "pragmatic liberalism" that Robert Eden has so systematically analyzed in his admirable exposition of FDR's Commonwealth Club

---

[11] David K. Adams, "The New Deal and the Vital Center: A Continuing Struggle for Liberalism," in Herbert D. Rosenbaum and Elizabeth Bartelme, eds., *Franklin D. Roosevelt: The Man, The Myth, The Era, 1882-1945* (New York: Greenwood Press, 1987), 103-117. Robert Harrison traces the rise and fall of liberal reform against the development of an administrative state in *State and Society in Twentieth Century America* (London and New York: Longman, 1997).

[12] Louis Brownlow, *A Passion for Anonymity* (Chicago: University of Chicago Press, 1958); Richard Polenberg, *Reorganizing Roosevelt's Government: The Controversy over Executive Reorganization* (Cambridge, MA: Harvard University Press, 1966).

[13] Samuel I. Rosenman, comp., *The Public Papers and Addresses of Franklin D. Roosevelt*, 1938 volume, *The Continuing Struggle for Liberalism* (New York: Macmillan and Co., Limited, 1941), xxix–xxx.

[14] "Policy as process" a phrase used by Eric Larrabee to describe FDR's foreign policy, *Commander in Chief: Franklin D. Roosevelt, His Lieutenants, and Their War* (New York: Harper and Row, 1987), 61, is equally applicable to domestic affairs. For the 1932 letter, see Frank Freidel, *Franklin D. Roosevelt: The Triumph* (Boston: Little Brown and Company, 1956), 253.

Speech of 23 September 1933, and the "programmatic liberalism" discussed by Sidney Milkis in his important study, *The President and the Parties*.[15]

The way forward was always through partnership, and "insistence," in the words of the First Inaugural, "upon the interdependence of the various elements in and parts of the United States—a recognition of the old and permanently important manifestation of the American spirit of the pioneer."[16] The way forward was to be encapsulated in David Lilienthal's dicta about TVA, that combined central direction with both local, grass roots responsibility, and cooperation with state and local authorities.[17] This was an established American tradition. It can be traced from the early twentieth century, for example, in the Department of Agriculture's support for the development of rural roads. Such programs "pulled the states out of the mud."[18] There were similar precedents for many of the New Deal's initiatives. Shelterbelt, sometimes thought of as just a fad of the tree-loving squire of Hyde Park, can be traced back not just to the Ukraine but to Secretary of Agriculture Morton's advocacy in the 1890s of tree planting on the plains, and in the experience gained by the Forest Service.[19] Emphasis upon partnership, between a national government that accepted the responsibilities of leadership, and state governments, local communities and interest groups all of which had legitimate concerns, is characteristic of the defining policies of the 1930s. Executive leadership, within an established if not universally accepted tradition, always subject to re-balancing, made the New Deal.

It was the re-balancing that was to cause problems with the United States Supreme Court;[20] but in the interim, executive prerogatives, confirmed to the president *by* the congress, enabled swift action in a situation akin to war that might

---

[15] Robert Eden, "On the Origins of the Regime of Pragmatic Liberalism: John Dewey, Adolf A. Berle, and FDR's Commonwealth Club Address of 1932," in *Studies in American Political Development* 7.1 (1993): 74-150; Sidney M. Milkis, *The President and the Parties: The Transformation of the American Party System Since the New Deal* (New York: Oxford University Press, 1993).

[16] Rosenman, *Public Papers of FDR*, 1933 volume, *The Year of Crisis* (New York: Random House, 1938), 14.

[17] David E. Lilienthal, *TVA: Democracy on the March* (New York: Harper and Brothers, 1944), 111-123.

[18] U.S. Department of Agriculture, *Century of Service* (Washington, DC: Government Printing Office, 1963), 55; President's Research Committee, *Recent Social Trends in the United States* (New York: McGraw-Hill Book Company, Inc., 1933), 2:1297-1298.

[19] *Century of Service*, 33-36; Wilmon H. Droze, "The New Deal's Shelterbelt Project 1934-1942," in Wilmon H. Droze, George Wolfskill, and William E. Leuchtenburg, eds., *Essays on the New Deal: The Walter Prescott Webb Memorial Lectures* (Austin: University of Texas Press, 1969), 23-48; Edgar B. Nixon, ed., *Franklin D. Roosevelt and Conservation, 1911-1945*, 2 vols. (Hyde Park, NY: Franklin D. Roosevelt Library, 1957) is a rich source of information on FDR's personal involvement. See also memorandum on shelterbelt by Earl W. Tinker, 15 August 1936, in Nixon, *FDR and Conservation*, 1:547-549.

[20] In a number of cases the Supreme Court found an unconstitutional delegation of legislative power by the Congress to the executive. See *A.L.A. Schechter Poultry Corporation v. United States*, 295 US. 495.

otherwise have been delayed and inhibited by a more rigid interpretation of the checks and balances of the constitution and by the slowness of established bureaucracies. The setting up of new agencies helped to secure immediate mobilization of resources in the counter-attack on the ravages of the depression; but at the same time Roosevelt relied on the great departments of state most directly relevant to the domestic crisis, and also enlisted Commerce, the Treasury and War.

To Agriculture Roosevelt appointed Henry Wallace, son of a former secretary of Agriculture in the 1920s, and himself a well-regarded plant geneticist and agricultural economist. To Interior he nominated Harold Ickes, a progressive Republican from Chicago. To Labor came Frances Perkins, an experienced social worker, campaigner for the rights of working people, and Roosevelt's industrial commissioner for the state of New York. These departments were the spearhead for the attack on the depression.

Agriculture had been established in 1862, the year also of the Morrill Act that granted parts of the public lands to support colleges for the agricultural and mechanical arts.[21] The department worked closely with the "Aggies," gathered and distributed agricultural statistics, engaged in soil analysis and the development of improved plants, and made available public information over a wide spectrum. It gained cabinet status in 1889 and was one of the most invasive of all federal departments, particularly through its national network of country agents.[22] Its primary concern became the development of more scientific agricultural practices to control and rectify the traditional rape of the land: "Because the USDA was the sturdiest, strongest structure in government when Roosevelt first took office, it was the place where ambitious planners like Tugwell—who knew he needed a bureaucracy in order to change the world—sought to be. That said, the USDA's only problem, through the Hoover Administration, was that all it knew how to do was to help, advise, and lobby on behalf of farmers who kept producing surpluses that buried them."[23] Raising farm income by destroying crops and taking land out of production represented radical policies which were difficult for many to understand.

The Interior Department was established in 1849 and embraced a number of federal bureaus: the Census, Indian Affairs, the Land Office, later adding the National Parks Service. There was scope for overlapping and conflicting jurisdiction with Agriculture, particularly in the west, and for competition rather than cooperation between the two departments.[24] This became clear in the Hundred Days,

---

[21] USDA, *Century of Service*, 415. Murray R. Benedict, *Farm Policies of the United States, 1790-1950* (New York: Twentieth Century Fund, 1953), 83-84.

[22] USDA, *Century of Service*, 63-88.

[23] "USDA had excellent field staffs, excellent regional staffs, excellent central staffs, excellent reporting and record keeping." Michael Lesy, *Long Time Coming: A Photographic Portrait of America, 1935-1943* (New York: W.W. Norton and Company, 2002), 9-10.

[24] For the Department of the Interior, see <http://www.doi.gov/faq/history.html>. The Forest Service and the National Parks Service represented different constituencies and often had conflicting interests. For insight into such rivalries, and for FDR's personal commitment to conservation, see Irving Brant, *Adventures in Conservation with Franklin D. Roosevelt* (Flagstaff, AZ: Northland Publishing, 1988).

when the spate of relief, recovery and reform legislation challenged the resources of all cabinet departments, and the creation of new executive agencies aroused understandable bureaucratic sensitivities. These were some of the jurisdictional frontiers that had to be crossed or redefined.

The Emergency Relief Act of 31 March 1933 established an agency for Emergency Conservation Work that soon became known as the Civilian Conservation Corps. Agriculture, Interior, Labor and War were all immediately involved. As noted earlier, there were both national and international precedents, as in so much of the New Deal. Both TR and FDR had long been associated with the domestic conservation movements, a major concern for progressives. Transnationally there were conservation projects for the unemployed in Austria, Bulgaria, Denmark, Germany, the Netherlands and Norway.[25] War and Interior were specifically designated in the act establishing the TVA (May 1933), and most federal departments and agencies featured in the omnibus National Industrial Recovery Act of 16 June. The creation of the Farm Credit Administration in March by executive decree received congressional authorization by the Farm Credit Act on 16 June, in a tidy-up at the end of the Hundred Days. An early example of departmental in-fighting came over the control of soil erosion. This had long been a concern of Agriculture; but partly because of the funding requirements of public works legislation, and the role of Harold Ickes as public works administrator, a Soil Erosion Service was established in Interior in September 1933, and the "old curmudgeon" was keen to keep that which he held against the claims of Agriculture. Ickes and Wallace discussed possible re-organization, with the transfer of roads from Agriculture to Interior, and reclamation, lands and erosion control to Agriculture. However Ickes firmly believed that all "conservation activities ought to be grouped in the Interior Department ... which is the natural home for such activities."[26] After intense negotiation over almost two years he lost this one. In 1935 the Soil Erosion Service was transferred to Agriculture, apparently by decision of the president, at a time when congressional hearings were under way to make Soil Erosion a permanent division of Interior, and when Harold Ickes was on vacation in Florida! Tensions continued to reverberate over this at least until 1939.[27]

This particular decision may have been "Rooseveltian," but he was well aware, despite many of the accusations frequently made against him, of the need for greater coherence in the administration and allocation of responsibilities for federal programs. It has been well observed that "there was little administrative precedent for what the Roosevelt Administration was trying to do. There was neither a corpus of wisdom nor a reserve of experienced personnel ready to direct this effort. Neither

---

[25] Leslie Alexander Lacy, *The Soil Soldiers: The Civilian Conservation Corps in the Great Depression* (Radnor, PA: Chilton Book Company, 1976), 17-18; Benedict, *Farm Policies*, 317-319; John A. Salmond, *The Civil Conservation Corps and the New Deal, 1933-1942* (Durham, NC: Duke University Press, 1965).

[26] USDA, *Century of Service*, 138, 192-193; Harold L. Ickes, *The Secret Diary of Harold L. Ickes*, vol. 1, *The First Thousand Days, 1933-1936* (New York: Simon and Schuster, 1953), 250.

[27] Ickes, *First Thousand Days*, 327, 339, 343, 398; Ickes, *Secret Diary*, vol. 2, *The Inside Struggle, 1936-1939* (New York: Simon and Schuster, 1954), 40-41, 566.

was there administrative machinery for a massive and far-reaching program."[28] An attempt to bring about coherence was the establishment in July 1933 of an Executive Council. This basically an enlarged cabinet, incorporating the heads of the new executive agencies. It proved cumbersome. A new National Emergency Council (NEC) was created by executive order in November 1933 with a core membership of only nine. NEC was greeted on all sides with enthusiasm as a much-needed planning agency that would bring cohesion and clarity to the New Deal administration. But Ickes saw NEC not just as a forum for mutual understanding but rather as an instrument for personal control by the president.[29]

The president presided at the regular meetings of the Council which received reports from, among others, the state directors of relief agencies. Roosevelt displayed an informed and perceptive understanding of the issues under discussion. At the Council's inaugural meeting on 19 December 1933 he had clearly read and absorbed the reports sent by Lorena Hickok to Harry Hopkins. Hickok had been sent off by Hopkins in July 1933 to cross the country reporting on conditions. Her mandate was "to look things over. I don't want statistics from you. I don't want the social worker angle. I just want your own reaction, as an ordinary citizen. Go talk … with those who are on relief and those who aren't. And when you talk with them don't ever forget that but for the grace of God, you, I, any of our friends might be in their shoes. Tell me what you see and hear. All of it. Don't ever pull your punches."[30] Her reports from the Dakotas in October/November 1933 are couched in the words used by Roosevelt at the NEC. In an apparent direct paraphrase of Hickok he described the new Democratic governor of South Dakota, Tom Berry, as a "darned good fellow" and concluded that though relief was terribly needed, "their machinery is clicking and everything is going fine."[31] But in reality it was not fine; conditions were not fine throughout the American farmland that "was the equivalent

---

[28] Lester G. Seligman and Elmer E. Cornwell, Jr., eds., *New Deal Mosaic: Roosevelt Confers with His National Emergency Council* (Eugene: University of Oregon Press, 1965), xiv.

[29] Seligman and Cornwell, *New Deal Mosaic*, xv; Ickes, *First Thousand Days*, 242-243. On this occasion in December 1934 Ickes was jealous of Donald Richberg whom he saw acting as "the fair-haired boy of the Administration." For a sensible discussion of Roosevelt and the NEC, see A.J. Wann, *The President as Chief Administrator: A Study of Franklin D. Roosevelt* (Washington, DC: Public Affairs Press, 1968), 50-71. Another instrument for coherent management was the National Planning Board established under title II of the NIRA. This became the National Resources Committee (1935-1939) and the National Resource Planning Board (1939-1943). See Marion Clawson, *New Deal Planning: The National Resources Planning Board* (Baltimore, MD: Johns Hopkins University Press, 1981).

[30] Richard Lowitt and Maureen Beasley, eds., *One Third of a Nation: Lorena Hickok Reports on the Great Depression* (Urbana: University of Illinois Press, 1981), ix-x.

[31] Seligman and Cornwell, *New Deal Mosaic*, 13-14; Lowitt and Beasley, *One Third of a Nation*, 85-88. Democrats swept the state in 1932, see Alan L. Clem, *Prairie State Politics: Popular Democracy in South Dakota* (Washington, DC: Public Affairs Press, 1967), 36.

of what would later be called a Third World nation."[32] Conditions in South Dakota were dire.

* * *

From its admission in 1889 there had always been two distinct parts to the state: the counties to the east and those to the west of the Missouri. The western section, containing the tribal lands of the Oglala and other tribes of the Teton Sioux, embraced some of the largest of the state's nine Indian Reservations, particularly Pine Ridge and Rosebud, Cheyenne River and Standing Rock. They were witness to the poverty of the tablelands that rose from the great river on an inclined plane to the Black Hills and the Rocky Mountains. Low precipitation, extreme temperatures and high winds always made arable farming a gamble and there was a distinct pattern of depression and revival.[33] It sometimes seemed that the region was only fertile in one respect: farmers protest movements, the Grange, the Farmers' Alliances, the Populists and, in the twentieth century, the Farmer-Labor Party and the Farmers' Holiday Association.[34] Lorena Hickok, who had spent her early teens in Milbank, Summit and Bowdle as a household drudge rather than a child, wrote on her return in 1933 that "It is the 'Siberia' of the United States. A more hopeless place I never saw."[35] This interior part of the country still bestrode a frontier, but it was a frontier of deprivation and desperation rather than of opportunity. There was a superficial promise to these dour lands but they so often betrayed their own enticements. During the drought of the early 1890s, 18,000 prairie schooners fled the neighboring state of Nebraska in 1891 alone, and South Dakota shared in the misery.[36]

This was a borderland of little hope, despite the resilience and faith of its inhabitants. Roads, such as there were, were either muddy or deeply rutted. The railroads tended to avoid the area because of the Indian lands, low settlement and the cost of bridging the Missouri. Despite the discovery of gold in the Black Hills as early as 1874 it was not until 1907 that the Milwaukee Rail Road crossed into the west country at Mobridge. The transcontinentals either followed routes through North Dakota or the traditional pathways of migration to the south along the Platte River.[37] The first transcontinental motor road from New York to San Francisco, the Lincoln Highway planned from 1912, was to follow this same route. There were

---

[32] Lesy, *Long Time Coming*, 10.
[33] Herbert S. Schell, *History of South Dakota*, 3rd ed. (Lincoln: University of Nebraska Press, 1975); Federal Writers Project of the Works Progress Administration, *South Dakota*, 2nd ed. (New York: Hastings House, 1952); Benedict, *Farm Policies*, 94-111.
[34] John L. Shover, *Cornbelt Rebellion: The Farmers' Holiday Association* (Urbana: University of Illinois Press, 1965).
[35] Doris Faber, *The Life of Lorena Hickok: E.R.'s Friend* (New York: William Morrow and Company, Inc. 1980), 13-39; Lowitt and Beasley, *One Third of a Nation*, 83-84.
[36] Federal Writers Project of the Works Progress Administration, *Nebraska: A Guide to the Cornhusker State* (New York: Hastings House, 1939), 74.
[37] John F. Stover, *American Railroads* (Chicago: University of Chicago Press, 1961); WPA Guide, *South Dakota*, 66-69.

some highway improvements consequent upon the federal highway acts of 1916 and 1921, but until the 1920s there were no road bridges between the eastern and western parts of the state, and the first hard topped federal highway (US 14) was not completed across South Dakota until 1938. Improved communications did something to open up tourism to the Badlands and the Black Hills, but the economic benefits were only modest. Low wage employment in the isolated clusters of gas stations, motor courts and diners, almost surreally planted as moments of transition on the bare landscapes, made small although important impact on the local economy.[38]

The new century had seen increased immigration of settlers into South Dakota, encouraged by the Homestead Act of 1909 that raised the acreage per claim from 160 to 320, provided that states acknowledged that they were "dry."[39] But then the great drought of 1910-1911 was catastrophic, with some counties losing half their population.[40] Farming prospered during the Great War but afterwards, when prices collapsed, land values fell and "the hard times of the early twenties set the tone for the remainder of the decade and for the even harder times to come in the thirties." The average value of west river farms dropped by 42 percent between 1920 and 1925, and by another 35 percent between 1925 and 1930.[41] Tax revenues fell, with consequent pressure on essential road maintenance and school provision. Tractors and trucks came to the region but farm work was desperate labor, only somewhat relieved by the threshing rigs at harvest; hygiene and health were poor, with malnutrition making even the daily haulage of essential water a debilitating task. In 1930 and 1931 further drought and a plague of locusts piled Pelian upon Ossa; state and local organizations did what they could but resources were inadequate. In 1929 the value of agricultural production in South Dakota in terms of cash income was $17 million. In 1932 it was $6 million.[42]

---

[38] Although the continent was first crossed by automobile in 1903 the trip took sixty-five days. "Most of the roads across the nation were just plain dirt. A rural road could be defined as the space left between fencerows that a farmer wasn't allowed to plow and plant. The term was 'natural road,' implying that nothing had ever been done to improve the thing, and each car and wagon that passed did its share to deepen the rut." Most of the roads were "phantom trails of mud," and did not go anywhere. Emily Post decided in 1915 to drive from New York City to California. She asked a friend for the best road and was told the Union Pacific. As for motor, as opposed to rail, roads, there were none. Military requirements and federal aid did allow completion of the Lincoln Highway by the late 1930s. Drake Hokanson, *The Lincoln Highway: Main Street Across America* (Iowa City: University of Iowa Press, 1988), xvi, 7-13, 83-85, 93; WPA Guide, *South Dakota*, 43, 45, 68-69, Nelson, *The Prairie*, 92-115. For the struggles to attract tourists, see Shebby Lee, "Travelling through the Sunshine State: The Growth of Tourism in South Dakota, 1914-1939," *South Dakota History* 19.2 (Fall 1989): 194-223.

[39] Nelson, *The Prairie*, xviii.

[40] Ibid.; xxii-xxiii; Schell, *History of South Dakota*, 348-349.

[41] Nelson, *The Prairie*, 5, 7, 12-13; Schell, *History of South Dakota*, 351-352.

[42] Schell, *History of South Dakota*, 283. For the vital role played by farm women, see Dorothy Schweider, "South Dakota Farm Women and the Great Depression," *Journal of the West* 24.4 (October 1985): 6-18.

In this desperate situation, desperate measures were proposed by desperate men. The Farmers' Holiday Association was organized. In South Dakota in 1932, it supported direct action to prevent foreclosure of farms, and also a farmers' strike to influence the state, regional and national authorities.[43] When Lorena Hickok visited the area around Aberdeen in early November 1933, a strike was in operation. She felt that the farmers *believed* that the president would help them although they were hostile to the officials who were trying to enforce the detailed requirements of federal legislation that had to be met before relief for crop and cattle controls could be paid.[44] In a letter to Eleanor Roosevelt from Winner, South Dakota she reported that she had spent much of the day on the Rosebud Reservation that had been opened up for settlement when she was a child: "it used to be grand grazing country, and it probably never should have been used for anything else." But New Deal programs were beginning to be felt and she talked with a farmer whose loans were coming though. He told her that he had always been a Republican but "I've got to hand it to this fellow Roosevelt. He's really trying to help us."[45] She wrote again to Mrs. Roosevelt from Huron, South Dakota, after driving through the grasshopper area; "miles of fields that look as if they had just been plowed. They haven't been. What happened was that the grasshoppers simply cleaned them off—right down to the earth, even eating the roots. And there they lie, great black patches on the landscape, completely bare ... people were afraid to hang their washing out. They even ate the clothes off the lines." That same day she encountered a dust storm: "We were being whirled into space in a vast impenetrable cloud of brown dust."[46] A week later she reported to Hopkins: "I think I'd be afraid too, were I a South Dakota farmer. The whole darned state apparently is drying up and blowing away."[47]

---

[43] Shover, *Cornbelt Rebellion*; Schell, *History of South Dakota*, 284-288; Michael W. Schuyler, *The Dread of Plenty: Agricultural Relief Activities of the Federal Government in the Middle West, 1933-1939* (Manhattan, KS: Sunflower University Press, 1989), 14-17; Arthur E. Burns and Edward A. Williams, *Federal Work, Security, and Relief Programs* (Washington, DC: Government Printing Office, 1941).

[44] Lowitt and Beasley, *One Third of a Nation*, 76-82. For details of agricultural policies, see Edwin G. Nourse, Joseph S. Davis, and John D. Black, *Three Years of the Agricultural Adjustment Administration* (Washington, DC: Brookings Institutions, 1937). In *The New Deal and the States, Federalism in Transition* (Princeton, NJ: Princeton University Press, 1969), James T. Patterson discusses how problems of implementation were frequently enhanced by Republican state and local officials.

[45] Lowitt and Beasley, *One Third of a Nation*, 88-90. For all federal policies concerning rural America, see Theodore Saloutos, *The American Farmer and the New Deal* (Ames: Iowa State University Press, 1928); for general applications in the West, see Richard Lowitt, *The New Deal in the West* (Bloomington: Indiana University Press, 1984).

[46] Lowitt and Beasley, *One Third of a Nation*, 90-92; "The US Dust Bowl," *Life Magazine*, 21 June 1937, 60-65; Stuart Chase's passion can be experienced in *Rich Land, Poor Land: A Study of Waste in the Natural Resources of America* (New York: Whittlesey House, 1936).

[47] Lowitt and Beasley, *One Third of a Nation*, 93; for a quite iconoclastic contemporary view, see James Rorty, "Drought and Planning," in *Where Life is Better: An Unsentimental American Journey* (New York: John Day, 1936), 211-215. For the effects of dust on livestock, see Michael Johnston Grant, *Down and Out on the Family*

The consequences of the destruction of the natural environment through use of inappropriate farming techniques were well understood in Washington. When a Harvard geologist tried to explain the droughts in terms of a geological cycle, Roosevelt was quite sure that in plowing up land that had never been plowed before "we have been using land for the wrong purpose. Instead of using it for pasture, we are using it for wheat."[48] This is why New Deal agricultural legislation, from the first Triple A to the Soil Conservation and Domestic Allotment Act of 1936 and the second Triple A of 1938, contained "set aside" and soil conservation provisions. It also underlines the thinking behind the Taylor Grazing Act of 1934, an often forgotten act whose purpose was to prevent over grazing and soil depletion in the remaining public lands. It also planned to take privately owned sub-marginal land out of production, with a first year target of seventy-five million acres. The Taylor Act has been judged "the most significant action with respect to lands of this class that has been taken since the public domain was established."[49] A National Grazing Division was set up in the Department of the Interior, and in South Dakota were located a number of National Grasslands from which the state benefited, as it did from the wide variety of federal programs. Even on her first tour for Hopkins, Hickok saw improvements under FERA, and believed that there was considerable potential under the Civil Works Administration during the critical winter of 1933-1934, although she added a poignant aside that the road improvement schemes were slowed down by the weakness of the near starved horses of the near starved farmers. CCC was also making a significant contribution, with an initial manpower quota that was the largest per capita in the nation.[50]

In that winter of 1933-1934, out of a total state population of circa 690,000, there were believed to be 40,000-50,000 people on direct relief under the Federal Emergency Administration. In 1934 farm income fell from $68 million to $55 million, of which benefit payments totalled $38.5 million. In December 1934 South Dakota had a greater percentage of its people in relief than any other state in the union.[51] Such payments continued to be essential to sustain life. In February 1935 a

---

Farm: Rural Rehabilitation in the Great Plains, 1929-1945 (Lincoln and London: University of Nebraska Press, 2002), 22.

[48] Edward Robb Ellis, *A Nation in Torment: The Great American Depression, 1929-1939* (New York: Kodansha International, 1995), 454.

[49] Benedict, *Farm Policies*, 320; Worster, *Dust Bowl*, 190. The Taylor Grazing Act, like most of the legislation of the New Deal, has stimulated debate about what George A. Gonzalez has called "Ideas and State Capacity or Business Dominance: A Historical Analysis of Grazing on the Public Grasslands," *Studies in American Political Development* 15.2 (Fall 2001): 234-244. The response by Christopher McGroy Klyza and a further reply by Gonzalez are contained in the same issue, 245-252. For the beginning of this debate, see Klyza's essay in *Studies in American Political Development* 8.2 (Fall 1994): 341-374.

[50] Lowitt and Beasley, *One Third of a Nation;* 92-93; Grant, *Down and Out*, 78-79; Kenneth E. Hendrickson, Jr., "The Civilian Conservation Corps in South Dakota," *South Dakota History* 11.1 (Winter 1980): 1-20.

[51] Schuyler, *Dread of Plenty*, 61, 111; Nelson, *The Prairie*, 157. South Dakota was one of eleven states in which the state authorities "carried no financial or administrative

farmer's wife wrote to the *Dakota Farmer* magazine: "we plan to live on our small income of $1 a week, besides $3,60 which we receive from the relief." In July 1936 under WPA Hopkins announced that seven thousand South Dakota farmers would be provided with work digging walls, building earth dams for controlling run-offs, and making farm to market roads.[52]

President Roosevelt visited South Dakota and other Great Plains states during his "non-political" drought inspection trip in August 1936, during which he received a report of the preliminary conclusions of the Great Plains Drought Area Committee. On his return to Washington he appointed a committee to recommend long term policies for the utilization of the resources of the area.[53] Its lengthy report, *The Future of the Great Plains* (December 1936) was to set the agenda for an immediate, continuing and occasionally bitter debate about land-use planning in the region, whose original inhabitants had lived in ecological harmony with their environment.[54] It had been the land hunger of the white man which had killed the buffalo, decimated the Indians, reduced those who survived to the reservations, and plowed the grasslands. It is not frivolous to include within the all-embracing strategies of the New Deal the Wheeler-Howard Act of 1934, generally known as the Indian Reorganization Act, that recognized the communality of tribal lands and the rights of tribal councils. This "Indian New Deal" owed much to the newly appointed Commissioner for Indian Affairs, the crusader for Indian rights John Collier.[55]

What can be felt in South Dakota by the mid-thirties is the rebirth of what has been called "a cooperative individualism that placed the individual within the context of a community," and a renewal of confidence.[56] This can be illustrated by the acceptance as a worthy native son of Hamlin Garland, the writer. In *A Son of the Middle Border* (1917) and its sequels he had traced his family's migration from the

---

responsibility for general relief." Donald S. Howard, *The WPA and Federal Relief Policy* (New York: Russell Sage Foundation, 1943), 54.

[52] Grant, *Down and Out*, 79-81; T.H. Watkins, *The Hungry Years: A Narrative History of the Great Depression in America* (New York: Henry Holt and Company, 1999), 432; Carle C. Zimmerman and Nathan L. Whetton, *Rural Families on Relief* (Washington, DC: Government Printing Office, 1938). In 1936 and 1937 South Dakota had the largest average monthly number of WPA employees of any state in the Union, 395 per 10,000 population in 1936, Howard, *The WPA and Federal Relief Policy*, 858-859.

[53] FDR made "rear platform" remarks at Aberdeen and Huron, and attended conferences in Pierre and Rapid City, South Dakota. Rosenman, *The Public Papers of FDR*, 1936 volume, *The People Approve* (New York: Random House, 1938), 293-316, 369-370.

[54] Worster, *Dust Bowl*, 192-197; Nixon, *FDR and Conservation*, 2:3-6. The Summary Final Report of the Great Plains Committee stressed the importance of "coordinated co-operation between Federal, State and local agencies," Nixon, *FDR and Conservation*, 2:4.

[55] Kenneth R. Philip, "John Collier, 1933-45," in Robert M. Kvasnicka and Herman J. Viola, eds., *The Commissioners of Indian Affairs, 1824-1977* (Lincoln: University of Nebraska Press, 1979), 273-282; Albert L. Hurtado and Peter Iverson, eds., *Major Problems in American Indian History* (Lexington, MA: D.C. Heath and Company, 1994), 442-482.

[56] Robert S. McElvaine, *The Great Depression: America, 1929-1941* (New York: Times Books, 1933), xxv.

old Northwest to South Dakota along with the westward moving frontier of settlement. From the publication of his first book, *Main-Travelled Roads* (1891), he had offended the pride of his fellow South Dakotans because of his portrayal of the loneliness and drudgery of farm life and the misery of the people. With the new cultural programs of the New Deal a marker was erected at the Garland Homestead Site in 1936, and he is also commemorated in Mitchell. One may expect the WPA State Guides to be boosters for their states, and writers on the federal payroll to be somewhat partisan in their appraisals, but their conclusions about South Dakota are unequivocal. "During the drought and dust storm years of the 1930s, thousands of destitute farm and town families required Federal aid for the necessities of life. Government-supplied employment on permanent improvements, such as water conservation dams, soil erosion projects, roads and public buildings, provided a tremendous boon to business and agriculture. It was the biggest factor in South Dakota's battle against the lean years." [57]

This verdict of the Federal Writers Project is later confirmed by the state's leading historian: "a total of $55,280,000 was distributed in South Dakota on benefit payments ... the Department of Agriculture between 1935 and 1942 planted 3,206 miles of shelterbelt in the central part of the state with a total of 41,599,000 trees.... About 87 per cent of the cultivated croplands in the state was covered by soil conservative programmes in 1936.... Under land utilization programs the Federal Government acquired title to 986,000 acres of sub-marginal land between 1936 and 1940." And every other federal program made its impact on the state. Indeed it has been estimated that the state received $46 per capita each year in research grants whereas Connecticut, for example, received less than $15.[58]

What was happening in South Dakota in the 1930s was also happening, with obvious local differences, in every state of the Union. The New Deal was nationalistic and all-embracing. Nationalistic in that there was national leadership, and that policies were directed from Washington into each state and community. But it was not nationalistic in that everything was "federalized." Roosevelt understood federalism to mean a partnership between the federal government and the states, and also with local communities. Such pragmatic realism, otherwise pragmatic liberalism, was its achievement. It did not, however, deny the requirement of executive leadership. Roosevelt took a broad construction of the constitution of the United States: "While it isn't written in the Constitution, nevertheless it is the

---

[57] WPA Guide, *South Dakota*, 6, 51, 97, 127, 345.

[58] Shell, *History of South Dakota*, 352-354; Paul A. O'Rourke, "South Dakota Politics during the New Deal Years," *South Dakota History* 1.3 (Summer 1971): 270-271. However, by 1938 South Dakota was returning to a long period of Republican ascendancy: Clem, *Prairie State Politics*, 38. One response to a later survey recognized that "As South Dakota people prosper, they favour the Republicans," Inda Avery, "Some South Dakotans' Opinions about the New Deal," *South Dakota History* 7.1 (Summer 1977): 318. Others, in an oral history exercise of the 1970s chose to remember climatic and economic hardship more clearly than government assistance. Gerald W. Wolff and Joseph H. Cash, "South Dakota Remember the Great Depression," *South Dakota History* 19.2 (Summer 1989): 225-258.

inherent duty of the Federal government to keeps its citizens from starvation."[59] He believed that the State was the "duly constituted representative of an organized society of human beings, created by them for their mutual protection and well-being."[60] This was the state that had a social, economic and moral obligation to provide "work and security." This was the state that had to make "a re-appraisal of values" and to "assist the development of an economic declaration of rights, an economic constitutional order."[61] This was the state that believed in leadership from Washington but within the confines of a democratic system whose particular characteristic was its nationalism within the fences of traditionalism.

In *The Federalist* number 70, Alexander Hamilton had declared that beyond "the dim light of historical research" there were the "dictates of reason and good sense." These dictates led him to the conclusion:

> Energy in the executive is a leading character of the definition of good government. It is essential to the protection of the community against foreign attacks; It is not less essential to the steady administration of the laws, to the protection of property against those irregular and high-handed combinations, which sometimes interrupt the ordinary course of justice, to the security of liberty against the enterprises and assaults of ambition, of faction, and of anarchy.[62]

Although Lincoln had been adopted by both parties it was impossible for Democrats to embrace Hamilton; but FDR was both Hamiltonian and Jeffersonian. He shared Jeffersonian ideals and his pragmatic understanding of the importance of party. He shared Hamilton's belief in the importance of executive power. Like George Washington he saw himself whilst not "the father of his country" at least as "Papa Roosevelt." Like Washington, at another time of new beginnings, he sought to build a structure of coherent administration to serve the interests of the American people.[63]

---

[59] Quoted in Charles McKinley and Robert W. Frase, *Launching Social Security: A Capture-and-Record Account 1935-1937* (Madison: University of Wisconsin Press, 1970), 7.

[60] "Message to the New York State Legislature," 28 August 1931, in Rauch, *Selected Speeches*, 62.

[61] Rosenman, *The Public Papers of FDR*, 1928-1932 volume, *The Genesis of the New Deal* (New York: Random House, 1938): Acceptance Speech, Chicago, 2 July 1932, 657; Commonwealth Club Speech, San Francisco, 23 September 1932, 742-756; Campaign Address, Detroit, Michigan, 2 October 1932, 771-780.

[62] Max Beloff, ed., *The Federalist, or, The New Constitution* (Oxford: Basil Blackwell, 1948), 358.

[63] Our understanding of the Roosevelt presidency has been considerably clarified by the recent work of a number of political historians and political scientists. See for example Stephen Skowronek, "Franklin Roosevelt and the Modern Presidency," *Studies in American Political Development* 6.2 (Fall 1992): 322-358; Milkis, *The President and the Parties*; Marc Landy and Sidney M. Milkis, *Presidential Greatness* (Lawrence: University Press of Kansas, 2000); David Plotke analyzes "progressive liberalism" in *Building a Democratic Political Order: Reshaping American Liberalism in the 1930s and 1940s* (New York: Cambridge University Press, 1996*)*. In his detailed and

FDR had moved a long way from his clarion call in 1923 for a new Jefferson. His ideas remained Jeffersonian but he was fully prepared to adopt Hamiltonian means, as he declared in 1936 when he defined his economic, social and political philosophy as "Nationwide Thinking, Nationwide Planning and Nationwide Action." Harold Ickes a year before, had suggested that "If Thomas Jefferson were alive today, he might want to rewrite for a second time the famous English declaration of men's rights to enjoy 'life, liberty and property' specifically to include the right to work." Ickes was also confident that "if private capital will not perform its functions, public capital must and will."[64]

Conclusion

The American presidency has been called many things. Roosevelt's was an American presidency of the Republic, that comprehended the whole country and its interests. Its achievements can be quantified. The literary genius of John Steinbeck and the cinematic brilliance of John Ford, who have made the Okies icons of popular and historical imagination, have distorted perceptions of the period. The frontiers and borderlands necessarily produced economic refugees like the Joads. It had always been so throughout the American experience. Roosevelt himself had encouraged a new westward movement in his speeches at the sites of the Bonneville and Grand Coulee dams in 1934, and newspaper reports of these circulated throughout the upper Mid-west. The Resettlement Administration issued a pamphlet on opportunities for settlers in the Pacific Northwest, and a druggist west of Spokane displayed a portrait of the president next to a sign reading "SURE YOU'RE WELCOME! F.D.R. SAYS SO HIMSELF."[65] And even the Joads to the south could marvel at the recovery of dignity and the promises of a better future when they reached FSA camps in California. These camps were existential symbols of an optimistic and caring government. Their purpose was to dispel the despair engendered by economic hardship, and to suggest an alternative to the deep seated

---

authoritative study, *The Exemplary President: Franklin D. Roosevelt and the American Political Tradition* (Amherst: University of Massachusetts Press, 1990), Philip Abbott blazed the trail that I have taken in this section.

[64] "Is There a Jefferson on the Horizon?" 3 December 1925, in Rauch, *Selected Speeches*, 43-47; Franklin D. Roosevelt, *Looking Forward* (London: William Heineman Ltd., 1933), 7-11; Franklin D. Roosevelt, *On Our Way* (London: Faber and Faber, 1934), ix-xiv; Jefferson Day Speech, 25 April 1936, in Rosenman, *Public Papers of FDR*, 1936 volume, 177-182; Harold L. Ickes, *Back to Work: The Story of PWA* (New York: Macmillan Company, 1935), 195, 233.

[65] John N. Webb and Malcolm Brown, *Migrant Families* (Washington, DC: Government Printing Office, 1938). In the "Letter of Transmittal" Corrington Gill accepts that a "high degree of population mobility is a basic necessity in America," iii. Rosenman, *Public Papers of FDR*, 1934 volume, *The Advance of Recovery and Reform*, 352-354; Richard Neuberger, *Our Promised Land* (New York: Macmillan Company, 1938), 35-64. James N. Gregory, *American Exodus: The Dust Bowl Migration and Okie Culture in California* (New York: Oxford University Press, 1989) discusses the stereotyping that resulted from Steinbeck's novel.

pessimism that, from the time of Thoreau, had been the underside of the myth of the west and of the moving frontier: "The demise of America is written in the orientation: in the west lies a bright place on the horizon—where the sun inevitably goes down."[66]

Roosevelt's "new frontier," whilst accepting that the search for economic opportunity could require the mobility of labor, rejected the traditional rape-of-the-land-and-move-on philosophy of the "old frontier." He was committed to the reintegration of domestic borderlands into the mainstream of American life through education, investment and scientific land use, accompanied by federal intervention to facilitate change and relieve distress. As the president himself said in 1936: "The period of geographical pioneering is largely finished. But, my friends, the period of social pioneering is only at its beginning."[67] This inevitably involved challenge to the shibboleths that had grown up around the Constitution, and jurisdictional boundaries that had become barriers had to be taken down. FDR had confidence that the sun was not to set, neither in South Dakota nor elsewhere in the Union during his watch.

---

[66] William Howarth, *The Book of Concord: Thoreau's Life as a Writer* (Harmondsworth: Penguin Books, 1983), 133.

[67] Address to the Young Democratic Club, Baltimore, Maryland, 13 April 1936, in Rosenman, *Public Papers of FDR*, 1936 volume, 165.

FRONTIERS AND BOUNDARIES IN HOLLYWOOD FILM: THE CASE OF *THE GRAPES OF WRATH*

Melvyn Stokes

The release of the movie *The Grapes of Wrath* in January 1940 provoked a heated debate. William R. Weaver, writing in the trade journal *Motion Picture Herald*, remarked that—like the John Steinbeck novel on which it was based—the film was "daring, significant and controversial." Although Weaver praised the technical aspects of the film, he thought it dealt with "a melancholy subject" and concluded that, in its attempts to be faithful to the original, it included "much that does not fit into the accepted conception of family entertainment." Martin Quigley, in the same issue of *Motion Picture Herald*, contributed a special editorial in which he condemned the film as "a new and emphatic item of evidence in support of the frequently repeated assertion in these columns that the entertainment motion picture is no place for social, political and economic argument."[1] Edwin Locke, writing for the liberal *New Republic*, emphatically disagreed, attacking Quigley's insistence that movies should offer only ill-defined "entertainment." To Locke, *The Grapes of Wrath* had "dramatized and memorialized one wretched section of the victims of American history," setting in the process a crucial precedent "for contemporary and historical honesty in movie-making."[2] Critical disagreements over *The Grapes of Wrath* went to the heart of the debate over what Hollywood films ought to be trying to do and the themes they could legitimately explore. At the same time, critics (including Quigley himself) often commented on the film's technical and cinematographic innovations. It was not simply that *The Grapes of Wrath* was on the boundary of what was permissible for a mainstream film in 1940, but it also extended the frontiers of movie-making in aesthetic terms too.

The man who decided to make a film of Steinbeck's novel in the first place was Darryl F. Zanuck, vice-president in charge of production at the Twentieth-Century Fox studio. Zanuck had begun his career at Warner Bros., where he had written films first for a dog (Rin Tin Tin), then for human stars, and finally—not yet thirty—had been promoted to head of production. At Warner Bros., he was primarily responsible for the cycle of "social exposé" films produced in 1931-1932: *The Match King* (critiquing business ethics), *Cabin the Cotton* (on the exploitation of Southern share-croppers), *Two Seconds* (attacking capital punishment) and *I Am a Fugitive from a Chain Gang* (dealing with the deficiencies of the penal system in the South).[3] Such films were by no means unusual for their time: other studios were producing movies that were—according to Terry Christensen—"questioning and

---

[1] W.R.W. [William R. Weaver], "*Grapes of Wrath* ... Movie of a Best Seller," *Motion Picture Herald* 138.4 (27 January 1940): 52; M.Q. [Martin Quigley], "*Grapes of Wrath*—An Editorial Viewpoint," *Motion Picture Herald* 138.4 (27 January 1940): 17.

[2] Edwin Locke, "*The Grapes of Wrath*," in Stanley Kauffman with Bruce Henstell, eds., *American Film Criticism: From the Beginnings to Citizen Kane* (New York: Liveright, 1972), 385, 391.

[3] Russell Campbell, "The Ideology of the Social Consciousness Movie: Three Films of Darryl F. Zanuck," *Quarterly Review of Film Studies* 3.1 (Winter 1978): 49-50.

pessimistic, torn between group solidarity and strong leadership as possible solutions to the crisis of the Depression."[4] By 1933-1934, however, the cycle of critical and socially conscious movies produced by Hollywood had practically come to an end. There were a number of reasons for this. The inauguration of Franklin D. Roosevelt in March 1933 brought about a major change in the political climate. However successful or unsuccessful New Deal programs were, they at least created the impression that the federal government was now actively involved both in fighting the Depression and attempting to alleviate its social consequences. Moreover, partly as a result of the Depression, the film industry had become extremely vulnerable to outside pressures.

Hollywood itself had been hard hit by the economic slump. Total box-office income fell from a peak of $732,000,000 in 1930 to $482,000,000 in 1933.[5] Such a 34 percent fall in income seemed even more disastrous because, as a result of the costs of acquiring theater chains and innovating sound in the late twenties, most of the major studios were under the financial control of their banks.[6] Conscious of its own weakness, the industry faced both public and private threats to its autonomy. During the 1920s, Protestant organizations such as the Reverend William H. Short's Motion Picture Research Council and Canon William S. Chase's Federal Motion Picture Council had pressed for federal censorship of films to be introduced. In 1928, Short managed to secure funding from the Payne Fund for a series of sociological investigations into the impact of movies. Most of the results of these surveys were published in 1933, together with *Our Movie-Made Children*, a book by popular journalist Henry James Forman summarizing the findings of the project. What the Payne Fund studies seemed to prove, through apparently impartial scientific research, was that the movies had a bad effect on young people, encouraging them to act and behave in anti-social ways. Their publication consequently gave an important boost to demands for federal regulation of the film industry as a whole.[7]

The Catholic approach to the problem of what to do about the movies was very different. Martin Quigley, publisher of the *Motion Picture Herald* (in which he would much later criticise *The Grapes of Wrath*), did not believe in government censorship (which was always vulnerable to pressure from corrupt politicians). He preferred to ensure that films were made without the inclusion of questionable material through a tighter system of movie industry self-regulation. In late 1929, he took the draft of a new "Production Code" written by fellow-Catholic Daniel Lord to

---

[4] Terry Christensen, *Reel Politics: American Political Movies from "Birth of a Nation" to "Platoon"* (New York: Blackwell, 1987), 43.

[5] Francis Bordat and Michel Etcheverry, eds., *Cent ans d'aller au cinéma: Le spectacle cinématographique aux Etats-Unis, 1896-1995* (Rennes: Presses Universitaires de Rennes, 1995), 203.

[6] Richard Maltby, "The Political Economy of Hollywood: The Studio System," in Philip Davies and Brian Neve, eds., *Cinema, Politics and Society in America* (Manchester: Manchester University Press, 1981), 46-47.

[7] Gregory D. Black, *Hollywood Censored: Morality Codes, Catholics, and the Movies* (Cambridge: Cambridge University Press, 1994), 32-34; Robert Sklar, *Movie-Made America: A Cultural History of American Movies* (New York: Vintage, 1994), 134-140.

Will Hays, chairman of the Motion Pictures Producers and Distributors Association. Hays quickly realized its usefulness and secured its acceptance by the major film producers. After its formal adoption in 1930, however, the Production Code was more honored in the breach than the observance. It was supposed to ensure that Hollywood produced only entertainment that was "correct" and "moral." The Code itself was overwhelmingly concerned with the treatment of sex, but it also insisted that good always be preferred to evil, that crime must not be presented sympathetically, and that the judicial system must never be represented as unjust.[8] Yet the period after 1930 saw the release, amongst many other examples, of the sex comedies of Mae West, a series of "fallen women" films and an early cycle of "gangster" films (*Little Caesar*, *Public Enemy* and *Scarface*); all of which, in one way or another, challenged aspects of the Production Code.[9]

This situation changed, however, in 1934. Catholics, disappointed with the operation of the Production Code, formed the Legion of Decency. This was a major force because the principal weapon it wielded—the threat of a boycott of some films by the U.S.'s twenty million Catholics—seemed particularly worrying to Hollywood at a time when audience figures were already depressed. (Because American Catholics were predominantly concentrated in urban areas, had their own national press and the disciplined leadership of a church hierarchy, they could threaten Hollywood with the possibility of impressively united action.) Moreover, 1934 saw the establishment of the film industry's own "alphabet agency": the Production Code Administration under Catholic Joseph Breen.[10]

After the introduction of the PCA, the Production Code itself was rigorously enforced for the first time. Some genres and film cycles were no longer made. Other subjects became taboo so far as the major studios were concerned. These included, for the most part, attempts at social exposures and anything to do with the consequences of the Depression. After 1934, as Robert Sklar has pointed out, most "of [the] important moneymaking pictures had little to do with contemporary life."[11] Most Hollywood movies of the mid to late thirties offered "entertainment" that allowed audiences to escape from the problems of the Depression years. "Nothing," Thomas H. Pauly has pointed out, "could have been further from the bread lines and the deprivation photographed by Dorothea Lange than the social comedies of

---

[8] Black, *Hollywood Censored*, 34-46; "The Motion Picture Production Code of 1930," reprinted in Gerald Mast, ed., *The Movies in Our Midst: Documents in the Cultural History of Film in America* (Chicago: University of Chicago Press, 1982), 321-333.

[9] Black, *Hollywood Censored*, 72-80; Lea Jacobs, *The Wages of Sin: Censorship and the Fallen Woman Film, 1928-1942* (Madison: University of Wisconsin Press, 1991); Melvyn Stokes, "The Gangster Cycle, the Impact of the Depression, and Cultural Struggles of the early 1930s," in Trevor Harris and Dominique Daniel, eds., *Le crime organisé à la ville et à l'écran aux Etats-Unis, 1929-1951* (Tours: Publications de GRAAT, 2002), 17-27.

[10] Black, *Hollywood Censored*, 149-192; James M. Skinner, *The Cross and the Cinema: The Legion of Decency and the National Catholic Office for Motion Pictures, 1933-1970* (Westport: Praeger, 1993), chap. 3.

[11] Sklar, *Movie-Made America*, 189.

Lubitsch, the slapstick of the Marx Brothers, and the polished dance routines of Fred Astaire and Ginger Rogers."[12]

Darryl Zanuck, who had left Warners in 1933 to found the new studio Twentieth Century (which merged with Fox in 1935), did the same as the rest of Hollywood. Turning his back on contemporary realism, he concentrated on musicals, Shirley Temple vehicles and genre pictures. One deeply unimpressed writer for the *New Masses* described Zanuck at this time as "a digger of some of the largest voids in the field of culture."[13] For all the complaints of left-wing critics, however, it is important to emphasise the fact that films produced during what David Bordwell, Janet Staiger and Kristin Thompson have called "Classical" Hollywood were industrial products.[14] They were produced by vertically-integrated corporations that existed solely for that purpose. The principal aims of these companies were to maximize the opportunity for profit and to minimize risks. Within this system, Zanuck was a highly-skilled operator. Under him, Twentieth-Century Fox achieved the third best financial record (after MGM and Warner Bros) for productions in 1938-1939. This success, together with the growing demand for A-class movies in first-run houses created by the beginnings of economic recovery, would create the conditions for the making of *The Grapes of Wrath*.[15]

Steinbeck's novel was published in March 1939. Two months later, Zanuck paid $70,000 for the movie rights, making it the most expensive cinematic property acquired that year.[16] His reasons for doing so may have included the desire to acquire a pre-sold property (Steinbeck's novel had swiftly become a best-seller) and awareness of a contemporary trend amongst the studios (as international tensions rose in Europe) to make films out of adaptations of novels and plays dealing with American subjects.[17]

But, in signing a deal that bound Fox to preserve the theme of Steinbeck's book (the only book he would later recall ever reading all the way through), Zanuck must have been aware that he was embarking on a deeply controversial project.[18] The California Chamber of Commerce was bitterly opposed and the representatives of large farmers in the state called for a boycott of all Fox productions if the movie was made. Twentieth-Century Fox itself and its main banker, Chase National in New York, came under intense pressure to abandon the project. Zanuck,

---

[12] Thomas H. Pauly, "*Gone With the Wind* and *The Grapes of Wrath* as Hollywood Histories of the Depression," *Journal of Popular Film* (Summer 1974): 204.
[13] Quoted in Campbell, "The Ideology of the Social Consciousness Movie," 50.
[14] David Bordwell, Janet Staiger and Kristin Thompson, *The Classical Hollywood Cinema: Film Style and Mode of Production to 1960* (London: Routledge and Kegan Paul, 1985).
[15] Rebecca Pulliam, "*The Grapes of Wrath*," *Velvet Light Trap* 2 (August 1971): 3; Thomas Schatz, *Boom and Bust: The American Cinema in the 1940s* (New York: Scribner's, 1997), 79.
[16] Pulliam, "*The Grapes of Wrath*," 3.
[17] Campbell, "The Ideology of the Social Consciousness Movie," 52; Schatz, *Boom and Bust*, 107.
[18] Pulliam, "*The Grapes of Wrath*," 3; Campbell, "The Ideology of the Social Consciousness Movie," 51.

strengthened by evidence from private investigators that the plight of migrant workers in California was even worse than Steinbeck had suggested, refused to back down. Opening a war on another front, he also threatened to launch a public campaign against the Hays Office if the PCA attempted to intervene.[19]

Throughout his career, Zanuck displayed an interest in making "social consciousness" movies. By the late 1940s, indeed, for reasons that will be examined later, he was probably the *only* head of production for a major studio with such an interest. In 1943, on his return from World War II duty as a colonel in the signal corps, Zanuck criticized the Hollywood obsession with films that "radiated sweetness and light" at a Writer's Congress meeting at UCLA. It was time, he urged, for the industry

> to move onto new ground, break new trails ... we must play our part in the solution of the problems that torture the world. We must begin to deal realistically in film with the causes of wars and panics, with social upheavals and the depression, with starvation and want and injustice and barbarism under whatever guise.[20]

Zanuck himself, worried about the possibility that the United States would lapse back into isolationism, produced *Wilson* in 1944 and considered filming a version of Wendell Wilkie's internationalist tract, *One World*.[21] Yet it would be wrong to perceive Zanuck as in any sense radical. A safe Republican in politics (he voted for Wilkie rather than Franklin D. Roosevelt in 1940), he championed "social consciousness" pictures only in part for idealistic reasons. He was also convinced that they appealed to the interest of audiences and, therefore, helped the studio's balance sheet. *The Grapes of Wrath* itself justified this belief, being Fox's most profitable production of 1940.[22]

Critics hostile to *The Grapes of Wrath* tended to perceive the film as an accurate adaptation of the book. Martin Quigley, in his *Motion Picture Herald* editorial, saw the screenplay as "guided by the heavy and designing hand of John Steinbeck." William R. Weaver, in his review, described it as "an extremely literal and very nearly complete transcription of the Steinbeck novel."[23] Other critics—while writing positively of the film as a whole—emphasized that crucial aspects of the novel had disappeared or been toned down. Some of these changes were inevitable. The Hays Code, for example, did not permit swearing in movies. More seriously, the still-birth of Rosasharn's child and her subsequent attempt to save the life of a starving man by permitting him to suckle her breasts were completely unacceptable (for a whole variety of reasons) to the PCA. Apart from such omissions, there were also a number of additions or changes that helped make the

---

[19] Campbell, "The Ideology of the Social Consciousness Movie," 52; Pulliam, "*The Grapes of Wrath*," 3.
[20] Ian Hamilton, *Writers in Hollywood 1915-1951* (London: Heinemann, 1990), 275; Campbell, "The Ideology of the Social Consciousness Movie," 51.
[21] Campbell, "The Ideology of the Social Consciousness Movie," 51.
[22] Ibid., 52.
[23] W.R.W., "*Grapes of Wrath*," 52; M.Q., "*Grapes of Wrath*," 17.

story less depressing. Although the adaptation of the novel was credited to Nunnally Johnson, a Fox contract writer, it was almost certainly heavily influenced by Zanuck himself. Traditionally, Zanuck involved himself closely in story development at the studio; his two- to four-hour daily story conferences were legendary. Johnson himself would later concede that he "was a collaborator on anything I ever did."[24] Consequently, it may well have been Zanuck who suggested transforming the Weed Patch Camp of the novel into the Wheat Patch Camp, and placing the Joads' arrival at the camp towards the end of the movie, thus setting the scene for a much more optimistic ending than in Steinbeck's novel. The clear association of the camp with the New Deal—from the sign at the entrance announcing it as part of a program run by the Department of Agriculture to the depiction of its director as a prototype FDR[25]—may also have been due to Zanuck. Aware that his film would be attacked by right-wingers, Zanuck may have thought that identifying it with the popular Roosevelt (who was triumphantly re-elected while it was in the middle of being shot) might make it less vulnerable to such criticism.

Once shooting actually started on 28 September 1939, John Ford and his cinematographer, Gregg Toland, had their own chance to put flesh on the bones of the script produced by Johnson and heavily influenced by Zanuck. Their movie differed from other contemporary American feature films not simply because of its social concern, but also through its visual appearance. "It has been photographed in the flat, newsreel technique," noted William R. Weaver on the film's release. "Similarly, the players wear no more makeup than flood sufferers." Philip T. Hartung, another contemporary critic, also applauded the absence of "Hollywood" production values: "No artificial make-up, no false sentiment, no glamour stars mar the authentic documentary form of this provocative film."[26] The film still appeared fresh and innovative several decades later. Terry Christensen writes that it "retains a documentary quality that is radically different from the style of other films but perfectly suited to *The Grapes of Wrath*."[27] One of Ford's biographers has suggested that the film's aesthetic style had its roots in several sources: contemporary photo-journalism, British and American documentaries, expressionism in the cinema, and the painting of Thomas Hart Benton.[28] Other students of film have underlined the efforts by the young and innovative Toland to expand the frontiers of film-making. Experimenting with wide-angle lens, high-speed film, new lighting techniques, "roofed-in" sets (as in the diner scene) and deep-focus cinematography, he was well

---

[24] Johnson quoted in Campbell, "The Ideology of the Social Consciousness Movie," 50.
[25] According to Jim Sanderson, the camp director (played by Grant Mitchell) "looks and acts like Roosevelt freed from his wheelchair, dressed for a summer evening in an upstate New York retreat, fearing only fear." Jim Sanderson, "American Romanticism in John Ford's *The Grapes of Wrath*: Horizontalness, Darkness, Christ, and F.D.R.," *Literature/Film Quarterly* 17.4 (1989): 241.
[26] W.R.W., "*Grapes of Wrath*," 52; Philip T. Hartung, "Trampling Out the Vintage," *Commonweal* 31 (9 February 1940), cited in Pauly, "*Gone With the Wind* and *The Grapes of Wrath* as Hollywood Histories of the Depression," 203.
[27] Christensen, *Reel Politics*, 50.
[28] Tag Gallagher, *John Ford: The Man and His Films* (Berkeley: University of California Press, 1986), 176-181.

on the way to developing the stylized form of realism that would soon impress the whole movie industry in *Citizen Kane*.[29] Certainly, in aesthetic terms, *The Grapes of Wrath* was very much on the frontiers of Hollywood film-making in 1939.

The fact that John Ford was the director of *The Grapes of Wrath* came about because Zanuck had formed a "Ford unit" at Twentieth Century Fox. Ford himself had just finished three films back to back—*Stagecoach*, *Young Mr. Lincoln*, and *Drums Along the Mohawk*. With *Stagecoach* he had made his first western since *The Iron Horse* in 1924 and, in the process, had reinvigorated a genre that seemed to have bumbled along on the lower half of the bill—the classic "B" movie—during the Depression years. *The Grapes of Wrath* itself, as some left-wing critics of the time perceptively noted, was itself in many respects a western, albeit a revisionist one. Instead of the pioneers moving West in wagon trains and menaced by Indians, it was the Joad family—together with countless other Okies—heading for California in their old jalopy, threatened this time not by Indians but by poverty and starvation. Moreover, unlike earlier westerns (including Ford's), *The Grapes of Wrath* dealt with the real social consequences of the western migration. Only with *The Grapes of Wrath*, argued Edwin Locke in his contemporary review, had Hollywood—"by touching on some of the results of land speculation, submarginal farming, agricultural mechanization, and the California latifundia"—at last "given us a picture that totalled, in human values, some of the results of our drive to the frontier."[30]

Almost certainly, Ford was sympathetic to the project of filming Steinbeck's novel. He was after all, as Robert Sklar observes, "a director with an unusual feeling for common life." Ford himself would later explain that "[t]he whole thing appealed to me—being about simple people—and the story was similar to the famine in Ireland, when they threw the people off the land and left them wandering on the roads to starve."[31] Certainly, the film that Ford shot seems to have stayed close to the shooting script written by Johnson and approved both by Zanuck and Steinbeck himself. It ended with Tom Joad going on the run from the law, leaving his family in the Wheat Patch Camp. In the scene in which he says goodbye to Ma Joad, Tom's discourse is heavy with references to startling injustices and social inequalities. It also demonstrates his new commitment to activism and collective action. At the end of this scene, Tom strides off into the dawn in order to become, it is clear, a radical agitator or a labor organizer. At this point, Ford turned over the cans of film he had shot to Zanuck for final editing and left to go on vacation. For Ford himself, this was standard practice. He hated cutting rooms and was happy that Zanuck (whom he regarded as "a great film editor") should take over responsibility for this.[32] But Zanuck was by this stage clearly worried about possible difficulties with the Production Code Administration, and his gut feeling was that a more upbeat ending was needed to expand the film's popular appeal. In Ford's absence (though probably

---

[29] Schatz, *Boom and Bust*, 93; Pulliam, "The Grapes of Wrath," 4; see also Locke, "The Grapes of Wrath," 388.
[30] Locke, "The Grapes of Wrath," 389.
[31] Sklar, *Movie-Made America*, 94; Peter Bogdanovich, *John Ford* (London: Studio Vista, 1968), 76.
[32] Campbell, "The Ideology of the Social Consciousness Movie," 51.

with his verbal agreement), Zanuck himself shot a new ending in which the Joads abandon the Wheat Patch Camp in search of work elsewhere. Ma Joad is now clearly the head of the family, and she delivers a long speech (written by Zanuck himself according to his biographer) in which she praises the qualities and staying power of "the people," suggesting that they—like the Joads—will triumph in the end.[33]

There can be little doubt that the new ending undermined the radical character of the film Ford had shot. It moved *The Grapes of Wrath* closer to the type of populist cinema produced by Frank Capra in the late thirties and early forties. Capra's populism showed how "the people" could be saved when one heroic individual took on the political and economic system and won.[34] There is no real suggestion, other than in Ma's speech, that this is likely to happen in *Grapes*. If anything, it is implied—in his goodbye scene with Ma—that Tom is most likely to suffer the same fate as Casey, who has been murdered for being a strike leader. Left-wing critics at the time of the film's release were unenthusiastic about Zanuck's new ending (Edwin Locke regretted "that the woolly lines about how the people go on and on are handed to Ma to end the picture").[35] Later scholars have been equally hostile. Tag Gallagher, in his study of Ford's film, declared that Ma's speech "virtually destroys the film's trajectory toward inevitable *disintegration*/revolution, in favour of *perseverance*/abidance."[36] Until Ma's homily to "the people" and their capacity for survival, the film had concerned itself primarily with what Thomas Pauly sees as "[t]he futility of individualism and the breakdown of the family."[37] Even Roosevelt's New Deal (the Wheat Patch Camp) is shown as offering only temporary respite, since Tom leaves it as a fugitive from justice and, soon after, the surviving Joads abandon it in a new search for (temporary) work.

If the final version of *The Grapes of Wrath* was less radical than Ford's film— itself considerably less bitter than Steinbeck's original novel—it was still unusual in being a Hollywood film that confronted some of the realities of the Depression. As Gallagher notes, it is "difficult to recall any other movie from a major studio whose

---

[33] Gallagher, *John Ford*, 179; Sanderson, "American Romanticism," 236; Pauly, "*Gone With the Wind* and *The Grapes of Wrath* as Hollywood Histories of the Depression," 208, 217 n. 13.

[34] Populism of the Hollywood variety revolved around the attempt to reassert traditional "American" values, including self-help and good neighborliness. Although it had some parallels with the Populist or People's Party of the 1890s, it lacked the ideology and detailed political program of the nineteenth-century Populists. See Wes D. Gehring, "Populist Comedy," in Wes D. Gehring, ed., *Handbook of American Film Genres* (Westport: Greenwood Press, 1988), 124-143. On Capra, see Jeffrey Richards, "Frank Capra and the Cinema of Populism," *Cinema* [UK] 5 (February 1970): 22-28; Glenn A. Phelps, "The "Populist" Films of Frank Capra," *Journal of American Studies* 13.3 (1979): 377-392; Wes D. Gehring, *Populism and the Capra Legacy* (Westport: Greenwood Press, 1995), 1-27.

[35] Locke, "*The Grapes of Wrath*," 387.

[36] Gallagher, *John Ford*, 180.

[37] Pauly, "*Gone With the Wind* and *The Grapes of Wrath* as Hollywood Histories of the Depression," 208.

tone was anywhere near so 'aware.'"[38] To the surprise and dismay of critics such as Quigley, the film proved popular with audiences (albeit more so in cities than in the countryside, where recollections of the sufferings of farmers were still raw). Premièred at the Rivoli in New York, it broke all of the theater's opening day records. In its eight-week run there, it made $273,000 (or one-seventh of the total cost of producing it.)[39] In his favorable review in *The New Republic*, Edwin Locke observed that "audiences ... are crowding the box offices and breaking into spontaneous applause after each screening of the picture." The manager of the Criterion Theatre in Oklahoma City (possibly reflecting the special interest of "Okies" in the film) greeted it as "[o]ne of the greatest pictures of all time. Honesty fearlessly on screen." What *The Grapes of Wrath* seemed to prove was that socially-aware movies could succeed at the box office. Its success, observed *Variety*, "may lead other producers to explore the rich field of contemporary life which films have neglected and ignored."[40]

A year later, Zanuck, pleased with *Grapes'* success, returned to the theme of dispossessed farmers and—again with a script by Nunnally Johnson and with Ford as director—set out to make a movie adaptation of another sensational novel, Erskine Caldwell's *Tobacco Road*. Shortly after the film's release, however, the United States became involved in World War II. Not only did the war itself distract attention from domestic problems, but the mobilization of millions of men into the armed forces and the conversion of the economy to full wartime production practically eliminated unemployment and most of the remaining effects of the Depression. In his speech to the Writers' Congress at UCLA in 1943, however, Zanuck looked forward to a post-war world in which Hollywood would no longer be afraid to deal with the darker and more problematic side of American life. Once the war ended in 1945, it looked for a time as if his hopes might be justified. A number of films were released that looked at social problems: alcoholism (*The Lost Weekend*, 1945, and *The Smash-up*, 1947); rehabilitating war veterans (*The Best Years of Our Lives* and *Till the End of Time*, both 1946), and anti-semitism (*Crossfire* and *Gentleman's Agreement*, both 1947). After 1947, however, the number of "social problem" films dropped, with Zanuck's Twentieth Century Fox and independent producer Stanley Kramer responsible for most of the ones that were produced.[41]

---

[38] Gallagher, *John Ford*, 176.

[39] Pulliam, "The Grapes of Wrath," 4; "*Wrath*'s Start Breaks Records," *Motion Picture Herald*, 138.4 (27 January 1940): 25.

[40] Locke, "The Grapes of Wrath," 385; William Nable, Criterion Theatre, Oklahoma City, Oklahoma, in "What the Picture Did for Me," *Motion Picture Herald* 138.12 (23 March 1940): 55; *Variety*, 31 January 1940, 14.

[41] Twentieth Century Fox released *The Snake Pit* (1948), dealing with mental illness, and two films on racism (both produced by Zanuck himself): *Pinky* (1949) and *No Way Out* (1950). Kramer's *Home of the Brave* (1949) dealt with racism in the army during World War II and *The Men* (1950) with the plight of paraplegics. Louis de Rochemont, who had pioneered "The March of Time" newsreels on the world situation, made two "problem" films: *Lost Boundaries* (1949), dealing with race, and *The Whistle at Eaton Falls* (1951), on the subject of labor relations.

There were two main reasons for this decline. The first was the state of the American movie industry itself. Movie attendance started to decline after 1946, its peak year. The post-war baby boom and the emergence of new leisure pursuits (there were one million television sets in the United States in 1948 and eleven million by 1950) undercut the profitability of Hollywood. By 1948, industry profits had halved since 1946. Overseas markets were also down, as countries such as Britain and France adopted policies designed to protect their domestic film industries from American competition.[42] In 1948, moreover, the Supreme Court issued its Paramount decree, undercutting the long-term stability and profitability of the major studios by forcing them to sell off their chains of movie theaters. The increasing economic vulnerability of Hollywood discouraged attempts at making movies that might alienate significant sections of the national audience.

The second reason for the fall in the number of social problem films was the advent of the cold war. With the Soviet Union as the United States' principal international adversary, right-wing Americans were eager to avoid anything that—by criticizing the workings of American capitalism—would give aid to the communist enemy. "Don't Smear the Free Enterprise System," "Don't Deify the Common Man," "Don't Show That Poverty is a Virtue ... and Failure Is Noble," warned a guide published by fervent anti-communist Ayn Rand in 1947.[43] In terms of *The Grapes of Wrath* (which was used in the Soviet Union to underline the extent of poverty in the United States), right-wingers adopted a dual approach. They tried to prevent it and other "critical" movies from being circulated abroad.[44] They also set out to make it impossible to make similar, unflattering films in future. "We'll have no more *Grapes of Wrath*, we'll have no more *Tobacco Roads*," declared Eric Johnston, president of the Motion Picture Association of America, in March 1947. "We'll have no more films that show the seamy side of American life."[45]

Perhaps the most effective of all right-wing organizations of the time, the House Committee on Un-American Activities (HUAC), began its investigation into possible communist subversion in the movie industry with secret sessions in Los Angeles in May 1947. In October of that year, it held public hearings in Washington with a number of "unfriendly" (communist or once-communist) witnesses. When they refused to co-operate, these witnesses—who quickly became known as the "Hollywood Ten"—were cited for contempt of Congress. In November 1947, in the "Waldorf Statement," movie producers introduced a formal blacklist of those with communist associations. The next step was inescapable. In December 1947, the

---

[42] Hamilton, *Writers in Hollywood*, 293, 301; Brian Neve, *Film and Politics in America: A Social Tradition* (London: Routledge, 1992), 84, 87-88.

[43] Ayn Rand, *A Screen Guide for Americans*, quoted in Lary May, "Movie Star Politics: The Screen Actors' Guild, Cultural Convention, and the Hollywood Red Scare," in Lary May, ed., *Recasting America: Culture and Politics in the Age of Cold War* (Chicago: University of Chicago Press, 1989), 145.

[44] Christensen, *Reel Politics*, 52. In the western-occupied zone of Austria, for example, the Information Services film section discouraged the distribution of critical movies such as *The Grapes of Wrath*. Reinhold Wagnleitner, "The Irony of American Culture Abroad: Austria and the Cold War," in May, *Recasting America*, 294.

[45] Schatz, *Boom and Bust*, 382.

same edition of the *Motion Picture Herald* that announced the re-release of *The Grapes of Wrath* also included news of the firing of the Hollywood Ten.[46]

In the climate of the time, it was now much harder to produce a film that dared to be critical of any aspect of American society. Journalist Lillian Ross, interviewing William Wyler, the director of *The Best Years of Our Lives*, reported "that he is convinced that he could not make [it] today and that Hollywood will provide no more films like *The Grapes of Wrath* and *Crossfire*."[47] Only Zanuck's Twentieth Century Fox, amongst the major studios, continued to produce a small number of "social problem" films.[48] Two of these—*Pinky* (1949) and *No Way Out* (1950)—dealt with race, the one area in which the Motion Picture Association of America (supported by the National Association for the Advancement of Colored People) resisted the attempt by right-wing forces to prevent the making of critical or controversial movies.[49] Otherwise, with the Cold War intensifying (in 1949, the Soviet Union exploded its first atomic bomb and China was "lost" to communism; in 1950, the Korean War began), the production of "social problem" pictures came virtually to an end. The rise of "McCarthyism" and the rumors surrounding the possibility of another HUAC investigation into the movie industry (which finally began in early 1951) made them too dangerous to handle.

From the introduction of the Production Code Administration in 1934 until 1939, Hollywood largely ignored the social and economic effects of the Depression, producing films that were primarily intended to distract Americans from their problems by offering pure entertainment. Two things changed this situation: the publication of John Steinbeck's best-selling novel in 1939 and the growing demand for A-quality pictures created by the start of economic recovery. In combination, these things gave Darryl Zanuck the chance to return to the "social consciousness" style of film-making he had once preferred. With the Depression at last starting to come to an end, it finally became practicable for a major studio to make a movie about it. If *The Grapes of Wrath* could not have been made earlier, moreover, it also could probably not have been made later, in the highly-charged atmosphere of the Cold War years. It was—and would long remain—very much on the frontier of what was possible for a mainstream Hollywood film.

---

[46] *Motion Picture Herald* 169.10 (6 December 1947): 3966 [sic], 20.
[47] Schatz, *Boom and Bust*, 383.
[48] *Fortune* magazine commented that Zanuck "could risk a *Snake Pit* [on mental illness] because he had twenty-five or more other pictures a year and Betty Grable." Schatz, *Boom and Bust*, 384.
[49] Richard Maltby, *Hollywood Cinema: An Introduction* (Oxford: Blackwell, 1995), 377.

scholarly fields is the absence of middle ground so pronounced. This atypical situation has existed in literature on the CPUSA for nearly fifty years, and balance is long overdue.

Only in America?

Before the 2000 presidential contest, few domestic adults could explain the Electoral College, and many friends overseas found it equally confusing. Thereafter, the public received a civics lesson. Scholars, who have always known democracy's limits, pointed out that illegitimate presidents are not new. Public reactions to elections of chief executives who had lost the popular vote have varied widely. At times, citizens have seethed with outrage; at others they have displayed the equanimity and resignation more associated with authoritarian regimes.

In 1825, Andrew Jackson, who received a popular and electoral-vote plurality in a four-candidate field, lost the contest in the House of Representatives. (That body chooses a president when no one receives an electoral majority.) In response, Jackson contended that a "corrupt bargain" had made John Quincy Adams president. Shortly thereafter Jackson and Martin Van Buren began building the modern Democratic Party.[4]

The disputed 1876 election took place at the end of Reconstruction. Three former Confederate states submitted two sets of results each, deadlocking Congress and threatening to leave the nation leaderless on inauguration day. C. Vann Woodward, one of the twentieth century's greatest southern historians, noted that "so dangerous was believed the menace of war or anarchy" that negotiations for the agreement that ended the crisis "were conducted secretly."[5]

President Grover Cleveland and his Democrats suffered an electoral-college defeat, despite their popular-vote plurality in 1888. But patronage, rather than burning fundamental issues, separated them from Benjamin Harrison's Republicans. Accordingly, the Democrats simply went home and began building stronger party

---

Labour History Review [United Kingdom] 68.1 (April 2003): 61-78. My purpose here is not to replow that ground, but to present a different point of view.

[4] Richard Brookhiser, *America's First Dynasty: The Adamses, 1735-1918* (New York: Free Press, 2002), 92-99; Robert V. Remini, *Andrew Jackson and the Course of American Freedom, 1822-1832*, vol. 2 (New York: Harper and Row, 1981), 74-148; Joel H. Silbey, *Martin Van Buren and the Emergence of American Power Politics* (Lanham, MD: Rowman and Littlefield, 2002), 44-73.

[5] C. Vann Woodward, *Reunion and Reaction: The Compromise of 1877 and the End of Reconstruction* (Boston: Little, Brown and Company, 1951), 7. Woodward cites two earlier, less-scholarly accounts that contend "with probable exaggeration" that more persons expected a civil war in 1877 than had been the case in 1861. Keith Ian Polakoff, *The Politics of Inertia: The Election of 1876 and the End of Reconstruction* (Baton Rouge: Louisiana State University Press, 1973), 13-315; Ari Hoogenboom, *Rutherford B. Hayes: Warrior and President* (Lawrence: University of Kansas Press, 1995), 256-294.

machines in crucial "swing" states such as Illinois, Ohio, and New York. These efforts returned Cleveland to the White House cleanly in 1892.[6]

No twentieth-century race produced an illegitimate presidency. Close contests in 1960, 1968, and 1976 raised that spectre, however. The 2000 election underscored America's anachronistic political system. Yet a media-savvy and personality-oriented public focused on the candidates' body language and "dimpled chads" in Florida. Somehow, the larger question of the process's legitimacy got lost.[7]

Decade after decade, usually during the year following a presidential election, proposals for a Constitutional amendment to require direct popular election have surfaced in Congress, only to die a quiet death. Similarly, today's citizenry does not consider inadequate democracy a problem, though in 2003 several million members demonstrated against Gulf War II. While Americans enjoy personal liberties, their ideological frontiers are constricted. Patriotic rhetoric constantly proclaims "freedom," but the public displays a primitive conception of representative government.

Was Communism "Twentieth-Century Americanism?"

Surprisingly, "bourgeois" political democracy's noisiest champion before the Cold War was the Communist Party. During the 1930s under its preeminent leader, Kansas-born Earl Browder, the CPUSA sought to modernize the nation's constitutional system. An examination of the complaints the Communists voiced, and the solutions they offered, may remind new generations how far the nation still needs to go.

The Party considered itself a revolutionary organization, but even during its most radical moments, its vision remained distant. Therefore its actions never included today's distressingly familiar tactics: stockpiling weapons and guerrilla warfare; much less suicide bombings. Joseph Starobin, a former foreign editor of the CP's national newspaper who had become a political scientist, perhaps best explained the strategy in 1972. Communists believed in V.I. Lenin's vanguard party concept. Starobin characterized the CPUSA's understanding of it as an organization "so intimately connected with the struggles of millions of non-Communists" that it could lead them beyond their immediate demands. Eventually they would follow the CP in a fight for "total social change."[8] Despite any logical problems in denying that

---

[6] Alyn Brodsky, *Grover Cleveland: A Study in Character* (New York: St. Martin's Press, 2000), 217-250; H. Paul Jeffers: *An Honest President: The Life and Presidencies of Grover Cleveland* (New York: William Morrow, 2000), 213-228; Harry Joseph Sievers, *Benjamin Harrison: Hoosier Statesman, From the Civil War to the White House, 1865-1888* (New York: University Publishers Incorporated, 1959), 329-429.

[7] Florida at the time still used a surprisingly primitive election-day process. Voters made their choice by punching a hole beside the name of their candidate. A validity question arose when the ballot was not cleanly perforated ("hanging chad"), or was merely dented ("dimpled chad").

[8] Joseph R. Starobin, *American Communism in Crisis, 1943-57* (Cambridge: Harvard University Press, 1972), 26.

piecemeal reforms might sate revolutionary appetites, the CP used the vanguard theory to rationalize its numerous tactical twists and turns.

For about forty years, Communist Party members, self-proclaimed heirs to American revolutionary traditions, called public attention to virtually every inequity. They contended that the nation's vaunted democracy was bogus, as a result of systemic features the general public typically left unquestioned. The CP condemned the two-party hegemony as offering a choice without meaningful difference. Communists argued that American schools, churches, and newspapers promoted an unquestioning loyalty—not critical thinking—thereby vitiating the entire process.

The CPUSA had a valid point. National election laws are determined by the fifty states, beyond the most general constitutional parameters such as the women's suffrage amendment. In most locales, a vote-counting system known as "first past the post" prevails. The term is borrowed from horseracing, a popular pastime during the nineteenth century, when most states entered the Union. Simply put, the candidate with the largest number of votes wins, even if the margin does not constitute a majority. Typically, aspirants who cannot finish first drop out, often endorsing a "major" contestant. Since the 1830s, federal law has required all states to use the single member district system to elect federal representatives. This practice carves states into territorial divisions, each of which sends only one woman or man to Congress. Again, minority parties usually receive nothing. Proportional representation remains unknown, even to millions of well-educated adults. Whether because of, or despite election laws, modern U.S. voter turnout hovers around 50 percent for presidential elections. It sometimes drops to single digits for minor municipal posts. These anemic figures may suggest widespread failure to understand the system, a perceived lack of viable alternatives, or an increased depoliticization. On the other hand, conservatives argue that apathy bespeaks general contentment.

Although the Communists championed political reforms to increase democracy, such as direct popular choice of the president, a Senate representing persons, not land, and reducing the voting age to eighteen, their critique of the regime went far beyond electoral mechanics. Virtually every Communist speech, like those of their competitors from the Socialist Party (SP), focused to some degree on the question of class. Except among the wealthy and some academics, that concept would virtually disappear after World War II. The Marxists always emphasized that the Constitution, written in 1787, was designed to protect contracts, property, and slaveholders; it equated democracy with mob rule. The SP and CP expanded the political discourse by demanding that democracy be given an economic basis, such as barely existed before 1933, and still remains woefully inadequate. Of course, parties having no chance to win elections can safely promise anything. The CP, however, supplemented its words with action. In the late-1930s, it played a positive and disproportional role in organizing the Congress of Industrial Organizations (CIO), the nation's first large unions of semi-skilled and unskilled workers. Indeed Communists, at their peak of influence, controlled the leadership of CIO unions representing 1.3 million members.[9]

---

[9] Harvey Klehr, John Earl Haynes, and Kyrill M. Anderson, *The Soviet World of American Communism* (New Haven: Yale University Press, 1998), 348.

During the dark days of segregation, while other parties shunned the subject, Communists—as the new abolitionists—pioneered for civil rights. An entire generation before the careers of Martin King and Malcolm X, the CP proudly labelled itself the "Negro Party," nominating African American James W. Ford for vice president of the United States in 1932, 1936, and 1940. Communists demanded toleration of interracial marriage, when few black groups dared to raise the issue.

The CP broke what it considered a conspiracy of silence regarding "southern justice." In two historic court cases, it paraded courtroom treatment of African Americans before a world audience. Members defended Angelo Herndon, an Atlanta, Georgia, radical sentenced to eighteen years' imprisonment for organizing an integrated 1932 unemployment demonstration. Charged under a nineteenth-century slave-insurrection statute, Herndon had received his verdict from an all-white jury.[10] More spectacular, however, was a case that had begun fifteen months earlier, known simply as "Scottsboro." On 25 March 1931, authorities at Paint Rock, Alabama, arrested nine black hobo males, all but one still in their teens. The state first brought them to trial in nearby Scottsboro, alleging they had raped two white female travellers atop a moving freight train. The alleged victims, Victoria Price and Ruby Bates, were unemployed textile mill hands who had long supplemented meagre wages through color-blind prostitution. In a noisy courtroom ringed outside by national guardsmen holding back ten thousand angry locals, a white jury convicted all defendants and mandated the death sentence. The prosecution continued to insist on execution though one defendant was virtually blind, another had advanced syphilis and gonorrhoea, and Bates recanted and testified for the defense in later proceedings.

The CPUSA and its affiliates looked to international opinion for justice. The International Labor Defense and Red Aid sent Ada Wright, mother of two Scottsboro defendants, on a European tour. Communist Louis Engdahl, who accompanied her, claimed she visited sixteen countries in six months, inspiring nearly two hundred demonstrations that included five hundred thousand protestors. Even allowing for exaggerations, she attracted massive support. Twenty-first-century historians have noted that she "broadcast her message from a Social Democratic radio station in The Netherlands;" in Belgium "the former president of the Second International, Emile Vandervelde, joined her on the platform."[11] The CPUSA established Herndon's innocence within five years and helped prevent execution of any Scottsboro defendants, though most endured long prison sentences.

From the Communist movement's very inception, it had championed the immigrants. Indeed, until the mid-1930s, most members were foreign-born. Even after natives became predominant, it provided a preview of modern multiculturalism. Such efforts would be more impressive had the CP not retreated

---

[10] Charles H. Martin, *The Angelo Herndon Case and Southern Justice* (Baton Rouge: Louisiana State University Press, 1976), 210.

[11] *Daily Worker*, 1 June 1931; Dan Carter, *Scottsboro: A Tragedy of the American South* (Baton Rouge: Louisiana State University Press, 1969), *passim*; James A. Miller, Susan D. Pennybacker, and Eve Rosenhaft, "Mother Ada Wright and the International Campaign to Free the Scottsboro Boys, 1931-1934," *American Historical Review* 106.2 (April 2001): 415-416.

during World War II, by failing to protest the government's internment of one hundred thousand West-Coast Japanese Americans. In addition, according to Karl Yoneda, the Party suspended "all members of Japanese ancestry and their non-Japanese spouses" for the war's duration to further "national unity."[12]

Similarly, the CPUSA had a mixed record on women's rights. Party head Earl Browder understood that in nearly every measurable way women workers, as a group, suffered more than their male counterparts during the Great Depression. He advocated liberalized divorce laws and, during World War II, demanded abolition of existing remnants of gender inequality. Historian Sharon Hartman Strom has shown that the Communists battled the notion that "work outside the home was a stage, not a right, and that the mature woman" was a housewife. Robert Shaffer has demonstrated that the party, through its Women's Commission, demanded repeal of laws against birth control, and advocated childcare and shared housework responsibilities. Yet Elsa Jane Dixler has painted a darker picture. She contends that during the Depression the CP "defaulted on its commitments to women" by seeking to ingratiate itself with the American mainstream, whose members mostly "wanted to improve their standard of living, not alter their way of life."[13]

Although the CPUSA successfully helped expand public discussion, it did far less to broaden the range of legitimate political behavior. American Communists constantly endeavored to make a world movement's concerns an acceptable part of domestic dialogue. Yet, instead of merely looking abroad for ideas, inspiration, and friends, the CP placed international goals above all else. During the 1930s and 1940s, when the Soviet Union was the only major Communist nation, the party cannibalized the democratic left. Soviet funding gave it a major advantage. Historians Harvey Klehr, John Earl Haynes, and Kyrill M. Anderson put the annual subvention at $10,000 to $15,000, an imposing sum at the time. The figure ballooned to three million dollars by 1988, thirty years after the CPUSA had lost all influence in U.S. life.[14]

During World War II, when America and Russia were allies, party members and sympathizers in high government office engaged in the sort of espionage used against an enemy nation. They maintained a clandestine relationship with the Soviet secret police (best known as the KGB) and Soviet military intelligence (GRU). Washington Communists and "fellow travellers" delivered information on U.S.

---

[12] Karl G. Yoneda, *Ganbatte: Sixty Year Struggle of a Kibei Worker* (Los Angeles: UCLA Asian-American Studies Center, 1983), 115.

[13] James G. Ryan, *Earl Browder: The Failure of American Communism* (Tuscaloosa: University of Alabama Press, 1997), 96; Earl Browder, *What Is Communism?* (New York: Workers Library, 1936), 154; Earl Browder, *The People's Front* (New York: International Publishers, 1938), 201; Sharon Hartman Strom, "Challenging 'Woman's Place': Feminism, the Left and Industrial Unionism in the 1930s," *Feminist Studies* 2 (Summer 1983): 359; Robert Shaffer, "Women and the Communist Party, USA, 1930-1940," *Socialist Review* 45 (May-June 1979): 73-118; Elsa Jane Dixler, "The Woman Question: Women and the Communist Party," (Ph.D. diss., Yale University, 1974), i-7.

[14] Harvey Klehr, John Earl Haynes and Kyrill Anderson, *The Soviet World of American Communism* (New Haven: Yale University Press, 1998), 138-142; 152-155; see photographs of party leader Gus Hall's signed receipts on page 158.

diplomatic strategy, results of top-secret jet engine tests, and the atomic bomb. In a project known as "Venona" the army intercepted, and the U.S. and British intelligence communities decrypted, Soviet cables revealing 349 Americans had ties to Russian agencies. Nearly two hundred individuals remained hidden behind cover names.[15]

So the Communists, as ideological pioneers, brought the United States an opportunity to broaden its constricted political spectrum and to increase voter turnout. Yet by advancing a foreign power's needs, they transgressed a boundary that even the most enlightened societies do not easily tolerate. CP actions provoked legitimate national security concerns, which led to the reaction known as McCarthyism. For many American leaders, the U.S.S.R.'s murderous nature and hostile espionage offensive provided handy excuses to brand the indigenous Communists as political frontier outlaws. Their marginalization, which at times approached a court-sanctioned lynching, created a void on the left that has retarded human rights growth in the United States for half a century.

The Party, Historians, and the Cold War Consensus

At no time have scholars provided a balanced view of the CPUSA. Instead, from the earliest studies, the historiography has swung from one extreme to the other. Since the mid-1990s, U.S. Communism has been a field in flux, with acrimonious debate more common than collegiality, partisans more plentiful than conciliators, and common ground seemingly out of the question. Nor has a healthy sense of humor typified the scholarship. Indeed, some specialists have received recent evidence as one might react to reports of a newly evolved disease.

Forty-five years ago, American Communism was hardly controversial at all. Best known of the early studies were works by Irving Howe and Lewis Coser (based on published sources) and Theodore Draper. The latter unearthed internal CP documents and conducted lengthy, probing interviews of prominent ex-Communists. Howe and Coser's polemic reflected the hostile public view of the CPUSA in the years immediately following Senator Joseph McCarthy's death. Draper's two volumes held to such rigorous standards as to establish the field in the scholarly domain. Such was the quality of his work that it remains a part of the debate a half century after his first book's publication.[16] These traditional accounts focused on party leadership, emphasized the Soviet tie, and rendered an overwhelmingly negative view of the CPUSA. Here one finds little discussion of rank-and-filers' idealism.

---

[15] John Earl Haynes and Harvey Klehr, *Venona: Decoding Soviet Espionage in America* (New Haven: Yale University Press, 1999), 8-13.

[16] Irving Howe and Lewis Coser, *The American Communist Party: A Critical History* (Boston: Beacon Press, 1957); Theodore Draper, *The Roots of American Communism* (New York: Viking Press, 1957); Theodore Draper, *American Communism and Soviet Russia: The Formative Period* (New York: Viking Press, 1960).

Revisionists Surpass Traditionalists

Later scholarship, by contrast, took a quite-different direction. A revisionist school emerged as the United States suffered defeat in Vietnam and endured the Watergate scandal at home. Even as the general public became more conservative, revisionists sympathetic to American Communism produced what quickly became a floodtide: literally hundreds of articles, dissertations, and books. These writers insisted the CP had been an indigenous, legitimate, and democratic participant on the political left. They anathematized earlier historians for omitting the party's achievements in making the nation less repressive. Social historians, intrigued by local struggles, have produced the bulk of revisionist literature (such as Robin D.G. Kelley's *Hammer and Hoe: Alabama Communists during the Great Depression,* and Mark Naison's study of Harlem Marxists).[17] Ironically however, perhaps the best-known revisionists, Maurice Isserman and Ellen W. Schrecker, wrote political history at the national level.[18] Although notable accounts from a traditionalist perspective continued to appear in books by John Earl Haynes, Harvey Klehr, and others, revisionists achieved overwhelming ascendancy in academia.[19] This victory was one of the U.S. left's few major triumphs between 1975 and 1995.

The Current Debate

Events of recent years have dramatically increased interest in, and the relevance of, American Communist history. They have also sharpened the rhetoric signally. The Soviet empire's 1991 collapse washed in every direction documents never meant to be seen outside party leadership ranks. A few years later, the National Security Agency and the Central Intelligence Agency added to the deluge by releasing Venona decryptions of approximately 2,900 Soviet spy cables. They complemented the Moscow materials, as did additional Federal Bureau of Investigation files. For Freedom of Information/Privacy Acts purposes, the FBI now considers anyone whose hundredth birthday has passed to have died, thereby removing from researchers a difficult burden of proof. All of the new records have stimulated a controversy over espionage. Previously, historians had avoided the issue, citing a

---

[17] Robin D.G. Kelley, *Hammer and Hoe: Alabama Communists during the Great Depression* (Chapel Hill: University of North Carolina Press, 1990); Mark Naison, *Communists in Harlem during the Great Depression* (Urbana: University of Illinois Press, 1983).

[18] Maurice Isserman, *Which Side Were You On? The American Communist Party during the Second World War* (Middletown: Wesleyan University Press, 1982) and *If I Had a Hammer: The Death of the Old Left and the Birth of the New Left* (New York: Basic Books, 1987); Ellen W. Schrecker, *No Ivory Tower: McCarthyism and the Universities* (New York, Oxford University Press, 1986) and *Many Are the Crimes: McCarthyism in America* (Boston: Little, Brown and Company, 1998).

[19] John Earl Haynes, *Dubious Alliance: The Making of Minnesota's DFL Party* (Minneapolis: University of Minnesota Press, 1984); Harvey Klehr, *The Heyday of American Communism: The Depression Decade* (New York: Basic Books, 1984).

paucity of available evidence. Now some traditionalists, reinvigorated if still outnumbered, argue that the CPUSA was never a normal participant in American life, and should not be so portrayed. Haynes and Klehr charge, "no responsible historian laments the collapse of Nazism or seeks to redeem the historical reputation of its domestic adherents. It would be a tragedy if academic historians rehabilitated American Communism through shoddy, error-filled and intellectually compromised scholarship." By contrast, acclaimed revisionist Isserman stresses that "however spectacular" the KGB's wartime record, its "successes within the United States were short-lived." The FBI had, by 1953, "quietly written off" the CPUSA "as a serious espionage threat."[20]

The field has grown in response to its expanded popularity. In 2002 a new, refereed journal, *American Communist History*, appeared. Its editorial board is balanced between traditionalists and revisionists, and also includes writers of Communist history from other lands. The following year, CPUSA studies acquired a list-serve, H-HOAC, thereby bringing communication among its scholars into the electronic communications age. Yet, as John Earl Haynes and Harvey Klehr point out in their latest book, neither of the contending perspectives has "managed to persuade the other of the error of its ways."[21]

A Synthesis Offered

This essay seeks not to convince either side to abandon its worldview. Instead, it looks to establish a common ground that will allow more-nuanced inquiry into the complex movement that advocated Communism in capitalism's most powerful citadel. All too often, proponents of each perspective have talked past each other. In the process, much has been present that both sides could have acknowledged. Yet points of agreement have gone unnoticed amid ideologically based fulminations and, sadly, personal recrimination. This no longer needs to be the case. There is much that all can recognize. Good, competent, honest scholars can learn from each other if we will all agree to follow the evidence. I made a similar argument, more tentatively, in a book that reached print in 1997.[22] The case for a middle path is even more compelling today, because intensified scholarly debate and media sensationalism during the intervening years have increased its need.

For instance, it does not hurt the argument of the traditionalists, who have clearly benefited from the past decade's revelations, to concede that most American Communists never came in contact with security-sensitive government documents and never personally knew anyone who did. Most party members met no Soviet citizens, much less KGB agents. Typical CP rank-and-filers planned nothing more violent than defending themselves against attacks by strikebreakers or police.

---

[20] John Earl Haynes and Harvey Klehr, *In Denial: Historians, Communism and Espionage* (San Francisco: Encounter books, 2003), 233; Maurice Isserman, "Disloyalty As a Principle: Why Communists Spied" <http://www.afsa.org/fsj/oct00/isserman.cfm>, 7.

[21] HOAC stands for Historians of American Communism, a professional organization that has existed for the past twenty years. Haynes and Klehr, *In Denial*, 3.

[22] Ryan, *Earl Browder*, 274-275.

In 1994, former Marxist Eugene Genovese was right to denounce many historians' "wilful refusal to examine the evidence that had been piled high from the beginning" concerning Russian Communism and human rights.[23] Toward the CPUSA membership, however, a more charitable view seems appropriate. Between 1919 and 1957, the vast majority did not have professional scholarly training and lacked sufficient information about events in the U.S.S.R. to make informed, critical judgments. Instead they accepted, for a time, the words of local party bosses, who dissembled and bombarded them with Stalinist propaganda. Although fewer than a hundred thousand persons belonged to the CPUSA at any one moment, it had an astronomical turnover rate. The average member stayed for only a few years. Because a majority left the movement, it is reasonable to conclude that many had lost trust in the leadership's mental gymnastics. In other words, instead of pressuring the CPUSA to cut the Moscow tie, typical workers simply voted with their feet. The best example of this phenomenon occurred after the Nazi-Soviet Pact of 1939, when thousands departed.

Equally, the revisionist case would not suffer from conceding that American Communist heads Earl Browder and Eugene Dennis betrayed rank-and-filers by using the movement to aid a foreign power. Browder, in particular, eagerly cooperated in an assault on the United States while the U.S.S.R. professed friendship and accepted American aid.[24] Common ground can acknowledge that there is still no record of any party member's refusing an offer to perform espionage. Of course, a most important step toward a middle path would be agreement that reasoned criticism of the CPUSA, based on evidence, does not constitute McCarthyism.

Haynes and Klehr's latest book charges that some of today's revisionists who color the party's history "in benign hues" see their work as "preparation of a new crop of radicals" to overthrow American capitalism.[25] However accurate this may or may not be, the struggle for a more humane and inclusive economy does not require defense of Stalinism or Marxism-Leninism, much less the CPUSA. The latter's long, shameful record of subordinating the class struggle to a foreign dictatorship's interests is an albatross from which honest advocates of socialism would do well to cut loose. Exposure of the American party's clandestine actions discredited global progressivism and gave its enemies an arsenal of ammunition. A political movement's record of failure could hardly be more complete.

In any event, the history profession's view of the CPUSA is likely to change significantly during coming decades. Time is not on revisionism's side. The viewpoint emerged as the generation that opposed the Vietnam War (and the bipartisan anti-Communist foreign policy seen as leading to it) earned its professional credentials. As that age cohort group gradually trades the joys of research for the remote control accessing five hundred high-definition television channels, inevitably historians too young to remember the anger of the nineteen sixties will take their place. Barring a catastrophic economic depression or

---

[23] Eugene D. Genovese, "The Question," *Dissent* 41.3 (Summer 1994): 371.
[24] James G. Ryan, "Socialist Triumph as a Family Value: Earl Browder and Soviet Espionage," *American Communist History* 1.2 (2002): 125-142.
[25] Haynes and Klehr, *In Denial*, 8.

disastrous foreign adventure, they are unlikely to share the revisionists' fundamental discontent with what we used to call "the system."

Conclusion

In the United States Communism has always dwelled on the ideological borderlands. The CPUSA, even at its height during the 1930s and 1940s, never fully crossed the barrier separating it from respectability. For a time, the party blurred the boundary of permissible political dissent in America. In the end, however, the movement did not become a durable element in society; much less challenge the hegemony of capitalist values. The Cold War era brought an initial scholarly interest in the CP. For the past thirty years, the word "fascination" better describes historians' behavior. Yet the field of study's current condition is not normal, nor is it healthy. A viable common ground exists; historians can reach it if they stop insulting each other. Change almost certainly will occur anyway. The proposed middle path can cause scholars to welcome new evidence, instead of seeking ways to deride and minimize it.

BETWEEN AVANT-GARDE AND KITSCH: PRAGMATIC LIBERALISM, PUBLIC ARTS FUNDING, AND THE COLD WAR IN THE UNITED STATES[1]

David Brian Howard

It is among the hopeful signs in the midst of the decay of our present society that we—some of us—have been unwilling to accept this last phase of our own culture. In seeking to go beyond Alexandrianism, a part of Western bourgeois society has produced something unheard of heretofore: avant-garde culture.

Clement Greenberg,
"Avant-Garde and Kitsch," 1939.

Kitsch has not been confined to the cities in which it was born, but has flowed out over the countryside, wiping out folk culture. Nor has it shown any regard for geographical and national-cultural boundaries. Another mass product of Western industrialism, it has gone on a triumphal tour of the world, crowding out and defacing native cultures in one colonial country after another, so that it is now by way of becoming a universal culture, the first universal culture ever beheld.

Clement Greenberg,
"Avant-Garde and Kitsch," 1939.

On 4 October 1957, a stunned American society reeled at the news of the successful launch of a Soviet earth orbiting satellite, *Sputnik 1*. The launch of this satellite, officially baptized as the "Artificial Traveler Around the Earth," recalled the nightmarish period of national insecurity that followed the successful Japanese attack on Pearl Harbor. A period of intense national self-examination queried both the domestic and foreign policy of the Eisenhower administration under the alarmist twin banners of the "missile gap" and the "culture gap," accurately reflecting the intertwining of cultural and Cold War policies in the political discourse of the period. This internal debate and self-analysis was to have tremendous implications for the moribund status of public funding for the arts in the United States, moving the debate over public arts funding from its peripheral status in the House of Representatives, to the center, cumulatively leading to the establishment of a National Endowment for the Arts (NEA), on 29 September 1965, under President Lyndon B. Johnson.

---

[1] A longer version of this essay will be published in the *Canadian Review of American Studies*.

The apparent impotence of the Eisenhower administration in the political fall-out from Sputnik reinvigorated a moribund debate about the role of the federal government in arts funding, a debate stultified by the red-baiting of the early 1950s, by aligning the debate about culture with the overarching debate about the national purpose and will of the American people in the Cold War. In effect, a revamped, and more conservative, American liberalism exacerbated the rents and fissures within the public discourse over the "missile gap" following *Sputnik,* to create the impression that only radical and dramatic surgery could "suture" these gaps and save the United States both militarily and culturally. This essay will examine the ways in which pragmatic liberal politicians and intellectuals in the United States ironically exploited what the postcolonial theorist Homi K. Bhahba (extrapolating from the psychoanalytic theory of Jacques Lacan) has labeled "the process of the gap," in order to promote both their military and cultural agendas. For Bhahba it is within this "process of the gap" that "the relationship of the subject to the Other is produced."[2] The intention is to destabilize or unsettle the binary or symmetrical logic by which identities are produced. This process therefore enables the articulation of new partial identities that can exploit these gaps through forms of political and cultural resistance.

While Bhahba draws upon this process as the basis for fomenting a politics of postcolonial resistance, this essay examines a different application of Bhahba's concept, considering the exploitation of "gaps" by American pragmatic liberals who also wished to destabilize established identities. However, unlike Bhahba, their intention was not to criticize the hegemony of liberal capitalism but to more effectively entrench their vision of American hegemony through an astute and flexible application of pragmatic liberalism. On the political battleground of American politics between 1957 and 1960, the Democratic pragmatic liberals and their moderate Republican allies reconceptualized the role of culture and public arts funding in order to exploit the gaps in American society that the Eisenhower administration seemed unwilling, or unable, to close or ameliorate.

In the immediate post-war period, government funding for the arts in the United States was a virtual impossibility. Funding for cultural programs, even when tied to propaganda campaigns against the Soviet Union, had to be arranged by private foundations or individuals: the Cold War effectively quashed hopes of a resurgence of government support for the arts, as had existed in the New Deal up to 1943, because of the tainted associations of public arts programs with Soviet-style socialist-oriented culture. On several occasions during the first decade after World War II, individual politicians, such as liberal Republican representative Jacob Javits of New York State, attempted to introduce bills promoting a new activist role for state supported culture only to be repeatedly defeated by more conservative right

---

[2] Homi K. Bhahba, *The Location of Culture* (London: Routledge Press, 1995), 54, and generally chapter 1. The refinements to pragmatic liberal ideology in the 1940s through to the early 1960s may help to explain why so many strategies of resistance under the rubric of postmodernism and post-colonialism would seem to so often function as ideological corollaries to capitalism.

wing politicians, such as George Dondero of Michigan.[3] Even up to 1957 Javits co-sponsored a bill calling for the formation of a federally funded arts foundation with grant-making ability modeled on the examples of the British and Canadian Arts Councils. In each instance, the proposed legislation was defeated, but the advantages of government support of the arts were perceived by individuals such as Jacob Javits, John and Nelson Rockefeller, Jr., and even Henry Luce, as a natural complement to the economic, scientific, and military struggle for U.S. superiority in the Cold War. The launching of *Sputnik*, however, threw the question of public arts funding into the limelight of public policy in the United States. In April 1959, one month after introducing a massive Defense Appropriations Bill in Congress, Javits criticized the Republican right wing by underscoring the need for a public cultural strategy in waging the Cold War:

> Our political institutions, our individual freedoms and our way of life serve as examples, even as an inspiration, to the peoples of the world. We have expended untold toil and countless billions to give our nation this stature and to preserve it. Yet in this tremendous progress, one vital element of our national character has been left to struggle with little public effort and assistance to aid it. The cultural heritage of America—one of the great building forces holding together and enhancing our varied national life—has been relegated to a lesser role in the pageant of America.[4]

In addition to *Sputnik*, two other major events after 1957 questioned the portrayal of American life being promoted by the Eisenhower administration in the Cold War and reinforced the Republican Party's image of being too reliant on promoting effete images of consumerism to counter the potent Soviet combination of national purpose and increasing scientific accomplishment. The first was the colossal propaganda failure of the American exhibition strategy at the Brussels Universal and International Exhibition of 1958. The second was the triumph of Vice-President Richard Nixon over Nikita Khruschev in the famous "kitchen

---

[3] For a discussion of the frustrations experienced by liberal advocates for government funding of the arts prior to the launch of Sputnik, see Gary O. Larson, *The Reluctant Patron: The United States Government and the Arts, 1943-1965* (Philadelphia: University of Pennsylvania Press, 1983), especially chapter 1. Jacob Javits was one of the cold warrior George Dondero's most ardent opponents on the arts issue. In 1949, in response to Dondero's art treatise "Modern Art Shackled to Communism," he stated, "In seeking to discredit modern art by its wholesale condemnation as communistic my colleague—I am sure unwittingly—falls in to the trap of the same propagandistic device the influence of which we have all decried in the Soviet Union, Nazi Germany and Fascist Italy, for it is condemnation by class and broad-scale labeling without a patient confidence in the ultimate judgement of our people and their capability for discerning the good from the evil, the artistic from the propagandistic and the true from the false." Cited in Elaine King, *Pluralism in the Visual Arts in the United States 1965-1978: The National Endowment for the Arts, an Influential Force* (Ph.D. diss., Northwestern University, Evansville, 1986), 45-46.

[4] King, *Pluralism in the Visual Arts*, 51.

debate" held at the 1959 American National Exhibition in Moscow in an exhibit promoting the "American Way of Life."

In the spring of 1960, *Life Magazine* took direct aim at the Eisenhower administration strategy by publishing a series of ten essays on "The National Purpose" which generally argued that "excessive materialism, complacency, flabbiness, selfishness, apathetic and aimless affluence, and moral confusion ... impaired America's global performance and reputation."[5]

John F. Kennedy's invocation of the New Frontier was a clever rhetorical device designed to prod and cajole the American public from their consumerist malaise by means of a complex renegotiating of the traditions of pragmatism, progressivism, and liberalism that retained many of the characteristics of the postwar liberal "vital center" tradition, re-tooled to capitalize on the political opportunities presented to liberals at the end of the 1950s and during the early 1960s.[6] For example, in the 1962 "Introduction" to the re-publication of *The Vital Center*, Schlesinger outlined the process of reconstruction that pragmatism, liberalism, and progressivism had undergone in the intervening thirteen years since his book was first published. According to Schlesinger, the day of monolithic communism was definitely over:

> History thus shows plainly that Communism is not the form of social organization toward which all societies are irresistibly evolving. Rather it is a phenomenon of the transition from stagnation to development, a "disease" (in

---

[5] John W. Jeffries, "The Quest for National Purpose," *American Quarterly* 30 (1978): 457. The ten contributors to the volume included John K. Jessup, chief editorial writer for *Life*; Adlai E. Stevenson, twice the Democratic presidential nominee who ran against Eisenhower in 1952 and 1956; Archibald MacLeish, poet; David Sarnoff, board chairman of the Radio Corporation of America; Billy Graham, evangelist; John Gardener, president of the Carnegie Corporation; Clinton Rossiter, professor of Government at Cornell University; Albert Wohlstetter, associate director of projects at the Rand Corporation; James Reston, Washington correspondent of the *Times*; Walter Lippmann, liberal social critic and writer for the *New York Herald Tribune*. Albert Wohlstetter is a prime example of the missile gap advocate working at the juncture between the aerospace industry, the Air Force and the Rand Corporation whose insights informed both Rockefeller's and Kennedy's criticism of Republican defense policy.

[6] The concept of the "vital center" was developed by Arthur Schlesinger, Jr., in his key text *The Vital Center: The Politics of Freedom* (Boston: Houghton Mifflin, 1949, reprinted 1962). Schlesinger rejected the extremes of left and right in American politics, those of the "soft" doughfaced progressives of the 1930s on the left and the capitalists on the right who had failed to to provide an "effective governing class," 13. "Midtwentieth-century liberalism," argues Schlesinger, "has thus been fundamentally reshaped by the hope of the New Deal, by exposure of the Soviet Union, and by the deepening of our knowledge of man. The consequence of this historical re-education has been an unconditional rejection of totalitarianism and a reassertion of the ultimate integrity of the individual, " xxiii. The reference to the deepening knowledge of man, in part, is an allusion to the pessimistic theology of Reinhold Niebuhr, whose writings tempered the optimism of the progressive tradition in America while reinforcing Schlesinger's desire to replace the "soft liberalism" of the 1930s with his concept of the "hard liberal."

Walt Rostow's phrase) of the modernization process. Democratic, regulated capitalism—the mixed economy—will be more capable of coping with the long-term consequences of modernization.[7]

Schlesinger's invocation of the mixed economy opened doors to the reintroduction of businessmen and business ideals to a liberal ideology that was distancing itself from the anti-business attitudes of the "soft liberals" in the New Deal:

> There are signs today, it is true, of a new spirit stirring in the business community. The stabilization of economic life has given some business circles, at least, a clearer sense of their responsibility to the general welfare. Indeed, the very withering away of capitalist motivation, while rousing intimations of death-wish in some businessmen, has served as a means of liberating others with the American liberal beliefs in person integrity, political freedom and equality of opportunity.[8]

The New Deal emphasized problems of essentially a quantitative character, focusing on the issues of production and consumption, not unlike the one-dimensional approach of the Republicans in the 1950s. Schlesinger, therefore, altered the major focus of liberalism under the New Deal and reoriented it towards the qualitative concerns of the earlier American pragmatic philosophers who pre-dated the New Deal as a way of tempering the materialist excesses of free enterprise as well as big government.[9] Schlesinger's call for a return to the spirit of the frontiersman in the modern age was exploited, in the Kennedy campaign, to promote a new individualism and activist-oriented philosophy that would help suture the wound in the national psyche with a rapid deployment of missiles, astronauts, and artists. By emphasizing the qualitative aspects of an engaged civic life for the citizen as opposed to the so-called quantitative bias of the Eisenhower regime, or of the "socialist" legacy of the New Deal, liberal intellectuals sought to re-define the parameters of the "vital center" in response to the era of the military-complex.[10]

Schlesinger unveiled the outline of his new formula for the interaction of culture, business, and government in an article entitled, "Notes on a National

---

[7] Ibid., xiii-xv.
[8] Ibid., 28-29.
[9] According to Schlesinger, qualitative liberalism focused on the proper balance between public and private enterprise: "The resulting improvements in opportunities in education, medical care, social welfare, community planning, culture and the arts will improve the chances for the individual to win his spiritual fulfillment." Ibid., xv.
[10] Michael S. Sherry notes that "militarization was taking on a life of its own apart from the world scene, becoming woven into the fabric of American life." Thus, Eisenhower left office warning Americans to "guard against the acquisition of unwarranted influence, whether sought or unsought, by the military-industrial complex. The potential for the disastrous rise of misplaced power exists and will persist." Cited in Michael S. Sherry, *In the Shadow of War: The United States since the 1930s* (New Haven: Yale University Press, 1995), 234.

Cultural Policy," published in the journal *Daedalus* in the spring of 1960. In this article, Schlesinger argued that reliance solely upon private initiatives to fund the arts was tainted by its "impotence" to maintain the economic support necessary for a national cultural strategy. Schlesinger avoided suggesting massive government intervention as in the New Deal by advocating a limited role for the federal government in the arts and giving particular attention to Western European models of government art support programs. Recognizing the historical opposition to arts funding in the post-war period, Schlesinger recommended a small first step in the form of a Federal Advisory Council on the Arts to develop avenues that would negotiate the delicate balance between public and private funding and the fine line separating qualitative from quantitative concerns. Pivotal to all these issues was a redefined individualism whose relationship to the frontier was not dissimilar from that of the frontier mythology characteristic of "American exceptionalism" in the nineteenth century, but now adapted to an urban as opposed to a wilderness, context.

While intellectuals were crossing the frontier dividing the ivory tower from state-power and assuming positions of responsibility within the newly elected Kennedy administration, it is important to recognize that these were intellectuals minted in the pragmatic liberal mould. Idealists were shunted aside on the road to the White House in favor of hard-nosed liberals, many of whom had served on the Rockefeller Commissions. From a cultural perspective, the most intriguing appointment was that of August Heckscher, Jr., the director of the Rockefeller-financed Twentieth Century Fund as well as a member of the Art Commission of the City of New York, and the chairman of the board of the International Council of the Museum of Modern Art, to a new role in 1962 as the president's special consultant on the arts. This appointment coincided with the publication of Heckscher's cultural philosophy in a book entitled *The Public Happiness* in which his diagnosis of the ills facing American society followed Schlesinger's schema: Americans had overemphasized the quantitative aspects of modernity at the expense of the qualitative. The central issue facing society was defined not as attaining material well-being but as avoiding the dangers of boredom, loneliness, and alienation which threatened to tear apart the fabric of post-war American society. The individual citizen, according to Heckscher, was experiencing the loss of his or her own individuality, becoming "an abstraction in the midst of meaningless change and activity."[11] Such a loss of individuality led to the loss of will to close the gaps and overcome the contradictions challenging the United States. The corrupting influences of materialism symbolized by the rapid advance of suburban middle-class lifestyles and value systems across the nation was, for Heckscher, the greatest challenge of modernity.[12]

---

[11] August Heckscher, Jr., *The Public Happiness* (New York: Atheneum Publishers, 1962), vii.

[12] In *The Public Happiness*, Heckscher states, "The danger today is that this comfortable middle realm will prevail over everything else in the social order, swallowing up the private man and the public man alike and making way for the great mass that in the end dominates all. Then everyone will have become so well adjusted to everyone else that no one can any longer be a person in the old sense. Compromise and conformity will have been so far developed that there remain no veiled issues worth compromising and

From Heckscher's point of view, materialism, consensus, and conformity had proliferated under the Eisenhower era but thanks to the persistence of non-conformists such as the Abstract Expressionists and the Beatniks, a breathing space for individualism had been preserved. However, the miniscule nature of these individualist practices within the overwhelming presence of mass culture emphasized the extreme nature of the gap separating the avant-garde and bohemians from the middle class and threatened to make critical cultural practices irrelevant to the culture as a whole. Heckscher advocated an inclusive conception of culture that promoted the heterogenous identities of the anti-social margins as integral to American life. He aimed at transcending the rigid separation of private and public life while attempting not to implode both spheres into one undifferentiated mass. Unlike the revolutionary efforts of the Surrealist movement in Europe to integrate art into life prior to World War II (and continuing into the 1950s and 1960s with other French avant-gardes such as the Situationist International) this pragmatic liberal strategy sought to bring the remote practices of the avant-garde into a form of critical relationship with middle class culture. In effect, by diminishing the gap between the avant-garde and mass culture vital center liberals could reinvigorate the role of culture as a key element in defining their opposition to the totalitarianism of the left and the right while, at the same time, dispensing with the anti-bourgeois posturing of the European avant-gardes. In addition, Heckscher argued that this dynamic interplay between such diverse expressions of American life corresponded to the myth of a frontier identity born out of the collision of European civilization and the North American wilderness: "Only then can we hope to lift ourselves out of the yawning pit which reduces all values to communal values, and loses both the citizen and the person in the mass man."[13] As one of the remaining vestiges of the frontiersman in modern society the avant-garde was now recruited into the defense of freedom as well as being an expression of the superiority of the American way of life.

Within Heckscher's version of Schlesinger's schema, the arts were a key factor in remotivating civic virtue and achieving public happiness. As Heckscher readily admitted, this implied an intimate link between art and politics that avoided both overt propagandizing and isolation within a formalist elitism (a charge to which America's leading modernist-avant-garde art critic, Clement Greenberg, was particularly vulnerable). High culture, the avant-garde and mass culture were to engage in a dynamic interaction characteristic of the great civilizations of Greece, Rome, and the Italian Renaissance that would provide a concept of creative leisure, thus keeping the division between work and play in a heightened state of tension and animating the individual out of his or her boredom.

Heckscher's pragmatic liberal aesthetics emphasized a playful, ironic and detached approach to art in order to realize the dream of a dynamic civic culture. He

---

nothing to conform to except a vague and general standard of mass morality. Unless there are countervailing forces drawing men strongly toward privacy on the one hand, and toward a meaningful political life on the other, the social sphere comes to be taken as an end in itself. Unless there are a few anti-social people, all is lost," 57.

[13] Ibid., 58.

was sympathetic to the frontiersman approach of the modernist avant-garde and the anti-social individuals who preserved a fragment of self-expression during the darkest moments of mass culture, but his civic-minded pragmatism required that an active civic culture must press beyond the defensive positions of the post-war American avant-garde and the anti-ironic position of the formalists, if a cultural renaissance cutting across all social layers of American society was to be achieved. This vision of cultural activism was sophisticated, flexible, and yet conservative because this model of culture always remained within the limitations of the enhancement of the leisure life of the citizen under the New Frontier and not the historical avant-garde's revolutionary mission of reintegrating art into life. Heckscher believed that, within capitalism, a defensive and offensive posture capable of preserving and expanding the frontiers of freedom and forestalling the decline experienced by previous empires such as Sparta and Rome was the new pragmatic role of avant-garde art within American culture.

Another research director of the Twentieth Century Fund who worked with Heckscher to formulate a liberal arts constituency in the Kennedy era was the noted scholar Sebastian de Grazia, whose book *Time, Work and Leisure* was published by the Fund in 1962. The book examines the differences in the concepts of work and play in capitalist society and analyses the consequences for a meaningful sense of leisure in a mass urban society. De Grazia notes that as consumerism gained momentum in the 1950s, the concepts of work and play became increasingly estranged from one another. De Grazia's text emphasizes the virtues of an elevated concept of leisure, a synthesis of work and play ideally achieved through the combined efforts of education and government-supported cultural programs.

De Grazia employed the historical analogy of the Spartan Empire to illustrate the dangers of the separation of work and play in the modern United States and to argue for the value of an integrated concept of leisure, making extensive use of Schlesinger's comparison of the crisis of masculinity to the sorry state of American culture. Sparta, successful at war, was a society with clearly defined gender roles: the male warrior waged war away from home while the female remained isolated in the domestic sphere with "no education in self-control." Thus the Spartan female resorted to a life of "license and luxury" in her spare time. Echoing the concerns of Schlesinger and Heckscher, the parallels with the Eisenhower era are evident in De Grazia's description of the decline of the Spartan Empire as being characterized by "… the growth of luxuriousness, avarice, mal-distribution of property, shortage of warriors, and a female population that in war caused more confusion than the enemy."[14]

Pragmatic liberal advocates of federal funding support for the arts, such as Schlesinger, Heckscher, and De Grazia, were continually stymied in their efforts to promote legislation authorizing the establishment of a federal arts agency, but the difference between the period prior to *Sputnik* and after the launch of *Sputnik* indicates a slow but progressive implementation of their recommendations. In 1962, for example, three separate bills promoting federal involvement in the arts were

---

[14] Sebastian De Grazia, *Of Time, Work, and Leisure* (New York: Twentieth Century Fund, 1962), 11-12.

introduced by Hubert Humphrey, Joe Clark, and Jacob Javits but each was in turn defeated by a skeptical Congress. However, on 28 May 1963, Heckscher's report to the president entitled "The Arts and the National Government" was released, following the conclusion of his first year as the first presidential adviser of the Arts. With its official backing from the office of the president, the proposed federal cultural policy carried more political clout than any cultural funding bill that had yet been sent to the Congress since World War II.

Heckscher's blueprint for a federal role in the arts highlighted the contradictory nature of pragmatic liberalism in the Kennedy era. Great care was taken to downplay the extent and role of the government's involvement while the private sector was still expected to carry the main burden of cultural patronage, as Heckscher clearly argued: "Although the government's role in the arts must always remain peripheral, with individual creativity and private support being central, that is no reason why the things which the government can properly do in this field should not be done confidently and expertly."[15] While downplaying the extent of the foreseeable role of the federal government in arts funding, Heckscher's advocacy of a national arts foundation represented a significant shift in the structuring of American culture. By dispensing federal funds to aid in the establishment of arts councils across the United States, Washington D.C.'s National Cultural Center would become the model of state supported culture "promoting cultural diversity, innovation, and excellence."[16]

In response to Heckscher's report, President Kennedy issued Executive Order 11112 on 12 June 1963, announcing the establishment of an important first step in the process by creating the President's Advisory Council on the Arts. Kennedy's statement (drafted by Heckscher), acknowledged the significance of the Council as "... the first time the arts will have some formal Government body which will be specifically concerned with all aspects of the arts and to which the artist and the arts institutions can present their views and bring their problems."[17] Unlike earlier rounds of the culture debate prior to *Sputnik*, proponents of government financing for the arts could now point to both presidential support and the visible success of the various pilot projects in cultural funding inaugurated by Nelson Rockefeller, Jr., elected governor of New York State one year after *Sputnik*. Now, for the first time, backers of government funding for the arts could take advantage of the combined Democratic and Republican support for such a program, enabling the arts bill to pass through Congress successfully. On 20 August 1964, the bill came before the House of Representatives and passed by a vote of 213 to 135, with many Republicans loyal to Rockefeller approving the Democratic bill in a show of bipartisan agreement. Passed by the Senate the following day, the arts bill paved the way for the establishment of a National Foundation of the Arts, which would finally put into

---

[15] Quoted in Vineta Colby, *American Culture in the Sixties* (New York: H.W. Wilson Company, 1964), 106.
[16] Ibid., 40.
[17] For an in-depth discussion of the political skirmishing around the issue of federal support of the arts, see Fannie Taylor and Anthony L. Barresi, *The Arts at a New Frontier* (New York: Plenum Press, 1984), especially chapter 2.

place the machinery necessary to establish the National Endowment for the Arts (NEA) in 1965 and realize the pragmatic liberal cultural agenda.

Conclusion

Between the launch of *Sputnik* in the fall of 1957 and the creation of the NEA in 1965, the barrier to a publicly supported federal arts program arose in a highly contested political environment. Yet arguably, the suddenly perceived "missile gap" created a political opportunity which was immeasurably enhanced by the wave of public anxiety which cascaded across American society and fuelled the perception that the United States was rife with social contradictions and discord. By exploiting their strategy of underscoring that "gap" in the period between the launch of *Sputnik* and the 1960 presidential election, pragmatic liberal intellectuals and politicians had the opportunity to draft a sweeping set of reforms that, in effect, would appear to suture the contradictions (and the gaps) in American culture and society while also re-drawing the focus of American foreign policy in the Cold War. The societal trauma of *Sputnik* created many of the pre-conditions necessary for just such a re-forging of liberal politics in America. Pragmatic liberalism utilized the appearance of decadence and loss of national purpose under the Eisenhower administration in order to launch the idea of the "new frontiersman," with the astronaut and the contemporary artist as prime examples. Therefore pragmatic liberals were able to provide a momentary and partial solution to American social instability by formulating a newly articulated sense of the avant-garde artistic movement and its role as modern American "frontier."

HAWAII, STATEHOOD, AND THE EAST-WEST CENTER: OPENING UP THE PACIFIC FRONTIER

Giles Scott-Smith

In our continuing effort to broaden our intellectual horizons, and to expand our educational frontiers, this still young center of research and study has already begun to play a leading role.[1]

In his ground-breaking thesis on the importance of the frontier for American development, Frederick Jackson Turner claimed that "the true point of view in the history of this nation is not the Atlantic coast, it is the Great West." For Turner, the decisive factor in the social and political history of the United States was thus not the influence of European thought and institutions, but the unique experience of gradually expanding its territory westwards over a period of two centuries.[2] In the context of this westward expansion, the annexation and eventual acceptance of the islands of Hawaii into the Union offers an added dimension to what Turner was referring to. Whereas the Hawaiian experience does not fit perfectly within the central points of his thesis, it does at least represent a further example of the connection between the frontier and democratization, and a further contribution to the myth of Manifest Destiny.

This essay will concentrate on how the extension of the United States' democratic frontier out to the Hawaiian islands became embroiled in major shifts within the American body politic during the 1950s. Although Hawaii was granted statehood by President Eisenhower in 1959, it was Lyndon Johnson and his allies who played a crucial role in manoeuvering the necessary legislation through Congress. Johnson's motives for this were complex. The interests of American foreign and security policy in the Pacific region, which had escalated since the Korean War, were certainly a prime reason. Connected to this was how the Hawaiian statehood issue was important in the context of civil rights, in terms of offering a symbolic display of the American democratic process standing up to its rhetoric. This required the "modernization" of the Democratic Party by breaking the power of the South, something Johnson, a Texan, was uniquely placed to achieve. Beyond these matters, Johnson also looked ahead to how Hawaii could be used as a jumping-off point for establishing contacts with the cultural, intellectual, and political elites of Asia. The need to combine a progressive development policy with efforts to nurture anti-communism became a vital element in America's security policy in the Pacific

---

[1] "Remarks at the East-West Center in Honolulu," 18 October 1966, *Public Papers of the Presidents: Lyndon B. Johnson, 1966* (Washington, DC: Government Printing Office, 1967), 2:1219.

[2] Frederick Jackson Turner, "The Significance of the Frontier in American History," in George Rogers Taylor, ed., *The Turner Thesis: Concerning the Role of the Frontier in American History* (Lexington, MA: D.C. Heath, 1972).

region. The plan for an East-West Center to provide high-level training for promising graduates, which was also pioneered by Johnson, was an important result.

Hawaiian Statehood

Hawaii's relation with the United States changed fundamentally at the end of the nineteenth century as a result of the expanding interests of the United States in the Pacific region.[3] On 7 July 1898 Hawaii, formerly an independent kingdom, was annexed to the United States by President McKinley. With the Spanish-American War beginning in April that year, Hawaii had become a vital staging post in the Pacific for the military. In 1900 Congress passed the Organic Act which established an elected state legislature, but ultimate executive powers, including use of veto, were placed with an unelected governor to be appointed by the president every four years. The electorate could also choose a delegate to represent them in the House of Representatives in Congress, but the delegate had no voting powers in Washington and was only able to contribute to debate. In addition to these limitations, the inhabitants of Asian origin were denied American citizenship. Therefore, while the islands were as a whole disenfranchised with respect to the ultimate powers controlling their territory, some groups were inevitably more disenfranchised than others.[4] The Act did, however, include the legal right for Hawaii to one day attain statehood as a part of the United States.

The first statehood bill was introduced in 1919, but it would be another forty years before any such act would be passed by both chambers of Congress. Several reasons accounted for this delay. Firstly, the statehood issue became caught up in partisan political calculations, based on expectations of whether Hawaii would vote Democrat or Republican. As Hawaiian delegate Joseph Farrington remarked to a Republican National Committee meeting in 1951, "I do not think it is impossible in the years ahead of us with the majority so close that the control of the United States Senate might be determined by the outcome of an election in Hawaii."[5]

Secondly, Hawaii became combined with Alaska in statehood negotiations, complicating the debate because of the different justifications for each territory. After 1954 the southern Democrats managed to combine Hawaiian and Alaskan statehood in one bill. Due to Republican opposition to Alaskan accession because of its small population and vital location for national security policy, the southerners thereby forced the Republicans to oppose Hawaii at the same time.

Thirdly, there were concerns about the degree of communist influence within the powerful Hawaiian branch of the International Longshoreman's and

---

[3] On the extension of the power and influence of the United States in the Pacific during the nineteenth century, and the reasons for this, see Frank Ninkovich, *The United States and Imperialism* (Oxford: Blackwell, 2001).
[4] Richard Borreca, "Annexation," *Honolulu Star Bulletin*, 12 July 1999.
[5] Western Regional Conference, Republican National Committee, 12 May 1951, *Papers of the Republican Party, Part I: Meetings of the Republican National Committee, 1911-1980, Series A: 1911-1960*, reel 11 (microfilm collection, Roosevelt Study Center, Middelburg, The Netherlands, hereafter referred to as microfilm RSC).

Warehouseman's Union (ILWU). Serious strikes had occurred, especially in 1949. While there were communists active in the union, this accusation was largely used as a cover for other prejudices, as confirmed in 1959 when the Department of Justice and the FBI rejected any notion that the ILWU was a threat to political stability on the islands.[6]

Fourthly, there was opposition from what might be termed Republican old-style conservatism. This involved the representatives of the bigger states such as New York, Illinois, and Pennsylvania, who disliked "disrupting" the make-up of Congress with new members. Another reason used was the fact that Hawaii would be an offshore state, arguing that the United States should remain as one territorial unit.

Fifthly, and most importantly, there was the opposition from the southern Democrats. This centred on the simple fact of Hawaii's multiracial population.[7] Already during the debates over the passage of the Organic Act it was remarked that Caucasians were not in the majority, and that this was likely to be an obstacle for statehood—which indeed it was. Intermixing between the different ethnic groups was also high, harmonious, and increasing. Between 1912 and 1945 interracial marriages increased from 14 percent to almost 40 percent, and there was no evidence that "block vote" tactics in the state legislature were common.[8] Yet from the perspective of the segregationist South, such a multiracial society was rejected out of hand, not only on principle but also because it would provide a threatening example. It was highly likely, after all, that the two new Hawaiian senators would be pro-civil rights, thereby tipping the balance in the Senate in favor of new legislation. Hawaiian senator Daniel Inouye later put in graphic terms that the statehood legislation

> was a pure and simple civil rights bill, and civil rights bills during those days just weren't passing. The argument against the statehood bill, although not said so loudly and publicly, was that if Hawaii became a state you would have representation by a strange looking people. As one senator said, "How would you like to be sitting next to a fellow named Yamamoto?"[9]

Eisenhower had been a supporter of statehood since his time as dean of Columbia University, largely based on his recognition of the war record of Japanese-American

---

[6] Richard Borecca, "GI Bill Propelled 1954's Democratic Revolution," *Honolulu Star Bulletin*, 18 October 1999; Report of the House Committee on Interior and Insular Affairs, 5 March 1959, code 9: Cultural Relations, file 02376: Hawaii, Archives of the Ministry of Foreign Affairs, The Hague, The Netherlands.

[7] The ethnic breakdown of the population of Hawaii in 1964 was as follows: 209,000 Caucasian; 206,000 Japanese; 99,500 Hawaiian (part); 71,000 Filipino; 40,000 Chinese; 9,900 Hawaiian (full); 19,000 Other. Total population: 654,000.

[8] Roger J. Bell, "Admission Delayed: The Influence of Sectional and Political Opposition in Congress on Statehood for Hawaii," *Hawaiian Journal of History* 6 (1972): 47-48.

[9] Daniel K. Inouye, *Oral Histories of the Johnson Administration 1963-1969, Part II: The Congress, the Judiciary, Public Figures, and Private Individuals*, reel 2 (microfilm RSC).

troops. He subsequently expressed to Congress his wish for this legislation in every year of his presidency until it was granted. In this respect, it is interesting to note how his presentation of the subject changed through the 1950s. In his State of the Union messages of 1953, 1954, and 1955 he proposed statehood in curt, matter-of-fact statements. In his message for 1956, however, with the Eisenhower administration beginning to take civil rights and its political consequences as a more serious issue, he expanded on the theme in dramatic fashion.

> One particular challenge confronts us. In the Hawaiian islands, East meets West. To the islands, Asia and Europe and the Western Hemisphere, all the continents, have contributed their peoples and their cultures to display a unique example of a community that is a successful laboratory in human brotherhood. Statehood, supported by the repeatedly expressed desire of the islands' people and by our traditions, would be a shining example of the American way to the entire earth.[10]

Eisenhower would maintain this theme in the coming years when referring to Hawaii, especially when traveling in Asia. In 1959 he reached new heights of rhetoric when he addressed the Indian parliament: "Hawaii cries insistently to a divided world that all our differences of race and origin are less than the grand and indestructible unity of our common brotherhood. The world should take time to listen with attentive ear to Hawaii."[11]

The use of such expansive language was particularly related to America's standing in the Far East. By the 1950s Hawaii was more than just an important naval base. It was a potential symbol of how the American democratic system was as respectful and protective of freedom *for all* as was consistently claimed, especially as a balance to the negative realities of the segregated and violent South. Developments in the emerging Third World were beginning to have an increasing impact on American foreign policy during this period. In June 1954 the United States had brokered the Geneva peace talks that paved the way for the withdrawal of France from Indochina. In September 1954 the Southeast Asia Treaty Organisation, involving the United States, Great Britain, France, Australia, New Zealand, Thailand, the Philippines, and Pakistan was inaugurated in Manila. In April 1955 the African-Asian Conference in Bandung, Indonesia, in which twenty-nine nations from those two continents participated, marked the potential sea-change in international politics brought about by post-war decolonization. With its harmonious multiracial population and mid-Pacific location, Hawaii could be the perfect "bridge" to reach out to these new nations; if it were to be granted full democratic rights as a U.S. state. Thus in 1951 Joseph Farrington had remarked to the same Republican National Committee meeting how, over the previous fifty years,

---

[10] "State of the Union Message to Congress," 5 January 1956, *Public Papers of the Presidents: Dwight D. Eisenhower, 1956* (Washington, DC: Government Printing Office, 1957), 25.

[11] "Address Given to Joint Session of Parliament of India," 10 December 1959, *Public Papers of the Presidents: Dwight D. Eisenhower, 1959* (Washington, DC: Government Printing Office, 1960), 831.

thousands of Japanese, Chinese, Koreans, Filipinos, and Pacific islanders had been united under the American flag on the islands, and that as a result "the people who live around the Pacific are watching to see what the United States does about Hawaii before they come to their conclusions as to whether we are sincere in our belief in the principles of democracy."[12]

Through the 1950s the battle over statehood was largely fought out in the Senate, because it was there that the southern Democrats had the most leverage when it came to a vote. If they could not block bills by influencing the legislative timetable via the powerful Rules Committees, there was always the fall-back to filibuster tactics. This was notably applied by senators James Eastland and John Stennis from Mississippi and Richard Russell from Georgia. In a March 1954 debate on Hawaii in the Senate, Eastland, one of the strongest advocates of continued segregation, spoke for four hours before remarking that he had not yet reached the "preface" of his speech and that he would require a further four days to complete it.

Lyndon Johnson entered the story in 1953 when he became Senate minority leader. Being a Texan, it was naturally expected that Johnson would side with the Dixiecrats on many issues, opposition to Hawaii included. As he later admitted, he was not an initial supporter of statehood. But he was more concerned about maintaining the cohesion of the party in a time when the divisions between its northern and southern wings were becoming more exposed. In 1954 the Democrats took control of Congress, but in the Senate by one seat. They also secured a majority for the first time in the Hawaiian legislature, and, combined with their existing control of the Alaskan legislature, these results raised the prospect that both territories might actually vote Democrat once they were admitted into the Union.[13] This was naturally not missed by the Republicans, who noted that "increasing Democratic recognition of the political implications of statehood for these territories ruled out any possibility of securing statehood for Hawaii alone."[14] But with this opportunity in front of them, the Democrats were far from united on how to proceed.

After the congressional elections of 1954 Johnson became Senate majority leader, at age forty-five the youngest ever. His Texan colleague Sam Rayburn, the House majority leader, was also opposed to statehood, and as a result it appeared as if all legislative routes were blocked. But over the next three years Johnson changed his mind, and he carried most of his party with him as a result. As Robert Dallek has commented, Johnson's u-turn on Hawaii was indicative of his broadening political focus.

> Lyndon believed that Hawaii's admission partly represented an opportunity to score propaganda points in the Cold War. The United States was showing the world that it "practices what it preaches." ... He believed that Hawaii was a standing symbol of interracial harmony among Americans that could

---

[12] Western Regional Conference, *Papers of Republican Party*, reel 11.
[13] Bell, "Admission Delayed," 56.
[14] Legislative Conference, 1 March 1955, *President Eisenhower's Meetings with Legislative Leaders, 1953-1961*, reel 1 (microfilm RSC).

encourage peace in the South and improve America's image in the underdeveloped regions of Asia, Africa and the Middle East.[15]

In many ways, Johnson's relationship with the South is one of the most interesting aspects of his political career. For many people Texas falls into the category of "the South," but as George Reedy, Johnson's long-time associate and "fixer," stated in his oral history, this is too simplistic an interpretation. Reedy made the point that Johnson was from the hill country of Texas and considered himself more a westerner, especially as he knew this was politically a more favorable image in the rest of the United States. Yet, to his advantage, as far as the South was concerned Johnson was one of them, and to several senior southern Congressmen such as Richard Russell and John Stennis he was also the best chance for a southerner to become president. For these elder statesmen Johnson offered a way to overcome the damaging north-south split in the party.[16] This opened the door for Johnson to pursue a more flexible path, presenting himself simultaneously as the best hope for the South and the best hope for *transforming* the South, depending on which constituency he may be dealing with. In 1956 and 1957 Johnson, using all his persuasive powers on southern Democrats and demanding unanimity under his leadership in the Democratic Policy Committee, convinced his party that a civil rights bill had to pass. Otherwise the Republicans were going to take over Congress for the foreseeable future. Thus, having manoeuvred against the Congressional Liberals in 1955 to save the right to filibuster, he insisted that the filibuster was no longer a viable weapon in the changing political climate.[17] The Republicans, noticing the gradual shift in favor of civil rights nationwide after Little Rock, were picking up votes in black neighborhoods and were looking to capitalize on the Democrats' divisions. A head-on collision with the popular Eisenhower administration would be a grave political mistake. The South, to save itself, had to follow Johnson and compromise.

Opinion is split as to Johnson's true beliefs on this matter. In the latest edition of his biography, Caro comments on the consistent support that Johnson received from "ardent racists" such as Mississippi senator James Eastland, who truly believed that Johnson in the White House would offer the best future for the South and the advocates of states-rights. Clearly this was the biggest weapon that Johnson used to keep them in line, and it worked.[18] The consequences of this were considerable. As one study has pointed out: "The very fact that by 1957 the anti-civil rights faction

---

[15] Robert Dallek, *Lone Star Rising: Lyndon Johnson and His Times 1908-1960* (New York: Oxford University Press, 1991), 554-555.

[16] George Reedy interview, 20 May 1992, John C. Stennis Oral History Project, Mississippi State University, Mississippi State, 20 May 1992, 11-13.

[17] Caro reports that Johnson made shrewd use of the offer of committee appointments to persuade newly-elected liberal senators that they should not vote against him on this issue. Robert A. Caro, *The Years of Lyndon Johnson: Master of the Senate* (New York: Alfred Knopf, 2002), 600.

[18] Caro also reports that this approach by Johnson left much bitterness and a sense of betrayal in the South later on. Ibid., 867-870.

was forced to compromise its position on racial issues in Congress had far-reaching implications for Hawaiian statehood."[19]

Having secured passage for a watered-down Civil Rights Act (which was nonetheless the first civil rights legislation to have been passed for eighty-two years), in early 1958 Johnson made his move on the blocked statehood issue. Johnson arranged a compromise strategy inside his party that involved moving first to accept Alaska into the Union before acting on Hawaii the following year. While the prospect of gaining two extra democratic senators gained many supporters within the party, the southerners accepted this proposal mainly because it further delayed Hawaiian admission and there was a chance that the plan would be frustrated if they could mobilize latent Republican opposition to Alaskan statehood.[20]

Now that Johnson had the South under control, he had put the Republicans in an impossible position. The GOP had supported Hawaiian statehood since the late 1940s. By 1957 the Eisenhower administration had also accepted Alaska as a credible candidate for statehood, since large areas of the territory would remain under Federal control for reasons of national security. For the Republicans, collaborating with the southerners to oppose Alaska would have blocked any further effort later on for Hawaii, and it would also have damaged the civil rights platform that they had been trying to cultivate. Neither could they adopt the Democratic policy that they had previously vilified, linking Alaska and Hawaii in one bill. There was no alternative but to follow Johnson's lead, and on 30 June 1958 the Alaskan bill passed the Senate. With two exceptions, all those who voted in favor of Alaska had voted in favor of the 1957 Civil Rights Act.[21]

There was considerable speculation as to why Hawaii was not dealt with immediately after the successful admission of Alaska. Yet it seems clear now that Johnson deliberately bided his time, wanting to avoid the mistakes of previous years when the Alaska and Hawaii statehood cases had become embroiled in an unresolvable legislative conundrum dominated by inter- and intra-party strife. William Quinn, who would beat Burns to be the first elected governor of Hawaii in 1959, was able to arrange a meeting with Johnson in late July through Johnson's advisor Jim Rowe. Quinn, a leading Republican in the bipartisan effort to get a Hawaii bill introduced into Congress before the end of 1958, tried to express the widespread support for immediate action that he was seeing in public opinion and in the press. Instead he encountered the full wrath of the Senate majority leader:

> We were seated about four feet apart. He leaned forward until his face was inches from mine. His voice rose, his face turned red, cords stood out in his neck and he shouted, "Listen, young man, no one tells me how to run this

---

[19] Bell, "Admission Delayed," 58.

[20] Letter from Minnich to Brundage, Legislative Conference Notes, 4 February 1956 and Legislative Supplementary Notes, 4 March 1958, both in *President Eisenhower's Meetings*, reel 1.

[21] Bell, "Admission Delayed," 60-61; "Statement by the President upon Signing Alaska Statehood Bill, 7 July 1958," *Public Papers of Eisenhower, 1956*, 525.

Senate, not you, not your President, not *Life* magazine; that bill will be considered only when and if I want it considered, understand?"[22]

The East-West Center

Further proof that Johnson had a wider vision in mind than simply the statehood issue is provided by the fact that early in 1959, prior to the passage of the statehood bill, he began to develop plans for consolidating the islands' key location in the mid-Pacific by establishing there an East-West Center for Technical and Cultural Exchange, which would serve as a high-level cultural and educational "bridge" between the United States and the nations of East and South Asia. In early 1959 John Burns, then the Hawaiian delegate in the House of Representatives, sent Johnson an anonymous report (with the note that "this is from a top-flight source. It is very much in line with my thinking") which outlined in no uncertain terms the geopolitical importance of Hawaii in the Cold War struggle. The report's recommendations were very clear.

> At a time when the West and the United States in particular are spending billions of dollars in often futile attempts to combat communist subversion in the under-developed areas of Asia and Africa, the US has overlooked an asset at its very doorstep which has tremendous potential at minimal cost—Hawaii; specifically, the University of Hawaii.
> The USSR and Communist China, through conscious and malicious misrepresentation ... are successfully exploiting the racial problems of the US. The end results of our billions of dollars of military and economic assistance and grants to the under-developed areas of Asia, Africa, and the Middle East are being negated by communist "Little Rock" propaganda. The feeble attempts of USIA and other government information media have made little headway in setting the record straight or explaining to the non-Caucasian nations of the world what this country is attempting to do in solving its racial problems.[23]

For this author Hawaii, with its mixed population of non-Caucasians and Caucasians living in democratic harmony, offered the perfect riposte, such that "the city of Honolulu would be worth millions of dollars as Western propaganda if its story could reach the millions of non-Caucasians whom the communists are subverting in the 'battle for the minds of men.'" However, instead of taking Honolulu on a world tour, the "young potential leaders" of Asia, Africa, and the Middle East could be brought to Honolulu. Therefore the University of Hawaii should redirect its curricula

---

[22] William F. Quinn, "The Politics of Statehood," *Hawaiian Journal of History* 18 (1984): 11. Quinn came away none the wiser about the delay, and concluded that "perhaps the real reason was that Johnson didn't think the Senate had time to consider the bill."

[23] Letter from Burns to Johnson, n.d., S.3385, US Senate 1949-1961, Lyndon Johnson Papers, East-West Cultural Center, Lyndon B. Johnson Library, Austin, Texas (hereafter referred to as LBJ Papers, EWCC).

towards the problems of the non-Western world and be developed into a University of the Pacific, focusing on training highly-regarded professions such as dentistry, medicine, and law. Such a move "could be a weapon more powerful than atomic missiles, General Motors Corporation, or surplus wheat."[24]

The Hawaii statehood bill eventually passed through Congress in an incredible three days. Having already prepared the way by putting considerable pressure on his Democratic colleagues, Johnson announced on 9 March that the Hawaii bill would be considered the following day. On 10 March, with the help of Sam Rayburn, he rammed a similar bill through the House Rules Committee (7 votes to 4) for debate in the House the next day. On 11 March the Senate voted 76 to 15 in favor, on the 12 March the House followed suite by 323 to 89. Again, the alignments in the voting matched that of the 1957 Civil Rights Act and Alaskan statehood. Of the 15 who voted no, 14 were southerners, 13 of whom had voted against the Civil Rights Act and 11 of whom had also voted against Alaska. On the Republican side, resistance in the House again came from representatives from the larger northern states such as Illinois, New York, and Pennsylvania. But the Conservative-Dixiecrat alliance was no longer enough to hold up legislation.[25] The Eisenhower administration lauded the bill's passage, with Secretary of the Interior Fred Seaton declaring in a speech at the University of Hawaii that "all of us together must keep before the peoples of the world the stark contrast between the Communists' International Exhibit A—Hungary and Tibet—and ours—Alaska and Hawaii." But the success was Johnson's, and everyone knew it.

A month later, on 16 April 1959, Johnson publicly unveiled his proposal for an East-West Center in Hawaii in a speech before the American Society of Newspaper Editors. He then introduced the bill himself on the floor of the Senate on 9 June, echoing somewhat clumsily the anonymous report he had received from John Burns. Declaring that Hawaii offered an "opportunity to perfect for the people of the East a showcase of Democracy," Johnson put forward the idea for the creation of an Institute of East-West Studies "as an intellectual bridge, joining together the best of the East and the West."

> It is a practical concept which can be brought into being at a fraction of the cost now spent on weapons shipped to other nations. We cannot take [Honolulu] to Japan, the Philippines, Indonesia, Southeast Asia, India, or Pakistan. But we can bring the potential leaders of the East of tomorrow to Honolulu. Today, from behind the Iron and the Bamboo curtains, universities in Moscow, Peking and Prague beckon the young Hong Kong Chinese, the Singapore Malay, the Burmese and the Indians. The opportunity to answer is ours.[26]

Over the next year Johnson had to keep the legislation on track as opposition was raised, mainly from Mid-western congressmen, about the legitimacy of direct Federal support for an ostensibly educational project, and whether this would make

---

[24] Ibid.
[25] Bell, "Admission Delayed," 62.
[26] Johnson Speech, S.3385, LBJ Papers, EWCC.

it look too much like a "government propaganda weapon" as Carl Marcy, chief of staff of the Senate Foreign Relations Committee, put it.[27] After a State Department report approved the Center in January 1960, Johnson assembled a heavyweight bipartisan group to support the reintroduction of the amended bill in April, including Democratic chief whip Mike Mansfield, Republican minority leader Everett Dirksen, and Republican leader in the Foreign Relations Committee Alexander Wiley.[28] By that stage the plan had received an unexpected boost. The *New York Times* had reported on 24 February 1960 that President Krushchev had announced the creation of a new University of Friendship of the Peoples (later the Lumumba University) in Moscow for the training of up to five thousand students from Asia, Africa, and Latin America in a wide variety of fields including engineering, medicine, economics, and agricultural expertise. Hawaiian Democratic Senator Oren Long drew attention to Krushchev's plan and claimed that the Hawaiian initiative would actually be more attractive to prospective students.

> Under the Soviet program, students from abroad would study apart from Russian students. They would get the word from the Russians, but the Russians would not learn from them. The program we are proposing for America, Mr. President, provides for a bridge of understanding, with traffic moving in both directions, from east to west, and west to east.[29]

On 11 May the project for an East-West Center was given the go-ahead as an amendment to the 1960 Mutual Security Act. Johnson then orchestrated the hearings before the Senate Appropriations Committee that followed, securing a ten million dollar grant for fiscal year 1961.

It is worth considering John Burns's testimony from 24 June 1960. Burns began by declaring that in 1959 Congress had accepted the new state of Hawaii as "an invaluable asset to the United States," and that the follow-up legislation for the East-West Center was the logical way "to utilize, practically and intelligently, the new resource" that Hawaii represented.[30]

The State Department, clearly avoiding taking a leading role, officially passed responsibility for the Center's management to the University of Hawaii in October 1960, and the first funding instalment of $1.1 million was transferred on 8 November "to provide for scholarships, grants, and operational costs."[31]

---

[27] Marcy to Johnson, 28 May 1959, S.3385, LBJ Papers, EWCC.

[28] Dirksen, the respected civil rights supporter from Illinois, had initially rebuffed Oren Long's request for sponsorship on the grounds of his "principle of not co-sponsoring bills that require the expenditure of money." However, Johnson's influence made him reconsider. Wilson to Johnson, 21 March 1960, S.3385, LBJ Papers, EWCC.

[29] *Congresssional Record*, 19 April 1960, page 7539.

[30] Statement of Hon. John A. Burns before Senate Appropriation Sub-Committee in Support of Appropriations for the East-West Center in Hawaii, 24 June 1960, 1960 Subject Files: Foreign Relations, LBJ Papers, EWCC.

[31] *East-West Center: The First Twenty-Five Years* (Honolulu: East-West Center Publications, 1985), 9; Report on Progress of the Center for Cultural and Technical Interchange between East and West, 19 December 1960, S.3385, LBJ Papers, EWCC.

Coordinating with U.S.I.S. offices across East and South Asia, the Center had received 183 student applications from eighteen Asian countries (and the United States) by the end of the year, with most applicants being interested in agricultural training, government, and English language instruction. The first student, Abdul Zia from Pakistan, had already arrived in September, and by the end of the year he had been joined by three others from India, Ceylon, and South Korea. Extra scholarships were being offered for admission in February 1961, with a noticeable focus on trying to reach Indian, Philippine, and Taiwanese students.

With Johnson becoming vice-president he passed a large part of the effort to push the development of the Center into the hands of the Hawaiian members of Congress, although he did take time out in early 1961 to travel to Hawaii for the "ground-breaking ceremony" and to receive an honorary degree from the university. Annual appropriations battles in Congress continued, yet by the end of fiscal year 1963 the Center had received a total of $21.6 million in appropriations. By 1970 the Center had hosted two thousand students at bachelors, masters, and Ph.D. level, and has continued to expand to this day.[32]

Conclusion

Whether the Center was ever able, or allowed, to match the initial vision of Burns and Johnson in 1959 is another issue. But its origins offer further evidence of Johnson's shifting priorities in the late 1950s. After years of deadlock, in 1958-1959 he pulled off a remarkable coup that introduced two new states into the Union within the space of a year, and in doing so he took all the credit for the initiative away from the Republicans. Daniel Inouye had since remarked on how, from a national political perspective,

> it would have been extremely easy for a man from New England or from the North to support Hawaiian statehood. It would have been in line with the advocacy of civil rights. But it would have been extremely difficult for a man from the South, looking at it practically from the standpoint of his constituency and considering the circumstances and events at that time in history, to support Hawaiian statehood.[33]

It is worth concluding by giving some attention to Johnson's comment on expanding the educational frontiers of the United States. Prior to World War II, international education was left as a responsibility of private institutions such as foundations and missionary groups. However, the American government took an increasingly active role in the post-war period, due to a willingness to make American expertise

---

[32] "Hawaii Nurtures US-Asian Amity," *New York Times*, 1 June 1963; *East-West Center: The First Twenty-Five Years*, 15.

[33] Daniel K. Inouye, *Oral Histories of the Johnson Administration*, reel 2.

available to others and the need to improve the image of the United States abroad.[34] The establishment of the East-West Center is a further example of both governmental intervention in international education and the communion of interests that often existed between government and private institutions (here the University of Hawaii). That Johnson pursued it with such vigor displays an interesting additional aspect to his views on world affairs. Later, as President, Johnson sought to capitalize on the huge expansion of student exchanges during that decade by introducing the International Education Act in 1966 to coordinate all governmental involvement in international education. Although the failure of Congress to provide the necessary appropriations led to its untimely demise, the Act demonstrated once more to what extent Johnson recognized the need to utilize education as a tool of American leadership, in "the certain knowledge that only a people advancing in expectation will build secure and peaceful lands."[35] While the impact of President Kennedy has been much greater in this area thanks to ventures such as the Peace Corps, Johnson's contribution has so far been underrated.[36] The East-West Center episode indicates at least that it should be taken more seriously.

---

[34] See Liping Bu, *MakingThe World Like Us: Education, Cultural Expansion and the American Century* (Westport CT: Greenwood, 2003).

[35] "Annual Message to the Congress on the State of the Union," 12 January 1966, *Public Papers of the Presidents: Lyndon B. Johnson, 1966* (Washington, DC: Government Printing Office, 1967), 1:8.

[36] For example, Robert Dallek makes no mention of the International Education Act in his *Flawed Giant: Lyndon Johnson and His Times 1961-1973* (New York: Oxford University Press, 1998).

THE "NEW" AMERICAN FRONTIER
IN REAL AND FICTIONAL LAS VEGAS

Ingrid Eumann

In his book *The New Western Frontier* of 1999 Gary E. Elliott sees modern Las Vegas as a sunbelt-frontier in economic terms.[1] However, apart from economic aspects, there are more, essential features in modern Las Vegas that call for an analysis of frontier impulses in the city. In examining elements of the historical and imaginary Old West in real and fictional Las Vegas, the intention of this paper is to show that, on the one hand, facts and the underlying psychology of residents, visitors, and fictional characters make Las Vegas a successor of the old frontier. On the other, the city's achievements in technology, services, and infrastructure, as well as various aspects of its fictional depiction, turn modern Las Vegas into a new frontier in its own right.

Before turning to our analysis, it should be made clear that both public and scholarly points of view will be explored. For this reason, diverse interpretations of the term "frontier" will be taken into account, including facts and myths, but also general definitions as found in the Webster's dictionary as well as academic concepts. A stronger focus on the scholarly positions than this paper is able to provide, along with a more comprehensive and detailed interdisciplinary analysis of the influence of the American frontier in Las Vegas, will be given in my forthcoming Ph.D. thesis.[2] This article will rather stick to James Oliver Robertson's statements that the truth is to be found both in myths and in realities, and that "myths are part of the world we live in."[3] Accordingly, the terms "old frontier," "Old West," "Wild West," and even "Western" will be used on an interchangeable basis to identify aspects of the American frontier of the nineteenth century.

Legacies

As to elements of the old frontier in the real Las Vegas of today, one of the most obvious is the city's boomtown status. Once a water stop on the Old Spanish Trail to California, Las Vegas, named for the meadows that the region's springs provided in the valley, became the site for a Mormon settlement in the mid-1800s and a ranching area in the century's later decades. In 1905, when the railroad route from Salt Lake City to Los Angeles made the tiny village a water and provisions stop again, the city of Las Vegas was officially founded. Since then, the city has undergone a remarkable development. It turned into a get-away destination in the 1930s, when

---

[1] Gary E. Elliott, *The New Western Frontier: An Illustrated History of Greater Las Vegas* (Carlsbad, CA: Heritage Media, 1999), 9.
[2] Ingrid Eumann, "'The Outer Edge of the Wave': American Frontiers in Las Vegas" (Ph.D. diss., Ruhr-Universität Bochum, to be published in the fall of 2004).
[3] James Oliver Robertson, *American Myth, American Reality* (New York: Hill and Wang-Farrar, Straus and Giroux, 1980), xv.

near-by Hoover Dam was completed and became a nationwide attraction, and, most important, when gambling was legalized in Nevada. In the decades that followed, Las Vegas saw a continuous growth in its popularity until recession hit in the late 1970s. In 1989, however, the opening of the casino-resort The Mirage by Stephen Wynn triggered an unprecedented boom and transformed the city into modern Las Vegas.[4] Apart from an enormous increase in casino construction, the number of residents and visitors has doubled in the past fourteen years, turning greater Las Vegas with its population of 1.4 million into the fastest-growing metropolitan area in the United States. Las Vegas has led the United States in job creation since 1987 and thus served as an economic safety valve. With more than 35 million visitors annually it is one of the world's leading vacation destinations, offering about 140,000 rooms in more than two hundred casino-hotels, many of which are themed megaresorts of more than three thousand rooms and hotels, casinos, entertainment complexes, restaurant clusters, and shopping malls all in one.

Old West imagery can be found in abundance in symbols, logos, names, and services in the tourist and non-tourist parts of the city. Immediately recognizable frontier architecture and interior design, however, is sought in vain in the tourist areas of modern Las Vegas, where the casinos have shed the last remnants of Old West architecture. Many neighborhood properties, in contrast, have held on to Western-style architecture whose Las Vegas tradition dates back to the 1930s and 1940s, when the city successfully marketed its image with the motto "Las Vegas, Still a Frontier Town."[5] Casino-hotels such as Arizona Charlie's, Wild Wild West, Silverton, and as the most recent and up-scale example, the Green Valley Ranch, offer a Western ambiance that suggests the idea of a homey saloon where time can be spent in a relaxed, truly American atmosphere. On downtown's Fremont Street and the Strip the names of only a handful of properties suggest a Wild West link: for example, the Golden Nugget or The New Frontier Hotel & Casino, which, apart from Western-style lettering in its signs and a saloon-nightclub, has done away with Western theming. However, regarding the Western architectural phenomenon of the false-front, which was often found on saloons or drugstores, many Strip and downtown casinos are still "decorated sheds," as Robert Venturi called them in the late 1960s, in modern attire.[6] One of the most recent examples is the new Aladdin Resort & Casino, which shows a perfectly Arabian-themed front on the Strip, but non-decorated, plain outer walls on the sides of the building.

Apart from imagery and false-fronts, gambling, entertainment and the sex industry are further obvious legacies of the American urban frontier West, all

---

[4] Unless otherwise indicated, all general statements about Las Vegas are based on Mark Gottdiener, Claudia C. Collins, and David R. Dickens, *Las Vegas: The Social Production of an All-American City* (Malden: Blackwell, 1999) as well as the media releases of the Las Vegas Convention and Visitors Authority (LVCVA), <http://www.lasvegas24hours.com/press/home.html>.

[5] Elliott, *The New Western Frontier*, 47.

[6] Robert Venturi, Denise Scott Brown, and Steven Izenour, *Learning from Las Vegas: The Forgotten Symbolism of Architectural Form*, rev.ed. (Cambridge: MIT, 1977), 87.

designed to cater to the millions of visitors.[7] Their flourishing success is supported by what insiders call laissez-faire politics, pioneer spirit, and a strong optimism about growth, characteristics also linked to the old frontier.[8] According to Las Vegans, all of these elements help to create an atmosphere of constant evolution, of movement, progress, and energy, features that not only Frederick Jackson Turner attributed to the nineteenth-century West.

In accordance with these characteristics, for more than six decades now Las Vegas has been promoting itself to potential visitors—and Americans willing to relocate—as a city of freedom, as an open space of opportunity where anything, but never the ordinary, can be found. By this promotion the city has retained an aura of "wildness" arising from associations with frontier images. New residents hope to strike it rich in terms of income and life-style. For their part, most visitors go to Las Vegas to take what David Spanier defines as "a detour from 'real' life."[9] They respond to the city's publicity campaigns and a deeply-rooted familiarity with frontier metaphors, and tend to act like modern versions of cowboys who come to town to do some "Hellin' 'Round" after spending a long time on the range.[10]

In fiction, this image of Las Vegas as an "anything-goes" frontier town located in the vastness of the Mojave desert was readily picked up. Since 1938 more than 220 works of literature have been published and even more fictional movies and TV-productions have been released, which are either completely or partly set in Las Vegas or in which Las Vegas plays a prominent role. The vast majority of fiction depicting the old as well as the modern Las Vegas incorporates typical metaphors and stereotypical characters of the Wild West, including the usual old gender and ethnic stereotypes. Apart from modern greenhorns, saloon girls, gamblers, sheriffs, and gunslingers, the private detective, who is a descendant of the original cowboy figure, is one of the most common examples of frontier characters in the fictional renderings of Las Vegas.[11]

---

[7] Cf. John M. Findlay, *People of Chance: Gambling in American Society from Jamestown to Las Vegas* (New York: Oxford University Press, 1986), 3; Elliott, *The New Western Frontier*, 75; Richard Erdoes, *Saloons of the Old West* (New York: Gramercy, 1997), 37.

[8] Gottdiener, Collins, and Dickens, *Las Vegas*, 258; Hal K. Rothman, *Devil's Bargains: Tourism in the Twentieth-Century American West* (Lawrence: University Press of Kansas, 1998), 320.

[9] David Spanier, *All Right, Okay, You Win: Inside Las Vegas* (London: Secker and Warburg, 1992), 1.

[10] Richard W. Slatta has elaborated on cowboy behavior in frontier towns in *Cowboys of the Americas* (New Haven: Yale University Press, 1990), 148.

[11] For the link between cowboy and private detective, see David Mogen, "The Frontier Archetype and the Myth of America: Patterns That Shape the American Dream," in David Mogen, Mark Busby, and Paul Bryant, eds., *The Frontier Experience and the American Dream: Essays on American Literature* (College Station: Texas A&M University Press, 1989), 16-17. Richard Slotkin also points out this connection in *Gunfighter Nation: The Myth of the Frontier in Twentieth-Century America* (New York: Atheneum, 1992), 139. Slotkin explains that in the detective story frontier wilderness was replaced by corrupt civilization, where the Indian turned into the "urban savage"

Most fictional characters are clearly depicted either as inhabitants of the Las Vegas frontier or as visitors experiencing it. Crossing into frontier territory by arriving in Las Vegas is often presented as a sudden exposure to visual and acoustic stimuli that characterize the hyperactivity and crowdedness of the tourist spaces, and which Tom Wolfe described in his famous essay of 1964.[12] This presentation of "otherness" immediately identifies Las Vegas as a frontier, a different space, a space of extremes, and a space in which movie protagonists in particular undergo a transformation based on mythical frontier concepts.

While the territory at first presents itself as a bright, magical place where anything positive seems possible and the conquest, dominance, or control of the "other" culture seems easy, the heroes soon discover that they have entered a physical and/or psychological wilderness that they are unable to master. The Las Vegas frontier that at first seemed to be familiar turns out to be dangerous and alienating. Only some protagonists, such as private-eye Mike Rose in *The Death of Frank Sinatra*, or the pet-detective in Carole Nelson Douglas's numerous *Midnight Louie Mysteries*,[13] find themselves in a position analogous to Richard Slotkin's definition of a typical Wild West character, "a frontier hero [who] stands between the opposed worlds of savagery and civilization," and actually feel comfortable with it.[14] Most characters in Las Vegas stories, however, are unable to cope with the city's "savage" systems of behavior and rules and soon lose control of the situation they thought they could handle. The nightmare into which most fictional characters in Las Vegas fall is often brought about by a combination of being too self-confident and being tempted by a Las Vegas insider. The vices of the city, often personified in this bad guy, cause protagonists to transgress the boundaries of their usual value systems.

Off balance, the characters are now ready to enter the next phase of their transformation, in which the city's bad influence often triggers the process of "making the man," so often found in Western movies.[15] They are forced to reposition themselves and redefine their goals. Often this is a process of regeneration achieved by introspection; for instance, when Jack Singer works hard on his attitude towards marriage after his girl seems lost in *Honeymoon in Las Vegas*, or when the couples in *Indecent Proposal* and *Fools Rush In* have to rethink

---

and the frontier hero "who knows Indians" became the detective figure who knows criminals.

[12] Tom Wolfe, "Las Vegas (What?) Las Vegas (Can't Hear You! Too Noisy) Las Vegas!!!!" in Mike Tronnes, ed., *Literary Las Vegas: The Best Writing About America's Most Fabulous City* (New York: Owl-Henry Holt, 1995), 1-24.

[13] Carole Nelson Douglas, *Midnight Louie Mysteries* series (New York: Tom Doherty, 1993-).

[14] Richard Slotkin, *Gunfighter Nation: The Myth of the Frontier in Twentieth-Century America* (New York: Atheneum, 1992), 16.

[15] A concept discussed by Philip French in *Westerns: Aspects of a Movie Genre* (London: Secker and Warburg, 1973), 70-73, and Lee Clark Mitchell in *Westerns: Making the Man in Fiction and Film* (Chicago: University of Chicago Press, 1996), 8, 159.

their relationship.[16] Many fictional characters struggle to live up to the American Puritan tradition of moral dignity and integrity, and try to restore their moral code, their system of law and social order by self-examination and self-mastery. By contrast, interestingly enough, the real Las Vegas, as David Spanier puts it, is "designed to undermine self-questioning and moral judgment."[17]

As they enter the final phase of their transformation, most fictional protagonists have learned from their Las Vegas experience. Some metamorphoses take a turn for the worse as in *Very Bad Things*, where the effects of the characters' wild behavior on the Las Vegas frontier brings out the killing potential in them.[18] Some stories have an ambiguous outcome as in Edward Allen's novel *Mustang Sally*.[19] While at the beginning of the book main character Professor Schmidt is certain that for him Las Vegas has a life-enhancing quality, at the end of the novel the reader is uncertain whether Schmidt's Las Vegas adventure has left him liberated or damned forever. For most fictional characters, however, their individual Las Vegas experience brings about the necessary impulse for them to give their situation a positive turn. In the end, they, as in *Honeymoon in Las Vegas* or *Indecent Proposal*, have *ex negativo* been taught how to behave "properly" or "better."

New Approaches

While features of the Old West play a major part in the real and the fictional Las Vegas, the city has also been aiming at exploiting other interpretations of the term "frontier" ever since its beginnings as a holiday destination. In striving for frontiers in the definition of "the limit of knowledge or the most advanced achievement in a particular field," the Las Vegas leisure industry has focused on setting new trends in entertainment, architecture, and the service sector.[20] From 1989 on Las Vegas has even intensified this effort and has turned into a "City of Spectacle" and has explored and designed new, state-of-the-art and high-end frontiers in architecture, theming, the service industry, experience culture, and tourist infrastructure, including shopping and fine-dining.[21] It is also for this reason, that, while the frontiersmen lived off the land, Las Vegas manages to live off the tourists and fare extremely well. The service industry is the dominating economic force and provides

---

[16] *Honeymoon in Las Vegas*, dir. Andrew Bergmann, perf. Nicolas Cage, Sarah Jessica Parker, and James Caan, MGM, 1992; *Indecent Proposal*, dir. Adrian Lyne, perf. Robert Redford and Demi Moore, Paramount, 1993; *Fools Rush In*, dir. Andy Tennant, perf. Salma Hayek and Matthew Perry, Columbia Pictures, 1996.

[17] David Spanier, "Art & Craft: Creative Fiction and Las Vegas," *Journal of Gambling Studies* 11.1 (1995): 89.

[18] *Very Bad Things*, dir. Peter Berg, perf. Christian Slater, Jon Favreau, and Cameron Diaz, USA, 1998.

[19] Edward Allen, *Mustang Sally* (New York: W.W. Norton and Company, 1994).

[20] *Random House Webster's College Dictionary*, 2nd ed., s.v. "frontier."

[21] For a definition of "City of Spectacle," see M. Christine Boyer, *The City of Collective Memory: Its Historical Imagery and Architectural Entertainments* (Cambridge: MIT Press, 1998), 46-59.

plenty of employment opportunities, including an enormous number of low-skilled jobs. In marked contrast with conditions on old frontiers, many senior citizens come to live in the Las Vegas valley, attracted by its climate and tax laws, and also by the peculiar work niche that the city's major economic activities offer them. They already account for more than 21 percent of the population, and many more are likely to come when the generation of so-called baby boomers reaches retirement age.[22]

In catering to the latter group, who for the most part are still visitors today, Las Vegas cultivates its malleability, always trying to balance its status as a mirror as well as a trendsetter of American culture, and in consequence it never hesitates to do away with historical landmarks. Especially since 1989 the theming of resorts in the city's main tourist areas has produced a reversal of the old Western theme in architecture. Instead, the megaresorts rely on creating scripted places that draw on imagery of the tropics (Mirage, Mandalay Bay), fairytales (Excalibur, Aladdin, Sahara), of Antiquity (Caesars Palace, The Luxor) and urban Europe (Monte Carlo, Paris Las Vegas, The Venetian). Holding on to the old frontier in spirit, however, the city is proud of what Mark Gottdiener, Claudia Collins, and David Dickens call its "est-philosophy," that is, its constant aiming at the superlative, boasting, for instance, "the world's largest hotel" or "the highest roller coaster."[23] Following this philosophy in spatial, urban-design dimensions, Las Vegas has managed to turn the southern part of the Las Vegas Strip, especially from Tropicana Avenue up to Spring Mountain Road—expressed in landmarks, from the MGM-intersection to the Fashion Show Mall—into a space no longer designed for automobiles as it used to be in old Las Vegas. In the past decade it has been redesigned for pedestrians, who are invited to bridge the distances between the interconnected casino-complexes by monorails, walkways above street level, or so-called people movers, escalator-like transporter belts built to transport visitors from the sidewalk into the resort or from resort to resort. The Southern Strip has thus turned into what could be called the largest mall worldwide.[24]

Modern Las Vegas's focus on simulated and fictionalized places, however, has caused the city to negate its natural setting; an attitude, as Hal Rothman explains in his book *Devil's Bargains*, that is typical of communities specializing in entertainment tourism, which "cease to … provide inspirational outdoor experience" and concentrate entirely on the desires and dreams of the visitors instead.[25] Living up to the "est-philosophy" in negative terms, Las Vegas's attitude towards water has made the city a modern example of the American tradition of wastefulness and exploitation that can be traced back to the pioneering experience.[26] Negating the

---

[22] Gottdiener, Collins, and Dickens, *Las Vegas*, 107; Patricia Nelson Limerick, *Something in the Soil: Legacies and Reckonings in the New West* (New York: Norton, 2000), 286.

[23] Gottdiener, Collins, and Dickens, *Las Vegas*, 121, 200.

[24] A trend already hinted at by Mark Gottdiener in his book *The Theming of America: American Dreams, Media Fantasies, and Themed Environments*, 2nd ed. (Boulder: Westview Press, 2001), 115.

[25] Rothman, *Devil's Bargains*, 288.

[26] Cf. Ray Allen Billington, *Westward Expansion: A History of the American Frontier*, 3rd ed. (New York: Macmillan, 1968), 750.

city's arid surroundings permits the megaresorts on the Strip to boast lakes, fountains, and tropical landscapes. Judging from the visitor profiles prepared for the Las Vegas Convention and Visitors Authority, this focus on urban tourist spaces including lush, non-indigenous, and thus simulated fauna, is successful: Only about 23 percent of the visitors in 2001 stated that they had visited nearby wilderness or park areas during their trip to Las Vegas.[27]

In the same way as Las Vegas promotion is eager to blend out the desert, it also succeeds in blending out the real Las Vegas from the tourist view. Supported by its unique infrastructure as a Strip corridor without any businesses catering to locals and no residential housing, the Southern Strip is a closed space for visitors only. This, of course, enhances the possibilities for promoting the well-known Las Vegas myth of a special place, a place almost on another planet. Creating this myth is even supported by recent academic writing. Providing insights into the real Las Vegas, the real city behind the tourist image, several authors have tried to juxtapose Las Vegas facts and myths including "civilizing" efforts that attempt to counter many negative aspects of the city's focus on the entertainment industry.[28] Being a Las Vegas insider, Hal Rothman claims to be able to investigate Las Vegas facts objectively. However, in his recent book published in 2002 facts and myth become blurred for although he gives an in-depth analysis of the locals' role in making Las Vegas a trendsetter of the postindustrial, postmodern future, he also applies labels to Las Vegas such as "the place where the twenty-first century begins," that "now symbolizes the new America," or a city that "characterizes American hopes and fears."[29] In doing so, he himself is an active player in the myth-making process.

Most Las Vegas fiction is not interested in the real city behind the myth at all. The tourist areas of Las Vegas are where the action in movies takes place for the most part, and the new frontiers in terms of architecture and tourist infrastructure are elements often depicted. In contrast to most protagonists of old Western literature and movies, fictional characters coming to the Las Vegas frontier hardly come to stay. Rather, they take a break from the constraints of their normal life as in *Honeymoon in Las Vegas*, *Indecent Proposal*, or Edward Allen's novel *Mustang Sally*. Most fictional characters hope to make some sort of dream come true in "Sin City," whether it is the American Dream or the search for love, luck, or splendor, or whether it is "just" the hope of experiencing the tourist Las Vegas total of "booze, sex, and gambling."[30] In contrast to their hopes, however, fictional Las Vegas often turns into a nightmare brought about by the protagonists' own naïveté, by temptation

---

[27] Las Vegas Visitor Profile: Fiscal Year 2001, 39, prepared by GLS Research for the LVCVA, available under <http://www.lasvegas24hours.com/press/home.html>.

[28] Rothman, *Devil's Bargains*; Hal K. Rothman, ed., *Reopening of the American West* (Tucson: University of Arizona Press, 1998); David Littlejohn, ed., *The Real Las Vegas: Life beyond the Strip* (New York: Oxford University Press, 1999); Hal K. Rothman and Mike Davis, eds., *The Grit beneath the Glitter: Tales from the Real Las Vegas* (Berkeley: University of California Press, 2002).

[29] Hal K. Rothman, *Neon Metropolis: How Las Vegas Started the Twenty-First Century* (New York: Routledge, 2002), xxvi-xxvii.

[30] This definition of the Las Vegas total can be found in Jonah Goldberg, "Living in Sin: Fantasy and Reality in Today's Las Vegas," *National Review* (20 May 2002): 35-37.

and crime, or by being confronted with a zone where nothing is for free and opportunity and control are only illusions.

Real Las Vegas is extremely successful because of the persistent hints of its dangerous side.[31] The truth, however, is that the city's overall crime rate is average, and the main tourist areas of Las Vegas, the Strip and the Fremont Street area are among the urban spaces best protected by police worldwide, guaranteeing an accordingly low crime rate there.[32] In most works of literature and film on modern Las Vegas, however, the danger is not just potential, it is a constant feature and often the cornerstone of plots. Crime on the Strip and Fremont Street, whether mob activities, casino robbers, the sex industry, cheating players, or visitors falling victim to criminal actions provide key elements in the scripts for productions such as *Vega$*, *Casino*, *Ocean's Eleven I* and *II*, or even *Star Trek: Deep Space Nine*, as well for recent publications like *You Bet Your Life* by the author of the *Murder, She Wrote* series, Jessica Fletcher.[33] They thus turn Las Vegas into a dangerous Wild West town, an image also underlined by the fact that fictional Las Vegas is a place designed almost exclusively for adults.

Even outside the city, fictional protagonists cannot escape this constant danger because there is no relief or innocence in the desert wilderness beyond the limits of the seductive frontier town. Any place outside of the city is either a place of hopelessness, or the burying ground for the dead that Sin City has produced, as in *Casino*, *Very Bad Things*, *The Winner*, or *The Death of Frank Sinatra*.[34] Probably the darkest rendering of Las Vegas as a city and symbol of crime and sin is Stephen King's *The Stand*.[35] In his book, King incorporates imagery of the Old West, however his depiction of cowboys and the traditional American West is an evil one. In the end, Las Vegas, as a twisted symbol of the old frontier faith, is destroyed by an atom bomb. King does not permit Las Vegas to be reborn, but establishes his rebirth-myth in the East instead. Although this example is extreme, a large part of Las Vegas fiction shares the sense that modern Las Vegas is a frontier that is similar or related to the Old West image, yet also very different from it.

Recent fictional productions also explore Las Vegas from the viewpoint of frontier as a meeting ground of ethnicities. In the film-noir-style movie *Very Bad Things* of 1998 the Asian American hooker and the African American hotel security officer fall prey to the Anglo-American bachelor party's desire to "enjoy"

---

[31] Kathryn Hausbeck, "Who Puts the 'Sin' in 'Sin City' Stories? Girls of Grit and Glitter in the City of Women," in Rothman and Davis, *The Grit beneath the Glitter*, 337.

[32] Cf. Rothman and Davis, *The Grit beneath the Glitter*, 13.

[33] *Vega$*, prod. Aaron Spelling, perf. Robert Urich, Bart Baverman, and Tony Curtiz, ABC, television series 1978-1981; *Ocean's Eleven*, dir. Lewis Milestone, perf. Frank Sinatra, Dean Martin, and Sammy Davis, Jr., Warner Bros., 1960; *Ocean's Eleven II*, dir. Stephen Soderbergh, perf. George Clooney, Brad Pitt, and Julia Roberts, Warner Bros., 2001; "Badda-Bing Badda-Bang," *Star Trek: Deep Space Nine*, dir. Mike Vejar, perf. Avery Brooks and James Darren, Warner Bros., 1999; Jessica Fletcher, *Murder, She Wrote: You Bet Your Life* (New York: Signet, 2002).

[34] *The Winner*, dir. Alan Cox, perf. Rebecca de Mornay, Vincent D'Onofrio, and Michael Madsen, Artisan, 1995.

[35] Stephen King, *The Stand*, rev. ed. (New York: Signet, 1991).

themselves in a typical frontier-as-battleground scenario. These fictional renderings of white dominance over characters of other ethnicities are, however, the exception. The African American police detective in the 2001 movie *Rush Hour II* requests political correctness in relation to ethnic groups on the casino floor in his "I Have a Dream" speech, modeled after Martin Luther King's famous address.[36] In the end, he is the one who gets to wear the cowboy hat that formerly belonged to the only white player, indicating his dominance of the scene. The 1996 movie *Fools Rush In* presents Las Vegas as *La Frontera*, on which older Anglo-American generations are reluctant to "melt" with the other culture while their children, after some difficulty, manage to embrace the frontier concept as an equal-rights multi-cultural meeting ground. In the last episode of the *Star Trek: Deep Space Nine* trilogy featuring a Las Vegas lounge singer, even the casino in the city, that was once called the "Mississippi of the West" because of its racial discrimination, is turned into a place where history is rewritten by means of fantasy and technology, permitting all ethnic groups to live on equal terms in their own fictional version of the 1960s.[37]

The Interplay of Concepts

From this discussion, it becomes obvious that Las Vegas, in reality and fiction, has retained much of the Old West but works with new frontier concepts as well. Thanks to its status as a cultural symbol and myth Las Vegas, like the Old West, offers ideal ground for interpretation. Hal Rothman complains that the city that non-residents see is nothing but "a reflection of themselves."[38] This claim is supported by the special status of the region, which Neil Campbell defines as a space that "has always been, by the very nature of its mythic representations, a type of hyperreality, a simulation reproducing images conforming to some already defined, but possibly non-existent, sense of Westness."[39] However, also within in the tradition of the myth of the American West, Las Vegas is not only a product designed from the outside inspired by a deeply-rooted sympathy with and psychological need for Western frontier concepts. Insiders too, as has been argued before, help shape the positive dreamscape of the "Entertainment Capital of the World." Thus, Las Vegas is reflection and projection at the same time.

Wooing visitors from all over the globe, promoters of the real Las Vegas are understandably eager to make sure that in their marketing concept the term Las Vegas "frontier" is no "f-word." Their positive projection of the city's *raison d'être*, however, often clashes with fictional renderings. Writers have developed the Las Vegas concept on other levels by elaborating on the city's function in contrasting

---

[36] *Rush Hour II*, dir. Brett Ratner, perf. Jackie Chan and Chris Tucker, New Line Cinema, 2001.
[37] "Badda-Bing Badda-Bang," *Star Trek: Deep Space Nine*. Because this aspect is not the only interesting link to Las Vegas established by the Star Trek series, this subject will be dealt with in more detail in my Ph.D. thesis.
[38] Rothman and Davis, *The Grit beneath the Glitter*, 13-14.
[39] Neil Campbell, *The Cultures of the American New West* (Edinburgh: Edinburgh University Press, 2000), 130.

ways; not only as a place to have fun in the sun, of achievement and rebirth, but above all as a territory of temptation and sins, of danger, alienation, destruction, and disillusionment. The possibilities offered in Las Vegas mean that fictional characters encounter no upright and bright frontier in Frederick Jackson Turner's sense.[40] But neither is it only the dark, tragedy-oriented frontier of many contemporary critics. Rather it appears to be a hedonistic and sinful environment rendered as the moral wasteland of American society, the necessary counterpart to the ideals and traditions of the rest of America. Fictional Las Vegas is a moral testing ground, testing the characters' personality, their integrity, their souls. After exposure to the different rules in the Las Vegas territory, along with the physical or psychological violence involved, only those who are or become insiders can contemplate staying permanently. Most fictional characters, however, find themselves defeated by the city's "otherness." They find the city to be the beginning of their road to perdition or they experience regeneration or rebirth only by leaving Las Vegas.

For real-life visitors to the city, the themed tourist scape overlaps with fictional renderings of Las Vegas. They do not care about the real city behind the façade but prefer to enjoy their vacation in an environment of pleasure without any second thoughts, just like tourists enjoying Disneyland's Wild West theme.[41] What they expect to find and what they are accordingly offered in Las Vegas's trendsetting environments is an up-to-date version of the mythical Old West promoting a space of freedom, opportunity, and fun. The discounting of the belief in the end of American frontiers by the American public enables Las Vegas to be what it is and to be perceived accordingly. The meta-narrative of the frontier is very much alive, though sometimes hidden, in the cultural icon Las Vegas. In fact, it is a crucial, if not the crucial, element in the city's popularity. Only by using old frontier concepts, by adapting them, and by introducing new ones, is Las Vegas able to sustain its megasuccess. In short, Las Vegas has managed to create a frontier all of its own.

---

[40] The label "metropolis of hedonism" is given to Las Vegas in Goldberg, "Living in Sin," 36.

[41] For tourist behavior in Disneyland, see Limerick, *Something in the Soil*, 75-79.

FRONTIER AND IDENTITY:
THE CASE OF ALASKA[1]

Tity de Vries

Alaskans like to present their state as "the Last Frontier state." This "Last Frontier" identity is presented in numerous ways, varying from the state's website which invites the visitor: "Travel Alaska—a Ticket to the Last Frontier,"[2] to businesses, tour operators, restaurants and lodging facilities which carry "the Last Frontier" in their names. Souvenir shops named "Trading Post" and hotels and restaurants turned into "Roadhouse," refer to the importance of these facilities during the heydays of the Alaskan Goldrush frontier in the late nineteenth and early twentieth century.[3] Browsing through Alaskan visitors' guides, tourist brochures and websites results in the overwhelming impression that the frontier is still as much alive in Alaska today as it was in the nineteenth century American West.

This Last Frontier image is not just for tourists, but rooted in Alaskan daily life and in (some of) its state symbols. From the early 1980s till the late 1990s the official Alaskan car license plate carried "The Last Frontier" as its logo[4] and Mary Drake, author of the "Alaska State Flag Song," proclaims the state flag to be "The simple flag of the last frontier," whose blue background stands for the wilderness elements (sea, evening sky, mountain lakes, flowers), and the yellow stars represent "the gold of the early sourdough's dreams."[5]

The numerous references to the Alaskan frontier identity contrast sharply with Alaska's position in the ongoing academic debate on the American frontier. In 1926, Frederick Jackson Turner himself acknowledged Alaska as a new frontier within the broad conceptual framework he had created. "The opening of the Alaskan wilds," he wrote, "furnished a new frontier and frontier spirit to the Pacific Northwest as well as to the nation."[6] However, it was not until the 1970s that historians hesitatingly started to include Alaska as a past and contemporary, and even post frontier[7] in frontier studies.

---

[1] The research for this article was done from January-May 2000, during my stay as a Fulbright scholar at the History Department of the University of Alaska Fairbanks.
[2] <www.state.ak.us> (2000).
[3] Alaska had several gold rushes. The Klondike Gold Rush, starting in 1896 was the most colorful and famous, followed by the Nome Gold Rush of 1900 and the Fairbanks Gold Rush of 1904.
[4] The logo was the outcome of a contest for school children in 1977. Around 1997 it was replaced by "Gold Rush Centennial," as part of the celebration of the centennial of the Klondike Gold Rush of 1897-1898.
[5] "Alaska State Flag Song," Postcard J&H Sales, Anchorage, Alaska 99501. Anyone who has survived an Alaskan winter qualifies as a sourdough, an old timer.
[6] Frederick Jackson Turner, "The West—1876 and 1926: Its Progress in a Half-Century," *World's Work* 52 (July 1926): 327.
[7] Peter A. Coates, *The Trans-Alaska Pipeline Controversy: Technology, Conservation, and the Frontier* (London and Toronto: Associated University Press, 1991), 319.

First, several historians pointed out that Alaska's history is indeed a frontier history which fits into the framework of the history of the West and its frontier. Alaska answers to the four criteria of Westerness: aridity, heavy dependence on the federal government, a fresh legacy of the frontier process (Prudhoe Bay oil fields exploitation) and a persisting importance of extractive industries. Arguments in favor of Alaska as a past and present frontier society are its immense uninhabited spaces (more than 50 percent of Alaska's nine hundred thousand residents are concentrated in or near Anchorage, Fairbanks and Juneau), its prolonged territorial status, the role of outsiders as the major protagonists in the state's development, and a political agenda which is dominated by energy issues. Two major differences from the lower forty-eight states' experience stand out: Alaska was never an agricultural frontier (except for the failed Matanuska Valley experiment in the 1930s) and the relation between Native Americans and Alaskan settlers has been less violent and disruptive.[8] With its inclusion as a frontier state, Alaska is linked to the history of the American West of the "lower forty-eight" states. In being the *last* frontier Alaska is seen as the last American region which can be identified as "authentically" American.

In the second half of the 1980s Western historians developed a new approach towards the history of the West and the frontier, resulting in the school of New Western History. A major protagonist of this new direction was Patricia Nelson Limerick of the University of Colorado, who published in 1987 *The Legacy of Conquest: The Unbroken Past of the American West* which was widely acclaimed as a seminal work, comparable to Henry Nash Smith's *Virgin Land* and other classic texts on the history of the West.[9] *Legacy* presented a new vision on the significance of the West, in particular its moral significance for the forces that shaped American character and American values. According to Limerick the West was not only the scene of America's national success, but also the scene of national failure because of the effects of the invading frontiersmen on resident native peoples, ethnic minorities and the environment. Limerick rebelled against the traditional Turnerian frontier history because it distorted the complexity of the American West. She proposed a different approach by constructing a new framework around the notion that the many elements of Western history can best be understood as a series of ongoing conquests or contentions for power, and their intentional and unintentional consequences. In fact, Limerick proposed a new paradigm for Western history to replace Turner's frontier thesis, and to rewrite Western history. Instead of frontier,

---

[8] See Orlando W. Miller, *The Frontier in Alaska and the Matanuska Colony* (New Haven and London: Yale University Press, 1975); Melody Webb, *The Last Frontier: A History of the Yukon Basin of Canada and Alaska* (Albuquerque: University of New Mexico Press, 1985); Frank J. Popper, "The Strange Case of the Contemporary American Frontier," *Yale Review* 76.1 (1986): 101-121; Michael P. Malone, "Beyond the Last Frontier: Toward a New Approach to Western American History," *Western Historical Quarterly* 20.4 (1989): 409-427; Peter A. Coates, *The Trans-Alaska Pipeline Controversy: Technology, Conservation, and the Frontier* (London and Toronto: Associated University Press, 1991).

[9] Donald Worster et al., "*The Legacy of Conquest*, by Patricia Nelson Limerick: A Panel of Appraisal," *The Western Historical Quarterly* 20.3 (1989): 303.

she preferred "conquest" as the key concept in the history of the West: "... 'frontier' is one of the most difficult concepts in the world to pin down, and its value for analysis is further compromised by the heavy load of ethnocentric, nationalistic, white-centered associations that it has to carry around, clinging to the hull like barnacles."[10]

The book was praised ("boldly imaginative and dazzlingly wide-ranging"[11]) and criticized ("descriptive, unsystematic, individualistic"[12]). "Obviously, this book expresses a considerable disillusionment with the western past," stated Donald Worster during a panel discussion on *The Legacy of Conquest* in October 1988.[13]

Except for some side-remarks, Limerick excluded Alaska from her "unbroken past of the American West." Nor was Alaska included in the New Western history that emerged from Limerick's approach. This omission was remedied in 1991 with the publication of *The Trans-Alaska Pipeline Controversy. Technology, Conservation, and the Frontier* by the British historian Peter A. Coates. In fact, Coates' book can be considered as an application of Limerick's plea to include in American frontier history the twentieth century West, the impact of technology and the vital importance of the exploitation of natural resources. Coates in particular focused on the debates and conflicts preceding and involving the building of the Trans-Alaska Pipeline (1969-1973, one of the most passionately fought conservation battles in American history) as a case study of the impact of frontier myths, images, and symbols in Alaskan history. Concentrating on the effects of the frontier on the Alaskan environment in past and recent times, he developed a methodology to unravel Alaska's identity as a frontier society. In his perception this identity has been (and still is) constructed by two different interpretations of the frontier image, that of the "boosters" and that of the "conservationists."[14] Both interpretations have a preoccupation with the significance of Alaska in connection with the frontier idea and its meaning for American history: both admire the frontier and agree on its importance for American and Alaskan culture and history, but in very different ways.[15] In the interpretation of the "boosters", Alaska is predominantly a source of swift economic success, with "frontier" being a metaphor for promise, progress and ingenuity with a positive connotation.[16] Alaska as the last frontier had developed in the same way as the Western frontier, including the exploitation of natural resources on a large scale. In fact, the "booster" interpretation of the Alaskan frontier is a variant of "old western history", in particular of Turner's perception of the evolution of the pioneer ideal. In his 1910 "Social Forces in American History" Turner states (without regret) that the old pioneer individualism had made way for the "forces of

---

[10] Ibid., 320.
[11] Ibid., 316.
[12] Ibid., 309.
[13] Ibid., 304-305.
[14] Coates, *The Trans-Alaska Pipeline Controversy*, 28-29.
[15] Ibid., 23, 28.
[16] Also Patricia N. Limerick, "The Adventures of the Frontier in the Twentieth Century," in James R. Grossman, ed., *The Frontier in American Culture: An Exhibition at the Newberry Library, August 26 1994-Jan 7 1995* (Berkeley: University of California Press, 1994), 66–102.

social combination": the self-made man had transformed himself into "the coal baron, the steel king, the oil king, the cattle king, the railroad magnate, the master of high finance, the monarch of trusts."[17] The same process, and much more compressed, had occurred on the Alaskan frontier: individual freedom and unrestricted competition for the control of natural resources had mainly resulted in fast and huge profits for fur traders and fish industries, and later in the twentieth century, for mining barons and oil companies. In the "booster" interpretation the story of Alaska's last frontier had been a success story because of the profitability of Alaskan resources.

The second interpretation of the Alaskan frontier image is that of the "conservationists," which is much more ambivalent in its approach to the historic frontier process and its pioneering mentality. The "conservationists" are highly critical of the damaging consequences of old-fashioned boosterism for the Alaskan wilderness. In this respect they are linked to New Western historians like Limerick who focus on the advancing frontier as an ongoing process of conquering and controlling nature and native people, often resulting in overexploitation of natural resources. In the case of twentieth century Alaska this "conquest" was even more damaging because of all the technology involved. However, for the "conservationists" Alaska is also a symbol of hope. They consider Alaska as a second chance for America to protect at least some of the original wilderness and native cultures of the American continent, a chance it had ignored in the nineteenth-century West. In Alaska the lessons of the past could be applied, and mistakes avoided.[18] Coates points to early-twentieth-century conservationists' efforts (with the support of the federal government) to prevent the extinction of wildlife, which resulted in Alaska's first game law in 1902 and in the establishment of Mount McKinley National Park in 1917. Both events can be considered as examples of trying to avoid a repetition of the mistakes in the West, like the near extinction of the bison.[19]

Coates' analysis of the different concepts of Alaska as a frontier society offers a workable methodology for analyzing other manifestations of the Alaskan frontier identity. One of these—and the focus of this study—is the history theme park Alaskaland (renamed Pioneer Park in 2002), located in Alaska's second largest city, Fairbanks. The representation of Alaska's past in this park makes it into a popular culture narrative of Alaska's identity as the Last Frontier state, positioning the Alaskan frontier theme at the intersection of history, collective identity and popular culture, with all the complex interpretations the frontier concept has. In concentrating on the historical development of the park and on the iconographic meaning of its main attractions, I will argue that this popular representation of Alaska's Last Frontier identity can be considered as another manifestation of the tension that has been caused by the conflicting "booster" and "conservationist" interpretations of the frontier in Alaska.

---

[17] Frederick J. Turner, "Social Forces in American History," in F.J. Turner, *The Frontier in American History* (New York: Holt, Rinehart and Winston, 1962), 318.
[18] Coates, *The Trans-Alaska Pipeline Controversy*, 29.
[19] Ibid., 43.

Presenting Alaska's History and Identity

All over Alaska museums tell the story of its frontier past. Balanced narratives can be found in the University of Alaska Museum in Fairbanks and the Anchorage Museum of History and Art. Both museums excel in exhibitions of Alaska's development from pre-historic times till the end of the twentieth century, with ample attention for Native history and daily life on the Alaskan frontier. On a smaller scale, local museums exhibit—often impressive—collections of historic artefacts, machinery, utensils and photographs. Reconstructions of trapper log cabins, saloons, grocery stores and school rooms are popular. Some of these museums, like the Juneau-Douglas City Museum, are professionally operated. The visitor is guided through exhibitions on the often glorious past by interpretive plaques and video presentations. Other museums are more amateurish operations of well-meaning and enthusiastic local historical societies, and show a considerable variation in approach and order. Admission is usually a couple of dollars, and the visitor can almost touch the nostalgia in the air. Memories of the hardships of the past (and of the Alaskan cold), and pride in the pioneer accomplishments, seem to be the main focus of the exhibitions.

Whatever their quality, museums are artificial constructions where the visitor is informed by watching exhibitions and reading interpretive texts. Historic locations offer a more direct and authentic experience of the Alaskan past. In the town of Eagle on the border of the Yukon River or in the old mining town of Ester near Fairbanks, civil and private enterprises like historic societies or tour operators restored the old buildings and now organize guided tours and activities. In Eagle, visitors can attend a trial in the historic courtroom and in Ester, the restored mess hall and bunkhouses of the former mining camp have been turned into a hotel and visitors can enjoy the famous Malamute Saloon Stage Show at night.

Former marked sites (of transport, trade, industry, or mining), like the Independence Mine near Palmer or Rika's Landing and Roadhouse close to Delta Junction, which were abandoned decades ago and deteriorated rapidly in the harsh Alaskan climate, have been designated as state historical parks and restored to their original condition. Volunteers and park rangers have turned them into living history museums, often with demonstrations of old-fashioned crafts and trades, and tour guides in period dress.

The history theme park Alaskaland is a combination of these presentations of the past. It is an artificially created park on a location with no specific historic meaning, set up with many original early-twentieth-century buildings and artefacts, and with an educational and recreational purpose. In other words, it is a cross between Williamsburg and Disneyland.

A Meeting Point of a Heroic Past and a Dynamic Future

Originally named A67 the park opened its gates on 28 May 1967 as the exhibition site of the Alaska Purchase Centennial Celebration. That day 12,000 people visited the park on the border of the Chena River near Fairbanks. More than three decades later the park is still one of the main attractions of Fairbanks, considered by some visitors "... a little corny, while others think it is an enjoyable step back into Alaska's history."[20]

Although Alaskaland was actually established as part of the 1967 Centennial, the first plans for a historic "Pioneer Park" emanated from the members of Igloo #4 of the "Pioneers of Alaska" in the late 1950s. In their perception this future "Pioneer Park" should "... change some of the misconceptions of Alaska and the life here in the far north, where it is so infernally cold."[21] They selected a lot on the south border of the Chena River which was to be developed as "a Pioneer Park and Museum for the preservation, conservation and display of items of an historical nature for the benefit of tourists, students and all Alaskan residents."[22] In their (successful) struggle for the purchase of this land from the State, the Pioneers showed a remarkable sense of "conservationism": "Because there were people here that were ambitious and greedy for the dollar and would have converted it for commercial use; as all of the rest of the recreation areas of this area have turned out."[23] The development of the site accelerated in 1964, when Fairbanks became the central exhibition site for the upcoming celebration of Alaska's Purchase Centennial in 1967.

The theme of the Centennial celebration was "North to the Future"; a slogan echoing the famous words of Horace Greely: "Go West Young Man" and aiming at the future economic opportunities of Alaska. It was a reminder that "beyond the horizon of urban clutter there is a Great Land beneath our flag that can provide a new tomorrow for this century's 'huddled masses yearning to be free.'"[24] The choice of this slogan indicates the focus on economic progress of Alaska's state policy during the 1960s.

The design of the logo for the Centennial shows us a second orientation: celebrating Alaska's heroic past. The 1967 Centennial was the beginning of an increasing historical interest in Alaska. For the first time, people in the state realized the potentials of Alaska's past and the need to protect its pioneer heritage. The logo is shaped like a circle, and its main eye catcher is a totem pole, composed of symbols referring to the highlights of Alaskan history: the onion-shaped roof of a Russian orthodox church indicating the Russian possession of Alaska before 1867, a bald eagle sitting on top of this church, symbolizing the U.S. purchase of 1867, a gold miner with his gold pan as a reference to the gold rushes, and a narrow gauge locomotive symbolizing the importance of railways for the state's development. On

---

[20] Jim DuFresne, *Alaska: A Travel Survival Kit* (Hawthorne: Lonely Planet Publications, 1994), 381.

[21] Adolf Stock (president of Pioneers of Alaska, Igloo # 4), "Introduction," *Alaskaland Scrapbook* 1 (1962): 2, Archives University of Alaska Fairbanks (hereafter cited as Archives UAF).

[22] "History: Alaskaland," undated, 2, folder 7, box 8, Alaskaland Commission Papers, Archives UAF.

[23] Stock, "Introduction," 2.

[24] *Centennial Press* 2.9 (September 1964), folder 2, box 1, Betzi Woodman Papers, Alaska Purchase Centennial Collection, Archives UAF. The translation of Alaska is the Great Land.

top of the totem is a large star with forty-nine written on it, Alaska being the forty-ninth state of the United States. In the background behind the totem pole we see a mountain range (Alaska's Mount Denali is the highest mountain of the United States) and a streaming Alaskan flag. Together, slogan and logo focus on future progress and on celebration of the past, in concurrence with the objectives of the Centennial.[25] In a brochure for the press it was formulated like this: "Alaska is changed and unchanging. The Exposition which will mark 100 years since the Alaska Purchase will feature the role of Alaska in the Space Age and as a vital link in worldwide air transportation. ... At the same time the Exposition will illustrate that the Alaska of yesterday still exists; that the adventure which drew the pioneers can still be found within a stone's throw of missile sites and satellite communication bases. This is Alaska 67—revealing the many faces of this magnificent land."[26] Or, in the words of President Lyndon Johnson in the same brochure: "The Alaska of 1967 is where our dynamic and prosperous future meets the last American frontier."[27]

The intertwining of past and future and of education and recreation is shown in the plan of the A67 park. The main, future oriented exhibit area was *Bartlett Plaza*, with its International House and two geodesic dome buildings which served as exhibition halls for the federal government and various enterprises and businesses. *Gold Rush Town*, representing the early 1900s, was the historic center, composed of authentic Fairbanks log cabins, the sternwheeler *Nenana* and the Pioneer Museum. Within the museum building visitors could also attend The Big Stampede Show, which consisted of fifteen murals on the Alaskan gold rushes, painted by the famous Alaskan artist Rusty Heurlin. In this historic section the emphasis was on the accomplishments of former generations of Alaskans. *Bonanzaland* was the main amusement center with rides, concessions and other attractions. On the border of the Chena River the *Native Village* was built, with Native sod buildings, a Native Museum and blanket tossing demonstrations. The *Wilderness Park* with its "zoo" offered the visitors an impression of Alaska's nature. Examples of mining operations took place in the *Mining Valley*, where visitors could also pan for gold.[28]

A Troubled History of Conflicting Interests

The Centennial park was not as successful as expected and hoped for. The situation grew worse after 14 August, when the Chena River flooded the A67 grounds and the park had to be closed down for the rest of the season. Debt-ridden and damaged by slick and silt, the park was taken over by the city in December 1967 and its name was changed into Alaskaland. Except for some minor alterations (one of the

---

[25] Advisory Memo # 32, 7 May 1964, folder 1 A: Advisory Memos 1-56, box 3, Alaska Purchase Centennial Collection, Archives UAF.

[26] *Press Information Alaska 67* (no date): 1, folder 8 Pamphlets, box 2, Betzi Woodman Papers, Alaska Purchase Centennial Collection, Archives UAF.

[27] Ibid., 2.

[28] Press information folder, folder 10, box 4, Alaska Purchase Centennial Collection, Archives UAF.

geodesic domes was removed together with their exhibitions and some of the attractions of Bonanzaland, and International House was renamed into Civic Center) the lay-out of the park stayed the same.

Alaskaland's operation became a recurring problem for the city. Several times during the next decades the future of the park was an issue of local public debate. Due to financial problems of the city, maintenance personnel had to be laid off and activities were often restricted. Vandalism in the park increased, as did complaints of the public on the deterioration of the park. After a couple of years of "muddling through," a dormant controversy on the destination and future of Alaskaland came into the open. The local *Fairbanks Daily News-Miner* put its finger on the sore spot: "There are two major drawbacks to the job—there is not enough money to do anything properly, and no one has ever defined exactly what is expected of the park."[29] The last critique expressed the core dilemma: should Alaskaland be mainly a tourist attraction or a community park, or both? In May 1979, the Alaskaland Commission (the advisory board of the park) presented its *Alaskaland Development Plan*, and recommended the hiring of a professional consultant who could draw a master plan for the future: "Alaskaland is directed toward being the image builder of Alaska and Alaskans."[30] In the fall, the city hired consultant Jack Pentes and for the first time since 1967 the planning and development of the park was given serious and professional thought.

In Pentes' evaluation, Alaskaland was at best a "themed public park, offering experiences based on the history of the state, its people and its legacies"[31] and it would never have the attraction of a Disneyland or Williamsburg. At most, "Alaskaland can hold enormous fascination for its out-of-state visitor while providing facilities for the pursuit of recreation, entertainment, learning and history for the people of Fairbanks and the State."[32] In other words: Alaskaland should be appealing to both the tourist and the resident.

The Pentes Master Plan was ambitious (as master plans should be), and emphasized the need for more sensational attractions and a profitable exploitation of the historic parts. Obviously, Pentes was in favor of a boosterish approach, aiming at more visitors by adapting the park to contemporary amusement standards. In the end just a few of his recommendations were accomplished, due to lack of support and money and the limitations of the Alaskan climate. A "Big Sluice" water-slide and an exhibition on the Alaskan Pipeline were never realized, but the infrastructure of the park was improved and most buildings were brought up to the building code. After the death of the park's mascot, Ed the Moose in 1980, the zoo was closed, which not only ended the citizen's complaints about the disgraceful living conditions of the animals, but also restricted the Wilderness Park considerably to some woods and

---

[29] "Editorial," *Fairbanks Daily News-Miner*, 30 June 1975.
[30] *Alaskaland Development Plan: Goals and Strategies for Course of Action for Alaskaland Park, Fairbanks, Alaska*, Report of the Alaskaland Commission (Fairbanks, 1979), chap. 7, folder Masterplan Alaskaland 1980, box 6, Alaskaland Commission Papers, Archives UAF.
[31] "The Consultant's Overview," in *Alaskaland Masterplan* (Fairbanks, 1979), 10, folder Masterplan Alaskaland 1980, box 6, Alaskaland Commission Papers, Archives UAF.
[32] Ibid., 11.

bushes. During the 1980s the Alaskaland Pioneer Air Museum was established in the geodesic Gold Dome and a Square Dance Hall was built near the entrance of the Mining Valley. In 1983 the sternwheeler *Nenana* was moved to a new location in the park and restoration of the vessel started.

Although the condition of Alaskaland improved considerably from the 1980s on, the park did not succeed in becoming a major tourist attraction of the state and its financial problems continued being a burden for the Borough administration. In the late nineties the future of the park again became the focus of local debate. This resulted in a different perception of the purpose of the park, which was partly due to a general, renewed interest in historic preservation and authenticity. Complaints on the condition of parts of the park, and accusations that taxpayers' money was being used to subsidize the tourist industry caused the Borough to install the Alaskaland Review Panel to develop recommendations for maintaining and developing Alaskaland for future generations. In March 1999, twenty years after the Pentes Master Plan, their report was published, emphasizing historic and cultural preservation as the park's primary use. Its secondary use should be a location for events and recreation, "if effectively integrated with the historic/cultural preservation use."[33] In this way, an explicit choice for the destination of Alaskaland was made: "The park cannot and should not attempt to be all things to all people."[34] In the near future the spaces of the Park designated for recreation use should be converted into historic and cultural preservation uses, and the Borough should continue to both own and operate the Park. The parameters of the historic and cultural attractions were to be set on Fairbanks and surrounding areas, and from pre-gold rush (1903) to present. Gold Rush Town, the SS *Nenana*, Mining Valley, the Gold Dome, Native Village and the Railroad Depot were designated as the main historic preservation use areas. The visitor's experience should be enhanced by the production of a video, telling the story of Fairbanks, and by guided and self-guided walking tours. A new name was to reflect this new historic preservation identity and prevent any further association with commercial theme parks like Disneyland. It seemed that finally, after more than forty years, the initial late 1950s intentions of the Pioneers of Alaska Igloo #4 were going to prevail over the uses of Alaskaland as playground, tourist trap, shopping mall, and festival grounds.

Nowadays the park is run by an impressive number of partners: public servants of the Fairbanks North Star Borough maintain and operate the park, the Alaskaland Commission serves as its advisory board, the Fairbanks Historical Preservation Commission restores and operates the SS *Nenana* and the Harding Railway car, the Tanana Valley Historic Society is responsible for the restoration and operation of the Judge Wickersham House (a State Historical Monument), the Pioneer Air Museum is operated by the Interior and Arctic Alaska Aeronautical Foundation and the Pioneers of Alaska keep the Kitty Hensely House, the Pioneer Museum and the Big Stampede Show open. Concessionaires sell food and souvenirs.

The history of Alaskaland resembles Alaska's history itself: a mixture of private and public initiatives and involvement in which the booster mentality with its

---

[33] Alaskaland Review Panel, *Final Recommendations* (Fairbanks, 1999), 8.
[34] Ibid.

focus on economic progress and profit dominated at first, and was supplemented in the 1990s by an approach with more and more emphasis on conservation and preservation. The changing perceptions of the preferred identity of the park also reflect shifting perceptions of the presentation of the past: in the 1970s and 1980s the park aimed to be a tourist attraction and a facility to house commercial and community activities, although efforts to commercialize the park successfully, with large scale rides and sensational attractions, have failed. In the 1990s there was an increasing shift to efforts to offer visitors a more authentic historic setting which would enrich their Alaska experience and knowledge. Eventually, in the latest plan of 1999, historic preservation is preferred to exploitation of the commercial potential of the park, a policy which is reflected in the new 2003 name Pioneer Park. Visitors of Alaskaland can still have fun playing mini-golf or riding the narrow gauge train, and they can buy Alaskan souvenirs, but at the same time they can learn a lot more about the region's history, by "taking a walk in the past" (with some imagination). This combination of commercial activities and historic authenticity in a cheerful cooperation makes the park exceptional. Compared to amusement parks, Alaskaland may look amateurish and even corny, and in comparison with official historic state parks or historic frontier sites Alaskaland is lacking in authenticity, but in its combination of both elements, Alaskaland is a valuable popularization of the (last) frontier experience.

Intermingling of conflicting interests, a dependency on high's and low's in the city's and borough's economy, lack of public funding for preservation projects and sometimes confusing responsibilities of the city and the borough made it hard to develop a consistent, long term policy for the park. Considering these restrictions, it is almost a miracle that the park has been kept open. One of the reasons that Alaskaland did stay open has been the steady support of the local Fairbanks community, even though its citizens were often critical towards the management of the park. This local loyalty indicates the pride that Fairbanks' citizens have taken in this presentation of their past. For them it represents much more than a not so profitable tourist attraction or a nice picnic location: it is a manifestation of the sense of continuity between past and present many Alaskans have, of being pioneers themselves, in spite of their much more comfortable life style than that of the early twentieth-century pioneers.

Icons of Boosters and Conservationists

In this study the booster interpretation of Alaska's frontier identity is taken as the emphasis on economic progress in Alaska's history and on commercial exploitation of the past in Alaskaland, while the conservationist interpretation is "translated" as the focus on preservation and authenticity of historic heritage. Both perspectives are reflected in the park's plan and in its simple attractions.

The plan of Alaskaland[35] maps the main elements of Alaska's historic development. Its location on the border of the Chena River refers to the historic

---

[35] Dated 2000.

reality of many settlements in Alaska. Close to the river, on the north side of the park, a fairly large area is marked out for the Native Village, set between the Wilderness Area and the Railroad Depot and representing the pre-white history of Alaska where Native people lived in harmony with nature. The Native Village is also a reference to the preponderantly peaceful relations between white Alaskan settlers and Native people. The south-eastern part of the park, its historic heart, is dominated by the romanticized construction of early-twentieth-century Fairbanks, Gold Rush Town. This section is surrounded by icons of historic boosterism: the railway station, the riverboat SS *Nenana* and the Harding Railroad car. In the south-western part the Mining Valley is located, representing gold mining as one of the main forces of Alaska's economic development. Situated in the north-west is the Wilderness Area, a very faint extract of Alaska's real wilderness and mainly serving as a setting for picnic facilities. The Aviation Museum, housed in the Gold Dome, is dedicated to the role of air transport in Alaska's quest for progress. Scattered in the central area are community facilities like the Civic Center and the Square Dance Hall, and children's attractions like a playground, an antique carousel and a mini-golf course.

Five attractions: the Harding Pullman Car and the Crooked Creek and Whiskey Island Railroad, the sternwheeler *Nenana*, Gold Rush Town with its Pioneer Museum and Big Stampede Show, and the Mining Valley are the most popular destinations in the park.

In which way do they reflect the tension between the two frontier interpretations?

Trains of Progress

Although railroads and trains are considered manifestations of boosterism, boosterism is completely absent in the presentation of the Pullman railway car "Denali." This was the car in which President Warren Harding traveled to the town of *Nenana* in 1923, in order to drive in the Golden Spike commemorating the completion of the Alaska Railroad, which joined Alaska's two major cities, Fairbanks and Anchorage. The event itself had meant progress: the railway connection ended Fairbanks's isolation, and linked the Interior[36] to the civilized world. Trade and industry increased, the tourist industry was promoted, and Fairbanks and its population grew. The Harding car had been a gift from Alaska Railroad to the Fairbanks branch of the Pioneers of Alaska in May 1961, to be exhibited in the future Pioneer Park. After years of damage due to negligence and the severe Alaskan weather conditions, the "Denali" is currently cared for by a volunteer group of the Fairbanks Historical Preservation Foundation (FHPF). The interior of the car is very austere, mainly due to lack of money to bring back the state rooms to a replica of their former condition. Visitors can enter the car, sniff the

---

[36] Alaska has six geographic regions: Southeast, Southcentral, Alaska Peninsula, Bering Sea Coast, the Arctic and the Interior. The Alaska Railroad was the only railroad ever built by the American government.

air and look around, read a few texts on its history and donate some money for further preservation.

The presentation of the "Denali" car is in striking contrast with the importance of the 1923 event and with the operation of another historic railroad relic in the park, a replica of steam engine #1 of the former narrow gauge Tanana Valley Railroad. Similar to the trains in Disneyparks, the Crooked Creek and Whiskey Island Railroad circles the park, and visitors enjoy a "fun" ride in modern open cars behind the steam engine. The current display and use of the train neglects the original meaning of the narrow gauge railroads for the development of the Fairbanks region in the early twentieth century. Back then they were the life lines for the gold miners up in the hills, which made it relatively easy to travel between the city and one's claim. Those trains and cars were dirty and smelly, breaking down all the time, while the Alaskaland visitor neither hears of nor experiences any of such discomforts.

"The Queen of the Yukon"

The pride of the park is the sternwheeler *Nenana*, sitting in a basin in the center of the park. From 1933 till 1955 the SS *Nenana* cruised up and down the Yukon River, serving as the link between the villages along the Yukon and Tanana River and the shipping center town of *Nenana*, located between Anchorage and Fairbanks. The sternwheeler was a provider of supplies, news, employment and transportation for these white and native communities: "She was the Queen of the Yukon—she meant everything to the old sourdoughs."[37] Steam boating on the Yukon River had started in 1869 when Alaska's rivers were the sole means of transportation into the interior. In Alaskaland the SS *Nenana* serves as an icon for the opening of large areas of Alaska to trade and industry; as a bringer of progress, with her 1,120 tons, 237 feet length, room for fifty-two passengers and three hundred tons of cargo, and capacity to push up to six barges.[38] After twenty-two years of service the vessel was herself a victim of progress when modern diesel riverboats, airplanes and highways took over the commercial transportation and she was taken out of service. The *Nenana* is an emblem of Alaska's past, although the sternwheeler never anchored in Fairbanks, nor sailed the Chena River.

After her retirement the ship was successively operated as a "boatel" and a public restaurant with bar and dance floor, the Sandbar Restaurant. Converting it for these uses required some restoration, which saved the boat from final decay and destruction.[39] The Centennial Exhibition A67 was a turning point for the future of the sternwheeler: the SS *Nenana* was recognized as a major Alaskan heritage icon. However, it took till 1982 before the restaurant was closed. It turned out that the

---

[37] *Fairbanks Daily News-Miner Visitors Guide to A67*, 24 May 1967, 5.
[38] Marilyn Jesmain, "Heritage Interpretation on the SS Nenana: The Last of the Great Riverboats in Alaska," (master's thesis, University of Alaska Fairbanks, 1994), 32.
[39] Rene Blahuta, "The Sea in Alaska's Past: The Preservation of the Sternwheeler Nenana," Report for the Alaskaland Commission, no date, folder Preservation of Nenana, box 4, Alaskaland Commission Papers, Archives UAF.

Nenana was in very bad shape, with a rotting bow and super structure and that she was close to collapsing.[40] Almost immediately the City of Fairbanks took action and started a program of stabilization and restoration. In the archival records of Alaskaland, this restoration process is an endless succession of bad luck, small successes and many demands for more money. In 1987 the title of the SS *Nenana* was transferred to the Fairbanks Historical Preservation Foundation, a private sector foundation that finished the restoration of the inner and outer structure for $1.7 million.[41] Visitors can take a guided tour of the ship, peek into the state rooms, marvel at the luxuriously decorated lounge and stand behind the steering wheel on the bridge.

However, in order to make the sternwheeler even more attractive to visitors the FHPF added a new element to the vessel: an interpretive diorama, positioned in the cargo hold and reconstructing on HO scale[42] the twenty-two villages along the banks of the Tanana River and the Yukon River, which were serviced by the SS *Nenana*. The diorama is surrounded by authentic sounds and narration.

For a long time the debate on the destination of the SS *Nenana* was undecided, varying between restoring the sternwheeler to its original state and operating it as a museum or historic site, or using the boat as an exclusive location for commercial enterprises like a restaurant and bar, souvenir shops, and so on. The restoration of the vessel into her authentic state during the 1980s and 1990s may indicate that preservationists have prevailed over commercial boosters. Partly this is the case, but at the same time the vessel can still be hired for private parties, and the diorama in its hull is aimed at enlarging the *Nenana*'s attraction for paying visitors. In fact, installing the diorama has been a missed opportunity for preservation: instead of filling the cargo hold with wood, machinery and other examples of cargo, which would give an impression of the efforts it took to operate a vessel like this, the hull was turned into an exhibition room reducing the historic authenticity of the vessel to almost nil. As has often been the case in Alaska's history, the commercial mentality was stronger than the preservationists' criteria.

Alaskaland's Shopping Village

A similar tendency can be seen in Gold Rush Town: two streets lined with original (early) twentieth century log cabins, some frame houses, a warehouse, a church, and the Palace Theatre & Saloon. Gold Rush Town was based on the original idea of the Pioneers of Alaska in the late 1950s: once Fairbanks was "the log cabin capital of America" and when in the 1950s downtown Fairbanks started to modernize and the traditional log cabins were replaced by brick and concrete buildings at a fast rate, the members of Igloo # 4 wanted to preserve them for future generations in a Pioneer Park.[43] During the course of years, from all over the state, in particular from

---

[40] Jesmain, "Heritage Interpretation on the SS Nenana," 55.
[41] Ibid., 58.
[42] 1/8 inch equals 1 foot.
[43] Stock, "Introduction," 3.

Fairbanks, some thirty log cabins, dating from the first four decades of the twentieth century, were relocated to the park.

Log cabins are a persistent icon of the Alaska frontier experience. Even more than in the lower forty-eight states, they are the embodiment of frontier ideals of rugged individualism and self-sufficiency, of freedom, pragmatism, perseverance and progress, an architectural symbol of the very essence of the American character. To this day they have stood as symbols for deeply revered "last frontier" values in Alaskan society: self-reliance, outdoor living, and independence.[44] Living in a log cabin, even when it has all the comforts of an apartment in Manhattan, is for many the ultimate Alaskan experience. Building it yourself is even better. The importance of the log cabin as a symbol of frontier life is reflected in Alaskaland's logo of the 1970s, which shows a sturdy log cabin against a background of mountains and spruce, indicating the original pioneer life in the unspoiled wilderness. In contrast with this image, the log cabins in Gold Rush Town have been subject to a metamorphosis, from icons of the Alaskan pioneer life in the wilderness into icons of Alaskan entrepreneurship.

In 1967 commercial activities in Gold Rush Town were diverse but limited: shops in some log cabins, an exhibit on the Klondike Gold Rush poet Robert Service, an operating post office, an old time ice-cream parlor, a dancehall and saloon, and a general store.[45] During the next decades Gold Rush Town increasingly commercialized: a 1978 advertisement announced: "Alaskaland Home of the 'FAMOUS' GOLD RUSH TOWN Shopping Village."[46] And a year later a newspaper report proudly stated: "This year there is a drive towards flourishing. For the first time all 28 cabins of Gold Rush Town are occupied by shops. Shopkeepers are urged to wear early 1900 clothes."[47]

Gold Rush Town turned into a shopping area during these years. Maintenance on the log cabins was low and at random, without considering preservation recommendations and regulations. The Alaskaland Commission tried to reverse this development by making an effort to get Gold Rush Town approved as a historical district. This would open the gates to a wave of new grants for restoration of the cabins, the members of the commission hoped. The plan failed: the status of historical district was denied on the grounds that the buildings were no longer on their original, historic location. Many cabins have been painted in bright colors, which make their significance as icons of the rugged, early twentieth frontier life almost a joke. Only the plaques next to the front doors, telling the cabin's colorful histories, refer to the times when these cabins were proof that their owners knew how to survive in the Alaskan wilderness. Exceptions to this boosterish treatment are two historic dwellings which are strictly operated as house museums: the Kitty Hensley House and the Judge Wickersham House (placed on the Historic National Register).

---

[44] Nathalie Gitto, *The Log Cabin as Myth and Symbol on the Northern Frontier* (master's thesis, University of Alaska Fairbanks, 1997), 92.

[45] *Jessen's Weekly*, 24 May 1967.

[46] "Golden Days Program," *Alaskaland Scrapbook* 6 (1978-), Archives UAF.

[47] Unidentified Newspaper Clipping, 26 May 1979, *Alaskaland Scrapbook* 6 (1978-), Archives UAF.

Showtime on the Last Frontier

A popular source of amusement and of information on life at the Last Frontier in the pioneer days is the "The Golden Heart Revue" in the (replica) Palace Theatre and Saloon with humorous acts and songs on the history of Fairbanks. On the painted curtain which serves as the background of the stage, all the facts and clichés associated with Alaska's Last Frontier image are pictured together. It shows a map of the state with its main towns, surrounded by sea with a whale and an oil platform; a sternwheeler is pushing up the Yukon, stampeders climb the Chilkoot trail of 1898; we see a gold panner, native totems, a moose, a train, salmon fishing, husky dog sleighs, caribou herds, canoes, and the nicknames Uncle Sam's Icebox (meaning all of Alaska's wealth goes to outsiders) and Seward's Folly (when Secretary of State William H. Seward bought Alaska from the Russians in 1867, he was called a fool). The show is meant for fun, and most of the songs and acts relate Fairbanks's history as a success story, with some serious undertones about the harshness of life in the Interior. This kind of show can be found anywhere in the West, its sketches and songs adapted to local circumstances, but with the same romanticized image of frontier life, and the same clichés and stereotypes.

A second, very different theatrical presentation of the early pioneer days is The Big Stampede Show, which focuses on the Klondike and Fairbanks Gold Rushes. The Big Stampede Show is located in the Pioneer Hall and Museum Building, which is operated by the members of the Pioneers of Alaska. The audience of the show is seated on chairs on a turntable. Turning slowly, and listening to the voice of narrator Reuben Gaines, the public watches the fifteen mural-sized paintings of famous-in-Alaska-artist Rusty Heurlin. The show begins with two large paintings showing gold seekers crossing the Chilkoot Pass and the Thompson Pass to reach the Klondike goldfields in 1898. As the platform turns, the audience progresses deeper into the story of the gold rushes. Many of the famous characters of the era are portrayed: Robert W. Service, poet of the Klondike; the Big Swede, who offered to give a dance hall lady her weight in gold if she would marry him; the writer Jack London; and pioneer Alaskans Frank Young and Robert Sheldon. Another painting shows twenty-one male pioneers, indicating at the same time the painter's opinion on pioneer women. "Those were days and those were men the likes of which we'll never see again," said Heurlin.[48]

To the contemporary visitor the paintings look romanticized and out of date, emphasizing the success stories of the stampeders. This effect is somewhat modified by the narration, telling about those who did not survive the hardships or turned back to their homes empty handed and disappointed. The Big Stampede is a homage to all those heroic gold seekers who tried and succeeded (or failed), the pioneers who faced Alaska as the Last Frontier, testing their strengths by braving mountains, rivers, lakes, snow, and cold in order to extract the gold from it, to strike it rich and to develop the Great Land into a civilized nation. However, in conquering the wilderness, those pioneers started the drive for economic progress and success

---

[48] "Foremost Alaska Painter, 'Rusty' Heurlin, Completes Canvas, Epic of the North," *Jessen's Weekly*, 14 December 1966.

without considering the consequences for the environment or the Native Alaskans. In fact, Heurlin's twenty-one pioneers were the predecessors of the large scale mining (gold, silver, copper) operations which not only contributed to Alaska's economic wealth and stimulated a boosterish mentality, but also caused severe damage to the Alaskan wilderness and often disrupted the traditional subsistence of Alaska's Native people. In both theatrical productions of Alaskaland these elements are left out.

Mining Junk

The Mining Valley is the most evident example of boosterism in Alaskaland. Here the pursuit of profit has expelled the historic narrative almost completely. Originally, this section was meant to show the visitor early gold mining techniques and machines, including a mechanical sluice box and other sophisticated equipment. Evaluating the Valley in 1980, consultant Jack Pentes had already concluded that it was in a deteriorated and unsafe condition, which gave the area "the appearance of a junk yard rather than an organized section of the park."[49] He advised the addition of a Mining Museum and the re-instalment of a gold panning facility for the revitalization of the Mining Valley Area. None of these recommendations were followed, and in the summer of 2000 it was an even more sorry-looking part of the park than it had been twenty years ago.

For twenty-five years now, Mining Valley has been dominated by the Salmon Bake and its smell, an open air eating facility where visitors can enjoy a hearty grilled salmon for a reasonable price. Eating at the Salmon Bake is often part of an Alaskaland package offered by tour operators. Some log cabins, housing souvenir or art shops, and a large scattering of rusty pieces of mining equipment complete the area. Central in the Valley lies the pond, surrounded by former sluice scoops. A mechanical sluice box and water canon that operates occasionally offers an impression of Alaska gold mining in the early decades of the twentieth century, although this is hard to tell for an uninformed visitor. The scarcity of adequate historical explanation and interpretation, the deplorable state of the mining equipment, the overwhelming smell of baked salmon and the abundance of shop cabins, have turned the Mining Valley into a pre-eminently commercial area. Until recently the visitor of Alaskaland left the park with a distorted and rather vague idea of the mining practices which had meant so much for the origins and development of Fairbanks and the rest of Alaska.[50]

---

[49] "Mining Valley," in *Masterplan Alaskaland* (Fairbanks, 1979), folder Masterplan Alaskaland 1980, box 6, Alaskaland Commission Papers, Archives UAF.
[50] Three years later, in 2003, the situation of the Mining Valley had improved considerably. The restaurant buildings and furniture had been replaced or renovated, and the smell seemed less penetrating. Mining equipment and operations were explained on large signs and more mining history was exhibited in the tunnel.

Conclusion

For more than thirty years the people of Fairbanks have supported the continuation of Alaskaland, considering it a valuable community facility, as a public park, as a tourist attraction and as a representation of their past and identity. Its history and its present situation, as well as the different elements of the park—recreational and historic heritage attractions—reflect this community and its Last Frontier identity. Alaskaland is in fact a correct popular construction of Alaska's past, mainly representing the "booster" interpretation of this history and approaching the subject much less from a "conservationist" perspective. Currently, commercial exploitation still prevails over historic heritage attractions, and the focus of the park's historic section is on the economic success story of Alaska. As in representations of the frontier elsewhere, Alaskaland idealizes the Last Frontier experience as a romantic and exciting adventure, an approach which is perfectly suitable as a marketing instrument. The emphasis on familiar icons of the frontier (trains, sternwheelers, log cabins, gold pans) reconfirms the identification of the Last Frontier with progress and wealth. A profitable exploitation of Alaska's natural resources has always been an essential part of Alaska's frontier experience, more dominant than the call for protection of the original wilderness and native cultures of Alaska. It has made the "booster" mentality fundamental to the Alaskan identity. Next to lack of sufficient public funding and a late developing sense of the need for historic preservation, the "booster" mentality seems to be one of the main explanations of the continuing commercialization of Alaskaland. This finding offers a different perspective on the concept of authenticity in this respect. In the park most of the historical attractions have been turned into commercial enterprises, even though they are original historic buildings and artefacts. Log cabins are used as souvenir shops, art galleries or food stands, the narrow gauge train offers fun rides without a historic context, the cargo hull of the SS *Nenana* has been distorted by a diorama, and the mining machinery in Mining Valley serves mainly as a decorative setting for the outdoor restaurant. However, although the original uses of these buildings and artefacts were different from their current uses in the park, they give the visitor an authentic flavor of the Alaskan frontier: in fact, by trying to make some profit out of history the operators of the park are not so different from their pioneer predecessors, who came to Alaska "to strike it rich." From the perspective of historic continuity, Alaskaland's boosterish approach to history is as authentic as the park's historic buildings and artefacts themselves.

NOTES ON CONTRIBUTORS

David Adams (dkadams@breathemail.net) is Emeritus Professor, University Fellow and Chair of the David Bruce Centre for American Studies at Keele University, United Kingdom. His research interests lie in twentieth century U.S. and international history, and he is the author, editor and co-editor of some forty books. His most recent publications are *Before the Special Relationship* (2002) and "FDR as Jeffersonian" in *"Nature's Nation" Revisited* (2003). He was appointed OBE on the Diplomatic List in 1997 and Hon.D.Litt. (Keele) in 2000.

Louis Billington (rosbgreen@rosbgreen.karoo.co.uk) is Senior Research Fellow in the American Studies department at the University of Hull, United Kingdom. He is the author of many articles on eighteenth- and nineteenth-century British and American history, and has a particular interest in the social history of religion. His paper on "The Churches of Christ in Britain: A Study in Nineteenth-Century Sectarianism" has been re-published in Michael W. Casey and Douglas A. Foster, *The Stone-Campbell Movement: An International Religious Tradition* (2002).

Michael Boyden (michael.boyden@arts.kuleuven.ac.be) is Research Assistant in the Department of Literary Studies at the Catholic University Leuven, Belgium. He has studied at the University of Edinburgh, Queens University Belfast, and the University of British Columbia in Vancouver. His doctoral dissertation deals with the differentiation of American literary history as a scholarly discipline. He is a fellow of the Salzburg Seminar and a grantee of the John F. Kennedy-Institut für Nordamerikastudien of the Freie Universität Berlin.

David Brown (d.brown@sheffield.ac.uk) is Lecturer in American History at the University of Sheffield, United Kingdom, where he teaches courses on slavery, the South, and the Civil War. He has published articles in the *Historical Journal* and the *Journal of Southern History*, and his book *Southern Outcast: Hinton Rowan Helper and the Impending Crisis of the South* is due to be published in 2005. He is secretary of BrANCH (British American Nineteenth Century Historians).

Graham Davis (g.davis@bathspa.ac.uk) is Course Director of the MA in Irish Studies at the School of Historical and Cultural Studies, Bath Spa University College, United Kingdom. His research interests are Irish Migration (Britain and the Americas), the American West, and the history of Bath. His publications include *The Irish in Britain, 1815-1914* (1991), *Bath: A New History* (1996), and his award-winning book (co-authored with Penny Bonsall) *Land!: Irish pioneers in Mexican and Revolutionary Texas* (2002).

Ingrid Eumann (ingrid.eumann@ruhr-uni-bochum.de) studied at Ruhr-Universität Bochum, Germany, and New York University. Her Ph.D. thesis "'The Outer Edge of the Wave': American Frontiers in Las Vegas" is scheduled for publication in late

2004. She co-edited essay collections on Las Vegas and Chicago and is currently teaching American Studies at Ruhr-Universität Bochum. Her research interests include the American frontier in fiction and film, Las Vegas, and American art.

Carmen de la Guardia Herrero (guardia@uam.es) is Professor of U.S. History at the Autónoma University in Madrid, Spain. Her books include *Proceso Político y elecciones en Estados Unidos* (1992) and *Conflicto y reforma en el Madrid del siglo XVIII* (1993). She is currently preparing a study of U.S relations with Spain, 1763-1800.

Sylvia L. Hilton (slhilton@ghis.ucm.es) is Professor of U.S. and Latin American History at the Complutense University in Madrid, Spain. She has published extensively on Hispano-Anglo-Native American borders and relations in colonial North America, and the nineteenth century. She is co-editor *of European Perceptions of the Spanish-American War of 1898* (1999), *Federalism, Citizenship, and Collective Identities in U.S. History* (2000), and *Nation on the Move* (2002). She is currently researching Spanish perspectives on the Louisiana Purchase of 1803.

David Brian Howard (david@nscad.ns.ca) is Associate Professor of Art History in the Department of Historical and Critical Studies at the Nova Scotia College of Art and Design University, Canada. He has published numerous articles on the history, politics, and theory of modernism in the United States and Canada after World War II and curated a critical retrospective exhibition on the Canadian modernist painter Arthur F. McKay.

Robert Lewis (r.m.lewis@bham.ac.uk) is Lecturer in American History at the University of Birmingham, United Kingdom, where he teaches American Studies. His particular interests are in nineteenth-century social and cultural history, especially private recreation and commercial amusements. Most recently, he edited an anthology of documents *From Traveling Show to Vaudeville: Theatrical Spectacle in America, 1830-1910* (2003).

Cornelis A. van Minnen (ca.v.minnen@zeeland.nl) is Executive Director of the Roosevelt Study Center in Middelburg, The Netherlands, and Professor of American History at Ghent University, Belgium. He published on Dutch-American relations and is co-editor of *FDR and His Contemporaries* (1992), *Reflections on American Exceptionalism* (1994), *Aspects of War in American History* (1997), *Religious and Secular Reform in America* (1999), *Beat Culture* (1999), *Federalism, Citizenship, and Collective Identities in U.S. History* (2000), and *Nation on the Move* (2002).

Paul Otto (potto@georgefox.edu) is Associate Professor of History at George Fox University, United States, where he specializes in early American and Native American history. His book, *The Dutch-Munsee Encounter in America: The Struggle for Sovereignty in the Hudson Valley*, is forthcoming.

James G. Ryan (ryanj@tamug.edu) is Professor at Texas A&M University at Galveston, United States. He received B.A. and M.A. degrees from the University of Delaware, and an M.A. and Ph.D. from the University of Notre Dame. He is the author of *Earl Browder: The Failure of American Communism* (1997) and co-editor of *The Historical Dictionary of the Gilded Age* (2003). He is currently working on a monograph on Soviet espionage in North America, and co-editing *The Historical Dictionary of the 1940s*.

Frank Schumacher (frank.schumacher@uni-erfurt.de) is Assistant Professor of North American History at the University of Erfurt, Germany. His publications include *Kalter Krieg und Propaganda: die USA, der Kampf um die Weltmeinung und die ideelle Westbindung der Bundesrepublik Deutschland, 1945-1955* (2000). He is co-editor of *Culture and International History* (2003) and currently at work on his book *The American Way of Empire: National Tradition and Transatlantic Learning in America's Search for Imperial Identity, 1870-1920*.

Giles Scott-Smith (g.scott-smith@zeeland.nl) is Senior Researcher with the Roosevelt Study Center in Middelburg, The Netherlands. His research interests are focused mainly on U.S.-European relations, in particular the importance of public diplomacy and cultural relations. He is currently working on a study of the U.S. State Department's Foreign Leader Exchange Program in Western Europe. His recent publications include *The Politics of Apolitical Culture* (2002), and he co-edited *The Cultural Cold War in Western Europe 1945-1960* (2003).

Marco Sioli (marco.sioli@unimi.it) teaches North American History at the Faculty of Political Science of the University of Milan, Italy. He won the OAH Foreign-Language Article Prize for 1996 and received fellowships from the International Center for Jefferson Studies, the Library Company, and the Gilder Lehrman Institute of American History. Most recently he edited the volume *Metropoli e natura sulle frontiere americane* (2003) and he is currently working on a book entitled *Exploring the Nation: At the Origins of American Expansionism*.

Joseph Smith (joseph.smith@exeter.ac.uk) is Reader in American Diplomatic History at the University of Exeter, United Kingdom. His most recent publications include *The Spanish-American War* (1998), *The Cold War, 1945-1991* (1998), and *A History of Brazil, 1500-2000* (2002). His book *The United States and Latin America, 1776-2000* will be published in 2005.

Melvyn Stokes (m.stokes@ucl.ac.uk) teaches American and Film History at University College London. He is the editor of *The State of U.S. History* (2002), and his co-edited books include *The Market Revolution in America* (1996), *The United States and the European Alliance since 1945* (1999), *American Movie Audiences* (1999), *Identifying Hollywood's Audiences* (1999), *Hollywood Spectatorship* (2001), and *Hollywood Abroad* (2004). He is currently completing a book on D.W. Griffith's controversial film, *The Birth of a Nation*.

Tity de Vries (t.de.vries@let.rug.nl) is Assistant Professor in Modern American History at the History Department of the University of Groningen, The Netherlands. The focus of her research is post-1945 Dutch-American intellectual relations. She was a Fulbright scholar at the University of Alaska Fairbanks in 2000. In 1996 she published *Complexe consensus. Amerikaanse en Nederlandse intellectuelen in debat over politiek en cultuur 1945-1960* and she co-edited *The American Metropolis. Image and Inspiration* (2001).

ACKNOWLEDGMENTS

The collection of essays in this book were originally presented and discussed at the Roosevelt Study Center's Sixth Middelburg Conference of European Historians of the United States on 23-25 April 2003. From the twenty papers presented at that meeting, sixteen were subsequently selected for inclusion in this volume, after careful revision and, in some cases, extensive rewriting. The conference and the publication of this volume were made possible by the generous sponsorship of the Roosevelt Study Center in Middelburg, the Franklin and Eleanor Roosevelt Institute at Hyde Park, New York, the U.S. Embassy in The Hague, and the David Bruce Centre for American Studies at Keele University, United Kingdom.

In our capacity as organizers of the conference and as editors of this volume, we gratefully acknowledge the indispensable and most efficient services of the Roosevelt Study Center's secretary Leontien Joosse throughout the project.

Cornelis A. van Minnen and Sylvia L. Hilton
Middelburg/Madrid, September 2004